9 TH EDITION

Public Relations Writing

Form & Style

Doug Newsom

Professor Emeritus, Texas Christian University

Jim Haynes

QuickSilver Interactive Group

WADSWORTH
CENGAGE Learning

Australia • Brazil • Japan • Korea • Mexico • Singapore • Spain • United Kingdom • United States

WADSWORTH
CENGAGE Learning™

**Public Relations Writing: Form & Style,
Ninth Edition**
Doug Newsom and Jim Haynes

Senior Publisher: Lyn Uhl

Publisher: Michael Rosenberg

Associate Development Editor: Megan Garvey

Assistant Editor: Jillian D'Urso

Editorial Assistant: Erin Pass

Media Editor: Jessica Badiner

Marketing Manager: Bryant Chrzan

Marketing Coordinator: Darlene Macanan

Marketing Communications Manager:
Christine Dobberpuhl

Art Director: Linda Helcher

Print Buyer: Justin Palmeiro

Permissions Editor: Roberta Broyer

Production Service: Pre-Press PMG,
Sini Sivaraman

Photo Manager: Mandy Groszko

Compositor: Pre-Press PMG

For product information and technology assistance, contact us at
Cengage Learning Customer & Sales Support, 1-800-354-9706
For permission to use material from this text or product,
submit all requests online at **cengage.com/permissions**
Further permissions questions can be emailed to
permissionrequest@cengage.com

ISBN-13: 978-1-4390-8546-2

ISBN-10: 1-4390-8546-3

Wadsworth
20 Channel Center Street
Boston, MA 02210
USA

Cengage Learning is a leading provider of customized learning solutions with
office locations around the globe, including Singapore, the United Kingdom,
Australia, Mexico, Brazil, and Japan. Locate your local office at:
international.cengage.com/region

Cengage Learning products are represented in Canada by
Nelson Education, Ltd.

For your course and learning solutions, visit **academic.cengage.com**

Purchase any of our products at your local college store or at our preferred
online store **www.ichapters.com**

Printed in Canada
1 2 3 4 5 6 7 13 12 11 10 9

Public Relations Writing

Form & Style

Dedicated to all public relations practitioners and students who care about communicating clearly and effectively.

Brief Contents

Contents

CHAPTER THREE
Persuasion   37

PART 2

Preparing to Write   59

CHAPTER FOUR
Research for the Public Relations Writer   60

CHAPTER FIVE
The Public Relations Planning Process   80

P A R T   **3**

Writing Principles   101

C H A P T E R   S I X
Writing to Clarify and Simplify the Complex: Style and Content   102

C H A P T E R   S E V E N
Grammar, Spelling and Punctuation   129

P A R T **4**

Writing for Traditional Media and Social Media   **149**

CHAPTER THIRTEEN
Writing Advertising Copy   264

C H A P T E R   F O U R T E E N
Newsletters   294

C H A P T E R   F I F T E E N
Brochures   314

CHAPTER SIXTEEN
Magazines   333

Preface

The information environment has changed tremendously since the last edition, so we knew this book would have to reflect those changes and their implications for public relations writers.

You'll find that the three chapters in Part 1, Public Relations Writing: Role and Responsibility reflect the impact of changes in their content and their organization as well. The writer's role today is more complex with legal and ethical responsibilities enlarged by instant global access and persuasion efforts not always clearly defined in an expanded, unmediated communication system.

Preparing to Write, the name of Part 2, includes chapters on research and the planning process.

Part 3, Writing Principles, contains the chapters on writing to clarify and simplify complex subject matter and reminders about grammar, spelling and punctuation.

The name of Part 4 reflects the changed media environment, Writing for Traditional Media and Social Media. The new demands on style and content of converged traditional media and social media are in the first chapter. The second chapter in this section includes media kits and media pitches as well as backgrounders and position papers.

Part 5, Writing for Select Publics, includes eight chapters. The subjects of this section are indicated by the chapter titles: message design; emails, memos and letters; reports and proposals; advertising copy; newsletters; brochures; magazines; speeches and other presentations.

Writing in Turbulent Times, Part 6, contains the crisis communication chapter.

These 18 chapters reflect best-practices approaches to style and content, so their content should assist beginning public relations writers and offer guidance and reference for practitioners.

A separate exercise book for this text offers practice problems in addition to the exercises suggested for each chapter.

We welcome your questions and feedback: d.newsom@tcu.edu; jhaynes1102@sbcglobal.net.

Acknowledgments

We would like to express our gratitude to colleagues, practitioners and students who offered informal comments on the book and to more formal directions from reviewers who suggested changes and offered guidance and suggestions for this edition: Meg Lamme, University of Alabama and Dr. David Ritchey, The University of Akron. We also are very grateful for the many who signed permissions for us to use materials that appear in the illustrations.

We'd also like to thank the dedicated team at Wadsworth for the support, mainly Michael Rosenberg, Publisher; Megan Garvey, Development Editor; Jill D'Urso, Assistant Editor, for her work on the ancillary package, and Bryant Chrzan, Marketing Manager. Thanks also to Sini Sivaraman, Project Manager at Pre-PressPMG.

PR Writing: Role and Responsibility

Finding facts, communicating effectively in all media, knowing the law and being ethical—all are essential for the PR writer.

Public Relations and the Writer

Public relations writing—that's all about putting a "spin" on things. Right? Wrong! It is about tailoring messages for particular media and publics. Clients and employers may not understand this, but it is imperative that you do, as a writer. Writing for public relations takes many forms, as you will realize as you go through these chapters. The more you know about different media and diverse publics, the more facile you are with all writing assignments, the better off you will be in the kaleidoscopic job market.

The changing job market is bringing together various demands on the writer that used to be more distinctly categorized along separate job lines. Some public relations people will tell you that they don't write advertising copy. Too bad for them. They may get into a job where that skill is needed. As more public relations units identify their titles as "strategic communication," that often indicates an integrated communications practice that involves both advertising and public relations.

Many public relations practitioners are still learning about preparing digital messages combining words, art and sound, such as material for websites. Some are just relinquishing the task to specialists. The results are dreadful if those specialists in design, video and sound are not strong word people too.

Always and remaining critical talents for public relations people are the ability to recognize potential news stories and anticipating how these might be received by global audiences. Choosing words and illustrations requires a keen understanding of the complex, and often conflicting, values held among diverse publics. The demands on today's writers are for more versatility, greater understanding of the repercussions of convergence among traditional media and the impact and connectivity of social media and the requirements of different media and increased competence in using visuals and sounds to help convey a message.

Source: Comerunspeedbump.com, distributed by American Creators Syndicate, 3/29/09. "Please visit
http://www.mrstillschalkboard.com."

At the same time the demand for versatility is growing, there is more emphasis on
accountability—evidence that the messages work. Employers want measured proof of results
from communication efforts. There is no open budget line for communication. Yet there is
no need to despair. The writer who is genuinely good at the task of researching information,
learning its meaning and communicating that effectively is and always will be needed. You
must understand what makes public relations writing different, though, from literary writing,
news writing or selling, although you may be involved in all three.

Public relations writers do prepare messages for any medium that can convey information. Furthermore, much of the time, these messages—words, images and often sound—are
conveyed electronically. Potentially these messages can be received anywhere in the world.

The difference for public relations writing lies in the power and responsibility of the
public relations person who is in the position of brokering goodwill between an institution and
its publics. There are two aspects to this responsibility. Strategically, public relations practice
involves the ways an organization's operations and policies affect people—the face-to-face interaction of employees with customers or clients and the organization's participation in the affairs
of the community. Tactically speaking, though, good policies and good performance are worth
little if people don't understand the policies and don't know about the performance. The heart
of public relations practice remains in communication, particularly writing.

Good public relations requires communication skills, expertise in dealing with all media,
the dynamics of public opinion and the principles of persuasion. Further, the communicator
must know when and what to communicate. This involves analysis, judgment, counseling
and planning—in addition to and prior to communicating. In this chapter, we'll try to clarify
the nature of this complex task and the writer's role in it, beginning with a definition of the
discipline, public relations.

Defining Public Relations

Even people who practice public relations don't all agree on just what public relations is. Each
practitioner probably has a slightly different definition, depending on his or her particular
public relations experience. That experience is affected by the social, political and economic
environment. Thus, the practice of public relations in many countries is different, and the

demands on the writers vary. Nevertheless, certain definitions express the meaning of public relations to the satisfaction of most professionals. Ingredients to look for are "ethical," "socially responsible," "trusting relationships,"

"reliable communication," "anticipation of consequences," "counsel to client/organization" and "evaluator of outcomes."

Definitions change, but one of the oldest, adopted in 1978 in Mexico City during the First World Assembly of Public Relations Associations and the First World Forum of Public Relations, still contains essential elements:

Public relations practice is the art and science of analyzing trends, predicting their consequences, counseling organization leaders, and implementing planned programs of action, which will serve both the organization's and the public interest.

It's a broad definition but a useful one. By examining it more closely, we can get a better understanding of what public relations is and where the writer fits in.

Analyzing, Predicting and Counseling

The central part of this definition of public relations outlines the main roles of the professional public relations person: "analyzing trends, predicting their consequences, counseling organization leaders." These roles fall into the management context, in which personnel help to frame, implement, adjust and communicate the policies that govern how an institution interacts with its publics. It is through public relations that a company acts with responsibility and responsiveness—in policy and information—to the best interests of the institution and its publics.[1]

Doing this job well requires a broad educational background, expertise in many areas and, most of all, good judgment. Unlike the corporate attorney or accountant, the public relations practitioner cannot refer to a body of laws or procedures that prescribe behavior under given circumstances. Instead, the public relations person must know human behavior and combine that knowledge with specific information about people within the institution and people outside whom the institution deals with. For example, the PR director for a bank must consider the views of bank officers and bank employees as well as those of customers, the community, legislators and government regulatory agencies. The public relations person for the local school district must be aware of the feelings of students, parents, voters and the regional accrediting agency. Any institution has many publics, and the public relations director must be able to advise management about the possible impact on those publics of various plans, policies and actions.

In addition to analyzing publics and counseling management on the effects of policy, the PR person must be alert for signs of change. The right policy today will not necessarily be the right policy tomorrow. People's attitudes and opinions evolve, and the composition of the public changes. The capable PR person notes trends in public opinion and predicts the consequences of such trends for the institution.

Usually, the public relations director also serves as a spokesperson for the organization and overseer of the entire public relations program. The PR person at the top of the department spends little time on basic public relations techniques such as writing. The basics are handled by entry-level people, the staff writers.

Frank Wylie, a former president of the Public Relations Society of America, describes the division of public relations labor in this way: Senior-level public relations people are likely to spend 10 percent of their time with techniques, 40 percent with administration and 50 percent with analysis and judgment; at entry level, it's 50 percent techniques, 5 percent judgment and 45 percent "running like hell."[2]

Advertising, Publicity and PR

Much of the "running like hell" is done to carry out those "planned programs of action" mentioned in the definition of public relations. These programs, the most visible part of public relations practice, usually reach the public in the form of advertising or publicity.

However, as the lines between publicity and advertising are increasingly blurred, there's room for confusion about these two terms. Strictly speaking, *advertising* is time or space in a medium, purchased to display a message that has been prepared or approved by the buyer. Both content and placement—time and place, as well as duration—are controlled by the buyer. *Publicity* is information provided to a public without charge. The supplier controls content but relinquishes further control. When information goes to a news medium, the decision whether to use the publicity and the determination of its final form are controlled by the medium. Only when the medium itself is controlled by the source of the information is there full control of the message. Examples of controlled media would be employee communications of all types from magazines, newsletters and annual reports to video presentations and web pages.

Confusion begins when advertising is not purchased but is donated by a news medium to nonprofit organizations. Is this advertising or publicity? Technically, it's advertising because it looks like commercial advertising and is used in the time or space reserved for advertising. Further confusion arises over promotional letters and brochures. Are these direct sales (and consequently advertising), or are they promotions?

Adding to the problem is the fact that image, identity or institutional advertising is usually written by someone in a public relations department. On the other hand, ads for products or services, marketing-type advertising, often are handled exclusively by advertising agencies and their copywriters. Catalogs, which require more promotional kinds of writing, fall somewhere between publicity and advertising.

In any case, both publicity and advertising demand strong writing and conceptual skills. Most business executives are able to identify what they expect out of both, even when the lines between them begin to blur. However, many still equate publicity with public relations. Again there's an important difference. A publicist merely disseminates information. A public relations person, as we discussed, is involved in the analysis, counseling and planning that precede the dissemination of information. Or as PR authority the late Edward L. Bernays said, "Publicity is a one-way street; public relations is a two-way street."[3] PR incorporates publicity, press agentry and public information, with the emphasis depending on the type of institution.[4]

The Two-Way Street

The last part of the Mexico City definition of PR speaks of serving "both the organization's and the public interest." Publicists who simply transmit their organization's views to the media are not likely to serve the public interest. As Bernays said,

> Public relations is not a one-way street in which leadership manipulates the public and public opinion. It is a two-way street in which leadership and the public find integration with each other and in which objectives and goals are predicated on a coincidence of public and private interests.[5]

| **T A B L E   1 . 1** | *Feedback/Behavioral Model PR*   This symmetrical feedback model goes beyond communication to behavior. |

Symmetrical Process Model

The five steps in this model are represented by circles, each of which gives a public the opportunity to respond so that goals can be adjusted, or some mutual understanding arrived at. The first step, *discovery,* is gauging existing levels of awareness and discovering conditions under which publics are likely to respond positively. The second is *investigation* of responses of various publics in an attempt to create, raise or sustain awareness and to determine any problems that might result in modifying goals or even abandoning some publics. The third, *measuring,* means evaluating the latent readiness to act so that action can be anticipated and the conditions under which it may be expected. The fourth is *monitoring* responses so that the level and direction of action can be anticipated and some intercession be planned if the action is undesirable or some reinforcement if the action is going in a positive direction. The fifth is *evaluating* the behavior to see what action was taken by which publics and how it can be sustained, if positive, or counteracted, if negative.

Source: Created by the late Patrick Jackson and printed in *pr reporter, 33*(30), Exeter, NH, July 30, 1990. The model appears also on page 121 of *This Is PR*, 10th ed. Doug Newsom, Judy VanSlyke Turk and Dean Kruckeberg.

This means that the task of PR people is not simply to communicate management's view to the public. The task also involves communicating the views of the public to management. The objectives of an institution and its public relations program must be designed with the needs and desires of the public clearly in mind.

Going one way, the PR person analyzes public opinion and the needs of the community, and opens channels of communication that allow such information to flow into the institution. Using this information, the PR person advises management on the policies that are likely to be of mutual benefit to the institution and the public—or at least acceptable, if not beneficial, to the public.

Then—going the other way down the PR street—the PR person opens channels of communication that reach out from the institution to the public. These channels are used to interpret the institution's policies and actions to its various audiences. Communication in this direction is largely the responsibility of the PR writer. (See Table 1.1 Symmetrical Process Model.)

Publics, Channels and the Role of the Writer

It is a simple thing to say that the task of public relations writers is to communicate with the public. But in practice, there is nothing simple about it. It's not as though there were one single "public" to write for. Rarely is a public relations message important to everybody in the "public."

News that a theme park is creating a new thrill ride is important information to youngsters who enjoy such entertainment, but what they want to know about it is quite different from what businesses and residents near the theme park want to know. Concerns of businesses and residents are about increased traffic to the area and more noise. What that group is concerned with is different from what the city's safety engineers and the theme park's insurance people want to know. These groups' needs are all different from what the local and state tourism departments want to know. The tourism departments' needs for information are different from those of investors in the theme park, and even those are not the same. If the theme park belongs to a publicly held company, its stock is traded on the open market, so securities analysts are another public. Publicly held companies are also responsible to the Securities and Exchange Commission. If the theme park is your client or your employer, you have to prepare information to reach all of these publics, and the information for each has a different focus. This focus is not a "spin." It is a responsible communication to satisfy the information needs and interests of particular publics.

A *public* is any group of people tied together by some common factor. And as public relations writers soon discover, there are many, many such groups. As some public relations people say, and as we've acknowledged through usage in this book, the *public* in public relations should really be *publics*.

The Public in Public Relations

In his book *The Mass Media,* the late Stanford professor Bill Rivers describes the endless variety of publics in this way:

> There are as many publics as there are groups with varying levels of income, education, taste, and civic awareness; as many as there are groups with different political allegiances, different religions and so on. What concerns and convinces one public may seem trivial to another. Furthermore, the definition of each public is never static; it changes as the issues change. When California is voting for a governor, a Los Angeles college student becomes one member of a large and diverse public that includes a San Francisco stevedore and excludes a college professor at the University of Maine. But, when higher education in the United States is the issue, the college student is one member of a public that includes the professor but excludes the stevedore—except that the stevedore's working partner may have a daughter who attends the University of Idaho . . . and so on in bewildering variety.[6]

Obviously, each of us belongs to many different publics. If you're a student, you're naturally a member of a public important to the university or college you attend. If you're about to graduate, you belong to a public important to prospective employers in the community. If you've just married, you're part of a public important to real estate agencies eager to sell you a house. If you belong to the local chapter of the Sierra Club, you're part of a public important to politicians and energy companies.

Just as each individual belongs to many publics, each institution must communicate with many publics—from customers and suppliers to employees and stockholders. A public relations writer for a university must write for faculty, students, administrators, alumni, financial benefactors, community leaders, legislators and sports fans. The public relations writer for a political candidate tailors messages to fund-raisers, voters, reporters and precinct workers.

The global proliferation of electronic technology also means that messages may be received by "unintended audiences," or nimbus publics.[7] An awareness of these publics, knowledge of them and sensitivity to their potential reactions are critical because misunderstandings, some of crisis proportions, can result. As an example, a casual comment in a speech by a high-level business or political figure might characterize the citizens of a nation in such a way as to cause outrage when it is seen by them on television or reported in their other news media. Such a communications misstep can jeopardize trade negotiations or business deals.

One opportunity of building relationships among broader communities, including news media, is through use of social media.

It's not just the reach that is important, or even the instant access, but the feedback, also instant, that is a barometer of public opinion from a multiplicity of groups. Reliable and responsible communication with them has the opportunity to build trust.

The variety of publics is so vast that PR people often find it useful to divide the publics they deal with into two broad classes: internal and external. *Internal publics* are groups within the organization (such as employees or the board of directors). *External publics* are groups outside the organization (such as the media, your company's customers or the state legislature). The distinction between the two is not always clear-cut; stockholders, for example, though essentially an external public, can have close ties to the institution. One definition of internal publics is "all those who share the institution's identity." Broad categories of publics appear in Table 1.2.

Priority Publics

On any one project it is impossible to direct attention equally to all publics. Therefore, PR people must select the publics that are most important for the communication effort. They may include the group that a new policy will affect the most or the groups whose opinions are especially important. In any event, the groups considered most important for a communication effort are called the *target publics* or *priority publics.*

But demographic information alone does not tell writers all they need to know about a public. Statistics such as age, gender and income are not useful in predicting whether a person would be likely to subscribe to the magazine *Dog World,* for example. Dog lovers come in all ages, both sexes and most income levels—groups that might seem totally unrelated if defined by demographics alone.

In fact, what public relations people call *psychographics* is frequently more important to the PR writer than demographics. Psychographics classifies people by what they think, how they behave and what they think about—their special interests, such as dogs. Psychographic information is not merely helpful to the PR writer; it is often necessary. Consider the public relations director responsible for a university's alumni association magazine, who admitted with some dismay that she didn't know how to appeal both to an 80-year-old graduate of the engineering school and a 22-year-old sociologist. She did a research study that revealed a psychographic pattern binding all the alumni to the institution. This information suggested the sorts of articles that would interest alumni. The public relations director was then able to make informed decisions—and she now felt a great deal more confident in her choices. (See Table 1.3 for a formula to prioritize publics.)

Channels

To reach different publics, the PR writer must choose channels of communication carefully. To get the message across, the channel must be one that the target audience will receive and believe. For example, the amusement park that wants middle-school students

T A B L E 1 . 2	*Internal and External PR*		
	Internal	**External**	
Publics	Management (top and middle) Staff and employees (union and employee organizations—nonunion) Stockholders Directors	**Direct** (marketing communications) Customers Sales representatives Traders and distributors Suppliers Competitors	**Indirect** (institutional communications) Potential customers Potential investors (stockholders) Financial community Special community of institution Government (local, state, federal) Community (environmental)
Media	Personal (person to person/person to group) Audiovisual (specialized media: films, slides, videotape, closed-circuit TV, computer networks—i.e., on intranet) Publications (specialized media: books, magazines, newspapers, newsletters) Direct mail Exhibits (including posters and bulletin board materials internally displayed as well as personalized items such as pins and awards) CD-ROMs Email Fax (or facsimile) Web pages	Personal (person to person/person to group) Audiovisual (Web pages with art and sound, films, slides, videotape, mass media, specialized media available to external audiences such as externally distributed CD-ROMs, videos, etc.) Publications (mass and specialized, including controlled and uncontrolled publicity as well as institutional and commercial advertising) Direct mail (personalized, institutional and sales promotion) Exhibits (mass and specialized externally displayed and product packaging, graphics, including point-of-sale promotions) Broadcast fax Listserve (email) Internet site (on World Wide Web)	

Source: pr reporter 33(30), Exeter, NH, July 30, 1990. Used with permission.

to try its new ride would be foolish to run an ad in *Harper's* magazine. Few middle-school students even know that *Harper's* exists. They would not receive a message placed in that medium. But they do listen to radio and watch TV, so programs in those media are the channels that the amusement park would probably use, as well as maintaining an Internet presence.

The channel must also be appropriate for the message. Radio and television are not good channels for conveying messages on complex subjects such as a university's endowment. These subjects are better suited to a magazine or the school's website, channels that readers can spend

TABLE 1.3	*Discovering and Prioritizing Publics* Prioritizing publics may be done in a number of ways. One informal method is called the PVL *P*, the Potential to influence a public, plus *V*, the Vulnerability of the organization to that public (which may change over time and in different situations), equals *I*, the Impact of that public on the organization. Here is a tabular form for "computing" a PVI index.

	P	+	*V*	=	*I*
Audience or Public	Potential for Organization to Influence (Scale 1–10)		Vulnerability of Organization to Be Affected (Scale 1–10)		Importance of Audience to Organization
————————	————————		————————		————————
————————	————————		————————		————————
————————	————————		————————		————————

Source: Jim Haynes, *Instructor's Guide for This Is PR,* 3rd ed. Doug Newsom and Alan Scott (Belmont, Calif.: Wadsworth, 1985), p. 63.

time with. Traditional broadcast media, though poorly suited for discussing endowments, work just fine for telling students about weather closings.

Channels may be individuals or media and may be mass media or specialized media. Each medium has characteristics that make it suitable for sending a particular message to a particular audience at a particular time.

People may be channels—for example, through social media, in person-to-person meetings or person-to-group interactions such as speeches, meetings or LISTSERVs. When communication media are mentioned, you are likely to think of publications and audiovisuals. Publications may be books, magazines, newspapers, newsletters or reports. These may be printed or online or both. Audiovisuals may be videos on disks, online or on television. But people, publications and audiovisuals aren't the only channels of communication. Other channels are direct mail or email of personalized letters or institutional or promotional pieces. Exhibits are another channel. They encompass everything from trade-show displays to campaign buttons.

Specialized Media   Media designed for a particular audience are called specialized, to distinguish them from media for general audiences. Specialized media include the internal publications or intranets that institutions produce to communicate with employees, staff, management and others close to the institution, such as directors and stockholders. Also included in specialized media are an organization's computerized message boards and audiovisuals intended for internal use only. Among these specialized media are electronic information networks of personal computer users. Most specialized media are controlled by the institution using them. Email is a good example. Although not usually heavily monitored, there often is a "postmaster" to watch for viruses and to clean up the network storage system periodically.

Mass Media   These mass media include magazines, books, newspapers, radio, television and the Internet. Because neither the circulation nor the audience of such media is controlled by the institution, mass media are mostly for communication with external publics. Public relations writers using mass media to reach large audiences must remember, however, that such media are seen by internal publics as well. For example, a leading metropolitan daily newspaper's female employees objected to a promotional campaign that displayed women as sex objects. French police did not like billboards portraying them as "helpful" rather than as crime fighters facing danger.

The Role of the Writer

Public relations writers must be knowledgeable not only about publics and channels but about all aspects of their institution as well. The PR writer for a social services agency must understand welfare eligibility rules and federal funding guidelines. A writer for the highway department must know about everything from road-building materials to traffic laws. PR writers must know enough about the financial aspects of a business to prepare the right message for securities analysts and to develop an annual report that stockholders can comprehend and auditors will approve.

In addition to possessing a broad knowledge of their company's business, public relations writers must be able to research specific subjects to determine what is and what isn't important. They must be able to borrow ideas from other fields—psychology, social psychology, sociology and political science, for example—to help put their research in perspective. PR writers must be alert to changing patterns of thought and behavior in society and must fully comprehend the issues of the day.

Finally, and most important, the public relations writer must be an expert in communication. If you want to be a public relations writer, you must know how to write effectively in many different styles and for all media. You must understand the principles of good writing and be familiar with the vast body of scientific research on communication, persuasion and public opinion. Your goal is to be an efficient, effective communicator.

You must accept that your writing is management-oriented, strategic communication and therefore likely to be persuasive in nature. Because of the scope of your communication, you must command a knowledge of publics and their cultures—their corporate or work environment culture, their personal or lifestyle culture and their indigenous or ethnic culture. Beyond that, you must know the international communication networks and media systems and how they operate. No matter what message you communicate, what audiences you communicate with and which media you use to reach those audiences, you have to know which words will work and why. You are critical to the PR function.

Preparing you for these varied writing tasks is what this book is all about.

Conclusions

- A kaleidoscopic job market demands increasing flexibility and a greater command of technical skills from writers.
- More accountability for results is demanded by today's employers and clients—they want proof that the messages worked.
- Messages—a combination of words, images and often sound—are frequently communicated electronically and may be received anywhere in the world, whether or not that is the intent of the sender.
- Always and remaining critical talents for public relations people are the ability to recognize potential news stories and anticipating how these might be received by global audience.
- A public relations writer is responsible for helping an organization establish good relationships with its publics.
- Choosing words and illustrations requires a keen understanding of the complex, and often conflicting, values held among diverse publics.
- There are two aspects to this responsibility: *strategy* of determining what and when to communicate to whom and *tactics* for handling that communication through the appropriate channels so that receivers understand the policies and performance of the institution.
- The lines between advertising and publicity are blurred and frequently not clear to clients or employers.
- Advertising is time or space bought to carry a buyer's message, but public service announcements, although appearing in the same time or space as commercial copy, are carried at the discretion of the medium.
- Publicity is information supplied to the public without charge but also without control unless the employer or client owns the medium. Information supplied as publicity can appear in any form, and whether it appears at all is at the discretion of the medium.
- Public relations communication is a two-way street, a conduit for incoming as well as outgoing messages.
- Publics are people tied together by some common factor(s).
- Factors binding people together as audiences may be uncovered through demographics (statistics such as age, sex and geography) and psychographics (interests and attitudes).
- Priority publics or target audiences are public relations publics selected for special attention and specific messages.
- Channels of communication may be specialized media or mass media.
- A public relations writer's role is to know about the institution for which that writer is working, the audiences or publics of that institution and the channels of communication through which to reach them.
- Public relations writers must be effective, efficient writers in all media.

Exercises

1. Collect materials from your admissions office about your school. Analyze them for message statements about the school. Are different appeals addressed to first-year students, transfers, graduate students, older-than-average students? What are these appeals?
2. Examine the different types of materials from your school's public relations office. List all of the publics these suggest.
3. Look at ads for your school (commercials, too, if you have them). Compare these message statements with the admission materials and the publicity about the school. What message statements are consistent? Are any of them inconsistent? For example, does admission material suggest it's easy to get into the school while publicity talks about the high standards for admission?

Use InfoTrac® College Edition to access information on topics in this chapter from hundreds of periodicals and scholarly journals.

Ethical and Legal Responsibilities of the PR Writer

Jobs in public relations generally are not high in status. Some individuals and organizations are clear exceptions to that indictment.

Why are they exceptions rather than the rule? Many reasons are possible, but we'll focus on just four. First, public relations practitioners have a highly developed sense of personal and professional ethics that drives them to meet the spirit of the law as well as its explicit provisions. Second, they believe that their highest professional obligation is to advocate policies and techniques that are socially responsible. Third, they uphold the idea that looking after the best interests of priority publics is in the best interests of their organizations. Fourth, the organizations for which they work are managed by people who are proactive in outlook and behavior.

Public relations professionals and their organizations that don't meet those standards often cause problems for themselves as well as others. They sometimes are cited by critics as the reason public relations practice is seen in a negative light. Critics can find plenty of things to cite in support of their view.

If anyone ever doubted that we live in a "wired" world, the troubles of this global society that were piled on the desk of the 44th president of the United States, Barack Obama, when he took office on January 20, 2009, are more evidence than anyone needs. The global economy was in serious recession due to many factors. Major financial institutions and their insurers went out of business or were propped up by infusions of government investments. USA industries, including cars and planes, either went under or were barely viable.

Why? In many cases, the financial chaos was the result of bad judgment and greed, but much of it was due to outright fraud and lack of transparency. The interconnectedness of global businesses and their financial underpinnings resulted in personal economic disasters for individuals and families. Global stock markets fell dramatically on a daily, sometimes hourly, basis with every revelation of another financial crisis.

If that were not enough, the world also was the scene of lethal combat in many parts of the world, conflicts that created refugees fleeing, when they could, to safer territory. Places that could provide a safe harbor suddenly found their economies, already seriously strapped, desperately trying to accommodate an influx of people with nothing but the clothes on their backs.

Nature didn't help either with a series of earthquakes, storms, floods and such all over the world that resulted in more needy survivors. World relief organizations were strapped for resources in a diminished economic setting. Then, there were health issues such as a form of influenza, A/H1N1, mistakenly labeled "swine flu," that swept the world. Mexico got the blame because the epidemic erupted in Mexico City, and so did pigs, although the virus has no relationship to contact with pigs, live or as food sources.

The global financial turmoil made it more difficult to cope globally with these other problems. Examining the root of financial issues turns a spotlight on business practices that were questionable, outrightly deceptive and relentlessly greedy. Some were actually illegal but not prohibited by regulatory agencies supposedly responsible for doing just that.

You might pass off situations such as the derivatives investments, hedge fund excesses or loose investment and insurance institutional practices as nothing more than "just doing business." Even if you set aside legal issues, the question remains: Do these practices reflect good business ethics? Perhaps the question should be: What *are* good business ethics?

John Wanamaker, a famous retailer at the turn of the 20th century, had his personal credo etched into a marble column in his Philadelphia store: "Let those who follow me continue to build with the plumb of honor, the level of truth and the square of integrity, education, courtesy and mutuality." That credo is as valid today as when Wanamaker penned it. It applies just as much to the professional practice of public relations as to the conduct of any organization that interacts with the public.

Embedded in that quote are two guidelines especially relevant to public relations. One is the idea of being genuinely *sensitive* to the feelings and needs of others. The other is the will to practice the *Golden Rule*, which says you should treat other people as you want to be treated by them. Although these two guidelines are at the center of responsible professional practice, they are too simple to fully describe the complex set of influences affecting how you approach and complete any writing task.

Public relations writers often initiate or implement practices that draw criticism, much of it justified. Although some public relations writing practices are legally prescribed, others are set by *moral principles*. Ethics are founded on moral principles that are themselves grounded in effects. Moral principles consist of a set of beliefs and values that reflect a group's sense of what is *right* or *wrong*—regardless of how these terms are defined in formal rules, regulations or laws.

This is the case whether you agree with the idea that a moral judgment must fulfill *formal conditions* or you think a moral judgment must also meet some *material conditions*. The difference is that formal conditions call for moral guidelines or rules that are regarded as universal and prescriptive. But material conditions represent considerations that deal with the welfare of society as a whole and emphasize basic human good or purpose. For example, agreements in the Geneva convention are prescriptive, but they do not address restrictions on the freedoms of individuals within a society such as apartheid or immigration quotas.

If you ask for a public's view of your ethics, don't be surprised if your organization is seen as unethical. The public view of an organization's ethics is likely to be based less on a definition of morality than on the consequences of what the organization says and does, which will be seen as either moral or not moral by each and all of its publics. This sense of rightness, even if it later proves to be in error, is the stuff of on which *public opinion* is formed.

Clearly, public opinion is important. Much of what you will do as a professional will be directed toward influencing, if possible, the opinion of publics. Since we live in a global society, you need to remember that, as a public relations practitioner, not everyone in the world is free to express a personal opinion.

For example, Singapore's attorney general wanted to charge a senior editorial page editor of *The Wall Street Journal* for contempt based on two of the paper's editorials and a published letter to the editor that the Attorney General said impuned the integrity of the nation's courts. (In Singapore, sedition laws prevent any criticism of the government.) The substance of the suit involved defamation (libel) court judgments against the head of the opposition Singapore Democratic Party, Chee Soon Juan, and his sister for publishing in the party's newspaper an article implying corruption on the part of government founder Lee Kuan Yew and the current prime minister, his son, Lee Hsien Loong.

In many parts of the world, some expressions of opinion, or even fact, are not legal. This will affect the way you as a public relations person do your research and communicate your messages, including illustrations.

In the USA, the country's First Amendment is treasured, in a real sense the product of public opinion. That's a sobering thought because it implies that the First Amendment can be abridged or voided if public opinion no longer supports it. So if you write, say or do something that violates society's sense of "rightness," you may be undercutting your constitutional right to free speech. That's a heavy responsibility. As a PR writer, how can you meet it?

Core Values and Personal/Professional Behavior

Our core values are based on our personalized belief system—what we believe to be right or wrong. We are influenced in these by our family, friends, education and a faith we endorse, if we do. This core of values we take into the world where it is often tried and tested, but probably no more so than in the workplace.

The reason is that organizations, like individuals, develop around a core set of values, often set forward in a mission statement or even a formal statement of values. These values are operationalized in the corporate culture that is often set by the organizational leadership. In looking for a place to work, you need to find an organization that fits within your own value system. In all probability, the organization that hires you will be looking also for a "good fit" between the corporate culture and a potential employee.

Even when there is a "good fit," initially, situations change and so may your level of comfort in working there. One way to understand ethical responsibility is to look carefully at the interplay of different levels of influence on your personal and professional behavior.

Dynamics

Pressures in the workplace come from the economic, political and social system in which the organization exists. As we live and work in a more global society, these pressures have increased significantly. It's an understatement to say there is little consistency in cultures. You are more likely to hear the term "cultural conflicts."

Governments are a big part of that. Governments change and with them the philosophy of governance as well as the laws themselves and the rules of regulators. Public relations is a recognized discipline, but it is practiced in many different ways around the world because it too must be responsive to the environment in which it functions in representing businesses and nonprofit organizations. Additionally, the organization itself for which you as a public relations person work is responsive to standards and practices set by its own industry. If you work for a PR firm or agency, you may have clients from a number of different industries. The relationship between you and an organization changes with time. Provisions of communication law are always in flux because a new court decision may put a different interpretation on a law, rule or regulation. And society's expectations and judgments about what is right or wrong are notoriously capricious. An example of changed expectations is the effect of what's happening in cyberspace to the old protocol of a clear division between advertising and editorial content. Website editorial independence is seldom carefully defined, and search engines finding information on a topic cannot sort out the independent news from the sponsored information.[1] Compounding the problem are the many organizations that have placed their websites in the hands of management information systems specialists instead of public relations people. Because building and maintaining relationships are not necessarily high on their list of priorities, the result can be damaging to the corporate image.[2]

Trying to follow your own moral compass in the swirl of this social, legal and economic storm is not easy. You can easily get "off course," confused in your ability to know with certainty your ethical and legal responsibilities as a writer. Adding to the confusion is the increasing diversity of the population, especially in the USA. With this mix comes a complexity of value structures. Although these may be difficult to tease out in research about your publics, it is crucial that you do so.

Things simply change. What is wrong today may be right tomorrow, or vice versa. It is your responsibility to be sensitive to these changes; otherwise, you and your organization may get into lots of trouble stemming from the volatility of today's values.

Values

The concept of *values* is another way of talking about ethics. The study of ethics falls into two broad categories: *comparative ethics* and *normative ethics*. Normative ethics are studied by theologians and philosophers. Comparative ethics—sometimes called *descriptive ethics*—are studied by social scientists, who look at the ways different cultures practice ethical behavior. Values form the foundation of our institutions and organizations, as well as of our informal and formal rules of behavior.

We're taught from an early age that some values are eternal verities. But if we see them violated repeatedly without sanctions, we begin to wonder whether they really are verities or eternal. A deceptive public relations practice, for example, may go unpunished or even unnoticed, and its users may gain significant advantages to the detriment of others. Which are the values we are expected to exhibit as responsible public relations writers?

Remember that ethics, being value based, are different in different cultures, something to be sensitive to when communications go to other countries and something to be aware of in other countries, such as the USA, that also have diverse cultures. When the *limits* of what your primary public will tolerate turn out to be narrower than those of your organization or yourself, your ethical behavior will be open to public debate, which may result in censure or withdrawal of support. In such cases, your first concern should be with examining your own personal and professional standards.

Influence of Personal Standards

Your personal and professional ethical standards come from your core values. If you find that your own standards are in conflict with those of your colleagues (especially your supervisor) in an organization, it can be personally and professionally upsetting.

Suppose that your task is to write, say or do something that, although legal, can't readily be reconciled with your own standards. What is your responsibility? To resolve this problem, you must explore your options realistically. Four basic strategies are apparent: (1) try to educate those in your organization to your standards; (2) refuse the task; (3) ask that you be given another task; or (4) take the assignment.

Educating

You can try to convert those around you to your point of view. The character of an organization tends to reflect its top leadership. The leadership hires managers, who then hire people whom they perceive as fitting into and contributing to the goals of the organization. To say that you must be a clone of the top leadership is absurd, but it is equally absurd to believe that you would be in the job if those doing the hiring had not assumed that you "fit the mold" to some extent.

That assumption will be in your favor as you attempt to educate others in the organization to your point of view, because you are presumed to be much like them. If you use this identification tactic, you'll probably find that some colleagues are open-minded but others aren't. If your organization encourages dialogue, however, your chances of getting a fair hearing are greater. But even with a fair hearing, you may not convert them to your view of the world; besides, you may be wrong. A lot depends on how carefully and thoughtfully you have drawn the personal and professional circles of influence around yourself.

How pliable is your position? What is the absolute limit beyond which you will not compromise? What justification can you offer to support your position? Is the basis of your justification appropriate to the situation? You must ask yourself and carefully answer these questions and many like them before you attempt to implement a strategy of conversion.

Suppose you ask and answer such questions to your own satisfaction and mount a campaign to change the organization's course of action. Can you win? Yes. Even if you aren't successful at converting your colleagues, you still may win in two important ways.

First, your colleagues will respect a well-articulated, well-reasoned argument, even if they disagree with it. That's because the subject of contention is a matter of judgment. Neither you nor they can be absolutely certain of the truth of the matter, but each of you may recognize and appreciate sincere efforts to divine it.

Second, you also win because, when you articulate a different or unpopular standard, you accept the highest responsibility of being a professional public relations person. You are expected to counsel your organization against doing something you believe is wrong. Any lesser standard of behavior is not worthy of being called professional.

If you don't convert the others to your point of view, you can then adopt a strategy of refusal.

Refusing

A position of refusal is often greeted with arguments that "It's OK because everybody does it." If those arguments don't succeed, they are often replaced by anger—even retribution—that may get you fired. Your willingness to risk being fired is the severest test of your conviction. If your belief is strong enough, getting fired may be a personal and professional favor to you. That's because it tells you clearly that the organization does not respect you or your professional judgment and abilities. You need to know this so you can find another organization that does. Also, you will not be subject to criticism when the action of the organization draws fire.

No one and no organization can make you do something you believe is wrong, even if it is not illegal. If you cave in because you need the money, you like your position, you're really counting on an attractive retirement program or the like, your convictions are mostly for show. That's your fault. Don't blame the organization, society or some generalized "other" for the bottom-line decisions you make.

If you don't have the courage of your convictions, you may tend to assume that others don't either. This may be true of some, but not of all. And such an assumption is likely to make you less sensitive to the feelings, needs and values of others. As a result, you may write, say or do things that are harmful to pertinent audiences, without even recognizing it. Thus you may feed on and perpetuate stereotypes, confuse form with substance and promote behaviors detrimental to the best interests of your target publics. If left uncorrected, this behavior can end in alienation and loss of support for your organization, thereby setting the stage for program or organization failure.

To paraphrase the Golden Rule, the way you are treated as a writer is a reflection of how you, as a writer, treat your target publics.

Requesting Reassignment

If you like what you are doing and your prospects for the future look good, you may seek an alternative to refusing the task. One approach is to ask that you be assigned to something else of equal or greater importance. The problem is that there may be no one else to take the assignment. Assuming that someone else is available, this strategy will produce three important results. First, by stating your case clearly, calmly and logically, you will find out just how persuasive you really are. Second, whatever the response to your request, you also discover how you are valued by your supervisor and organization. Third, you'll get a clearer picture of the people you work with and for—what their values are and how they relate to the organization and industry with which they are identified.

Taking the Assignment

Taking the assignment, even if you are sincerely opposed to it, labels you as a team player who puts the values and needs of the organization above personal values. You are seen as fitting into the culture of the organization. You won't rock the boat. You will safeguard the values of

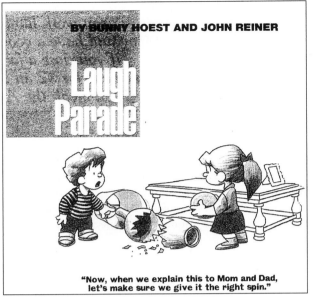

Source: Reprinted by permission of Bunny Hoest.

the organization because you are loyal and trustworthy. You may even get a raise, a promotion or both.

The problem with all this is that you may be expected to write, say or do things that, although not strictly illegal, may violate a primary public's sense of right and wrong. If you push beyond what your target public will tolerate, you are likely to find yourself on trial in the court of public opinion. The judgments can be harsh. Even if you later clean up your act, you may never win an appeal or get a pardon. That will depend to some extent on the values and standards of practice exhibited by your organization and industry.

Influence of Organization and Industry Standards

Will having high personal and professional standards mean that you'll always be swimming upstream in your organization? That depends on the organization you work for and the industry sector it is part of. Some organizations and industry sectors are seen as monoliths whose only purpose is to make more money or gain additional power and influence. Such perspectives often are based not on facts but on perceptions that masquerade as facts. Some organizations and industry sectors seem more gifted than others at keeping facts and "facts" in close harmony.

Perceptions

Johnson & Johnson (J&J) is remarkably successful at marketing a wide range of medical products and supplies. This long-term success can be traced in part to its standards of practice, as explained simply in its corporate credo. (See Figure 2.1.)

Our Credo

We believe our first responsibility is to the doctors, nurses and patients,
to mothers and fathers and all others who use our products and services.
In meeting their needs everything we do must be of high quality.
We must constantly strive to reduce our costs
in order to maintain reasonable prices.
Customers' orders must be serviced promptly and accurately.
Our suppliers and distributors must have an opportunity
to make a fair profit.

We are responsible to our employees,
the men and women who work with us throughout the world.
Everyone must be considered as an individual.
We must respect their dignity and recognize their merit.
They must have a sense of security in their jobs.
Compensation must be fair and adequate,
and working conditions clean, orderly and safe.
Employees must feel free to make suggestions and complaints.
There must be equal opportunity for employment, development
and advancement for those qualified.
We must provide competent management,
and their actions must be just and ethical.

We are responsible to the communities in which we live and work
and to the world community as well.
We must be good citizens—support good works and charities
and bear our fair share of taxes.
We must encourage civic improvements and better health and education.
We must maintain in good order
the property we are privileged to use,
protecting the environment and natural resources.

Our final responsibility is to our stockholders.
Business must make a sound profit.
We must experiment with new ideas.
Research must be carried on, innovative programs developed
and mistakes paid for.
New equipment must be purchased, new facilities provided
and new products launched.
Reserves must be created to provide for adverse times.
When we operate according to these principles,
the stockholders should realize a fair return.

Johnson & Johnson

FIGURE 2.1

Johnson & Johnson Credo   *"Our Credo" is Johnson & Johnson's attempt to state clearly its standards of practice with reference to its primary publics.*

Source: Reprinted with permission of Johnson & Johnson.

The credo places top priority on the welfare of its customers. Most organizations say no less, but J&J is perceived as really meaning it. That's because J&J tries to respond quickly and responsibly to any threat to the welfare of its priority publics. This was demonstrated dramatically when the company immediately removed all Tylenol (made by a subsidiary company) from retailer shelves after a psychopath laced some capsules with cyanide, resulting in the random deaths of several people.

The economic loss to the organization was enormous. But the decision in 1982 to remove Tylenol from the public was both quick and decisive because management believes the J&J credo means what it says. More importantly, the public perceived the decision as the "right" thing to do. It was not mandated by law; it was simply the most responsible thing to do. Performance that is perceived positively earns lots of favorable support. That support has carried J&J through subsequent crises as well.[3]

On the other hand, Exxon's response in 1989 to the aftermath of the Valdez oil spill provoked extensive criticism from many quarters. Whether Exxon did everything it could do as quickly as possible will likely be debated for years. But Exxon was perceived as not responding quickly and responsibly. In fact, you expect to see comments about Exxon on every anniversary of the spill. Remember that perceptions become "facts" in the court of public opinion. Once those judgments are made, they may be very hard to overturn. And even when they can be overturned, the process is usually slow.

Organizational Culture and Values

When you start a new job, you'll go through a period of training in the culture and values of the organization. This may include attending a formal training program whose announced purpose is to acquaint you with the principal processes, techniques and policies that are to guide your behavior as an employee. These also reflect, but often not as obviously, the values and culture of the organization. But much of your training comes from simply watching and interacting with your new associates. That's how you learn the rules governing how you should behave in an organization. These rules of conduct may become so much a part of you that you hardly notice them. You may even respond automatically to new cues.

Automatic Responses

When you do things automatically, you're less likely to question your behavior or that of the organization. And if you don't question how, what and why you do things, you aren't much more than an automaton. The only real difference is that you draw a salary. Automatons are machines whose greatest expense comes in the form of an initial capital investment, supplemented by routine maintenance to keep them productive. When they wear out or become outdated, they are simply replaced.

A responsible public relations writer should be a thinking, constructively critical and contributing member of the organization. In fact, the highest contribution you can make is not your technical skill but your sensitivity to the needs of your organization's relevant publics. If you become so immersed in the culture and standards of the organization that you lose touch with the values of those publics, you can do little more than a machine can do.

Problems may arise when the messages you shape undergo significant changes in the process of obtaining necessary approvals. The challenge for you is to see that these changes don't affect the sense of what must be communicated. This problem is aggravated by "editors" who excise segments or change things just to prove they can. You are supposed to be good enough with words and language that you can retain the sense of the message without compromising its integrity and without challenging the ego of those who have authority to approve what you write.

Because you are part of your organization, you are expected to know as much about what you write as anyone in the organization. You can't rely on your wordsmithing skills alone. You must know your organization and its industry thoroughly. You won't get much support or respect if you repeatedly make simple mistakes, such as using jargon incorrectly. You are supposed to know, and you shouldn't have to be told over and over. That's part of an organization's culture and values. But the practice of professional public relations also has its own culture and values, thus representing another area of influence on your behavior.

The complexity of this overlay of influences makes ethical decisions anything but clear-cut.

What Happens When You Aren't Told?

Unfortunately, there's yet another scenario to consider. One has to imagine that many investor relations people experienced this during the recent global financial meltdown. You are not told about decisions that have moral, and sometimes legal, consequences.

The reason that "best practices" in public relations has the top PR person reporting directly to the top manager of the organization is that to communication responsible, you have to know the facts. Some top managers don't agree and hide facts from their public relations people assuming that "what they don't know won't hurt them," and certainly won't "get outside." They are just wrong.

When a crisis is brewing, or even seems likely, the public relations person has to know as much as can be known, and as soon as it is known. It is the responsibility of top management to tell its board of directors, even if it is a nonprofit organization, and to arrive at an action plan that should be shared with the top public relations person immediately. Be sure that such procedure is in place before you take a job or you are accepting unnecessary personal and professional risk.

Source: "Shoe" © MacNelly. King Features Syndicate.

If you are not told, what do you do when you find out? You have to meet with top management to determine why you were not told and then evaluate your situation. If you can't persuade management to take an ethical and responsible communication of the situation, you are better off leaving. Leave gracefully, without accusations or threats. If legal possibilities are involved, you also need to get a lawyer. Yes, you'll have to bear the cost, but whatever that is, it is not as costly as the loss of your reputation, which could make you unemployable in the industry. Or, the result could be a substantial fine or imprisonment, if the event involves legal matters.

Influence of Public Relations Standards of Practice

The reason you could find yourself unemployable is due to a tainted professional performance. Every professional field has its own code of ethics and standards of practice. One of the most widely acknowledged codes in public relations is the one adopted in 2000 to replace the 1988 code. (The Public Relations Society of America adopted its first code in 1950.) The code has much to say about the standards of practice, but a few key points are especially pertinent to your role as a writer.

Accuracy

Credibility with primary publics is probably the most important asset a writer or an organization can have. Without credibility, it is very difficult to succeed at what you want to do. Factual inaccuracies usually are pretty easy for primary publics to detect. The more difficult such inaccuracies are to discover, the more damaging they may appear in the eyes of your audience. Publics may conclude that you have deliberately distorted or misrepresented the facts for some ulterior motive.

They may label you and your organization as dishonest—and you are, if you misrepresent the facts. But you and your organization can also make "honest" mistakes. These may seep into your writing as a result of rushed, sloppy editing, failure to verify details and the like. But if you simply rationalize them as "honest" mistakes, you're really not being very responsible. You are paid to do things correctly, and this includes preventing "honest" mistakes from getting by.

To illustrate, the annual report of a major oil company contained an out-of-place decimal that dramatically reduced estimates of its oil reserves from those it had claimed in previous reports. The financial community immediately became alarmed because it feared the company had been puffing up earlier estimates of its reserves. Frantic phone calls and a dramatic drop in share prices ensued. The company quickly issued a corrected estimate, so the damage, though costly, was temporary—all because the writers, editors and proofreaders made an "honest" mistake. You can also bet that market analysts and brokers looked at the next year's annual report with an extra dose of skepticism. "Honest" mistakes are sometimes no less damaging than dishonest ones.

Honesty, Truth and Fairness

The concept of honesty goes beyond the idea of accuracy and raises questions of truth and fairness. You can deal with documentable facts as a writer and still be dishonest, untruthful and unfair. So factual accuracy is not enough. The selection of facts and the way you weave them into the fabric of a message are what establish you as honest, truthful, fair and credible.

Must you use all the facts, even the bad? No. But to ignore the negatives is not fair. Even if members of your primary audience are not highly sophisticated, they are not dumb. If you fail to acknowledge damaging information, you simply invite disbelief. Not only will you not be believed, you may also be perceived as unfair. Honesty and forthrightness served American Airlines well when one of its jets ran into a mountain in Colombia. The airline's chief pilot said, "Human error on the part of our people may have contributed to the accident."[4] Years ago, the legal department might have been in an uproar because of concern over protecting the company from liability. Now most organizations see that a greater loss may come from a failure to speak out. A loss of credibility translates to a loss of customers.

Illustrations matter too, and often that is a question of fidelity to truth rather than an attempt mislead or deceive. A digitally altered photo released from the USA's Army regarding promotion of Ann Dunwoody to four-star general involved keying in the USA flag as background instead of her desk in front of a bookcase. The USA's Department of Defense claimed not to have violated Army policy in altering the photo, but the Associated Press (AP) suspended use of photos from the USA's Department of Defense as a result of its policy of not altering any content from an image.

That situation probably is a more ethically defensible one than another issue involving the USA's Department of Defense. The Pentagon Public Affairs office had sent around retired military officers as spokespeople supporting the government's military decisions. Many of the retired military analysts were said to have undisclosed ties to military contractors. Many retired military officers have gone to work as advisors to companies that are defense contractors. The uproar that disclosure of this practice created was over the law against "domestic propaganda."

False or Misleading Information

Misleading information can lead audiences to make bad decisions. When they discover they have been misled, they withdraw their support. Although you and your organization may enjoy some advantage because of a deception, the advantage is usually temporary. And the consequences of misleading people can be enormous as well as long term. In fact, disaffected audiences may seek retribution through legal actions, boycotts or other means.

The excesses of false and misleading information that came from Enron and WorldCom provoked the Sarbanes-Oxley Act of 2002 designed to make publicly held companies more accountable. As a result, the Securities and Exchange Commission (SEC) and the New York Stock Exchange issued new orders. Although the public relations implications fall largely on the investor relations specialists, other corporate communications people must also be watchful. One has to wonder about some deliberate and confessed decisions during the financial meltdown that are in direct contradiction to Sarbanes-Oxley and even SEC regulations.

The Sarbanes-Oxley regulations requiring more explicit information about earnings emphasizes the SEC fair disclosure regulations made in 2000. That SEC regulation requires that investing decisions be made more accessible to the public and that anytime material information is intentionally disclosed, it must be made available simultaneously to all publics. That did not happen when Bank of America acquired Merrill Lynch. The bank officer blamed the regulators for telling him not to make the disclosure. So that action was intentional. When unintentional, the undisclosed information must be made public as soon as possible. Disclosure also has to be made through a combination of means to reach as broad an audience as possible. Many Investor Relations (IR) officers now post news releases immediately on the corporate website as well as sending them on the Dow-Jones wire, the AP wire and the PR newswire.

Public relations practitioners also were affected by the Campaign Reform Act of 2002 that created new disclosure requirements and requires prompt compliance with earlier regulations so that there's more public information available about politically active groups and individuals.[5] Truth has a way of emerging in spite of extraordinary efforts to keep it hidden. In the vast majority of cases, false information is destined to fail. PR writers who knowingly write and distribute false information, for whatever reason, violate one of the trusts explicit in the Public Relations Society of America (PRSA) code and risk losing the respect and acceptance of their primary publics. False information corrupts not only a writer but also the channels of communication used to distribute it. Hence, false information supplied to a newspaper and relayed to readers damages the reputation of the newspaper, as well as the primary source, in the eyes of the readers. The result is that the newspaper may be reluctant to accept subsequent information from you. Moreover, not only will you find it more difficult to get information into that newspaper, but also will all other public relations people. The assumption will simply be that all public relations professionals are alike, and you can't trust any of them.

Influence of Laws and Regulations

Everything you write has the potential to spark litigation. You must know your freedoms under the First Amendment (if you are in the USA) and the laws governing commercial speech as well to bulletproof your writing as much as possible. If your material is going into other countries, check on your rights and restraints there too. You can't fully immunize it from legal action, but you can minimize the potential for losses. And you don't have to be an attorney to do this. Just follow some simple guidelines.

Negative Laws

The first guideline is to realize that laws are generally negative. They define what is not legal. They generally don't define what is. You may suppose that something is legal because it has not been defined as illegal. But although that may be true at the time, you may be in for a surprise later.

A further guideline is to remember that case law is built on a series of court decisions, each citing previous decisions. Even when a substantial line of cases evolve from a seminal decision—often one that turns on some question of constitutionality—each new case has the potential to produce a different interpretation of what is illegal, thereby setting a precedent. One thing you should guard against is doing something that will turn you or your organization into a legal precedent.

A case in point was a U.S.A.'s Supreme Court decision in 1989 declaring that the copyright of creative work is the property of the freelancer or vendor unless its ownership passes to someone else in a legal contract at the time the work is authorized. Organizations and

PR agencies have sometimes acted as if they owned such creative work, even when no contract existed. The only way they can own it now is to contract for it ahead of time or to obtain permission to use it, which may involve paying fees for each additional usage. That now includes making the print version available on a website.

Simply because you or an organization has always done things in a certain way does not mean that those procedures will be acceptable tomorrow. It is your responsibility to keep up with court decisions and new laws affecting communication in general and your organization and industry specifically. Copyright laws continue to change regarding materials available through cyberspace.

That brings us to another guideline. Read and study each new issue of *Media Law Reporter*. This publication specializes in timely reports and summaries of laws and court decisions affecting every aspect of mass communication, including public relations. If you have any doubts about a new law or court decision, consult an attorney who specializes in communication law. Don't depend on other attorneys, because they may know no more about communication law than you do.

Contracts

You'll find that your organization probably uses lots of outside vendors—writers, producers, photographers, printers and the like. Because they are working for you, you are responsible for their actions in the process of preparing and presenting their material. You must know the nature of agreements with each of these suppliers. Otherwise you are liable to make a grievous error that may cost your organization lots of money and perhaps you your job. One of the most important contract areas is work done "for hire." Unless a vendor signs away ownership of his or her creative work to your organization in a legal contract, you may not use it for any additional or subsequent purpose unless you get legal permission and, sometimes, pay additional fees. This applies to all kinds of creative work.

Additionally, any time a photographer—whether staff or freelance—supplies you with pictures, each one that includes people (especially professional models) must be accompanied by a photo release form duly signed, thus "releasing" his or her likeness for use in the specified situation. If you're using a freelance photographer, determine who owns the rights to the images before shooting begins. Ownership of the images may fall under the "for hire" provision, too. But unless a contract says otherwise, the photographer retains the negatives and controls subsequent uses of them.

One contractual arrangement now simplified is for the organizational use of music—either for meetings or to entertain phone callers put "on hold." The American Society of Composers, Authors and Publishers now has an umbrella contract covering the playing of copyrighted music in public. Some organizations play their own promotional jingles, which for copyright reasons they usually have written especially for that purpose unless they use music "in the public domain," music on which the copyright has expired. There are some risks here because special arrangements of such music and performances of it may still carry a copyright, especially now with changes in the USA and the European Union (EU).

In addition to explicit contracts governing outside vendor relationships, there is an implied contract between you and your employer that you will maintain confidentiality. Some firms actually write this into a separate employee contract, although most of the time it's understood that you will keep to yourself what you learn about a client or an organization.

That you will protect confidential information is an implied contract. You won't share information with anyone outside the organization and will use a "need to know" basis inside. Such discretion is especially important when you're dealing with financial matters that may constitute "insider information" and thus be of concern to the Securities and Exchange Commission (SEC). The fact is that if you tip someone who uses that information for personal gain in the stock market, you are as guilty of "tipping" as they are of "insider trading."

Commercial Free Speech

In the USA, no First Amendment rights for organizations are constitutionally guaranteed. However, over the years, a commercial free speech doctrine has evolved. Advertising is clearly covered. The doctrine is less clear about public relations communication, as Nike discovered in defending itself from a lawsuit filed by activist Marc Kasky. Nike had been accused of using sweatshop labor in contracting factories abroad to make its shoes and not monitoring working conditions there. Nike wrote letters to educators and opinion leaders defending its operations and also wrote op-ed commentaries for newspapers as well as sending news releases to the papers.

The USA's Supreme Court has always supported First Amendment privileges for *political* free speech, even when it is inaccurate. But, Kasky sued Nike for false *advertising*. So, the question really is the definition of Nike's action: commercial speech, as Kasky claimed, or noncommercial, as Nike claimed. Commercial speech is held to high standards of truth so consumers will not be deceived. Earlier cases, like the 1983 Texas Gulf Sulphur case where a news release was held to be "false and misleading," suggest that news releases are also under the umbrella of truth.

The problem is that commercial free speech is determined by case law, to which the Nike case contributes. In the past, decisions have moved back and forth across the spectrum of just how free are organizational and institutional voices.

Beyond case law, organizations and institutions also have to deal with possible contempt of court in trying to defend themselves in lawsuits. Litigation journalism (or litigation PR as some prefer to call it), has relaxed some earlier threats. But all it takes is for the opposing side to make the case to the judge handling the case that anything being said about the case is likely to prejudice the jury. When that occurs, you can't write a position paper about the case that you make public or write commentaries or interpretations of the case for public consumption without inviting a contempt of court charge. Furthermore, you can't go on talk shows, issue news releases, buy advertising space or time or take other actions to convey the position of your organization on the case. This can be very frustrating because it effectively gags an organization until the case has been decided.[6]

Libel Laws and Privacy Issues

When you defame someone in writing, it's libel and to do so in speech that is not written is slander. Defamation is an attack on someone's character, good name or reputation.

If people believe they have been libeled by what you have written, they can bring legal actions for actual and punitive damages. Your best defense against libel is to be accurate and truthful to a fault—so much so that you can document anything you say. Public figures (elected officials and people in the public eye) who bring libel actions must prove you libeled them "with malice." You should realize, however, that current case law makes it difficult to determine exactly who is a public figure.

You need to be very careful when dealing with both public and private figures. Stick with provable facts. You can't play fast and loose with words and avoid libel actions. Look at the list of "red flag" words in Table 2.1. Any time you use them, you are inviting a court appearance.

Privacy laws are most often of concern when you want to use a person's likeness and name in publicity, advertising or other promotional materials. People in pictures of crowds at public

TABLE 2.1	*"Red Flag" Words* Words can be semantic land mines. It is best not to step on them.

These "red flag" words and expressions are typical of ones that may lead to a legal action if they are not carefully handled in news releases or other messages from an organization.

adulteration of products	co-respondent	gay (in context of "homosexual")	mental disease	smooth and tricky
	corruption		moral delinquency	sneak
adultery	coward	gouged money	Nazi	sold his influence
altered records	crook	grafter		sold out to a rival
ambulance chaser	deadbeat	groveling office seeker	paramour	spy
atheist	deadhead		peeping Tom	stool pigeon
attempted suicide	defaulter	humbug	perjurer	stuffed the ballot box
bad moral character	disorderly house	hypocrite	plagiarist	
bankrupt	divorced		pockets public funds	suicide
bigamist	double-crosser	illegitimate	price cutter	swindle
blackguard	drug addict	illicit relations	profiteering	
blacklisted	drunkard	incompetent		unethical
blackmail	ex-convict	infidelity	rascal	unmarried mother
blockhead		informer	rogue	unprofessional
booze-hound	false weights used	intemperate	scam	unsound mind
bribery	fascist	intimate	scandalmonger	unworthy of credit
brothel	fawning sycophant	intolerance	scoundrel	vice den
buys votes	fool	Jekyll-Hyde personality	seducer	villain
cheats	fraud		sharp dealing	
collusion	gambling house	kept woman	short in accounts	
communist (or red)	gangster	Ku Klux Klan	shyster	
confidence man		liar	skunk	
			slacker	

Any words or expressions imputing: a loathsome disease; a crime, or words falsely charging arrest, or indictment for or confession or conviction of a crime; anti-Semitism or other imputation of religious, racial or ethnic intolerance; connivance or association with criminals; financial embarrassment (or any implication of insolvency or want of credit); lying; involvement in a racket or complicity in a swindle; membership in an organization that may be in ill repute at a given period of time; poverty or squalor; unwillingness or refusal to pay or evading payment of a debt.

Source: Bruce W. Sanford, *Synopsis of the Law of Libel and the Right of Privacy,* rev. ed., Scripps-Howard and World Almanac, 1981. Used by permission.

gatherings represent fair use, but you can't single out people in the crowd and use them for promotional purposes without their consent. If they happen to be celebrities, you'll also need a legal contract to back up the usage. Otherwise, you may be guilty of invasion of privacy.

Libel is another issue, and one that is changing, in many ways due to the Internet. First of all, the person or institution suing for libel must prove damage. In the defense of libel claims, the documentable *truth* must be admissible in court, and that's up to the judge.

If a Massachusett state court judge's decision holds up at the federal level as precedent, a judge might even determine that if truth is spoken or published maliciously or due to "ill will" on the part of the speaker, it still is libeleous. "Actual malice," from the *New York Times v. Sullivan* case, has consistently been interpreted to mean "reckless disregard for the truth," leaving provable truth a defense. Libel lawyers as well as all supporters of the First Amendment's doctrine of free speech are watching the *Noonan v. Staples,* February 13, 2009, ruling by the U.S. Court of Appeals in Boston, based on state law that predates the *New York Times v. Sullivan* decision.

Privilege, another defense, is a fair and true report of a public, official or judicial hearing, but who determines whether the report is "fair"? The *fair comment* defense, which used to protect people such as reviewers and columnists who often exaggerate statements about public figures for humor, has suffered some severe blows in the courts. Some claim that now such protection doesn't exist. At the federal level, public figures still must prove malice in their libel suits, although, in some instances, their defense has been privacy. The privacy issue is often ignored within organizations when they assume that because people work there it's all right to use their names and pictures without permission. This is not true, and problems multiply if the representation is in something designed to make money for the organization, such as an ad or a brochure. There are also problems if the employee no longer works for the organization. The protection is a release form giving you *permission*.

Copyrights and Other Rights

A 2003 USA Supreme Court decision upheld a 1998 congressional action that extended all existing copyrights by 20 years. The premise of a copyright is that creators of creative works should own what they create. Consequently, it provides a means of protecting a person's or organization's creative property against unlawful appropriation and use by others. By copyrighting what you write, you serve notice that the work is yours. Always use the copyright symbol (©) with the word *Copyright* adjacent to it. Copyrighting does not automatically invoke legal action in instances of suspected infringement. It only makes it possible for you to seek legal redress. The initiative lies with you, not the law. Copyright protects the specific expression of an idea, but ideas, as such, are not protected.

The extension of copyrights means that the works of individuals on which the copyright would have ended in 50 years after the creator's death, now are still in effect for 70 years. If a creative property, such as songs and compositions, movies or cartoon characters, is owned by a corporation, the previous 75-year copyright protection is now 95 years. There is a Digital Millennium Copyright Act of 1988 that outlaws electronic copyright infringement, at least in the USA. When the EU was created, it brought the diverse copyright laws of its member nations under one umbrella. The result was a 70-year rule that began in 1995. File for copyright protection with the Library of Congress (http://www.loc.gov/copyright/).

You should also be aware that many publications routinely copyright their contents. However, unless the individual messages in these publications were written by staff personnel, their creators retain ownership of what they have created.

Violations of copyright often take the form of plagiarism. Public relations writers have to be acutely aware of not usurping other's creations while doing research. If you quote a source, put your notes in quotation marks, and register all of the information you will need for attribution. Furthermore, if you want to use more than 100 words from one source, less if it is a song, poem or relatively small work, you must get legal permission from the copyright owner of the source.

Much to the dismay of fans of historian Doris Kearns Goodwin, in 2002 she admitted to copying passages from other sources and using them in her own. She was asked to take a leave of absence from PBS's *The News Hour* and resigned from the Pulitzer Prize Committee. She is not the only high-profile public figure to admit to incorporating others' work into her own. In the election campaign for the 44th president of the USA, artist Shepard Fairey created a poster based on a photograph taken by an AP photographer of the then candidate Barack Obama. Neither the photographer nor the AP was given credit. Fairey's position was that artistic license changed the image so substantially that no permission or credit was needed. The AP then countersued Fairey and his companies claiming they knew the image was copyrighted by AP and still used it as a basis for posters and other merchandise sold and distributed through various channels without permission or compensation.

If you, as a public relations person, plagiarize someone's work, not only will you be fired when it is discovered, you will also have to find your own attorney and pay all of the expenses. Furthermore, it is highly unlikely that you will be able to find PR employment again.

When you use somebody's trademark, service mark, trade character or the like, make sure that you show the ownership. For example, the ™ symbol must appear immediately after the mark, usually accompanied by a line of small type that says something like "[product name] is a registered trademark of [company name]."

You do need to realize that many individuals and countries see copyrights and trademarks as unfair protectionism and argue for more freedom of appropriation of creative work.

Government Regulators

Most of the things you write will fall under the purview of four major government agencies. One is the U.S. Postal Service. That agency is concerned with classes of mail, fraud, lotteries and the like. The range of regulations is staggering. And you'll find the interpretation of some of them varies significantly, depending on whom you ask. So, if you're not sure about something, ask the postmaster at the site where you expect to do a mailing. That's the only way you can really be sure.

The SEC is especially concerned with information dealing with or relating to the stock market and the financial community in general. Particular concerns that may affect you as a writer involve executives and their compensation, annual reports and news releases dealing with the financial condition or direction of your organization and potential opportunities for insider trading. The Internal Revenue Service also watches financial reports.

The Federal Trade Commission (FTC) has a wide range of interests. In relation to writers, however, the FTC is most concerned with maintaining fair competition. Hence, seemingly deceptive advertising or other promotional materials draw FTC attention and action.

The Food and Drug Administration (FDA) watches over information from food and health industries and is very protective of the consumer. In fact, it considers information drug companies circulate about their products to be promotional, and it closely monitors educational or scientific activities.

Other regulatory groups can affect what you write too. In fact, the Bureau of Alcohol, Tobacco and Firearms threatened to close Leeward Winery in California because the winery quoted in a newsletter to customers information from a CBS *60 Minutes* show that suggested red wine may help reduce the risk of heart disease. Another winery got into trouble for using similar information in an ad. A liquor store was also stopped from using an in-store wine sales campaign that had heart signs reading "Wines to your health" and "Be heart smart."[7]

Your responsibility is to know the applicable rules and regulations affecting your organization and industry. If you don't know the answer, ask someone who does. But you'd be wise to go to the original source, rather than risk acting on someone's well-intentioned but possibly wrong advice. For protection, some advertising/public relations agencies and other profit-making companies have internal legal counsel and a policy of reviewing all information, especially public announcements of any kind.

Influence of Primary Publics

Although the four major areas of influence already mentioned are vital to your success as a writer, none is more important than the influence of primary publics. Every organization, public or private, profit making or nonprofit, must be keenly aware of the influence of its primary publics. Indeed, the organization can exist only with their permission.

Permission does not always mean approval of all that the organization is doing. However, the critical limits of an organization's ethical and legal behavior are determined by its primary or closest publics—those who share organizational identity, such as employees and (often) former employees, and those with whom it has an ongoing relationship, such as suppliers, distributors and customers.

Shared Values

The stronger a public's identity with the organization, the stronger its reaction will be to what the organization is saying and doing. Primary publics perceive themselves as having shared values with the organization. Any violation of these values is often reacted to very strongly and personally.

Relationships can be considered at three different levels: developmental, sometimes called the cultivation stage, the maintenance level and the quality level or strength of the connection of an individual to the organization.

To have a strong connection to the organization, people need to feel they have easy access, are being listened to in a positive way and are responded to honestly and fairly. The underlying consideration is trust in the organization and the credibility of its communications, both created by transparency.

Transparency is an expectation of openness and disclosure of information that significantly affects all publics. The Internet provides multiple opportunities for any organization to develop unique and personal connections. These are easy to establish but are of high maintenance.

Nevertheless, the quality of an organization's relationships with its publics is a measure of good management. Even those who may not agree with the organization should respect it.

Adversarial Groups

Maintaining connections with and respect from adversarial groups is critical, and therefore, their reactions are anticipated in the planning process and closely monitored thereafter. Adversarial groups may include regulators, competitors, special-interest groups and activists concerned about certain aspects of society (the environment, endangered species, animal rights and so on). These groups typically perceive themselves as having a different, not shared, set of values. That's not always the reality, but it is almost always the perception. For this reason, adversarial groups exhibit little tolerance for "mistakes" or "poor policy decisions."

Source: DILBERT: © Scott Adams/Dist. by United Feature Syndicate, Inc.

Although the closest publics may respond quickly and personally to something they don't like or something they see as a violation of shared values, they are much more forgiving than adversarial publics. These two groups set the boundaries within which an organization must operate to be successful. Understanding their ethical standards and values is therefore crucial to planning and setting policies.

Conclusions

- You have to be genuinely sensitive to the feelings and needs of others, and you must treat others as you want to be treated.
- Public relations writers often initiate or implement practices that draw criticism of public relations.
- Some public relations writing practices are legally prescribed; others are set by moral principles.
- Moral principles consist of a set of beliefs and values that reflect a group's sense of what is *right* or *wrong*, regardless of how these terms are defined in formal rules, regulations or laws.

- *Formal conditions* call for moral guidelines or rules that are regarded as universal and pre-scriptive. *Material conditions* represent considerations that deal with the welfare of society as a whole and emphasize basic human good or purpose.
- The public view of an organization's ethics is likely to be based less on a definition of morality than on the consequences of what the organization says and does, which will be seen as either moral or not moral by each and all of its publics. This sense of rightness is what creates public opinion.
- If you write, say or do something that violates society's sense of "rightness," you may be undercutting your constitutional right to free speech.
- One way to understand your responsibilities is to look carefully at the interplay of several levels of influence on your personal and professional behavior.
- Society's expectations and judgments about what is right or wrong are notoriously capri-cious, so it's your responsibility to be sensitive to changes and even to anticipate them.
- The study of ethics falls into two broad categories: comparative ethics and normative ethics. Normative ethics are studied by theologians and philosophers. Comparative ethics—sometimes called descriptive ethics—are studied by social scientists, who look at the ways different cultures practice ethical behavior.
- Remember that ethics are culture-bound. This can create controversies in ethnically diverse societies like the USA and provoke problems in other countries where values are different.
- Because your own ethical standards are at the core of your behavior, you have to decide what to do when your standards conflict with those of the organization. You have four strategy options: (1) educate the organization and persuade them to accept your standards; (2) refuse the task; (3) ask that you be given another task; or (4) take the assignment.
- Publics work with perceptions of facts, and these perceptions become the "facts" on which opinions are based.
- When you go to work for an organization, you may be given formal training in the cor-porate culture or value system, or you may pick it up informally by watching and inter-acting with new associates.
- Your real worth to an organization consists of your ability to be in tune with relevant publics. When you know these publics well, you can construct messages that are valued and accepted by them.
- Professional associations of public relations practitioners have standards with which you must comply in order to be accepted.
- Credibility with publics is essential for the success of an organization, and this quality depends on accuracy, honesty, truth and fairness.
- False and misleading information destroys credibility, and truth has a way of emerging. Besides, in some cases, giving out false information is against the law.
- This is a litigious society, and you need to bulletproof your writing as much as possible.
- Most laws are negative, defining things you cannot do. In addition to the laws them-selves, there is a body of case law consisting of judicial decisions interpreting these laws. Because case law is in flux, you have to keep up with the changes.
- Watch for changes in the laws, especially those governing materials available in cyberspace.
- Contracts can keep you out of a lot of legal difficulty, but you must know what you need to specify in contracts and what is bound by contract.
- Commenting on a situation that is under litigation can earn you a contempt of court charge.
- Libel laws and privacy considerations can cause you legal problems if you don't under-stand them thoroughly, even when you are dealing with public figures.

- Copyrights protect your creative works but not your ideas. You need to be sure that you observe the copyrights of others. The trademarks and such of an organization are protected by law, but legal protections are sometimes difficult to enforce. You need to get permission when using materials protected by such registry. Plagiary is a violation of copyright.
- Federal government regulators that figure most prominently in public relations writing are the U.S. Postal Service, the SEC, the Federal Trade Commission, the Internal Revenue Service and the Food and Drug Administration.
- When in doubt, consult a good attorney who is a specialist in communication law.
- Relationships with publics can be considered at three different levels: developmental, sometimes called the cultivation stage, the maintenance level and the quality level or strength of the connection of an individual to the organization.
- To have a strong connection to the organization, people need to feel they have easy access, are being listened to in a positive way and are responded to honestly and fairly.
- The underlying consideration is trust in the organization and the credibility of its communications, both created by transparency.
- Transparency is an expectation of openness and disclosure of information that significantly affects all publics.

Exercises

Situation: You are the vice president for corporate communication at Enodyne, a conglomerate. You are in a corporate board meeting, having just finished presenting the budget for next year, when an emergency phone call from Ben McConkle—the public relations director of a subsidiary, Fielding Works, which manufactures industrial solvents and other chemicals—advises you that a Fielding transport on its way to a toxic waste dump had an accident near North Platte, Nebraska, about three hours ago. The truck turned over three times and several containers of toxic chemicals ruptured, posing high danger to people on the scene and to people within a five-mile radius, depending on the speed and direction of the wind. No one was injured seriously, but the driver and his companion suffered minor abrasions and bruises. The driver is Burl B. Benton, 33, an employee of 10 years with a spotless record. The companion is Helene A. Haven, 30, a female nonemployee. McConkle wants quick guidance on how to handle inquiries, especially those related to these facts: (1) tests showed that Benton and Haven had been drinking; (2) neither was legally drunk; (3) tests showed that Haven had traces of cocaine in her system; and (4) McConkle has not yet notified Mrs. Benton and her two children of the accident. McConkle needs your advice now, not later, because the news media will pick up these facts very soon.

1. What guidance will you offer McConkle? Is your guidance fully responsible to Enodyne, to the driver and his family, to the driver's companion and her family, to the people in the area of the accident and to others? How so? Why so?
2. Write a one-page summary of the ethical problems involved in this situation, and explain how they might affect you as a PR writer.
3. Write a one-page summary of the potential legal problems in this situation, and explain how they might affect you as a writer.

Use InfoTrac® College Edition to access information on topics in this chapter from hundreds of periodicals and scholarly journals.

Persuasion

W hen you identify yourself as a public relations writer, some people may regard you with skepticism because they think of what you do as manipulation. Be prepared for that, but there's no need to apologize for it. Persuasion is implicit, if not explicit, every time a person tries to communicate with another. It is just that public relations is widely known for trying to persuade publics to a particular point of view.

Persuasion is explicitly part of the public relations fabric. If it is done ethically and legally, it logically is no more objectionable than most other human activities. Persuasive efforts now may seem more focused than in the past. That's because more and more companies are taking an *integrated* approach to planning and implementation. Integration simply means that a single communication strategy undergirds all messages from an organization. It is intended to give them unity and consistency.

The literature labels this approach variously as *integrated marketing communication, marketing communication* or simply *integrated communication*. We prefer integrated communication because it seems to encompass a range of activities not often central to the selling emphasis of marketing. The term used is not important, but it is important that you recognize that public relations efforts by many companies now seem to have a sharper focus than in the past. That tends to sensitize people to the persuasive role of public relations.

This integrated approach affects every public relations writer in at least two ways. First, writers will be expected to adapt any message to any medium. That certainly is not a new development, but an integrated communication philosophy will make it far more common than in the recent past. Second, writers who can think about persuasion at the strategic level will be at a premium. It is clear that a writer who knows how will always have a job. But the writer who knows why will always be the boss. That piece of wisdom is the focus of this chapter. Although persuasion has always been important in public relations, now it is critical that you understand the why, as well as the how, of persuasion. To begin, consider the following scenario.

A nuclear engineer especially good at explaining technical matters once gave a talk to a civic club in a small town. He used dozens of slides, charts and graphs to describe the operation of nuclear power plants and to explain how safe they were.

At the end of his talk, an elderly lady thanked the engineer for his presentation. "I don't understand anything you said," she told him, "but I agree with you a hundred percent." The point: People rely on information and logic in forming their opinions, but only up to a degree.

It is true that people are rational. But that only means they can think. People are also emotional. Were people driven only by logic, there would never be a need to persuade. The fact is, however, that people in economically advanced societies such as USA base most of their decisions and behaviors on emotion rather than logic. Most of us don't have to spend every waking hour just getting enough food, clothing and shelter to sustain life. As these things are easier to attain, we spend more and more time on improving their quality. That's where emotion comes in. And it is the context in which persuasion is most often used.

As we pursue our enlightened self-interest, we are often motivated more by emotions than by logic. Nevertheless, we place great value on information. It is the stuff of which good public relations is made. But a lot of public relations writing also attempts to persuade people to adopt a particular point of view.

To be a persuasive writer, you need to have some idea of the arguments—both factual and emotional—that will work best with your target publics. Common sense can give you some clues, but you'll do a much better job if you know something about the science of persuasion. Common sense is no substitute for what decades of research has revealed about how and why people form their opinions. As public relations pioneer Edward L. Bernays put it, "Like Columbus, you can sail west and reach new land by accident. But if you have charts, you can do better; you can arrive at a destination decided upon in advance."[1]

When engineers design bridges or buildings, Bernays pointed out, they apply a knowledge of physics, chemistry and other sciences. Doctors treat patients using a knowledge of biochemistry and medical research. In the same way, public relations people should apply the relevant findings of social sciences such as psychology, sociology and communication when they embark on efforts to persuade.

Persuasive writing focuses attention on these message areas: *recipients* of the message, intended and unintended; message *construction* with the emphasis on what consequences are intended—increased knowledge, attitude or behavior change; *source* for the message—who the source is and the credibility of that source with the intended recipients and the credibility of the organization identified with the source. Decisions have to be made at every level.

Primary, though, are the recipients: Who are they? What do they know or think they know? What do they believe about the issue/the organizations involved? You can't construct a message until you know that. The message construction then has to have a purpose: What do you want to happen as a result of communicating that message? What effect is it likely to have on each of the intended recipients? What about unintended recipients such as competitors, activists or other critics? Then there's the choice of a source: Who is the most credible, overall, with particular publics? In a crisis, there is another consideration of source because there will be many message sources from all parties involved. You know from personal experience that coverage of an apartment fire means you're likely to see and hear statements from fire officials, police, hospitals, owners of the apartment complex, residents as well as their friends and relatives.

The intent of maintaining credibility is to be sure there is consistency in the message statements. Many questions come up time and again in persuasive writing. Should you give both sides of the story or only your side? If you give both, which side should you give first?

Should you draw an explicit conclusion, or is it better to let the audience figure it out for itself? Which should you give first, the good news or the bad news? How effective are fear techniques? Should you make a point once or repeat it several times to make sure it sinks in? These are the sorts of questions that social scientists can *help* you answer.

Of course, research findings can only help you answer these questions. Research results can be valuable guides in planning persuasive communication, but they are not laws of nature. In many cases, the findings collected so far are not conclusive. At times, you have to rely on personal experience and knowledge of your audience.

Nevertheless, social science has found out a lot about the nature of persuasion, and it would be foolish not to put that knowledge to use. Research data is better than off-the-top-of-the-head speculation about the how and why of opinion formation.

Opinion Formation and Change

The first thing you need to know as a persuasive writer is that you are not going to gain many converts to your point of view, at least not immediately. The reason is simple. The few minutes a person gives to reading your message are not likely to change attitudes built up over a lifetime. If you're going to make headway at all, you need to know something about what attitudes and opinions are and how they are formed.

Opinion, Attitude and Belief

Some authorities see little or no need to distinguish among opinions, attitudes and beliefs, at least in theory. On the practical level of trying to understand how and why people behave as they do, however, it may be useful to you to make such a distinction. (See Table 3.1.)

In this context, opinions are temporal, fleeting and unstable. They can change on a whim. Attitudes are a little more stable and are less likely to change immediately. Beliefs, however, are very stable, and they are very resistant to change. To illustrate the different levels involved, suppose we get in a time machine and travel back to 1950. At that time, products made in Japan were generally believed to be of poor quality. Opinions in the USA of products with the "Made in Japan" label were not charitable. With the introduction of import cars, a variety of electronic gear and camera systems of high quality, however, attitudes began to change. Now we believe that many brands of products made in Japan in these categories set the standards of quality against which all others are judged.

TABLE 3.1	*From Opinions to Attitudes to Beliefs*

Accumulation of information and experiences—Opinions (conditional, temporal, fleeting and unstable)

Clusters of opinions relevant to a specific way of thinking about something compared with personal experience = Attitudes (relatively stable)

Attitudes currently held measured against values = Beliefs (less flexible or subject to change, except over time)

How did this change come about? As we began to experience products of higher quality from Japan, our opinions shifted to the extent that favorable attitudes began to be common, and these eventually came together in support of a belief that the label "Made in Japan" deserved respect.

When we accumulate information and experiences, we form opinions. Some of these opinions tend to cluster as especially relevant to a specific attitude. Attitude clusters then tend to gather in support of a specific belief. As used here, belief is the same thing as *engaged attitude* in Table 3.1 because the emphasis is on the effects. The point is that opinions can change with the wind. Beliefs can change, too, but they are slow to do so. Attitudes fall somewhere between these extremes. In many respects, opinions, attitudes and beliefs are closely linked, so it makes sense for us to discuss them as one, using the term *attitude* to signify all three.

Models of Attitude Formation and Message Recipients

To begin with, an individual's personal background or historical setting plays an important role in his or her behavior. Where was the person born? Where did he or she grow up? What were the social and economic conditions of the day? These and similar factors help to shape personality. Historical factors also shape the issues that persuasive writers deal with—not only those of their audience, but their own as well.

All of these considerations are part of the social environment in which communication and persuasion take place. Individuals belong to groups with social norms that affect their opinions. A person's life experiences also play a large part in attitude formation. And naturally, the characteristics of the issue at hand are important.

One other major element of the social environment influences attitudes: available information. Here is the one door open to the persuasive writer. The writer has no power to change a person's personal history or the norms of social groups, although persuasive messages may be woven into those fabrics of experience. You can't expect to change someone's life situation or provide a significant new experience with your message. As a writer, however, you can hope to add to the information on which attitudes may be based.

If you look at the situation objectively, it does not appear to be encouraging. Why spend all the effort and resources necessary to shape and send persuasive messages if there isn't much hope for change? The fact is that providing information is your only chance of making an impact. Even if the impact is minimal, you have to try. That's why you need to understand the nature of persuasion.

The Nature of Persuasion

As a writer, you can look at persuasion in three basic ways. One is as a learning process, whereby you impart information and members of your audience seek information because they want to know something. The second way of looking at persuasion is as a power process, whereby you attempt to "force" information on someone. The third broad view is that persuasion is simply an emotional process. No single perspective of persuasion is likely to be adequate, because the formation of attitudes is a complex process. But we can outline some aspects of the process that, when taken together, offer some useful insights.

Aspects of Persuasion

One of the best outlines of this process appears in Otto Lerbinger's *Designs for Persuasive Communication*. Lerbinger describes five "designs" of persuasion: (1) stimulus-response, (2) cognitive, (3) motivational, (4) social and (5) personality.[2]

Stimulus-Response   The concept of stimulus-response is the simplest approach to persuasion and, perhaps, the least useful. It is based on the idea of association. If two things are seen together many times, people tend to think of one when they see the other. Clearly, stimulus-response behavior does not involve any intricate thought on the part of the audience. It is useful only when a low level of response is acceptable. It seems to work as well with animals as it does with people, or perhaps even better. The classic illustration of this approach is Pavlov's experiments with dogs, in which a tuning fork was struck each time meat powder was fed to the dogs. Soon, whenever the tuning fork was struck, the dogs began to drool in anticipation of food. Similarly, a cat owner (a nonscientist) discovered that she could call her cats from any hiding place by starting up the electric can opener. The cats associated the sound of the can opener with food and thus with dinner.

Obviously, this design is not a very good way to persuade someone regarding a complex issue. If, however, you simply want to establish an "association" between an idea and your organization in the public mind, stimulus-response may provide an adequate model to follow. For example, Avis has been successful in associating its name with the idea of trying harder. But this design seems not to be as effective with internal audiences. The reason appears to be that they usually have much more cognitive information about the organization, so they tend to regard such low-level messages as fluff.

Cognitive   The concept behind the cognitive design is that people can think and reason about what they read, see or hear. And they will come to the right conclusion if they are given the right information in an understandable way. The "right conclusion" is not necessarily the one you advocate, but it is the one that is "right" by the standards of individual members of the audience.

The cognitive approach can be effective in many situations. If a person has no personal stake in an issue, for example, or has no preconceived notions about it, the simple presentation of information may be effective. Also, if you have a complex story to tell, a cognitive approach may be your best choice. People like to think of themselves as fair and reasonable, and if you provide reasonable arguments, they are likely to agree with you—other things being equal.

Of course, other things seldom are equal. You can't expect to dump your message (whether stimulus-response or cognitive) into people's heads without considering what is already in them. To persuade someone to take a certain position, you have to know what will motivate the person to take that position. This idea is the basis of the motivational design of persuasion.

Motivational   Generally, the motivational design is based on the idea that a person will change an attitude to fulfill a need. In essence, your message to the audience will offer some kind of emotional reward for accepting your message and responding to it as you suggest.

What are some needs that motivate people? A convenient outline of human needs was devised by the psychologist Abraham Maslow, who grouped human needs into a hierarchy ranging from the most basic to the least tangible. At the bottom of the hierarchy are physical needs such as food, water, air and sleep. One step up is the general need for safety, or the need to be free from fear of harm. Then come social needs: the need to belong to groups, the need to associate with others, the need for love. Next come personal needs, such as the desire for self-respect, the desire to feel important, the need for status. At the top of the scale are the self-actualizing needs: to fulfill potential, to be creative and to have a rewarding life.

Whether these needs are being fulfilled—and in what measure—may play a major role in an individual's response to your attempts at persuasion. Persuasion that ignores these needs in order to concentrate on reason and logic is not likely to get very far. It is also important for you, as a writer, to identify the relevant needs of the members of your audience. If your target audience is mostly at the social needs level and you're appealing to them at the ego level, your chances of success are diminished. Attempts at persuasion that do not meet individuals' needs will fail.

Social   Closely related to the motivational design is the social design of persuasion. This design takes into account an individual's background, social class and group norms. Often, group membership is the most important element in determining attitudes. On issues in which attitudes are closely tied to social conditions, persuasion must be designed to address the social factors that influence the individual.

Essential to this design is the idea that we learn from society which values are best and worst and which patterns of behavior are most acceptable. The key point here is that if you are trying to persuade across major regional, ethnic or national boundaries, the same message is unlikely to be appropriate in every case. You'll have to prepare separate messages, based on different social influences.

Continuous monitoring of program effectiveness is recommended for all of these designs, but it is especially important with the social design because norms change. They are dynamic. It is necessary, then, that you continue to take the pulse of your public. The norm today may not be the norm tomorrow. You'll need to know when, why and how the norm changes so that you can adjust your messages to the new conditions.

Personality   Finally, you can't ignore the fact that each individual is unique. Personality characteristics can determine which arguments will work best with a given person or public. Of course, a persuasive message is frequently directed at a large group containing a number of different personality types, so the personality design cannot be used effectively in many instances. Even if your message is directed at a large group—that is, it is designed for the masses—you should always remember that it will be received separately by individuals. As a writer, you need to remain aware of how personality characteristics affect persuasibility.[3]

Rokeach's Value Hierarchy

Values are a major contribution to the way recipients of messages respond to them. A hierarchy of values developed by Milton Rokeach complements, rather than competes, with the Maslow hierarchy.[4] Rokeach says that values are more important than attitudes and beliefs as primary influencers of our behavior. His values system, however, is based on attitudes and beliefs that cluster together to form values that are even more resistant to change than needs in the Maslow construct.

Rokeach thinks of values as specific clusters of attitudes and beliefs that act as long-term goals. He further asserts that values fall into two categories: *terminal* and *instrumental*. Terminal values represent ultimate life goals, but instrumental values are the tools we use to achieve terminal goals. Rokeach divides his values system into five levels.

Primitive values exist on two levels. At the first level are those core beliefs that are seldom challenged such as expectations that the sun will rise in the east. Writers are wise not to challenge messages that contradict basic beliefs because these disturb people who will dismiss them. At another level of primitive beliefs are values that are somewhat idiosyncratic and personal and for which there is no consensus. We may feel undervalued by our employer and/or family, for instance, but we seldom articulate these beliefs. Instead we hold them internally, but seldom do we change them very much. Such values are difficult to change, and the most effective messages are those that reinforce these values rather than contradict them.

Authority values depend upon our interaction with others, parents, friends or colleagues. An example may be the parental advice not to lie because then you don't have to remember the fiction you created. While beliefs on which these values are founded can change, the values may not change much. The writer may challenge the beliefs with persuasive messages but don't directly challenge authority values.

Derived values are ones we develop from our vicarious interaction with trusted sources such as books we read, Internet sites we have bookmarked, television or radio shows we listen to regularly. These derived values are better targets for persuasive messages because they are more easily influenced.

Inconsequential values are those based on individual preferences and tastes. These are more easily changed because they express a personal preference, such as preferring to live in a warm, dry climate, but they are not so substantive as to be self-defining.

Taken together these values, beliefs and attitudes define our self concept—the way we see ourselves. If something arises that challenges our self-concept, we move quickly to reestablish our sense of well-being. Shifts in beliefs or attitudes ordinarily result in short-term changes in behavior, but the values on which they are based seem to control our lifelong set of behaviors.

Steps in the Persuasion Process

Once you have considered all the different designs for the art of persuasion, how do you actually go about persuading someone?

To answer that, we must first identify the steps in the persuasion process. Social psychologist William McGuire lists six such steps: presenting, attending, comprehending, yielding, retaining the new position and acting.[5]

Presenting   You can't persuade anyone of anything unless he or she is in the right place at the right time to perceive a message. A person who does not own a television set probably will not see your public service announcement on TV. If he or she has a set but it is tuned to another channel, the result will be the same. In both cases, it will not matter how beautifully you have written the announcement. The same is true of the story in the newspaper about the benefit concert to help the hospital. If a person does not subscribe to the paper in print or at the on-line site and does not buy one at the newsstand, your message is not going to penetrate and persuade that individual at all.

Attending   The nonviewer's next-door neighbor probably has a TV set, and he might see your announcement. But he might not pay the least attention to it. He might be looking straight at the screen but thinking about who's going to win the upcoming football game. If so, he's not getting your message either. He must attend to the message—that is, pay attention—if you're to have any hope of persuading him.

Comprehending   Suppose this guy's wife is paying attention. She is watching the screen and listening intently to the sounds. But she's Belgian and does not speak a word of English. She likes to watch football games even though she can't understand the announcers. But she can't understand the public service announcements either, so there isn't much chance that you'll persuade her. The point is, you have to use message symbols that your audience can comprehend. If you don't, your message, even if delivered and technically defined as sent, will fail to communicate.

Yielding   In the house next door is another woman who sees the same message. She understands English, so she comprehends what your announcement says about the concert and its benefit to the hospital. And she happens to work at the hospital. But her reaction is somewhat neutral because she isn't very fond of the musical group. "They just try to make up for a lack of talent by playing and yelling louder," she says to herself. She got your message, but she did not yield to it. Although communication occurred, persuasion did not.

Retaining the New Position   Let's assume that the first woman's husband isn't daydreaming about football scores after all, but sees the commercial and is impressed. "That looks like a great idea," he says. "I think we should go to the concert because it will not only be fun, it will help the hospital." But the concert does not happen for another month. By that time, he may have forgotten about the concert and the benefit to the hospital. Your attempt at persuasion has been successful in getting the viewer to accept it. But because the viewer didn't retain his new attitude, for all practical purposes this attempt at persuasion has failed.

This element, of course, represents one of the main arguments for sustained public relations programming. It is not enough to get the message through. The message has to be retained by the audience long enough for the desired action to occur. Frequent repetition of the message and in different media is necessary to reinforce the adopted position until a person can act on it.

Acting   Now let's assume that the viewer didn't forget your message. Perhaps he saw the same announcement again and once more expressed a desire to go to the benefit concert. He may even have gone downtown with the intention of buying tickets, discovering when he got there, to his surprise, that his favorite pop singer was scheduled for a concert on the next weekend. So rather than buying the benefit concert tickets, he opted for the pop concert. Your announcement, then, did persuade him to a new attitude, but the persuasion was not strong enough to get him to act on it.

To be successful, persuasion must accomplish all six of these steps. McGuire calls the relationship between the steps in the persuasion process and those in the communication process the "matrix of persuasive communication." You must get your message to the audience. More important, you must get someone to pay attention to it. And the message must be understandable; people are more likely to read things that are easy to understand. In any event, they aren't likely to come over to your side if they don't understand what your side is. But understanding isn't enough. Your arguments must be convincing. The audience must be willing to give in, or yield. Then they must remember that they gave in, and then they must act.

You'll need to consider all these steps when designing persuasive messages. Techniques that work well for some steps might be useless for others. Some persuasive writing gets people to pay attention, but it might not be memorable. Messages designed only to produce yielding might not get the audience to act. For example, one research study tried to decide which persuasive methods were best for getting new mothers to go to the maternity ward for examinations. As it turned out, the best method depended on how the results were measured. One method got the most mothers to say they would come back a month later, but another method produced the most mothers who actually did go back a month later.[6] Obviously, one method was good at inducing yielding, but the other was better for retention and action.

Typology of Steps in Persuasion

A typology of steps in the persuasion process by David Therkelsen relates each step to the content areas of social science, communication, psychology and marketing and to such root functional areas as segmentation and writing. For example, his typology shows demographics, for instance, as relevant primarily to the first four steps in the persuasion process.[7] But writing relates mostly to the attention, comprehension and memorability steps.

A persuasion model with which you are probably familiar is a list of steps in the adoption process—adoption of a product, practice or idea. The first step is awareness, followed by interest, then some evaluation of the new information. If it is a product or a practice, this is followed by a trial, and if that works to the benefit of the experimenter, adoption follows. The model attracted more attention in public relations where it became known as the diffusion model.[8] This model indicates some elements that affect steps along the way as well as the personality of individuals taking those steps.

Persuasion and Logic

Although strategies and the steps in the persuasion process are easy to grasp, another element is often ignored. This element often makes people uncomfortable, because in its purest form, it demands rigorous thought. We're talking about *logic*, specifically *applied logic*. To understand the idea, consider this scene. A grandfather standing on the porch of his country home remarks to an adult grandson, as they peer into a cloudless sky, that a storm is coming. The grandson says that it is amazing how older people can predict weather. "How do you do it, Gramps?" he asks, adding, "Is your arthritis acting up?" To which the grandfather replies, "Nope. The TV just went out."

Although fiction, the scene symbolizes what applied logic is all about. Look again at how the characters interact. If you analyze them closely, you'll see that several major principles are illustrated.

Expectations

The elder character may be a little flighty, especially in the eyes of the grandson. The young man *expects* his grandfather to behave in certain ways. His expectations seemed to influence his view of his grandfather's behavior. Like this young man, audiences have expectations. If these expectations are met, your message clears one major hurdle toward effective persuasion. If these expectations aren't met, or if messages tend to contradict expectations and experience, the opportunity to persuade may be nil or, at least, quite limited.

This means that you must know the expectations of your audience. You have expectations, too, so don't let them blind you to what an audience wants. These expectations are formed from applied logic—that is, thinking about experiences and observations of life around us.

Experience

Perhaps the TV system failed often at the grandfather's house and he'd noticed that this failure was sometimes followed by a storm. Therefore, he concluded that the failure of the TV system was the result of a distant storm that would soon come his way. Never mind that it is not fully logical for him to conclude this cause-effect relationship. His experience tells him that it is a fact of life. Applied logic tells him that it is the way the world works.

You'll find that the quirkiness of the applied logic of your public may keep you from a real understanding of that audience. That means that you must work hard to grasp what goes on in its collective head. One key to this understanding is to recognize how perceptions influence reality for publics.

Perceptions

Perceptions are tricky. Both grandfather and grandson looked out on a cloudless sky. One saw nothing but an aging grandparent, the other, saw a storm coming. Perceptions are like that. They are individual, not collective, visions of the world around us. What we perceive may have little or no basis in reality, because our perceptions are our realities. Therefore, when the TV system goes down, it is perfectly clear, from the grandfather's perspective, that a storm is approaching. Because he had not had the same experience or concluded that there was cause and effect involved, the grandson could not perceive what his grandparent perceived.

One reason we can't fully perceive what others perceive is that we think in abstractions. We use verbal language as a tool inside our heads to give meaning and value to the reality around us. Because words merely represent reality, our understanding of reality is limited by our command of language. As a writer, you can only be as successful as your ability to select words that represent basically the same thing to your audience as they do to you. If you don't, you'll see a sky that has no hint of a storm. Therefore, you may fail to see the connections between things that your public sees. A semanticist will tell you that words are symbols with dictionary definitions, often more than one, but have value-laden meanings to individuals, based on experience, education, culture and beliefs. These associations are connections.

Connections

The principle of connectivity is simple, although vexing at times. The concept of connection is self-descriptive—that is, it refers to the way people see relationships between ideas, events, issues, processes and so on. Obviously, connectivity relates closely to perception. In fact, you can think of it as the next step after perception. It is the idea of "What does this mean?" or "How is this related to that?" or "What does this mean to me?" When the TV system went out, it meant to the grandfather that a storm was coming. That the system went out meant nothing to the grandson because he had not made a connection between the two events.

If strict rules of logic are applied, there may be no connection between the two events. Our experience is not that of the older man, so we can understand the grandson's skepticism. But if the grandfather is in your target public, you must make every effort to understand how he may have made that connection. Otherwise, you're not likely to frame a message that is meaningful to him. Meaningfulness suggests that you must also look at the values of your audience.

Values

Our personal values are always important to us. And they become even more important, and more rigid, as we age. The grandfather's observation that a storm was on the way may seem trivial to us. That may be because we tend to forget that he lives in a rural area where weather is an important part of his daily existence. Developments that reinforce our values are welcome. Those that contradict them, or call them into question, are often ignored as not worthy of consideration.

Values are at the core of our behavior. They are rooted in our basic beliefs, such as our convictions about what is right or wrong, important or unimportant, valuable or not valuable and so on. Value systems, once formed, remain pretty much unchanged throughout our lives; they are much like the leopard that can't change its spots. It is our value system that influences the way we apply logic to what we experience and perceive and the kinds of connections we make between our perceptions of reality.

Applied logic—the way we see relationships between developments, things or issues—often provides the motive behind our own efforts to persuade others to our points of view.

Persuasion and Communication

Persuasion is a special type of communication. To understand the persuasion process fully, then, we must understand something about communication. Like persuasion, the communication process can be divided into a number of elements.

As with persuasion, the communication process has many models. None of them is adequate in every situation. Some are clearly more relevant than others in certain situations. However, the principal paradigm of the communication process, as formulated by Harold Lasswell, is this: Who says what, through what channel, to whom, with what effect?[9] By using this paradigm, we can say that communication involves a source, a message, a medium (channel), a public and an effect. Changes in the characteristics of any of these elements can cause differences in the communication's persuasiveness.

Source

At first, it does not seem likely that you can change the "who"—the source of the message. You're stuck with who you are or who employs you. But then again, it is sometimes possible to change some of your characteristics (or some characteristics of your company). At the very least, you can design your messages to take advantage of any helpful qualities that your organization has.

What qualities of the source of the message influence the effectiveness of persuasion? One of the most important is credibility. Usually, the more credible a source, the more persuasive it is.[10] This means that your organization must constantly strive to remain believable if your message is to be effective. And the best way to remain credible is to tell the truth—even when it hurts. Thus, even if you are trying to persuade, you must remember to be honest and accurate. What you write must correspond to your company's actions. If the organization is not acting the part of a good member of the community, it does not really matter much what you say, because your message won't be believed. As Lerbinger puts it, "The communicator realizes that what he says must correspond to the realities of a given situation. The management he represents cannot be doing one thing while he is saying something else."[11]

Credibility can be viewed as having two major elements: *expertise* and *objectivity*. The audience is more likely to believe you if its members think you know what you're talking about. But to believe you completely, they must also think you are telling the truth. If you have a vested interest in an issue, your objectivity will be suspect. McGuire says, "For maximum believability, the source must be perceived as not only knowing the truth but being objective enough to be motivated to tell it as he sees it."[12] Research indicates that people tend to rate expertise higher in writers who use big words and longer, more involved sentences, compared to those who use common words and simpler syntax, especially when dealing with complex issues. The same study also indicates that people who already have a fairly clear understanding of an issue are more critical of what they read and who writes it.[13] Also, several research studies have confirmed that disinterestedness makes a source more persuasive to audiences. In fact, a source is most persuasive of all when arguing *against* his or her own best interests.

Credibility isn't the only source characteristic that can aid persuasion. Your audiences are likely to be persuaded, too, by sources they like. Often that means someone "like them" or someone they want to be like. Of course, the audience's feelings about the source aren't always clear. Is an audience persuaded by a source because it feels something in common with and likes the source, or does it like the source because it agrees with the message? In any event, being liked helps make persuasion more successful. So does *being similar* to the audience members in some way, especially when the similarity is ideological and not merely physical or social. Your persuasion, then, is more likely to be effective if you can establish some *ideological similarities* between yourself and your audience.

A third source characteristic that leads to effective persuasion is perceived power. Put simply, this means that your boss is more likely to persuade you than your neighbor is. Your boss has power over you; your neighbor does not.

Because many different source qualities affect persuasive success, it isn't always possible to predict what will happen when one of these qualities is changed. For example, if you work hard to appear to be an expert, your audience may very well perceive your expertise but may not agree with you as much as they would otherwise. By becoming more of an expert, you have become less similar to your nonexpert audience. The increase in agreement produced by greater expertise can be more than offset by the loss of agreement caused by the decrease in similarity. In many cases, then, some intermediate level of expertise is probably best. Audiences tend to believe people who know more than they do, but not too much more.

Although these points are all supported by contemporary research findings, it is worth noting that the value of a reputation for personal truthfulness and expert experience was treated long ago by Aristotle under the general term *ethos*.[14]

Most of the time, you can choose your sources for expertise and credibility. However, in a crisis, that may not be the case. Others involved in the situation will be speaking out, and still others may be sought for their views. The proactive public relations practitioner gets those others involved in the situation to help tell the story and goes forward with the first news of the crisis, incident or situation in order to frame the issue in the minds of those hearing the news either through mass or specialized media or interpersonal communication.

Message

From the standpoint of the persuasive writer, the message element in the process is often the most important. At least, the message is the one element of communication over which the writer has complete control. In writing the message, you have to decide what things to say and how and when to say them. In doing this, you will be faced with many difficult decisions. Here is what communication research says about some of the questions surrounding those decisions.

Should you give one side or both sides?

In general, studies show that it is better to give both sides of the story. One-sided arguments are frequently dismissed, especially if a public is highly sophisticated or tends to oppose your point of view at the beginning. If the public does not like you, or if the public does not already agree with you on the issue at hand, it's usually best to give both sides. It's also better to give both sides if the public is likely to hear the other side of the story.

Is there any time when stressing your side of the story *only* is a good idea? Possibly, if circumstances include *all three* of the following conditions: The public is poorly educated, the public is friendly to you, and the public probably will not hear any arguments from the other side. Only rarely, however, are all of these requirements met. Generally that means you must introduce and refute other points of view.

A related question is occasionally faced by public relations writers: Should an issue be raised at all? Sometimes people (especially corporate executives) prefer to "let sleeping dogs lie" and not bring up a potentially controversial subject until somebody else does it first. This is usually a mistake. If there is any chance at all that someone will bring up an issue in the future, you should strike first with your side of the story. In fact, most research indicates that the first communicator has a significant advantage in winning over public opinion because of the inoculation effect. That is, you can try to "inoculate" an audience against the opponent's views, just as a person can be inoculated against a disease by an injection of a weakened form of the same disease. Thus, it is generally more effective to raise the issues yourself, before your opponent does, but don't expect "inoculation" to work miracles. In fact, many scholars question its value.

Nonetheless, a smart public relations writer will supply a weakened form of the opposition arguments and then refute them before the opposition can present its case. The public will resist persuasion by the opposition at a later date. This strategy, studies show, works better than providing the public with large amounts of propaganda designed merely to promote the persuader's point of view while ignoring the existence of conflicting opinions.

Which side should you give first?

If, as in most cases, you use both sides of the story, whose side should you give first? Unfortunately, the evidence on this question is not conclusive. Giving the opposition arguments first is apparently better when dealing with controversial issues but not when dealing with noncontroversial ones.

Which should come first, the good news or the bad news?

In general, give the good news first. This approach will probably get you the widest overall agreement with your message.

Should you make conclusions explicit or let the target public draw its own conclusions?

In essence, this question asks whether it's better to tell people what to think or to offer the facts and let them figure it out. It's true that a person drawing his or her own conclusions is likely to hold the new opinion more strongly. The problem is that the conclusion might not be the one you are after. Generally, then, it is safer to make the conclusion explicit, especially when the issue under consideration is complex.

There are exceptions to this general guideline, however. A highly intelligent public can probably be trusted to form an obvious conclusion, based on the weight of evidence presented to it. In fact, such a public may consider an explicit conclusion in such situations insulting. Sometimes, an initially hostile public reacts negatively to explicit conclusions. And when the issues are very personal and members of the target public have a high ego involvement with your conclusions, it's definitely wiser not to make the conclusions explicit.

Do fear techniques work?

Research on this question seems to indicate that fear appeals do enhance persuasion, but only up to a point. Mild fear appeals seem to be more effective than strong fear appeals. Even then, you need to offer a resolution to the fear.

McGuire offers an explanation for this. Fear may be effective in passing the yielding step of persuasion. But high fear levels may work against other steps in the process, such as comprehension or remembering. If you scare people too much, they won't get the substance of your message, they will put it out of their minds and forget it or they will modify it to a less threatening form. Thus, as with expertise, some medium level of fear is probably the best approach. Keep in mind, though, McGuire's observation that the more complex the message, the less fear arousal is desirable.[15]

Is it better to use emotional or factual arguments?

Evidence on this question is simply not conclusive. Sometimes emotional appeals are the most persuasive, and sometimes factual ones are. It all depends on the issue involved and the composition of the public. There are no good general guidelines to follow.

It is probably safe to say, however, that the best persuasive writing employs both factual and emotional arguments. Because information by itself seldom changes attitudes, some writers tend to rely on emotional presentations. But information is also important to persuasion, if only to provide people with a rational basis for justifying attitudes that are primarily based on emotion. Information can strengthen or weaken attitudes. It can blunt the criticism of a public opposed to your position. It can strengthen the opinions of those already on your side. Furthermore, providing information to supporters of your view gives them a way to verbalize their feelings—and to defend them. This reduces the chances that subsequent persuasion from the opposition will undo what your message has accomplished.

Medium

Although it may be a bit of an exaggeration, Marshall McLuhan's contention that "the medium is the message" certainly responds to the question of how the channel, or medium, can influence a persuasive outcome.

It should be obvious that the medium is important in both the presentation and attention steps of persuasion. As a writer, you must use a medium that will get your message to the target public, and the medium has to be one that the audience will pay attention to. But research studies indicate that the medium is also important for other steps of persuasion.

One finding is that spoken communication is usually more likely than written communication to bring about yielding.[16] This does not mean that you should spend all your time writing speeches while ignoring print media. But it is useful to keep in mind that speech has more power to change minds than writing. The pen might be mightier than the sword, but the tongue can outdo both.

This is not an endorsement of "fiery oration," either. In fact, studies have been unable to show much difference between the persuasive effects of intense, enthusiastic speeches and more subdued ones. In both cases, however, the spoken word wins over the written word in persuasive power.

On the other hand, studies also show that the written word achieves better comprehension. But complete understanding is not always needed for successful persuasion. The spoken word diminishes understanding a little, but it increases yielding a lot.

These findings seem to recommend television and radio as media for carrying your message. But though the evidence shows that oral persuasion is more effective than written persuasion, it also shows that face-to-face encounters are more persuasive than messages in the mass media, especially in attempts to influence voting behavior.[17] This evidence suggests that spending a lot of money on media time and space may not be worth the price. But if mass media messages aren't effective, then the nation's businesses are wasting billions of dollars annually to promote their products, services and ideas via mass media. And there are reasons to believe that the media can play a role in persuasion, though perhaps an indirect one such as reinforcement. Some of the debate on this issue may simply reflect the fact that the effects of the media are too difficult to isolate and to measure. The ongoing process of convergence in the mass media is making it even more difficult to tease out effects peculiar to a specific medium.

Studies show that the mass media can successfully convey information to people (though not in all cases, and not always to the extent that the communicator would like). And though information alone is usually not enough to get people to change their attitudes, it does play a part. Even if most people are not persuaded much by news media, opinion leaders—those who influence others in face-to-face contacts—do pay attention to news media and base their opinions at least in part on media messages. The messages that are most successful, though, are electronic ones.

The idea that opinion leaders transmit media messages to others is usually described as the "two-step flow" of mass communication. More recent research has cast some doubt on some of the details of this idea. For example, many people do receive input from the media, but they turn to opinion leaders for interpretations of facts more than for the facts themselves. Furthermore, the opinion leaders may receive information from sources other than the mass media.[18] Nevertheless, opinion leaders do provide a possible avenue for mass media to influence public opinion.

Another important influence of the media has been described as "agenda setting." Research seems to show that issues considered important by the population often are also issues that the media devote much time and space to. Thus, it has been suggested that even if the media don't tell people what to think, they do tell them what to think about. Of course, it is possible that the situation is the other way around—that people decide what's important first, and then the media begin to run stories on those subjects. The more recent studies of agenda-setting do indicate that media do influence what people think. So if your intention is to raise an issue to public consciousness, you must first get the attention of the media.

The question, though, is what media? It's not all news media. Social media provide instant, unmediated (not edited) delivery to particular groups that cluster around certain social media sites. Twitter seems to have the broadest network, others have particular audiences and special uses, such as for video, music, etc.

Given that all media can be used as channels for your messages, which media are best to use? That's a difficult question to answer. Because the media's measurable effects on attitudes are small, it isn't easy to tell if one medium is more effective than another. Looking at the credibility for traditional media separately, the evidence suggests that people are most likely to believe what they see and hear. People go to online media sites, so they are more likely to get both. Television news offers not only its broadcast information, but also websites that give more information, such as a complete interview or more video. For traditional media, television is generally given the strongest believability ratings. However, members of higher socioeconomic groups usually rate newspapers and magazines higher for accuracy and truthfulness.[19] Looking at the question from the standpoint of complexity of message, highly complex messages are generally more understandable and believable in print media. Messages charged with emotion appear to work best in broadcast media.

The problem with such a simplification is that familiarity with technology has made skeptics of consumers of most media messages. People know how to use photoshop, how to record video and sound and how to transmit messages. People are carrying around a versatile message generator—their mobile phones. As experienced creators and editors of content, they are aware of how messages can be transformed and are thus somewhat skeptical of any information from untrusted sources.

Public

The greatest lesson of social science research on the question of persuasion is one that all good writers should already understand: Know your public. Techniques that will work wonders persuading a football team may flop with a group of engineers. Most of the guidelines for preparing a message or choosing a channel depend on the characteristics of the public. Publics that always have been fragmented are even more so. Any connectivity among them comes not from exposure to traditional media, but from conversations with family and friends, online and face-to-face.

Any public is made up of individuals. And all individuals, as receivers of your message, possess a common characteristic: They tend to forget things. This fact usually works to your disadvantage, because you must repeat messages often to combat forgetfulness. But attitudes built up over a long period of time are hard to forget. If your organization has a long history of exploiting employees or making a poor product, and if the company is perceived this way by your audience, you will have a difficult job writing credible messages. Before you can ever hope to be believed and accepted, your company will have to clean up its act. And you will have to tell the "good news" often over a long period of time before the new truth about the company will replace the old perceptions.

On the other hand, if your organization is generally perceived as a good place that is sensitive to employee and customer needs, you'll be able to weather a lawsuit filed by an employee or a customer with only moderate and temporary damage. A major part of that recovery is each individual member of a public's direct interaction with the organization.

That means organizations have to be involved with individual members of all of its publics. The one-line conversations may be one-on-one with members of a public, but are posted for all others to see and react to. Listening is more important than talking. Listening means paying attention to offline and informal discussions as well as online ones. You can learn whether or not your message was received and retained.

The point is that the "retention" step in the persuasion process is a particularly difficult one.

The human tendency to forget can sometimes be helpful, especially to communicators with low credibility, perhaps because of real or perceived bias. Messages from low credibility sources may not induce any immediate change, but months later, a public may show some agreement with that same source's point of view. It is possible that they will remember the message but forget where it came from. Thus the message, no longer associated with the low-credibility source, may now be believed. It just takes a while for it to happen.

This is sometimes called the *sleeper effect*, and whether it actually exists is a matter of some debate. Nevertheless, it's useful to know that even a low-credibility source can be effective in persuasion under some circumstances.

Forgetfulness probably carries no such benefits for high-credibility sources who want the target public to remember everything. High-credibility sources often repeat their messages over and over to make sure the point is retained. Research on this issue indicates that repetition (as with a commercial announcement presented many times) may indeed achieve greater effects, but mostly because it increases the likelihood that more people will hear the message.

On this point, however, it is wise to remember that people tend to forget information at about the same rate as they learn it. Hence, if you stop the flow of messages about your organization, you can expect awareness of your company to drop, though it apparently never goes back to zero. This point, viewed from the stance of economy, supports the idea of sustained programming, because it is more efficient to sustain awareness than to build it in the first place.

Effect

When you begin writing a message about your company to its publics, you have some objective in mind. You want those publics to think about an issue in a certain way, or you want the them to do something. In other words, there is a motive, or intent, not only behind the message you want to convey but also behind the way you will formulate and deliver it. Thus the overall "effect" question is: Did the message do what you wanted it to do?

You begin the process of writing with an intended effect in mind. It has to be "intended" because you don't know what the actual effect will be ahead of time. You can only guess—and hope. Nevertheless, you must ask yourself how your intended effect influences your success in persuasion.

The most obvious intention of any persuasive speaker or writer is to persuade. If the audience knows it is being persuaded, its resistance may increase. If, however, people merely overhear a message, without knowing that the message is intended for their ears, they might be more susceptible to the argument.

This fact suggests that it might be helpful to disguise your persuasive intent. Some evidence supports this view, but some does not. At times, the opposite effect can be seen. Although there is little doubt that disguising the intent to persuade enhances yielding, such a disguise may hinder presentation, attention and comprehension. The benefits of making sure your audience gets the message may outweigh the disadvantages of letting your intent be clearly seen.[20]

A companion issue regarding intent is the matter of how extreme your appeal should be. Should you try to persuade people to change their minds just a little or a lot? This question has been the focus of many research studies. It seems, generally, that increasing the level of intended change helps to increase persuasion, but only up to a point. If you ask for too much attitude change, effectiveness decreases.[21]

An Alternative Theory

Because of conceptual problems with certain methods by which some of the foregoing ideas have been tested, you will be wise as a writer to use them simply as guidelines, not as gospels. Some research findings are contradictory or, at least, inconclusive. James E. Grunig has introduced yet another perspective that may help us to better understand the effects of persuasion.

Put simply, Grunig proposes a situational theory asserting that "how a person perceives a situation explains whether he will communicate about the situation, how he will communicate, and whether he will have an attitude relevant to the situation."[22] This perspective involves six key concepts: problem recognition, constraint recognition, referent criterion, involvement, information seeking and information processing.

Problem Recognition   A person must perceive that something is missing or indefinite in a situation in order to stop and think about it. The importance of this to the public relations writer is that recognition of a problem or issue increases the chances that a person will respond to a situation or express a need for more information about it. This idea is closely related to the *attending* and *comprehending* functions cited earlier.

Constraint Recognition   If the receiver of a public relations message thinks his or her options to respond to the situation are limited by group, institutional, legal, economic or other external constraints, there is less need for information about the situation. These constraints may be perceived as so compelling that people simply ignore the information because they feel impotent to use it or, perhaps, to do anything about it. Therefore, even if your message is loaded with relevant material, it may have little impact because the receiver is resigned to a limited response or no response at all. This idea is related to the *retaining* and *acting* functions discussed earlier.

Referent Criterion   A person brings to a situation some prior information that is relevant to the situation. If the situation is common, the prior information tends to lessen the person's need for additional information. This suggests that the person probably won't be very open to new information from a public relations writer. On the other hand, if the situation is new, related prior experience tends to serve initially as a guide to seeking information about behavior pertinent to the situation. This referent concept suggests that a public relations writer should be prepared to provide extensive information in new situations. This concept is related to Lerbinger's designs of persuasion, especially cognitive, motivational and social.

Involvement   The more salient or important the issue is perceived to be, the more likely a person will be to respond to it. Involvement seems to suggest not only if a person will respond but also *how*. Remember to attempt in every message to make its importance clear to the public.

Information Seeking   Deliberate acts by a person to get more information about the situation are characterized as information-seeking behavior. A need is perceived and behavior is directed at fulfilling the need. The concept of information seeking tends to suggest behavior that has risen to a higher level of involvement. Persons with these higher levels of involvement are much more eager to receive and accept your persuasive messages. As a public relations writer, you won't have to work as hard to communicate with these persons, but they will probably demand a lot more salient material.

Information Processing   Information processing implies a much lower level of involvement because some—maybe a lot of—information is encountered and processed incidentally, if not accidentally, about the situation. A large proportion of information acquisition is unplanned. It arises in the context of other behavior. For example, if there's nothing else to do, a person may switch on the television set and watch whatever appears on it, including your public service announcement on your community's blood drive. To reach this segment of your public, you will have to work especially hard to make your persuasive messages relevant. That's why we emphasize repeatedly in this book how important it is to know your audience. If you don't know your audience intimately, you probably will not be successful as a persuasive writer.

Conclusions

Because the results of research in persuasive communication are inconclusive or contradictory in some cases, the following conclusions should be interpreted as general guidelines, not rules, that may apply in many situations.

- Behavior is both rational and emotional. Effective persuasion uses appeals based on one or both characteristics.
- Attitude formation is a complex process. It involves our personal experience and history, social environment, personality characteristics, predispositions and communication.
- Persuasion can be viewed as a learning process, a power process or an emotional process.
- The communication-design aspects of persuasion include stimulus-response, cognitive, motivational, social and personality.
- The six steps in the process of persuasion are presenting, attending, comprehending, yielding, retaining and acting.

- As it involves the communication process, persuasion has five major considerations: source, message, medium, public and effect.
- It is generally better to give both sides of an issue rather than just your side, especially if your public is sophisticated.
- If there is a chance that the opposition will raise an issue, it is generally better for you to raise it first and try to "inoculate" your public against opposing views.
- When dealing with controversy, give your opponent's views first; then follow with your own.
- In general, tell the good news first and then the bad.
- It is safer to draw clear conclusions in your messages than to let the public draw its own.
- Mild fear appeals seem to work better than strong ones, but a resolution to the fear should also be offered.
- Use both factual and emotional appeals.
- The spoken word is more persuasive than the printed word.
- Conversations that occur online are next to word-of-mouth delivered messages.
- Opinion leaders often base their views on information in mass media, then use face-to-face contact or personal electronic messaging, such as blogs, to persuade others.
- If you want to raise an issue for public debate, you have to get the attention of the media, because they set the agenda. One way to do this is by blogging because news media reporters often scan blogs for topics.
- The ongoing convergence of traditional media and the explosion of social media make guidelines for particular publics difficult to evaluate.
- You must know your public very well to be able to shape effective persuasive messages. The best way to do this is through interacting with individuals in those publics when that interaction is posted for others to see, perhaps hear and respond to.
- Attitudes built up over long periods of time are resistant to change. Even if you appear to be unsuccessful at promoting change in the short term, change might occur much later.
- A persuasive writer must know clearly what he or she wants to happen before writing the message. This intended effect may be quite different from the actual effect.
- If you ask for major attitude change, you will get more results than if you ask only for a little, up to a point. However, asking for too much change diminishes your effectiveness.

Exercises

1. You came to college, with a laptop and a mobile phone, both with the latest technology. Now, you find that both need upgrading. Some new software for the laptop you really need in order to manage your classes and get your assignments done. You've been thinking about this for quite a while, and now you've decided to ask your parents to underwrite the costs of these upgrades. Although the style of your letter can be fairly informal, it needs to be persuasive enough for you to get the money to buy what you need. You have all of the information, including the prices; now you must apply persuasive writing. Before starting this assignment, you might want to take another look at the chapter on letter writing. Remember: message, sources (quote experts?) and the medium, paper or email?

2. You have been working as an intern this semester for a small public relations firm that has given you a great deal of responsibility. However, two of their clients are in the retail business, and you know that November and December are going to be extremely busy for you in working with them. You are concerned that if you devote the time the clients need, your grades will suffer and you may lose a scholarship. You want to write your employer a letter that will persuade your boss to give you a week off before exams. You know that others who have asked for favors have been told they are "not professional," and one was even fired. How can you write your letter so you won't suffer such consequences? This needs to be fairly formal.

3. Write a persuasive piece on any topic you know a great deal about but something that is fairly controversial. This will be an opinion piece for the student newspaper. Analyze how you constructed your argument and explain the rationale for your choices based on some of the theories in this chapter.

Use InfoTrac® College Edition to access information on topics in this chapter from hundreds of periodicals and scholarly journals.

PART 2

Preparing to Write

You wouldn't begin a long journey without knowing where you were going, what you would take and where you would stay. Preparations—research and planning—also are necessary before writing is begun.

Research for the Public Relations Writer

You conduct research every day. Of course, it's more commonly called "information gathering" or "fact finding," so it includes checking the time, looking up a phone number and checking an email address. Admittedly, the research that we conduct in public relations writing is a bit more detailed. We use research mainly for two purposes: (1) to gather information for writing of all kinds and (2) to measure how well we've succeeded in achieving our public relations goals. (See Chapter 5.)

Other purposes for public relations research exist, of course. James E. Grunig, Professor Emeritus at the University of Maryland and "one of the most respected research minds in public relations,"[1] describes three kinds of public relations research: research *in* the profession, research *on* the profession and research *for* the profession:

> "Research *in* the profession is research that communication professionals use in the practice of public relations," he said. "It includes formative research to learn how publics are affected by organizations, to find out how publics view organizational actions, and to plan communication programs to build relationships with publics. It also includes evaluative research to measure the effectiveness of communication programs and to determine what contribution the public relations function makes to organizational success. Research *on* the profession is conducted by scholars who explain, evaluate, and criticize the behavior of public relations practitioners. Research *for* the profession also is mostly done by scholars, although many professional consultants and counselors conduct it also. The purpose of research *for* the profession is to build from research *on* the profession to develop and test new ideas and techniques that practitioners can use to improve their effectiveness."[2]

Interestingly, many companies don't rely on research in developing public relations strategies. *PRWeek*'s CEO Survey 2008 asked 200 corporate chief executive officers, "How frequently does your company invest in market research to formulate its PR strategy?" The results? 16 percent said "Never"; 19 percent said "Rarely"; 29 percent said "Sometimes"; 16 percent said "Usually" and 10 percent said "Always." The CEOs were asked, "How frequently does your company attempt to measure the success of its PR programs?" 15 percent said "Never"; 10.5 percent said "Rarely"; 19 percent said "Sometimes"; 26 percent said "Usually" and 29.5 percent said "Always."[3]

It is much easier and quicker today, but a lot riskier, to find information. You simply tell a search engine what you're looking for, and it will scour the Internet for the information. The problem is that the search engine can't recognize the difference between biased and unbiased information. Only you can make that distinction.

You must develop basic strategies that help you select and use information. One approach is to rely on information from reputable sources, including the websites of organizations such as the USA Bureau of the Census and other government agencies, *The New York Times* and *The Wall Street Journal.* Even then, the information may be less than dependable.

The point is that when searching for facts, be prepared for ambiguity that sometimes may be hard to reconcile. It's important to keep careful records of where the information you use came from, quote the sources and use footnotes when appropriate for the type of writing that you're doing.

Information from newsgroups and independent electronic newsletters may or may not be biased. That doesn't mean you can't use it. It does mean, however, that before you use it you must seek other sources to confirm it.

Getting information from the Web is problematic, because there are no traffic cops on the information superhighway. Wikipedia.com, which bills itself as "the largest reference website on the Internet,"[4] is "the communal encyclopedia that anyone can edit." Using Wikipedia is convenient, but it provides no way to track the source of information it contains, making accuracy iffy at best. You may find that you still must visit a traditional library now and then, or do some original research on questions that can't be answered by existing information.

Keep in mind that action data, according to the newsletter *pr reporter,* is what is needed by public relations writers, including data that

1. *Answers questions essential to planning projects, programs and campaigns.* The most desirable research methods focus on the latent readiness of audiences to behave in certain ways and on how audiences get information and how they use it to arrive at decisions.
2. *Tests, if possible, and deflates assumptions.* Conventional wisdom—often what leads senior management to decisions—may be wrong.
3. *Produces baseline data that permits accurate evaluation.* Good baselines help us know how far we've moved, if at all, whether a process is working and whether behavioral change goals are met.[5]

Research, then, is the key element in professional success—research at the beginning and at the ending of any endeavor. Research is as important to a beginner as it is to a senior counselor, although the focus of research may change as you move up the career ladder. Because most entry-level jobs in public relations are directly related to the writing process, it is important for you to learn as much as you can about research and how to use it as a writer.

For this reason, you should review and remember the prewriting checklist in Table 4.1.

TABLE 4.1	*Prewriting Checklist*

1. Gather the facts of the matter and get them right.

2. Gather authoritative opinions and interpretations of the matter.

3. Evaluate facts and opinions for their pertinence. Discard those not directly related to the matter.

4. Synthesize the remaining facts and opinions into a cohesive body of information.

5. Organize the information for writing.

6. Develop a writing outline that moves logically from one point to the next.

7. Write. Edit. Rewrite.

Research in Public Relations

Careful planning is central to the process and practice of professional public relations. Plans are generally successful in direct proportion to the quality of the information on which they are built. That's why research is so important to the overall success of a public relations plan. Planning usually begins with what is known as a *situational analysis.* This is where answers are sought for all sorts of questions.

What are the significant trends? What is the overall economic situation? What are the political considerations for the action we are contemplating? How is our organization perceived by target publics? How are our competitors viewed by target publics? How much support can we expect from affected publics? These and other questions unique to the situation must be raised and answered.

Two Basic Types of Research

The two basic types of research are *quantitative* and *qualitative.* The research that results in numbers, such as a survey, is quantitative, because we can attach quantities in response to questions: How many people think the product is superior, or inferior, to the competition's? And so on.

Qualitative research includes interviews, focus group interviews (FGIs), case studies and pilot studies. Although the results of qualitative research often are used as a part of the decision-making process, it is most common in exploratory research, where a problem or its scope is being defined. For example, FGIs often are used to explore what questions should be asked in an upcoming survey. In marketing, in-depth interviews and focus groups are used for input in deciding characteristics, and even names, for products being developed.

Although analysis of survey data requires training and experience, the results are statistical, more objective and thus less likely to be influenced by prejudices of the researchers. A thorough research study, such as a communication audit, often incorporates both qualitative and quantitative research methods in evaluating an organization's public relations or internal communications program.

Planning for Research

You may not be directly involved in public relations planning, especially early in your career, but you still need to know a good bit about research because you'll use a lot of information unearthed through research. This information generally falls into six broad categories:

1. Policy and purpose
2. Background material
3. Public
4. Message
5. Media
6. Program evaluation

All six are important in every PR situation, but rarely are they all equally important. Your sensitivity to the problem at hand will help you determine which category or combination of categories is especially important in a particular case.

Categories of Research for the PR Writer

Policy and Purpose The "company line" is a euphemism that hardly does justice to the full concept behind the term *policy*. Policy is a considered statement of purpose, position or direction that is expected to guide the behavior of those it covers.

Every organization in both the public and private sectors has a set of policies. Anyone working for or with the company or organization is expected to know the provisions of applicable policies.

Policy is of two general types: internal and external. *Internal policy* is that of your employer. It is a set of guidelines that directs and controls the collective behavior of the organization and the job behavior of each employee. Such policies may range from a policy governing employee benefits to a policy of public candor in the face of a community crisis.

External policy comes from a source outside the organization's immediate control but bears on the organization's behavior toward its constituencies. For example, if you are writing the annual report for a publicly held company, you must know and observe certain Securities and Exchange Commission policies and requirements. It is critical that you know applicable policies in order to avoid problems. This not only may save your job, it may even get you promoted.

Some policies you may need to know are available to you only in oral form. Oral policy can be especially frustrating, for three main reasons. First, oral policy is easily distorted. What you believe today to be a clear understanding of the policy may be completely obsolete a year from now. Second, management may be unsure of itself and thus reluctant to put a decision in writing. Third, management may have a hidden agenda. To understand this point, suppose you are about to write a series of releases for the local media about your country club's gala next month, some proceeds of which will go to the United Negro College Fund. Club policy does not bar blacks from membership, but there are no blacks in the club. And you are told, when you ask the club manager, that no blacks are invited to or expected to attend the gala. Written policy may say one thing, but unwritten policy may say something else.

If you find yourself relying more on oral than written policy, urge management to put the oral policy in writing. If management resists this suggestion unreasonably, start looking for another job.

Background Material   Successful public relations writing is based on a solid, fully developed body of facts. The kinds of facts needed will vary, depending on the situation.

For example, suppose you are retained to write a brochure in support of a bond election to double the community's hospital bed space. What facts do you need to know before you begin to write?

For starters, here are a few: What has been the community's rate of growth over the last 20 years? How much is the community expected to grow in the next 20 years? What accounts for this rate of growth? What is the ratio of community patients to patients from outside the community? Why? Has this ratio changed in the last few years? Is the ratio expected to change in the future? Why? Is the interest rate on the bonds favorable? How do local financial leaders view the bonding program? Why?

The questions you might ask about this project may number into the hundreds. The number is not the issue. The point is that public relations planning, decision making and writing depend on the careful accumulation of facts and ideas.

As you begin the task of assembling background materials, you should assume the traditional role of the news reporter by asking who, what, where, when, how and why—especially why. As you ask these questions, you'll begin to build an elaborate, sophisticated, project-specific system of information that will help you handle assignments ranging in diversity from staging a small symposium to handling a crisis at a chemical plant.

If your search for the proper background material leads you into legal or government documents and you find that an office or agency is uncooperative, you may want to request the needed information, if it qualifies, under the Freedom of Information Act (FOIA). For guidance and materials on how to make an FOIA request, contact the Freedom of Information Clearinghouse at (202) 588-7783, go online to http://www.citizen.org/litigation/free_info or write to 1600 20th St. NW, Washington, DC 20009.

One of the key points to remember about background materials is that, even if the public relations situation is new to you, it is not new. Others have faced the same situation or a similar one. Learn from their experiences if you can.

Public   As noted earlier, public relations professionals are fond of talking about publics, audiences or constituencies. These terms are used synonymously. It is rare in public relations that you will deal with a single public. Even when it appears that way, closer examination usually turns up two or more subsegments, each with its unique characteristics, concerns and needs.

Thus the question is: How can you identify the public or subsegments? This requires research, perhaps at different levels of sophistication. To illustrate this point, consider the following situation.

You are director of public relations for a new bank with a national charter in a metropolitan area. The bank's management is aware that deregulation allows savings and loans and investment companies, such as Fidelity, to provide many financial services previously available only at banks.

Your management decides to market the bank to certain types of potential customers—specifically, those whose annual incomes are $100,000 or more. This rules out many potential depositors from your target audience. And it focuses attention on specific segments of the community, such as physicians, dentists, attorneys, retailers, owners of manufacturing or service companies, architects, designers and engineers.

In this situation, you will first try to divide the priority public into segments by using demographic information—income, sex, education, occupation, marital status, home ownership and the like. Once the demographic profile is complete, the picture of this public comes into sharper focus. But does it tell you all you need to know? Perhaps. Perhaps not.

What you may need now is psychographic information—information about lifestyle, attitudes and behavior. Information of this type may give you important clues indicating that your public relations program should communicate differently with, say, physicians and dentists than with retailers and manufacturers. For example, physicians and dentists may be more concerned with long-range financial planning, whereas retailers and manufacturers may be more concerned with managing cash flow. If so, messages going to these two groups must be different.

Research helps you understand to the fullest extent the needs of your public and its components so that you can shape messages that speak to their distinct needs.

Message   What you say and how you say it may have a great deal to do with your success. Recall our discussion about publics. If you are lucky enough to have a single public with which to communicate, your job will be easier. But when you have several publics, your job can be complex.

Whether it is one public or several, you are generally well advised to begin by reducing your message to a single simple idea. Remember, though, that a single simple idea is not necessarily an insignificant or simpleminded idea. Reducing what you want to say to this level is necessary to help keep you on the right track as you shape your message.

Because different methods can be used to construct a message for maximum impact, you should select an approach based primarily on your purpose for the message. Is the purpose to change or to reinforce behavior? If it is to change, you must remember to make a reward obvious to the receiver of your message. If it is to reinforce, your message must avoid information that contradicts current behavior.

Should you use a conclusion-drawing technique? In this method, you select and present information that will lead your audience to draw the conclusion you want it to draw. Communication-research literature suggests that this is a good method of communicating with sophisticated audiences. However, this technique can be fatal if used with unsophisticated audiences.

There are many techniques of message presentation in addition to the ones discussed. You should review the communication-research literature and develop a personal understanding of these methods. What are they? How do they work? Under what conditions do they appear to work best? A good way to begin is to review Chapter 3.

Media   As you work your way through a public relations problem, you will have to make choices about which channels of communication to use and how to use them. Before you can make these decisions, however, you need to know the characteristics of the various media available to you. What are their technical qualities and requirements? What can they or can't they do? What are their emotional qualities? How do people react to them? How and why do people use them as they do? Should you use general media, specialized media, social media or a combination of the three types? These are serious questions, the answers to which are not easy and may involve large amounts of time and money. But you need to know, not guess.

Once you have chosen the media, you'll need to assess whether they are effective and efficient in implementing this particular public relations program. This suggests that you'll need to monitor progress and evaluate success. Four questions are important here. Did you reach your priority public? Was your message really heard and accepted? Was your message acted upon? Was the use of the media cost-effective?

Program Evaluation   Public relations programs have to prove their worth. This means that one of your tasks as a writer is to evaluate the cost-effectiveness of the program. You will need to know what worked well, what did not and why. Most of the techniques discussed earlier are used in this phase too. It is simply a matter of employing surveys, interviews and secondary sources to evaluate what has been accomplished. Of course, such common pieces of physical evidence as how many people attended an event, how many people were exposed to your message and how many people responded to a special coupon offer are critical in basic program evaluation.

Research for Storage and Retrieval

Public relations professionals would have more serious communication problems if intensive spadework in policy, background material, public, message and media were fresh with each new program. However, professionals routinely accumulate pertinent research information, initiate research for later use and plan for future research needs.

A large proportion of public relations research is borrowed from the social sciences, especially from behavioral areas. Useful research studies are accumulated and indexed for future use. Research about publics and about media is continually reviewed and stored. Much of the information about publics comes from comprehensive studies done by the commercial media about their audiences. Other studies come from product and service institutions concerned about their own publics. Research on internal policies is mined from organizational sources, whereas external policies are gleaned from various municipal, state and federal organizations, professional or associational groups and the like.

A particular public relations situation may require some original fact-finding. In conducting original research or in hiring a research company to do it, the public relations practitioner must know clearly what is needed. Otherwise, the resulting information may be imposing but inadequate.

Organizing   Because public relations information comes from such a wide variety of sources, organizing it can be a problem. One common organizational pattern is to categorize information according to policy (pertinent internal and external guides), background material (substantive facts bearing on the situation), public (facts about the people you want to reach), message (facts about successes of message types in similar situations) and media (the most effective ways of delivering your message).

Presenting   The organization of the research should reflect the ways in which it will later be presented and used. In presenting this information, it is important to explain the implications of the findings when these are not obvious and to suggest what bearing the research has on the situation. The information should also indicate what other research is needed to make the picture clearer.

Updating   Organization of the research should allow for easy updating, especially when ongoing research, such as periodic opinion measurement (as in an election campaign), is critical. Today, most organizational information is stored in computers, and the PR professional must know enough about the method of storage to use the system effectively. What works best for information technology (IT) people may not always be what works best for the public relations person trying to use the information.

Reusing   Adding to or reusing research information is difficult if the information is not readily accessible. The retrieval process, therefore, is critical. PR professionals must work with IT people to tell them how the information will be used—what will be needed, under what conditions, when and in what form. Don't be timid about asking for help. For PR research needs, the system must be designed so that data is well organized, is presented in a meaningful way and can easily be updated.

Sources for PR Writers and Researchers

Writers and researchers of all types—not just public relations professionals—depend on research from two basic sources: paper and people. Of course, "paper" doesn't always mean books. It can mean Internet sites, CDs, magnetic tapes or disks, films, DVDs or videotapes, audiotapes, or some other forms of storage. The important point to remember is that sources are either secondary (paper or other form of stored information) or primary (people).

Secondary Sources for Research

Every public relations writer should have at least a working library in the office that contains a dictionary, a thesaurus, appropriate reference volumes and bibliographies and pertinent professional and technical journals and documents. Completing this working library is a file system where information can be placed for easy and immediate access. This office library will be your first line of attack when you need secondary information. For some writers, all of this will be in one place—their computer. Computer software and the Internet can include many language references and fact-storage packages. Computer access to databases also is available.

If you need help, call a reference librarian. You will save time if you can succinctly describe the information you want. Some reference librarians will answer simple questions on the phone.

Library   Most universities and metropolitan areas have public libraries containing resources for basic research. They also usually have cooperative agreements with other libraries to get information on loan. College and university libraries contain scholarly material you may need. Some university libraries are repositories for government documents. These documents represent a large body of research in many different areas. Some churches have substantial holdings of religious works, and many cities have law libraries. Some libraries have special collections that are open to qualified researchers.

Reference Works   The primary tools of both the reference librarian and the researcher in the library are collections of information and reference works. These are "maps" that enable you to find the treasures of information you seek. Standard reference works include encyclopedias, biographical dictionaries, dictionaries of quotations, concordances of the Bible and other famous works, atlases and gazetteers, chronologies or other books of dates, handbooks and sourcebooks such as dictionaries of all languages and areas of specialization.

Bibliographies   One reference source that is especially important is the bibliography. In compiling and categorizing bibliographies, authors provide you with paths through mazes of footnotes. Bibliographies usually identify reliable sources of information that you will want to tap. Many libraries offer electronic access to stored bibliographies so that you can call up on a screen all the most likely sources. Hard (printed) copies also are available from material listed in these databases.

Periodicals/Databases   One resource accessible in electronic systems is *The New York Times Index*. Using this database, online at http://www.library.wwu.edu/ref/howtoguides/nyti.htm, you can track, call up and read any story that has appeared in *The New York Times* within a specific number of years. Because *The New York Times* makes an effort to be a newspaper of record, it is possible to do a great deal of research through this index alone. LexisNexis, CompuServe, Dow Jones News/Retrieval Service and others are electronic databases that can be tapped through the Internet by public relations writers for research purposes. Many newspapers in addition to *The New York Times,* such as *The Washington Post, The Oklahoman* and *The Fort Worth Star-Telegram,* provide database services that may be helpful. For commercial publications, the most useful index is the *Readers' Guide to Periodical Literature*. AdTrack is a database consisting of all ads of a quarter page or more in 148 USA magazines. You can also find indexes and databases that focus on highly specialized fields, such as law (LexisNexis®) or medicine (MEDLINE®).

An extensive database on public opinion is available from Pew Research Center, one of the world's leading archives of social science data, specializing in data from surveys of public opinion. Pew is a nonpartisan "fact tank" that provides information on the issues, attitudes and trends shaping America and the world. It does not take positions on policy issues. Other good references for events and issues of the day are *Facts on File* and encyclopedia yearbooks. The database for most communication materials is ERIC—the Education Resources Information Center.

Public Records   Government records at all levels—local, state and federal—are available to you unless they contain classified information. Some government agencies offer significant research assistance. For example, the Library of Congress (LOC) is helpful in locating information and will often offer advice to put you on the right trail.

Government Records   Most government offices are storehouses of information, and many government offices distribute their own materials. The federal government has published its materials by the USA Government Printing Office (GPO). A central store in Washington, D.C., contains information on every imaginable subject, as do GPO regional offices in cities with federal centers. Ask to be put on the GPO's mailing list. One essential source of information for PR people is the *Statistical Abstract of the United States,* published annually by the

USA Bureau of the Census, even though it is said to underestimate minorities. Much data is available on the www.census.gov website. For information about countries around the world, the Central Intelligence Agency (CIA) *The World Factbook* is an excellent online resource.

Public Access to Information FOIA has opened many files of both public and private institutions to examination. This means that normally you now have access to all documents— titles to property, budgets of state institutions, court proceedings and the like—that have been filed in a public place. A wealth of information exists in these documents.

Primary Sources for Research

When you must research primary sources, generally you have two ways of gathering information from people. One is the interview, and the other is the questionnaire. Whether you're asking questions face-to-face or through a questionnaire, you must prepare yourself ahead of time so the answers you receive will give you the information you want. Let's look at each of these methods.

Interviewing After you have done some fundamental research, you are ready to begin asking questions of people who might be knowledgeable in your subject. In any interview you may want to begin by asking yes/no questions, but always use these as the basis for asking open-ended questions in the body of the interview. Find authorities through your research, then develop questions for them and follow up any leads they may give you.

Although some people seem to have a natural talent for getting information from others, every public relations person should develop and practice interviewing skills. Like people who play musical instruments by ear, natural interviewers—and all others—become even better with practice.

Go to an interview prepared with questions on paper, and be sure to explain how and where the information will be used. As the interview proceeds, keep information in mind that you have gained from your research. Then, if the opportunity arises, you can follow a different line of questioning. Take notes and use a tape recorder, and try not to rely solely on one or the other. It is unquestionably ethical to advise your interviewee that you want to record the conversation and to seek consent. No federal law requires prior consent in a face-to-face interview, but if the interview is recorded via interstate telephone, prior consent is required. A few states require prior consent to record intrastate telephone conversations. Be sure to check out legal provisions in the state where you work.

Listen to what the person is telling you, and try to remember the information by putting it into the context suggested by your prior research. Encourage full responses by asking relevant questions and by participating in the conversation. Avoid being judgmental. You are asking, not telling. Table 4.2 provides an interviewing checklist.

Some of the important information you get from the interview will come from keen observation of the behavior of the person you are interviewing. Watch for nonverbal communication cues, and note both physical characteristics and environmental factors that could be telling. In particular, note gestures that indicate personality characteristics and remember emotional emphases. The latter are particularly evident in the way something is said: the inflection of the voice, the expression on the face. Be cautious, however, about reading more into these details than is there. Be aware of your own bias and involvement with the subject, so you don't

T A B L E 4 . 2	*Checklist for Interviewing*

1. Research your subject before the interview.

2. Know something about the person you are interviewing.

3. Prepare a list of questions in advance.

4. Inform the interviewee in advance of the kinds of questions you will be asking.

5. Whenever possible use a tape recorder *and* take notes. Never put complete trust in a machine or in your memory.

6. Ask for explanations if you don't understand something.

7. Ask specific questions. Vague questions elicit vague answers.

8. Ask one question at a time. Don't throw several questions into the same sentence and expect the interviewee to answer—or even to remember—them all.

misinterpret what you experience. To safeguard against misinterpretation, some researchers prefer to videotape interviews so that they can capture this information and isolate it later.

Keep in mind that there are several characteristics of a good interview. First, you need to present yourself as a warm, responsive person to the interviewee. If you cultivate that impression consistently, people you interview will respond warmly to you. That goes a long way toward convincing respondents that their interaction with you will be both pleasant and personally satisfying. Second, you need to create a permissive atmosphere in which the person being interviewed does not feel inhibited by your questions but that invites candid responses. If respondents see your interview as important, they'll tend to be more cooperative. Third, you must be sure not to apply pressure of any kind, real or implied, on the person you are interviewing. If you maintain a detached but permissive posture in the interview, respondents are more likely to "open up" with more candor than you may have expected.

To achieve these purposes, it is recommended that you follow these steps:

1. Introduce yourself by name and explain your affiliation (show documentation if it is needed or is asked for).
2. Explain clearly what it is that you are doing.
3. Explain to the interviewee how he or she was chosen to be interviewed.
4. Adapt your behavior to the personality of the person being interviewed.
5. Build rapport.

Focus Group Interview   A focus group interview, or FGI, is with a group, not an individual.

Its original intent was as a preresearch tool to help researchers identify and use terms in their questions to respondents that had common meanings to people in a target public.

The procedure for an FGI is to select 8–12 people from a target public, bring them to a central location and talk with them for about two hours on some topic. While the atmosphere should appear to be casual, the moderator always works from a prepared list of questions designed to get participants to begin talking and interacting with each other. Their conversations often are recorded, sometimes with video. A transcript of the dialogue can be analyzed

"I thought you did fine, but I'm afraid you didn't test well with the focus group."

Source: Reprinted with permission of Mike Baldwin and Cartoon Stock,
www.CartoonStock.com

to identify words or phrases that people use consistently to mean certain things. These words and phrases may then be used to form questions to be asked in a survey.

Suppose your client is a materials testing laboratory that does nondestructive and destructive testing for a wide variety of clients. Tests might range from stress tests on alloys to air quality. Many lab personnel become expert witnesses, especially in product liability cases. Your client wants feedback from quality control engineers representing a broad range of manufacturing in which testing is both routine and regular. Further suppose that you know nothing about how a materials testing laboratory operates. How can you shape appropriate questions to a sample of quality control engineers? Don't try until you've done an FGI. You should then have enough insights to put together a group of unambiguous questions that get the information you need.

Survey   The second means of getting information from people is the survey, which is a research workhorse. Drafting a questionnaire for a survey is difficult, however. Several simple questions are sometimes necessary to get a single piece of information.

It can be difficult to ask a question so that the respondent knows exactly what you mean by it. For example, a national survey once asked a question about "consumer movement leaders." Another researcher, attempting to replicate part of the study, used the same expression with different audiences and was asked by one respondent for a definition of "consumer leader." Did the researcher want to know about movement activists, government appointees or civil servants involved in consumer information, or corporate employees charged with responding to consumers? The question was invalid because it was being interpreted in different ways. One technique that helps to safeguard against this is to pretest the questions with focus groups before actually using the questionnaire.

All questions should be phrased in such a way that they are bias-free. Consider this question: Do you still drink too much? Even a negative response signifies that the respondent drank too much at some previous time, though in fact the respondent may have never indulged in liquor at all. Questions asked in this fashion are not only ineffective but also unethical.

To develop a questionnaire, begin by simply listing all the information you want to know. Then begin to draft questions that will get at the information. Next, consider your respondents. Who will be responding to these questions and under what circumstances? Some people get impatient with long telephone questionnaires, especially if the questions are on a topic that is personally uninteresting. An online questionnaire or one that can be returned by mail gives the respondent the choice of answering on his or her own schedule. However, because you cannot control who responds, problems may arise regarding the representativeness of the sample.

The age and educational level of respondents may also be factors in how questions should be phrased. Familiarity with the subject is another possible factor. The less familiar respondents are with the topic, the simpler the questions and the longer the response times need to be. It is also important to arrange questions in logical sequence so that answers develop naturally in the respondent's mind.

In writing the questions, it is also important to consider how the questionnaire will be administered and scored. If a questionnaire is to be used in a busy shopping mall, for example, or in a phone call, the respondent may not want to take time to answer long or involved questions. Open-ended questions are difficult to evaluate and score. How you ask a question affects the response, and that determines whether the information you get from the questionnaire will be valid and useful.

Some open-ended questions and some interview responses are later subjected to content analysis. This means that words are counted to see how often they appear, and in what context. At least two national research agencies use in-depth interviewing and content analysis extensively. The system involves transcribing oral interviews and entering these in the computer, as you would other open-ended responses. The computer can rank the words by their frequency of usage, and a social science software program can be used to analyze each word in relation to others. Subtle themes often emerge from such analyses, making it possible for researchers to determine accurately what people *mean* by what they say. Table 4.3 presents pros and cons of surveys and FGIs.

Caveats   Much of the information you get from secondary and primary sources will be in simple statistical form that relies on your understanding of concepts like sum, mean (average), median and mode. If you are not familiar with these terms now, get a mathematics book and study it until you are. Otherwise, you run the risk of misinterpreting factual information, drawing poor conclusions and eventually misleading your public.

Research information that infers cause-effect relationships usually entails more sophisticated statistics and research methodologies. There are several good books you can consult for help in these areas. One is Frederick Williams and Peter Monge's *Reasoning with Statistics,* a

T A B L E 4 . 3	*Pros and Cons of Surveys and Focus Group Interviews*
Pros	**Cons**

Surveys

Pros	Cons
Good when definitive numbers are needed	Can be expensive and time consuming
Recognized (i.e., by management) as solid research technique	Usually do not uncover new information
Can disclose source and scope of problem	Data can be easily misinterpreted
Excellent way to track *trends*	Results are not necessarily indicative of the "truth" but do reflect *perceptions*

Focus Group Interviews

Pros	Cons
Provide the possibility of learning completely new information	Information obtained is subjective
Can be modified as needed during process	Results cannot be charted and graphed
Facilitate obtaining information on "WHY?"	Management may not accept results as well as they would survey data
Can be relatively inexpensive	Good results depend heavily upon experience and objectivity of person conducting the focus groups

paperback designed for people who lack a statistical background but who need to know how to interpret and use information that is available only in statistical form.

Whether you are using secondary or primary data, be skeptical about its meaning, especially if the compilers claim that it is based on a random sample. The term *random* has a very strict scientific meaning when applied to survey research and is a *probability sampling* technique.

Probability sampling means that every person in your public should have an equal and known statistical probability of being included in the sample. The key point to remember here is that only when the sample is truly random can the findings be generalized to the total public being researched. For example, if you were conducting a survey of employees in an organization, a valid random sample of all the employees could be obtained by selecting every "Xth" (perhaps every third or fourth) employee. Using this simple random sampling technique, each member of the population has an equal chance of being included in the sample.

In *nonprobability sampling*, there is an assumption that there is an even distribution of characteristics within the population being surveyed. Since samples are chosen arbitrarily, there is no way to estimate the probability of any one element being included in the sample. An example of non-probability sampling is the "shopper-intercept survey" in which shoppers in a mall or store are asked to participate in a survey. Using this technique, sometimes called "convenience sampling," samples are selected only if they can be accessed easily. The obvious advantage is that the method is easy to use, but that advantage is greatly offset by the presence of bias. Although useful applications of the technique are limited, it can deliver accurate results when the population is homogeneous.

Source: Reprinted with permission of Cartoon Stock, www.CartoonStock.com

You should look for certain research protocols in every piece of research data you use. These are listed in the form of questions in Table 4.4. If answers to these questions are missing from the research report or if they are so vague, you can't get a clear view of how the information was gathered, be wary of the data and of any conclusions based on it. It is possible, of course, that the information is reliable, but you should still use it with caution.

TABLE 4.4	*Checklist of Research Protocols*
1. What is the name of the person(s) or organization that did the research? What was the date on which it was done? For whom and why was it done?	
2. If a sample was used, what steps were taken to ensure randomness?	
3. What steps were taken to validate the questions before they were asked of respondents?	
4. What steps were taken to ensure the reliability of the research methods?	
5. Is a copy of the questionnaire (or measuring instrument) included in the research report?	
6. How will this material help you or your organization to make a decision?	

Verifying

When you start putting information together from all your sources, you will want to cross-check your sources. Check primary sources against each other. If you find areas of conflict, look for more primary sources so that the weight of information will clearly support your conclusions.

In addition, check primary sources against secondary sources. People have fallible memories. In attempting to check out information, you'll often find conflicts among secondary sources. Historians, for example, sometimes spend years tracking down an elusive date for an event. Most PR researchers don't do that type of research, nor do they have the time for it, but it pays to be careful, especially now that so much information is highly specialized and technical. If authorities disagree, you need to know it and to find out why. Check and keep checking until a pattern emerges.

Communication Audits

A special kind of research is the communication audit, sometimes called a customer satisfaction study. It's an analysis of how well information flows from one place to another in an organization and, sometimes, to special external publics such as selected financial analysts and media representatives. A great deal of emphasis also is placed on the credibility of sources. When an organization takes stock of its communication functions, it must rely on a wide range of research approaches, including individual interviews, content analyses, FGIs and surveys.

A lot of information can be gleaned from simply reading, analyzing and systematically evaluating newsletters, employee publications, intranets, emails, memos, letters, announcements, websites and other sources. An audit also produces a lot of empirical evidence. For example, it may involve FGIs with representatives of employee groups at various organizational

"I just feel fortunate to live in a world with so
much disinformation at my fingertips."

Source: Reprinted with permission of Cartoon Stock, www.CartoonStock.com

levels. Several surveys may be used and may be posted on intranet or Internet sites, sent through the mail, or distributed in person at meetings. Some Web-based software allows survey participants to complete the online questionnaire in a choice of numerous languages.

The reason for using a variety of research devices is one of the maxims of research: People sometimes are guilty of telling you what they think you want to hear rather than what they really think. This can be a significant problem when employees believe their responses may be monitored, even if that is not possible. Personal in-depth interviews also are necessary, especially when you're looking for blockages in information flow.

A well-executed communication audit can yield a wealth of information that can help you as a public relations writer and also help all levels of management. Its results usually cause an extensive review of communication policies and would investigate the following:

- Management's communications philosophy
- Management's goals and objectives
- Communications goals and objectives compared with communications staff's goals and objectives
- Identification of internal constituencies
- Flow of information from management to communications staff and from communications staff to various internal constituencies
- Existing communications programs and vehicles
- Employee attitudes toward existing communications
- Employee needs and wants in the area of communications

Research Using Social Media

Attitudinal research involves *listening to people*. Interviews, FGIs and surveys have made listening more efficient in gathering information, but they're not particularly good at gaining insights into what people are really thinking. Social media offer some new opportunities to do just that. Here are two examples:

In 2006, Trudy Hardy, head of marketing for MINI USA, the American arm of BMW's MINI Cooper brand, set out to make the MINI more competitive. She had confidence in "her little car," and she knew that MINI owners loved their vehicles. "But what did they love, and how could the MINI take advantage of that? To understand and answer this question, MINI decided to monitor online chatter about its cars.[6]

MINI and its agency hired MotiveQuest, "one of half a dozen companies, including Nielsen's BuzzMetrics and TNS's Cymfony, that offer brand-monitoring services." All of these companies use automated monitoring of not only blogs but "of the entire online chatter associated with a brand: discussion groups, forums, MySpace pages, and so on."[7]

What they learned totally changed MINI's communications strategy. Other cars' owners talked about their *cars*—the power, the styling, the comfort, the speed. But MINI owners talked about the *culture* of people who owned MINIs. "As the first buyers of this odd little car, they bonded with each other. They identified themselves—and each other—*as* MINI owners. This insight led Trudy and her agency to a radical conclusion: it was time to market to MINI *owners,* not prospective *buyers.*"[8] A typical activity in their new program included a series of MINI rallies across the country that resulted in more than 2,100 photos posted on Flickr and eight YouTube videos. In a year, they sold 38,000 cars.

Setting up a social media *private community* is another approach. Communispace, a rapidly growing "listening" company, "has set up hundreds of private communities for its clients, which include over 75 companies, ranging from hair care and breakfast cereal to financial service and IT advice. The company recruits 300–500 people in the client's target market . . ." These "form a community that looks like any other online social network . . . but this is a *research* network. No one can see it except the members, the moderators from Communispace, and the clients." It's a listening machine that generates insight. Usually thanked with inexpensive Amazon certificates, the members "look" and act like social media participants, but they pledge to spend an hour a week on a site, interacting with others.

It's not inexpensive. But a group 21 of cancer centers across the country formed a group to share expenses, since they all needed the same information, and recruited more than 300 cancer patients to join the community.[9] Interacting with this community changed the way New York's Memorial Sloan-Kettering Cancer Center approached its communications. Previously, the center had been focusing on touting its excellent worldwide reputation, believing that patients made decisions on where to seek treatment based on the best chance for a successful outcome. But they learned that when a patient hears a diagnosis of cancer, "you go into a tailspin." They want as much information as they can get, but they rely on their doctor to make a recommendation on a treatment center. With this insight, Memorial Sloan-Kettering switched the definition of its main target audience from cancer patients to primary care physicians.

Skepticism—A Requisite for All Research

Research involves digging, thinking, verifying and analyzing. It is the act of deciding between the probable and the improbable, the true and the false, the likely and the doubtful, the acceptable and the unacceptable and the right and the wrong. These acts are vital decisions in any PR situation. They call for sustained reasoning, a dedication to knowing the truth and a determination to be satisfied with nothing less.

Questions to Ask

Every writer should be from the "Show Me" state, because skepticism is the hallmark of all successful writers, including those in public relations. Skepticism should not be confused with cynicism. The former is a mind-set that says, "I will believe but you have to prove it to me." The cynic often rejects proof without considering it.

This skeptical approach is especially important for you to adopt as a public relations writer, as it is for other writers in mass communication, even when presenting your side of the story, because you are legally accountable for false information. You simply can't afford to take the word of any one person as "the truth." You should always insist on documentation and then cross-check the documentation just to be safe, even if the information comes from your senior management.

Even résumés are not exempt from careful scrutiny. A CareerBuilder.com survey of hiring managers uncovered tall tales and even bold lies that job seekers have constructed on their résumés. One candidate listed military experience dating back to before he was born!

Probe with questions such as these: Who says this is true? What documentation is available? Where is the evidence? Is there any outside authority to substantiate this? What is the experience within the industry? Can I test this myself? What does other research suggest might be the case? What is my instinctive reaction to the credibility of each source? Just remember that the only dumb question is the one not asked.

Answers Prompt Questions

When you begin researching secondary and primary sources, you'll discover that answers to your questions suggest more questions. These questions become an agenda for future research. The point is that, if you expect to make it in PR, you'll need to dedicate yourself to being a good researcher who is always pursuing new questions.

A good model is to use FGIs to frame questions for a survey, prepare the questionnaire, test and revise it (perhaps using FGIs), launch the survey and tabulate the results, then use post-survey FGIs to gain insight into why questions were answered the way they were.

Conclusions

- Computer-accessible data is easier to use but can be less reliable, depending on its origin.
- Public relations planning generally succeeds in direct proportion to the quality of the information on which it is built.
- Research is vital to the public relations writer.
- The focus of research for the public relations writer is on applicable internal and external policy, relevant background material, appropriate publics, methods of message presentation, the most effective media for delivering the message and evaluation of program success.
- Research information must be stored in such a way that it can be easily accessed, updated and used.
- The most common sources of secondary information include Internet sites, libraries, reference works, bibliographies, periodicals, databases and government records.
- A principal use for FGIs is to help identify words and phrases used commonly by a target public regarding a topic.
- An FGI can give insights into a situation, but results from it can't be generalized to a target public.
- Primary information is developed mostly through interviews and questionnaires. To get information by these means, you must prepare yourself carefully to ask good questions of the right people under the right circumstances.
- Gathering information is not enough. The data you collect has to be cross-checked and verified before you can base decisions on the data. Be skeptical.
- It is in the nature of research that answers to questions prompt still more questions.
- You can secure a place in public relations by becoming a skilled researcher.
- Communication audits are used to evaluate how well information flows within an organization.
- A great deal of emphasis is on credibility.

- Communication audits use a full range of research techniques to get answers to questions.
- Employees sometimes tell researchers what they think the researchers want to hear rather than what they really think.
- Social media offer some new opportunities to gain insights into what people are really thinking.
- Skepticism is the hallmark of all successful writers. You simply can't afford to take the word of any one person as "the truth." You should always insist on documentation and then cross-check the documentation just to be safe.

Exercises

1. You are employed by a small company that recently moved to its present location. The owner of the business asks you to locate a form that she can use to assign legal authority to her son, who lives near the company's previous location. You know that the form is called "Power of Attorney." Explain how you would determine which form is appropriate and legal in the state and how you would evaluate the source.

2. After doing necessary research, draft a questionnaire for a survey to probe attitudes toward physical fitness. The target audience is young men and women, ages 21–35, upwardly mobile in their professions, with college degrees or some college experience, living in metropolitan areas. They lead very active social lives, but their careers are generally stressful.

3. Analyze the bias in the following questions. Rewrite them as necessary to eliminate bias.
   a. What did you like about the product you just tried?
   b. How good a job do you believe the USA president is doing?
   c. Do you believe that jogging does serious damage to the bone structures of the foot and joint?

4. Locate 10 websites for reliable reference material.

5. Compile a bibliography of at least 10 publications whose primary emphasis is on public relations.

Use InfoTrac® College Edition to access information on topics in this chapter from hundreds of periodicals and scholarly journals.

The Public Relations Planning Process

There is a process called "matchbook planning" that involves outlining a plan on the inside of a paper matchbook. In a pinch, that's better than no planning at all. But the public relations planning process is considerably more complex.

In planning a public relations event or campaign, it's good to keep in mind that it is impossible *not* to communicate, whether your organization is dealing with a crisis situation, a short-term public relations campaign or an ongoing public relations program.

As an individual, everything you wear, everything you do and everything you say communicates something about you. The same is true of organizations. The way buildings, signs and office decor look, the way telephones are answered (or not answered), the logo, the letterhead, the annual report, the website, everything communicates something about your organization.

So we can't choose whether or not we want to communicate. What we *can* do, though, is decide *how* to communicate and whether we choose to *manage* communications.

That's what public relations planning is all about. An organization without a written plan is like a runner in a race without a finish line. There's a lot of activity, but without a plan, there can be no success—no "finish line."

For you as a public relations professional, writing a plan is *defining success for yourself;* a good plan gives you measurable goals—"finish lines," so to speak. For your organization, planning is a lot like drawing a *map*—providing a direction toward a desired destination. A plan can equip the organization to speak with one voice, like a choir whose members sing from the same page of music.

A public relations campaign or program is a series of coordinated, unified activities and messages, driven by a single strategy, delivered to relevant publics by a variety of means. These activities and messages are intended to inform, educate or persuade those publics to buy, use or support something. So the public relations plan should fit properly into an overall strategic

Source: Reprinted with permission of Gary Larson and Cartoon Stock, www.CartoonStock.com

plan. A strategic plan and its public relations component focus the resources of an organization on a particular purpose. It is a way to use resources—human, financial and physical—to help an organization accomplish its purposes. A plan defines first *what* is to be done, second *how* it will be done, third *who* will do it, fourth *when* and/or *how often* it will be done and fifth *how much it will cost*. Resources are deployed in what is believed to be the most effective and efficient way to accomplish an organization's purpose.

A plan's design is dictated by the organization's strategic objective. What the organization wants to achieve determines the priority publics. Once the publics are identified, the media to reach them are clear, or should be. Thus a campaign might be designed that involves no mass media at all, either for publicity or for advertising. The whole effort might be carried out through specialized media or social media, if that's the most effective way to reach the publics.

On the other hand, the primary publics might best be reached through the mass media, and the mass media they hold credible may be needed for one or both of two public relations purposes. One is employing publicity to give third-party credibility to other messages originating from the organization. The second is advertising to give guaranteed exposure in targeted media.

If the latter is more important—the case with introducing new ideas, services or products—then the campaign is primarily an advertising campaign with publicity and special event support. If the campaign is primarily information centered or focused on conveying complex messages, then publicity is the driver of the campaign.

When a campaign is primarily directed to specialized audiences, there may be little or no use of mass media. Some ads may be bought in trade or professional journals supported with publicity in the same media. Or the campaign may be entirely driven by presentations. (See Chapter 17.)

But in public relations, *anything* can be used as a channel for communications—doorknob hangers, mayors' or governors' proclamations with related publicity, open houses, marathon races, parades, social media and so on—the list is almost endless. The most effective public relations programs encapsulate the individuals composing the target publics in carefully selected messages delivered through channels that are highly believable and credible to the individual public.

A public relations writer usually is directly involved only in helping to review or craft message strategies and in the implementation phase. Does that mean a public relations writer need not be too concerned about the overall thrust of a campaign? Certainly not. The public relations writer is a vital part of the total success of a campaign, because it is the writer, more than anyone, who interprets the objectives, goals and strategies to relevant publics. So a writer must be fully aware of what the campaign is expected to accomplish and why. The entire campaign plan must be studied carefully and understood exactly to ensure that the writing supports the total effort.

Often the most workable planning strategy is to develop numerous "mini" plans—one for each aspect of the public relations program. One international corporation has separate plans for employee communications, marketing publicity, community relations, media relations, urban affairs, government affairs, investor relations and customer relations.

Let's take a step-by-step look at how a public relations plan is put together. (See Figure 5.1.)

1. Review, Revise and Affirm the Mission Statement

The organization's mission statement establishes the scope, domain and fundamental purpose of the organization and provides a guiding philosophy. It should be a clear, simple statement of the overall purpose of the organization, provide a focal point for objectives, goals and activities and define success for the organization.

Southwest Airlines' mission statement meets those criteria: "The mission of Southwest Airlines is dedication to the highest quality of Customer Service delivered with a sense of warmth, friendliness, individual pride, and Company Spirit."[1]

The mission statement should be in place long enough to be identified with the organization, and it should be regularly reviewed and updated as the organization changes. The beginning of a public relations planning process is an excellent time to do just that.

To review the mission statement, answer the following questions:

- Is it current? Does it reflect the organization as it exists today?
- It is explicit? Is there any room for misinterpreting what the organization is all about?
- Is it understandable?

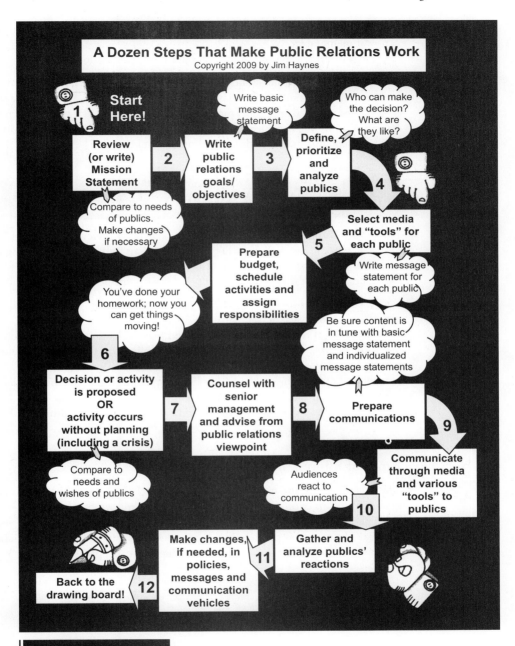

A Dozen Steps That Make Public Relations Work.

Source: Copyright © 2009 by Jim Haynes, APR, Fellow PRSA. Used with permission.

- Is it brief?
- Is it memorable?
- Does it contain the key words that reflect the organization's focus?

If these questions can all be answered "yes," then the mission statement can be affirmed, and the public relations planning process can proceed. If there is a "no," the statement should be modified. Once this is done, most organizations require that the revised mission statement be approved by the organization's senior management or board of directors. Such approval will represent affirmation of the revised mission statement.

2. Examine the Present Situation

Now that the mission of the organization has been reviewed, changed if necessary and affirmed, you can begin the task of gathering relevant information, analyzing it and preparing forecasts. You might want to review Chapter 4 on research before you read further.

Questions you will want to answer in this work include:

- What are our strengths?
- What are our weaknesses?
- What might restrict our success in accomplishing our objectives and goals?
- Will we have the support of our internal publics (board of directors, senior management and employees)?
- How about our main external publics (shareholders, contributors, media and others)?
- What level of financial support can we expect?
- Will we be working within the boundaries of the current cultures in the areas where we operate?

Kinds of Information

The overall quality and effectiveness of a public relations program depends heavily upon the quality of information on which it is based. There are two broad kinds of information available. The first is secondary information. This is information available to you from existing sources. The second is primary information. This is new information generated by original research, such as surveys, interviews or meetings. (See Chapter 4.)

3. Analyze the Data

The next step is to analyze the information gathered from secondary and/or primary sources. Gathering much more information than you may use is a good idea, because it is better to have too much than too little. The first step in analysis is to sort the information into categories. This information may fall naturally into quite a range of categories, such as audience, market, geographical area, product, service, economics, politics, behavior and so on.

Each piece of information in each category then is reviewed carefully for its direct relevance. Duplicate information is discarded. The least useful information is set aside for further research, if needed. Information judged most important is extracted from the rest and put into usable form. Much of it is converted into tables and graphs, especially if the information is complex. Tables and graphs help people "see" things they might overlook if the information is reviewed only in narrative form. All of the information is carefully documented as to its original source. This is necessary because during the analysis you may find that you must refer to an original source for additional information or to clarify a technical point. Returning to original sources also may be necessary to resolve contradictions in information between sources.

It is also common at this stage to look especially at an organization's *strengths* and *weaknesses,* as well as those of the opposition or competition. Strategic planners covet information that leads them to match one of their strengths against a weakness of an opponent or competitor.

Then efforts are made to synthesize these groups of information into a cohesive set of documentation that is linked by a terse narrative. Synthesizing is simply the art of tying diverse pieces of information together in some unique way so that it leads to clear, new insights as to what may be ahead in the near future for the organization.

4. Prepare Forecasts

If the information is well defined, it will lead management to draw better conclusions about the future. For example, if the data indicates the economy is static or in a downturn, this might be interpreted to mean that an organization may have a hard time reaching its profit or fund-raising goal. This might lead to a reduction in the goals. On the other hand, if the economy is heating up, the organization might adjust its target upward.

The point is this: Objectives, goals and strategies adopted for a program should be based on solid information, not whimsy, that supports the clearest possible view of the future. After the information is gathered and analyzed, conclusions can help you set achievable objectives, goals and strategies.

5. Write Statements of Objectives

In some organizations, the term *goal* is used to denote long-range outcomes desired, while *objective* is used for short-term outcomes. Other organizations reverse the meaning, with objective meaning long range and goal referring to short term. Neither is incorrect, but it is important to clearly identify the meaning of each as you go into a planning activity.

Using the latter definition, an objective should be:

- A long-term outcome desired
- An open-ended statement of purpose
- Based upon the organization's mission statement

Each objective should add value to the organization and should:

- Be feasible
- Be acceptable to those involved. Most public relations plans have only a few long-term objectives—often only one—and numerous short-term goals.

6. Prepare Statements of Goals

Whereas objectives are long-term and open-ended, goals are:

- Short range
- Specific as to time and degree
- Fully measurable
- Finite extensions of objectives

A goal should answer the question, "What one result do you want to accomplish?" Well-written goals are close-ended statements of purpose oriented toward an *end result*. (What happens *after* the special event occurs or the newsletter is delivered?)

Each well-written goal contains the following four components:

1. What is being measured (awareness? attendance? contributions?)
2. A starting point or base against which to measure
3. Quantities or percentages to be achieved
4. A deadline or amount of time for accomplishment

Evaluation of success is only as good as the quality of the goals. By including these components, you're setting the stage for measuring your success.

Here are two examples of how a weak goal can be made stronger by including these components, as in the following example:

Example 1

Weak: "Enhance our public image."
Stronger: "Improve recall of important facts about our organization—from three to five—among key media representatives by June 1 of next year."

Example 2

Weak: "Improve media relations."
Stronger: "Increase by 10 percent—from 60 percent to 70 percent—positive media coverage on 10 key issues by the end of the year."

As you see in both examples, the intangibles—"public image" and "media relations"—have been converted to terms that are measurable.

7. Develop Strategies

Once objectives and goals are spelled out, you're ready to take the next step toward a plan—the development of a basic strategy. A strategy is an approach to solving a problem or capturing an opportunity and should answer the following questions:

- How shall we proceed?
- What approach will guide us?

For example, a nonprofit organization could adopt a strategy of public recognition of donors, calling attention to the benefits of their generosity to individuals and to the community. Good news and feature stories could be developed around success stories. If these could be tied to current programs in the community, the general awareness of both the organization's focus and the organization itself could be increased, thus making it easier to raise money.

Other strategies for both nonprofit and profit-making organizations might include training and rehearsing the staff for group and one-on-one presentations, coordinating the timing of all presentations, coordinating invitations to and dates of group presentations, providing model scripts to follow when making phone contacts and a range of other activities.

8. Define, Prioritize and Analyze Publics

The next step in the planning process is to define your publics or constituencies. Each public is a group of people with similar characteristics (demographic and/or psychographic) that can help your organization achieve the objectives you have set, hinder your organization in achieving its objectives or hurt your organization in some way.

The basic questions to be answered are, "Who can make the decision (or take the action) that I want made? And what are those people *like?*

Identifying the characteristics of publics—whether the public is employees, shareholders or others—allows the public relations person to make communications more personal and relevant and therefore more memorable to the individuals composing the public. For example, if you work in public relations for an organization that sells pet-related products, knowing who owns pets can help you target your efforts and make your public relations program more effective. Or if you work in a corporation, you know that the company's shareholders have in common the ownership of shares of stock in the corporation.

Further segmenting each public into homogeneous segments who will respond in similar ways can help you make communications more targeted and effective. This kind of segmentation is accomplished using one or a combination of two criteria—demographics and psychographics or lifestyles.

Demographics

Demographics are the statistical characteristics of human populations and include such factors as:

- Age
- Gender
- Race
- Geographic location
- Occupation
- Marital status
- Education
- Household size
- Income or household income

Knowing any of these factors about the members of a target public can be of great help in public relations planning. For example, if you work for a grocery retailer, marketing research might indicate that the company's target audience is a married female between the ages of 26 and 34. The research might also indicate that a typical shopper is employed as a professional, has one or two children and prefers to shop at the end of her workday, stopping at a store on the right side of her homeward drive. With this information, you could develop a public relations plan for new store openings focused on events to include children and emphasizing products that offer both nutrition and ease of preparation. One large grocery chain that determined that its target public fits this demographic profile decided to build new stores on the right-hand side of evening drive-time traffic arteries to make stopping on the route home from the office more convenient for the women shoppers.

However, if you work for an organization making pet food, you are interested in reaching people whose lifestyles involve pets, regardless of the people's age, sex, race or other demographics.

Psychographics and Lifestyles

Psychographics involve identification of personality characteristics, interests (like children, music, art, pets, travel or hobbies) and attitudes that affect a person's lifestyle and purchasing behaviors. Psychographic data points include opinions, attitudes and beliefs about various aspects relating to lifestyle and purchasing behavior.

Prioritizing Publics

Once you have identified your main publics and conducted as thorough an analysis as time and budget allow, you'll find it's helpful to list the groups in order of priority, with the most important first on your list. This small step will equip you to always consider your most important constituency first—when you allocate budgets and staff time. (See step 11.)

9. Prepare Message Strategies and Statements

Notice that deciding what to say, how to say it and in what media messages should be conveyed are *not* decisions made at the outset of the planning process. Making those decisions before steps 1–8 have been completed would be like a physician prescribing medications before examining the patient.

Yet another step—developing message strategies—is important before messages are conceived.

Organizational, business and functional strategies collectively influence and shape message strategy. A basic message strategy focuses on what is the basic message to be conveyed to target audiences in every message. A good message strategy is simple, adaptable to any medium, applicable to all messages in the campaign and durable.

Simplicity

There is a temptation to overwrite message strategy. One way to avoid that is to look carefully at all three levels of organizational strategy in the plan. Think about your organization's purpose and the precise nature of the problems it tries to solve.

The Texas Education Agency called upon LaMancha Group, a small not-for-profit organization dedicated to working with nonprofit organizations, to assist the agency with a statewide program called "Child Find." Challenged to devise a public relations plan for implementation through the state's 20 Education Service Centers, LaMancha Group did just that.

In its planning process, the group developed the following message strategy:

> Child Find is a federally financed program designed to locate handicapped children who are not in school, assess their individual needs and provide them with the educational services they need.

That simple statement captures the essence of the program's strategy. It is neither fancy nor especially memorable. It is, simply, the basic message that was to be conveyed in every message from and about Child Find.

Adaptability

The Child Find message was unusual because it was adaptable and was used as an "umbrella" statement with a "tag" for each major public. For example, for a religious organization presentation, the statement might be:

> Child Find is a federally funded program designed to locate handicapped children who are not in school, assess their individual needs and provide them with the educational services they need. *We want to allow each child to develop to his or her fullest potential.*

For a Rotary club or other business group, the statement might be:

> Child Find is a federally funded program designed to locate handicapped children who are not in school, assess their individual needs and provide them with the educational services they need. *We want to help these handicapped children become voters and taxpayers.*

The statement cannot appear as written in every message. The medium used to carry the message may not be able to carry the message that way. For example, you could not use posters effectively if you had to carry that message statement as it appears. So the posters used in the program carried a large photo of a hearing-impaired child and the message:

How do you find the children
who stay at home all day
because their parents don't know that
free education is guaranteed to every child
by our state laws?

YOU ASK EVERY PERSON IN TEXAS TO HELP.

Maybe you know a handicapped child who needs
Help. Maybe you can help.
Call 1-800-XXX-XXXX

Applicability

Functional message strategies must apply to every message. This is one criterion, perhaps more than any other, that keeps writers from straying from the strategic fold. You may write a perfectly good news release about the record gifts coming in to a nonprofit organization. But if you fail to get across why they are coming in at record levels, then you're not being faithful to the organizational, business or functional strategies. That's when your supervisor gives the release back to you, tells you to remember what it is we're trying to do and suggests that you review the strategy and rewrite the piece. If that happens often, your supervisor soon knows that, although you may be a gifted wordsmith, you really aren't wired into what the organization is doing. That may lead to a suggestion to look for another job.

An illustration may be wonderful in all details except that its content does not communicate the central message strategy in any form. That's an illustration that should not be used. Clearly, the message strategy should be a central thrust of both the verbal and nonverbal portions of every message. If it isn't, the message should be scrapped or modified to make it applicable.

Durability

Durability may be the toughest part of evaluating the usefulness of a potential message strategy. Who can predict with accuracy when a message strategy reaches its wear-out stage? When does it become trite? When does it become boring to audiences? No one really knows. What *is* known is that a good message strategy will easily last a year without wearing out or becoming trite or boring. Walmart, the world's largest retailer, uses a straightforward line: "Save money. Live better." General Electric's message is a classic: "imagination at work" (with lower-case letters).

If the organizational strategy changes, then even the most durable of message strategies must change to remain consonant. Durable message strategies are sometimes changed only because organizations, not their audiences, get tired of them. That can be a mistake, because a really durable message strategy may be difficult to replace with one of equal or better quality. Building recognition levels so there's instant awareness also takes time. This sometimes leads an organization to seek another agency to come up with better creative work. That can be elusive. And costly.

To be durable, each message must meet the following guidelines:

- Be consistent with and supportive of all other messages
- Be tailored especially to a particular public
- Be written to fit the format of the medium used to deliver it

Now that you have a basic message strategy, you can turn to another important segment of the communication plan—media strategy/mix.

10. Develop Media Strategy/Mix

Media strategy/mix represents one of the most important areas of a public relations plan. However, it sometimes does not get the careful attention it deserves. It deals with what kinds of media will be used to deliver campaign messages, which specific media will be used and how they are mixed. It also deals with the timing of the delivery of messages and the frequency of delivery.

According to Forrester Research, "Media planning is ever more complex and dynamic. Americans use many different media—from TV to blogs—and their usage changes every year. Some media help drive brand awareness, and some drive loyalty. Some media have a young, urban audience; some have an older, rural one. Some media generate high consumer trust, some low. Some media form great cross-channel combinations; some don't.[2]

To select an appropriate media mix, you first would make a list of all the kinds of media— mass media, specialized media and digital media—that you can possibly use to effectively reach the publics that have been defined. In public relations, almost everything is a communications medium—from doorknob hangers to videos. The list might include such things as all of the local mass media and such specialized media as face-to-face contact, brochures, annual reports, backgrounders, position papers, newsletters, direct mail, ads, public serevice announcements (PSAs), faxes, email, news releases, social media and so on.

You then would apply several criteria to each of these media before you begin to make strategic decisions about them. These criteria are: attending, persuasiveness, credibility, timing and effective reach.

Attending

The first consideration is to review who the target publics are so you can identify which media each public "attends to" most. A fund-raising nonprofit organization has two primary publics: current donors who make the largest gifts and potential donors who are capable of making large gifts. Because you know who they are, you can now judge which kinds of media they pay attention to. You might then review the media list and rank-order these media in terms of their ability to draw the attention of our target publics.

Persuasiveness

The next step is to look at the persuasiveness of these individual media. Some media inherently are more persuasive than others. For example, the most persuasive medium is face-to-face delivery. After that, a presentation to a small group is most persuasive. Then come such media as the telephone, email and social media. The latter media also tend to impart a sense of urgency to a persuasive message. In a nonprofit's program designed to raise money, persuasiveness implicit in the media can be a critical factor. When you look at our priority list of kinds of media, you may produce a different rank-order because some kinds of media may be fairly low on attending but high on persuasiveness or vice versa.

Credibility

A message posted on the Internet may be believable but certainly not to the same degree as one delivered face-to-face by someone you know and trust, or even by someone who is an authority but whom you don't know personally. Most people would agree that the same message appearing in *The Wall Street Journal* is more credible than if it appears in the *National Enquirer.* Some media tend to impart more credibility to the messages they carry than do other media. If you expect to set the stage to raise money, you must consider carefully the credibility of the media used to deliver the organization's messages. That may cause you to change your rank-ordering a little.

Timing

Proper timing of the delivery of messages can affect the overall productivity of a campaign. For some aspects of a campaign, it may be important to control message delivery down to the hour. Such media as face-to-face, small group and telephone give us the greatest control. On the other hand, a news release does not. In fact, it may never appear in the media. So we have to score traditional mass media as fairly low on timing. If timing is not critical, however, local mass media can provide wide exposure.

Effective Reach

It isn't enough to deliver a message to massive numbers of people. For example, we might get *Time* magazine to run a public service ad on what a nonprofit organization is doing. That would be impressive to many people, and it would give us a potential reach into the millions. Suppose that our two target publics number only 3,600 people, and all of them subscribe to and regularly read *Time* (which is improbable). The fact is that maybe no more than a quarter of those who read *Time* can recall seeing the message. Of those who recall seeing our message, perhaps no more than 10 percent can recall substantial parts of it and connect it with the organization. That means that we communicated effectively with only about 90 members of our target public, yet the readership of the medium is in the millions. The difference between potential reach and effective reach often is dramatic. Of course, we didn't pay for the space in *Time,* but it did cost us a good bit to prepare the message to *Time*'s specifications. The idea of slippage, or waste, in this example applies equally to other mass media.

Effective reach relies on the economic efficiency of reaching the target public with messages that break through the clutter of other messages and cognitively penetrate so that the information is correctly associated with its source. And it must do that with the maximum persuasive impact and at the right time. The lesson is: Don't be mesmerized by massive numbers. More and more PR people have turned to social media to deliver messages at no or very low cost.

Strategic Use of Media

Having evaluated the different kinds of media that could be used, you now can begin to create a basic strategy for your organization. Three communication guidelines should be kept in mind here. First, you stand a better chance of getting the message across to your target publics if you use a multimedia approach. Research shows that people learn easier and retain information better if they get the same message from different kinds of media. Second, the media chosen should engage as many as possible of the human senses. Research indicates that this improves both learning and retention. It is easy to see how sight and sound can be involved in many of the media we've discussed. But what about touch, smell and taste? Are there things that can be done to engage those senses also? Third, some media should be used with messages designed to get the target publics intellectually involved.

Repetition

Repetition and engagement are key to building memory. Of course, we remember information that is *personal* and *relevant* to us, so making information as personal and relevant as possible to members of selected publics should be a priority in planning. Engaging members of a target public should also be a priority. Repeating the message in various formats and through a variety of channels is critical.

To achieve repetition in an acceptable way, using a strategy with three tiers is often appropriate. Let's assume our client is the APEX Foundation, whose mission is to provide community grants to nonprofit organizations and institutions to help children overcome learning disabilities caused by dyslexia. For its fund-raising campaign, we might use the following three-tier approach.

Tier One   The first and most important tier is to develop well-scripted presentations for small groups and one-on-one presentations. Everything thus far points to the fact that if these aren't done well, the fund-raising campaign may fizzle, because it is here that we should make our most eloquent pleas for help. Note that these two media or communications channels score very high on persuasiveness, credibility and effective reach. The highest quality of support materials must be developed for these sessions. These support materials might include such things as a video, tent cards, name badges, brochures, pledge cards and website content. The website should have the capability of accepting contributions online, but only if a secure server is used.

Tier Two   This tier might include the development of a series of information pieces that can be used as direct-mail items, as well as for other purposes, such as backgrounders, fact sheets, position papers and other items. We might also try to design some sort of crossword puzzle that is provocative enough to get people in the target audience directly involved in its solution while learning about dyslexia. Most or all of these should be loaded onto our organization's website. We might stage an event like a celebrity golf tournament in which the flags are tampered with so hole 6 looks like hole 9 and hole 12 looks like hole 21. For a special event like this, we also would prepare a media kit. (See Chapter 9 for media kit information.)

Tier Three   Here we could rely on a range of news releases—print and broadcast—to local media. We'd work to get spokespeople on local talk shows. And we could provide a series of coordinated PSAs to the local media. We also would provide tip sheets to editors and make sure they had a continuing supply of newsworthy art about APEX and its campaign. We would be sure that the slogan we use is part of every activity. We could even put the line on our standard news release letterhead. Certainly we would want to begin and/or join social media conversations about various aspects of the campaign.

11. Develop Schedule, Assign Responsibilities and Establish Budget

Having made those decisions, you would now develop a schedule or time line. You could divide the year into weeks and list them in columns across the top of a planning board or a spreadsheet software program. Down the left side you'd list the various media and activities that will be used, thus forming a grid. You'd then insert dates into appropriate blocks in the grid. When timing is critical, you may want to create specialized subschedules. For instance, you may want to create a special schedule that deals only with the days, times and locations of group presentations. Similar schedules might be made for individuals who will make the one-on-one presentations. Other subschedules can be developed as the need arises. A schedule grid makes it easy to track activities very closely. Of course, much narrative material about each of these activities will accompany the plan.

For each activity, one person with overall responsibility should be identified. Other people probably will be involved in various parts of the activity, but they do not need to be named in this overview of the plan.

A budget for each activity also should be included. Arriving at a budget may involve obtaining estimates from outside suppliers for printing, still and video photography and so on. Preparation for mailing and postage can be major costs in large projects such as annual reports and printed brochures. It's a good idea to add a contingency of 10–15 percent for unexpected costs. And be sure to add amounts for taxes as appropriate.

12. Devise Monitoring and Measurement Systems and Procedures

Control

When functional plans are presented for review, management looks for, among other things, methods of controlling the campaign so that everything is done when it is supposed to be done and in the way it's supposed to be done. Under normal operating conditions, lines of responsibility and authority remain unchanged. For example, the directors of internal and external communications both report to the vice president for corporate communications, who in turn reports to the president. Copywriters and designers both report to their supervisors, who in turn are responsible to the creative director.

However, if a campaign has unique features, it may be necessary to designate unusual responsibilities to certain staff. For example, if a plan calls for a major special event, but the organization has never before developed such a large event, explicit assignment of responsibility for its management and implementation is necessary. This might be handled by assigning this duty to a current staff person, or it might require creating a new permanent position. It also might be done by an outside vendor specialist. Some organizations don't try to produce their own media kits, for example, but give that task to people who specialize only in doing them. Decisions such as these are an organization's first line of control: assigning responsibility.

Budget is another means of control. As expenses are incurred, they must be paid. It should be clear who approves payment and who has the responsibility for making payments. Rules on bidding, working with vendors and work-for-hire employees should be spelled out clearly. Production control is yet another major area. Everything in a plan is supposed to happen as scheduled. A figurative time line is established, and particular activities are inserted at various places on that line. Elements of a campaign happen in prescribed sequences. Some elements overlap. So several or a great many activities may be unfolding simultaneously. Each is to be finished at a certain time.

From the point of view of the communication function in an organization, perhaps the most significant control is the degree to which the communication program consistently and effectively supports organizational strategy. Really good top management teams know how important it is for communication strategies to be carried out at the highest levels of quality. In the review process, they often look at the functional communication plan with especially critical eyes, because they know that problems in communication may put the organization at risk quicker than problems in some other areas. Less sensitive managements learn that lesson the hard way.

Control is also closely related to our next topic of coordination.

Coordination

Coordination relates to control, of course, but it is a much broader, richer concept. Every organization, even very small ones, is divided into functional areas. Each of those areas has its own roles to play and its own contributions according to the mission of an organization. Even if they are separate functional entities, they are also interdependent. Suppose that a new product rollout is scheduled for the first of the month. The public relations people have been busy placing news and feature stories in trade magazines and in the mass media and producing sales training aids and brochures. The marketing people have been working with distributors to negotiate shelf space, passing out product specifications, pricing sheets and brochures. The special promotions people have a sweepstakes program ready to launch with the new product. When the magic day comes, more than half of the distributors don't have the new product on their shelves because someone failed to make sure that all truckers knew the last date on which the product was to be delivered. The buildup for the rollout was terrific. There was excitement about the new product. But the new product didn't get to all the destinations on time. Consumers came to stores but didn't find it. They got angry at the stores and decided to shop elsewhere. The stores got mad at the company for letting them down and causing them to lose sales. That illustrates what coordination is all about: Making sure all the players know what they are supposed to do and when. Control is following through on the schedule.

But coordination can include even more than the preceding scenario, especially when the campaign involves working in tandem with other organizations. Suppose APEX works out a cooperative arrangement with American Airlines for six free round-trip airfares for two to Honolulu. Hertz is brought in to provide free rental cars. And the Hyatt Regency agrees to provide free luxury suites for one-week vacations. Winners of these prizes will be drawn at a victory banquet at the conclusion of a successful campaign. That's a nice way to say "thank you" to donors. The catch is that none of the promotion from APEX notes that these vacations are good only from June 15 to August 15 of next year. Winners may be elated, but three of them may find that other obligations will keep them from enjoying the prize. That isn't a tragedy, because they can give the vacations to their children or friends. That's when it's discovered that clauses with Hertz and Hyatt Regency prevent transfers. These problems arose because there wasn't clear coordination on every detail of the agreement.

Coordination may be the most difficult aspect of any campaign. It might appear that because all functional areas are within the same organization that coordination would just happen because each functional area is working according to its plans. And those functional plans are supposed to be driven by a single organizational strategy. That's theory. In practice, top management must regularly check to see that things are working as they should and to take corrective actions when they aren't. It should be remembered that an organization can act only through people. People make mistakes. They sometimes forget. Knowing that, the top management must be constantly alert.

Tactical Implementation

When functional strategic plans are finished and approved, it is time to set them in motion. This is when the public relations writer begins to play a major role. Assignments are made for a range of tasks. Copy supervisors do careful reviews with the writers to make sure they know what they are supposed to do, what the basic message strategy is and how it can be interpreted in particular writing tasks.

Suppose you are assigned the task of writing a brochure that explains to current donors and potential donors the background and philosophy of APEX. There are countless ways this task could be approached. Because this brochure will be used as a "selling tool," you'll probably want to avoid a chronology, preferring to concentrate on the philosophy behind the organization that created its unique history. That provides a context in which you can tie APEX's history and philosophy to the new campaign. Of course, your work must be coordinated with that of designers and production people.

A key element, regardless of the writing task, is to make sure that what you write is consistent with the strategic thrust of the campaign. That's what makes a campaign a campaign. As more and more messages are created and distributed, awareness of what APEX is doing begins to rise.

Another requirement is that each message must be written so it will fit the format of the medium used to deliver it. Of course, every message should be directed especially to the target audiences. Yes, other people will see many of these messages. But it is a good idea to regard them as incidental receivers. Don't let them divert you from the basic strategy.

While you are writing, others are designing, recording videos and doing myriad other tasks, such as negotiating with vendors about printing a brochure or producing a PowerPoint-type slide show. At the same time, people in other functional areas of the organization are doing their own things, such as arranging for financing, clearing legal requirements for the use of copyrighted materials, securing releases from models and doing various other tasks.

Monitoring and Evaluation

Monitoring a program is essential. Functional strategies collectively define what is expected to happen to achieve stated goals. One of the primary functions of supervisors at all levels in every area is to monitor progress. This is a routine part of their jobs, but their efforts are mostly focused inside the organization. What about monitoring things that go on outside? That's a different situation. Certainly, the leadership of the communication program should routinely and regularly scan the environment for problems, issues, developments, trends, opportunities and other things that may affect the organization or the campaign in progress.

How can we tell whether the program is working? Do we go by intuition, or do we set some routine procedures to take the pulse of our target publics at regular intervals? One measure we might consider is to review progressive reports on the number of inquiries. If there is an increase in inquiries, how can we be sure the increase is a result of the campaign? Another measure might be to count the house at special events to gauge how well people are responding to the campaign. It may be that an overflow crowd attended a concert simply because of the quality of the singer but they will soon forget the sponsor, even if they ever realized who the sponsor was. If we are selling a product or service, weekly sales reports can give us some insights. But are sales or the number of orders a clear indication of how effectively we are communicating with our audience? Lots of variables affect sales and orders other than messages. If we are promoting a candidate or a political issue, telephone canvassing can tell us a lot, but can we predict with great accuracy a victory at the polling booth?

Although those indicators, as well as many others, may be prominent parts of many campaign plans, the information they yield is ambiguous about what the target public knows about us or whether there have been any shifts in attitudes toward us because of the campaign. These two issues deal exclusively with the communication function. The only way they can be evaluated objectively is to do systematic research on relevant publics at regular intervals. That means that we need incremental research on our relevant publics to get a clear picture of how the campaign is doing. Such information may help us spot problems that can be corrected during the remainder of a campaign.

The monitoring process results in an assortment of writing tasks. Prominent among them are emails, memos and letters. Analytical reports may also be written, along with cover letters. If something is awry in the campaign and ways of righting it are found, then recommendations or proposals for specific actions will need to be written. Monitoring should be, of course, a part of every functional plan.

When a program is completed, it is necessary to evaluate its productivity. The most effective evaluations are those with known benchmarks in place at the time the campaign begins. For example, pertinent data gathered in support of the strategic plan would ordinarily contain a good bit of benchmark information. Depending on the nature of the organization, this information might be found in measures of attitudes and behavior, brand shares, market shares, sales volumes, unit sales, contributions and pledges received, aided and unaided recall scores and others.

Particular measures should be selected that are uniquely appropriate to the campaign and its parent organization. In the case of APEX, a critical measure is the dollar volume of contributions and pledges. This can be compared directly to the level from the preceding year. It is easy to see whether the organization met its goal. If it did not, efforts must be made to determine why so that those mistakes will not be made in future campaigns. If the goal was exceeded, we need to know why. Is the greater-than-expected increase due to the campaign, or is it attributable to some influence beyond the scope of the campaign? Is the awareness of APEX higher now than when the campaign began? Do people have more appreciation for APEX now than before the campaign? Clearly, many of these questions, and many like them, can be answered only if we expand the systematic research program that we used during the monitoring phase. Both monitoring and campaign evaluation cost money. This needs to be provided in the campaign budget. If there is not enough money for good monitoring and effective evaluation, then we can't really do these tasks correctly. An absence of evaluation cripples strategic planning for future campaigns.

Although many emails, memos and letters will be written as part of a campaign's final evaluation, the most daunting writing task is likely to be a thorough, lengthy report that summarizes the results of the campaign. Such reports must be highly persuasive, yet be careful not to mislead management as you try to marshal your arguments in support of conclusions. Much of the information in these reports is complex. That may make it useful to break out some pieces of information and recast them into backgrounders, position papers, letters and memos in support of forthcoming planning efforts. The reason for doing that, of course, is to make sure that the responsible managers get information that is in its most usable form without having to wade through a lengthy report.

Conclusions

- Writing a public relations plan is *defining success for yourself;* a good plan gives you measurable objectives and goals.
- Effective campaigns or programs are built around a unified message strategy. The organization must speak with one voice.
- A campaign is a series of coordinated messages and activities, driven by a single strategy, delivered to relevant publics by a variety of means.
- A campaign intends to inform, educate or persuade its relevant publics to buy, use or support something.
- The writer's primary role in a campaign is to craft messages that are consistent with campaign strategy.
- A campaign plan defines what is to be done, how it will be done, who will do it, when or how often it will be done and what each activity will cost.
- Public relations writers are involved in campaign planning mostly at the stage of crafting creative message strategies and in tactical application of those strategies.
- An effective organizational strategy is rooted in the mission of the organization.
- A mission statement must be explicit. It should be reviewed at the outset of strategic planning.
- A good mission statement leads to a clear understanding of the business mission of an organization.
- Organizational and business missions collectively give focus to the information-gathering process.
- Information in support of strategic planning is of two types: secondary and primary.
- Information must be analyzed carefully, put into usable form, synthesized and used as a basis for forecasting.
- Be sure you understand the meaning of "objectives" and "goals" in your organization.
- Relevant information is reviewed before setting objectives. Objectives are long range, are unspecific as to time and degree and are not measurable.
- Goals represent incremental movement toward fulfilling objectives. Goals are short range, are specific as to time and degree and are measurable.
- Strategy is shaped directly by an organization's mission, objectives and goals.
- Organizational strategy defines what is to be done that will help to meet the goals specified.
- Coordination of activities and messages is important to build unity and credibility.
- Functional plans for each area of operations are developed in support of the organization's basic strategy.
- A communication plan takes its strategic cues from organizational strategy.
- Good message strategy is simple, adaptable, applicable and durable.
- Good media strategy/mix considers who in the target audience pays attention to which media, how inherently persuasive the media are, how credible the media are, how easy it is to achieve precise timing of delivery of messages and whether the media provide effective reach.
- Effective management of campaigns depends on control so that what is to be done is done as it should be and when it should be.

- Coordinating communication campaign activities is a major challenge, especially if it involves working with other organizations.
- Tactical implementation is that stage at which writers and other creative people craft and distribute campaign messages.
- At the monitoring and evaluation stage, writers are most likely to be called on to write memos, letters, short or long reports, proposals and the like, most of which must be highly persuasive.

Exercises

1. Select a public relations campaign that is now under way in your area. Get as many pieces of campaign materials as you can. Work out a clear set of statements that reflect that organization's mission, objectives, goals and strategy.
2. Using your work from Exercise 1, identify the message and media strategies in use by this organization. Write a short evaluation that judges the degree to which these strategies support what appears to be the organization's mission, objectives, goals and strategies. Is that the best plan for this organization? Why? If not, why not?

Use InfoTrac ® College Edition to access information on topics in this chapter from hundreds of periodicals and scholarly journals.

Writing Principles

Remember that all readers, listeners and viewers of PR writing are volunteers! Make their experience rewarding.

Writing to Clarify and Simplify the Complex: Style and Content

Public relations writers seldom prepare materials that are required reading, listening or viewing. Occasionally, as a PR writer, you may prepare a handbook or manual or training video that eventually is required consumption for some audience. Even if it is "required" reading, you still have to make it accessible. The point of these materials is usually instruction, so the audience must be able to comprehend the message.

Most audiences for which you research and write, though, are volunteers. You have a great deal of competition too, at all levels. You have to compete for attention with all kinds of compelling messages. A primary source for information about your company, its products and its services is on a website. That website won't have many visitors if it isn't viewer-friendly and offers information that is easy to understand. When you are trying to get messages into a medium over which you and your organization have no control, just to get the material accepted you have to compete with materials prepared by skillful staff writers and freelance sources from all over the world. That means you have to be a very good writer, offering excellent information in an extraordinarily interesting way.

Most important, you need to remember that good writing is writing that succeeds in communicating. Bad writing is writing that fails to communicate.

Writer and teacher of writing at Yale, William Zinsser, says that every successful piece of nonfiction should leave the reader with one provocative thought not previously held. Not two thoughts or five, just one.[1] But all the advice in all the books about writing is worthless if you don't learn the most important point first: *Write so people will understand what you mean.* That is the one provocative thought you should take from this chapter. To do that, you must consider both style and content.

You won't be very successful in communicating if you simply enter words into a computer without giving them much thought beforehand, or if you are more concerned with displaying your vocabulary than with communicating with your readers. You have to think about who your readers or listeners are. What do they know? What do they think they know? You can't get by with just telling them what you want to do in the words you choose. Furthermore, much of what you write is expected to have a specific effect. PR writing is results-oriented, and it is a craft that must be learned and practiced.

How do you produce prose that succeeds in communicating? There is no magic formula, but you start with the basics—message, public, medium. Then be sure the message, however complex, is simplified.

Message, Public, Medium

An important part of good writing is being properly prepared before you start. You must do the necessary research on the subject matter so you will understand the material, know what is important and have in mind just what you want to communicate and what results you want. You must also know who will receive your communication and how best to reach them. In short, you must know your message, your public and your medium.

Message

Most writing, whether for public relations purposes or otherwise, has one goal: To convey a message. The goal of any writer is to transfer thoughts to other people's minds, whatever the medium. Step one, then, is deciding just what you want to say. If you don't understand what you're trying to say, neither will others.

This means you must know exactly what you are trying to say. Don't express your message in hazy, abstract terms. Make sure you understand the message before you begin to write. If you can't write a short, simple sentence that summarizes the point you want to make, you probably need to do a little more thinking. Remember: What do you want to happen as a result of your communication effort?

Public

It is not enough, however, for you to understand your message. You must phrase it so the public will also understand. You must know who your readers or listeners are (see the discussion of priority publics in Chapter 1), and you must know something of their characteristics, values and beliefs so you can reach them (see the discussion of demographics and psychographics in Chapter 4).

Otherwise, you won't be able to communicate effectively. In short, you must tailor your message to the public. Tailoring also means realizing that even publics able to read and comprehend complex information have too much to read and too little time in which to read or pay attention to a specific message that is being offered, but not necessarily sought.

Medium

An important part of tailoring your message consists of choosing the right medium to reach that public. In addition, different media are appropriate for different types of messages. Choosing the right medium is an important aspect of successful communication. (See Chapter 1.)

The choice of medium in turn affects the way you should frame the message. Articles written for magazines are done in an entirely different style than public service announcements for radio. You must use the style appropriate for the medium, being aware of the medium's technological advantages and limitations.

These three rules—know your message, know your public and know your medium—will take you a long way toward successful writing. Both the substance and the style of what you write depend on them.

These rules, however, apply only to the planning stages of writing. Even if you know your message, your audience and your medium, your writing may fail. The execution is just as important as the preparation. So add three other rules for successful execution: Write clearly, make what you write interesting and simplify the complex to make information easily accessible.

Style

Clarity, of course, is the number one aim of writing style. If your audience doesn't understand what you've written, your efforts will have been wasted. But even if your writing is clear, a dull style can put your readers to sleep, and your message still won't get across.

Readability/Listenability

Given a strong enough motivation, a person will "plow through any complexity of words, signs or hieroglyphs," says readability expert Robert Gunning.[2] That's true. Someone intensely interested in a subject will read through the worst writing trying to glean the slightest bit of new information. Usually, though, interest is not that high. People bombarded from all sides with innumerable public relations messages from different communicators are likely to ignore any messages that demand too much time or effort.

The problem today may be that although the desire to understand may be strong, the ability is inadequate. It is for 47 percent of the population. In the USA, 20 percent of the population read at or below the fifth-grade level and another 27 percent have reading challenges. These may be medical, such as dyslexia, a lack of educational opportunities or due to having English as a second language.[3]

What qualities make writing "easy to read"? This question has been the subject of a vast amount of research, finally focusing on two key qualities: Sentence length and word length.

Sentence Length   The first principle of readable writing is to keep most sentences short. For the meaning to be clear, the reader must be able to grasp at once the relationship among the words in a sentence. Long, tangled sentences tend to obscure those relationships.

Of course, not every sentence should be short. An endless stream of short sentences makes for dull reading. And it is possible for long sentences to be clear—if they are properly constructed.

The key to readability, then, is average sentence length. An occasional long sentence is no problem. But a never-ending series of long sentences leaves readers dizzy. According to Gunning, modern prose read by the public has an average sentence length of about 16 words.[4]

If your sentences are much longer than that on the average, your prose probably isn't as readable as it should be.

There are two major reasons why sentences are too long. One is that writers tend to connect independent clauses with coordinating conjunctions or add details that could be left for later sentences. The other is that too many unnecessary words are present. The cures are easy: Use more periods and fewer words.

Some long sentences, for example, can simply be cut in two with a period at the right spot. Avoid connectives like "however." Use a period and start a new sentence. Look at this example:

> Students inclined to fall into the habit of binge drinking are very likely to become alcoholics; however, students who are willing to learn how to drink responsibly and moderately may require external pressure and special incentives to change a habit perhaps learned in high school or earlier.

A revision might be: Binge drinkers are inviting alcoholism. A habit of alcohol abuse learned an an early age may require incentives or external help to change.

A sentence of 47 words becomes two, one 5 words and another 18. See if you can trim the second sentence to a desired maximum of 16 words.

Excessive words in much writing result from temptations to overwrite—overusing modifiers, especially words that intensify and may be redundant. Some modifiers are so trite they are meaningless, such as "spectacular" or "amazing." Some are redundant, like "dog puppies" or "young children." The fewer the words, the stronger the statement. Look at this example:

> The Provost said he never in his 10 years at the university ever had witnessed such a debacle, and he was surprised and shocked by the students' outrageous and destructive behavior at the game, although he realized it was not all students, just a disruptive few.

It is better to say, "The Provost said the students' outrageous and destructive behavior at the game shocked him."

The original sentence would have been worse if the attribution had not been clear. Much writing is made murky by needless attribution. Introductions and personal commentary also inflate, and commentary is not welcomed in news releases. These writing flaws are quite common in what is euphemistically called "business writing."

An example is: "Structural integrity has been found to be difficult to measure." All you need is: "Structural integrity is difficult to measure." If the statement is something that needs documenting, cite a source, don't write around it.

Weak information also causes protracted introductions. Another cause may simply be a lack of focus. People are in a hurry and if you want to be on their agenda, you have to earn the right with a clean, clear appeal.

Look at this example:

> Students, faculty and staff are asked to provide their cell phone numbers by email to the university's safety alert email address (safety@xxx.edu) so they can be called in the event of severe weather. A notice of when the university will be officially closed due to severe weather will be on the university website and on the university's main phone as well as given to the local news media to announce.

Try this: "University closings on bad weather days will come as a direct call to registered cell phone numbers. To be notified, send your cell phone number to safety@xxx.edu. Weather closings will also be announced on the main university website and phone and by local radio and television stations." The 70-word message was cut to 48 words and made more specific. Can you make it even better?

The personal commentary problem is so common in letters that one of the authors forbids students from using "I" to begin any sentence in a cover letter, memo or media advisory. The reason? People are likely to intuitively respond with "Who cares?" Of course few are rude enough to express it, but the reaction is there. It disengages the reader, whereas a "you" involves the reader.

Keeping sentences short is just the starting place in writing clearly, though. Short sentences won't make reading easy if the words within those sentences don't make sense. You can't write clear sentences if you don't use clear words.

Word Length   A student with an exceptional vocabulary once turned in what he thought was an especially well-written paper. The professor's comment scribbled across the top of the paper was simply: "Avoid sesquipedalianism." Because the student's vocabulary wasn't *that* large, he scurried to a dictionary to look up *sesquipedalianism*. He found it to mean the excessive use of long words.

The professor could easily have written, "Don't use so many long words," and the student would have understood immediately. The point for public relations writers is twofold. First, if you use long words, some readers won't understand them. Second, even if the long words you use have well-known meanings, they slow the reader down.

There is no need to say *precipitation* when you mean *rain*. There is nothing wrong with saying *use* instead of *employ* or *utilize*. *Fair* is just as good a word as *equitable*.

Some writers can't resist filling their prose with important-sounding phrases like "integrated conceptual analysis" or similar verbose nonsense. At least twice in every sentence they use words ending in *-ment*, *-any*, *-ial*, *-ization*, *-action* and *-ability*. Avoid such words when you can. They make reading more difficult and diminish the forcefulness of your statement. As public relations writer Alden S. Wood asks, who would have responded to these words?

> Retain your earth! Abstain from engagement in interpersonal ballistic relationships unless these relationships are initiated by the power incumbents. If, however, it becomes apparent that overt hostile interaction is to commence, let this commencement have its genesis in this geopolitical region.

The average sentence length in this paragraph is less than 14 words. But the words are so foggy that the meaning is completely lost. Fortunately, Captain John Parker didn't talk like that. Instead he uttered the famous command, "Stand your ground. Don't fire unless fired upon. But if they mean to have a war, let it begin here."

Why do long words make reading more difficult? One reason is that long words tend to be abstract. Readers comprehend more quickly if words are concrete—that is, if they evoke visual images and avoid ambiguity. If an oil company says it's spending money on "petroleum exploration facilities," for example, the average reader won't have a very clear notion of what the company is buying. They will, however, if the company says "drilling rigs."

Long words are often unfamiliar to readers. Common words, which readers recognize immediately, are usually short. Why say "remuneration" when "pay" will do?

Readability Formulas   Short sentences and short words are the prime ingredients of clear writing. These ideas have been incorporated into various formulas to gauge the readability of a piece of writing. Such formulas—notably those devised by Gunning and Flesch—can be very useful to writers who want to check the clarity of their prose. Readability is much easier to check now that most word-processing software comes with readability formulas. Everything from the technical writing of industry to the often-obscure prose of accounting is now being measured for clarity by using readability formulas. This shift toward plain language almost demands that writers measure their writing for level of comprehension. Keep in mind, though, that a high readability score doesn't guarantee good writing. Readability formulas are actually nothing more than measures of structural simplicity, and as Gunning points out, "nonsense written simply is still nonsense."[5]

Besides, clarity may be the first goal of writing, but it's not the only one. Clear writing can be stilted and unnatural. Writing can be so simple that it's just plain boring. Clarity is worthless if the writing isn't also interesting, because writing that isn't interesting usually isn't read.

What makes writing interesting? Primarily, the subject matter. Some subjects are interesting to some people but not to others (which is why you should know your public).

Here, though, we're concerned with style. The basic goals of style are, in addition to clarity, the logical development of ideas and a smooth transition from one idea to the next. Of course, style must also help maintain the reader's interest. Writing must be lively, with generous use of active verbs and vivid phrases. Interesting writing sounds natural, is not monotonous and, in general, is "pleasing to the ear." Interesting writing uses personal words such as you and people to enhance human interest. Thus besides the fundamental goal of clarity, good writers strive for naturalness, variety, euphony and human interest.

Naturalness

Reading is easiest if the style is conversational. Readability experts agree that one of the basic rules of readable writing is "write like you talk." Of course, you can't write exactly like you talk. There is a difference between written and spoken language. Spoken sentences are not carefully structured, and they often contain much repetition. In speaking, meaning can be shaded by intonation, inflection, facial expressions and gestures. You can't duplicate such features of the spoken language in your writing. But you can write prose that sounds natural, as though someone could have spoken it.

The following sentence, for example, is clear, but it sounds like a written, not a spoken, sentence:

> Smith was not disturbed that Johnson had submitted his resignation. He said that the position held by Johnson was not of high significance.

The same thing could have been written in a more natural, conversational manner:

> Johnson's resignation didn't bother Smith. He said Johnson's job wasn't important, anyway.

A good test of naturalness is to read aloud what you've written. If you stumble over phrases and your tongue gets twisted, the sentence is not easy enough to read. Try again. If you still have trouble writing sentences that sound natural, try this approach. Write what you want to say as you would say it in conversation. Then go back and rewrite the sentence with proper syntax, making sure the pronouns are in the right place and the meaning is clear. Part of making writing conversational is using active, not passive, verbs.

Notice the improvement that results when we substitute the active voice for the passive in the following sentences:

Passive: Everything possible was done by company engineers to restore service.
Active: Company engineers did everything they could to restore service.
Passive: It was requested by the company president that the exhibit be kept open by the museum officials.
Active: The company president asked museum officials to keep the exhibit open.

Another device that helps writing sound natural is the contraction. Use contractions freely. Everybody uses contractions in speech, and no matter what your grammar-school teacher told you, there is absolutely nothing wrong with using them in writing. You suffer no loss of meaning when you use *don't, won't* or *can't* instead of *do not, will not* or *cannot.* Avoiding contractions does nothing but slow the reader down, and readers don't like to be slowed down.

Variety

Monotony can poison an otherwise good style. You haven't gained anything by stringing clear and natural-sounding sentences together if their structure and vocabulary are so similar that readers get bored. You enrich meaning and help comprehension when you search for different words. Refreshingly new words help the pace too. The style must push readers along and keep them going. Readers shouldn't feel they have to force themselves through sentence after sentence.

Variety means following the rules wisely. For example, we already mentioned that not all sentences need to be short. True, a series of long sentences makes it hard for a reader to follow the flow. And it's easy to get lost in a maze of adverbial and prepositional phrases. But an occasional long sentence, if constructed properly, can improve the flow of the narrative. A compound sentence can take the reader from one idea to the next. An occasional inversion of subject and verb reduces monotony and can emphasize the action in the sentence. You need to be cautious with this technique, however, to avoid altering meaning.

Many writers, although aware of the need for judicious variety in sentence structure, still go too far in trying to achieve variety in word choice. This leads to the use of three or four words to describe the same thing. For example,

When my books arrived, I took the hardbound texts from the package and placed the treasured volumes on my bookcase next to my other bound publications.

Usage experts call this pitfall "elegant variation." "There are few literary faults so widely prevalent," says one expert.[6] No doubt the problem stems from the widespread belief that you should never use the same word twice in one sentence. But no such prohibition exists in any rule book, and a single repetition is seldom as terrible as some writers think. Of course, repeating the same word several times can get boring. But you don't have to thumb through a thesaurus to find a synonym. And often a pronoun works well enough: "I took the books out of the box and put them on the shelf with my others."

In other cases, there's no need to repeat the word at all: "Jones, Smith and Brown all won races; it was Jones' first win, Smith's third victory, and Brown's fourth triumph." But the vocabulary lesson is unnecessary. It's just as clear to say, "It was Jones' first win, Smith's third and Brown's fourth."

If there's no way to get around repetition, go ahead and use the same word again. It won't hurt you. And the reader won't have to figure out whether you used different words because of some real difference or because you were trying to avoid repetition at all costs or, worse, trying to show off your vocabulary.

As for the thesaurus, don't throw it away. But use it only when you are looking for a specific word, the exactly right word, which you know but just can't think of at the moment. It is rarely wise to pick a word you've never heard of or used before. Always check a dictionary to make sure the word you choose is appropriate.

Euphony

The main reason so many writers worry about sentence uniformity and word repetition is that they want to achieve euphony in their writing. Indeed, writing that is rhythmic and makes proper use of figures of speech is usually more enjoyable to read than straightforward stilted prose.

The only way to achieve euphony is to read good writing and develop an ear for it. If you discover a good style that is used successfully by someone else, don't worry about copying it. Just don't get carried away. As one observer puts it, a "concatenation of mellifluous phrases may indicate more polish than insight."[7] First make sure your thoughts are clear and your message is pleasing to the mind. Then worry about pleasing the ear.

Human Interest

If you are writing about people, your writing will naturally contain elements of human interest. But if your subject is something mechanical, impersonal or abstract, your task will be more difficult. How can you achieve human interest when writing about inanimate objects? The trick is to remember that you're writing *to* people even when you're not writing *about* them. When appropriate, address the reader as *you*. Use the pronoun *we* to refer to people in general when discussing common knowledge, as in, "We know today that the world is round." Rhetorical questions and direct quotations help give writing a personal sound. If you don't find any and you never use *we* or *you*, your prose isn't likely to be very interesting.

Trite Expressions

"The performance *highlights* . . .," "The series *features* . . ." and similar noun-into-verb conversions are trite. News releases burdened with such creaking turns of phrase as "colorful scenery," "dramatic new move" and "spearheading the effort" deserve their usual fate—a quick trip to the trash. Clichés make your copy seem old because the words are so familiar. Public relations writing demands freshness and vitality. But don't try to freshen a cliché. And don't try to be coy by putting it in quotes—as though you really know better but are speaking colloquially— as that just calls attention to its triteness. Simply avoid using expressions you constantly hear or read.

Eliminating Bias

A writer's word choice can be unintentionally disparaging. A careless construction can offend people with disabilities, members of ethnic groups, people in certain age groups—especially the very young and the very old—or women. Using gender-neutral language should become routine for you. Avoid expressions like business*men*, which excludes businesswomen. Use "businesspeople" or be specific: "merchants," "retailers" and so on. Avoid using the masculine pronoun in a generic sense. Either use a noun or use the nongeneric plural pronoun (they, them, their). Gender-neutral language is much more common now as state constitutions have adopted changes as have most businesses.

You need to watch titles too. Don't make assumptions about gender in addressing a letter. Be sure your professor has an earned doctorate before using Dr., but if he or she has a Ph.D., use it. Some women on campus find students using Dr. for all male instructors and using Mrs. for females, when that is inappropriate. More than one student has been castigated for using a social title in a business setting by a female professor. Having students use Dr. in addressing them has embarrassed some male instructors without the doctorate.

When you are writing about a couple in a story, be sure you give equal identification to each partner. For example, in a story that appeared in the business section of a newspaper, a couple who are partners in a real estate development company that bought a downtown property were not equally identified. He was identified as an accountant, but she, also a CPA, was only identified as his wife. It would have been just as easy to eliminate the bias by writing: Accountants Jane and Jim Smith, partners in the Heritage Building Co., are listed on the deed as new owners of a parking lot across the street from their downtown building at 500 Main Street. Although this example of bias is probably the fault of the reporter, you will be writing news releases, so don't make a similar mistake.

Don't mention ethnicity or disabilities unless they are important to content. Be careful not to use stereotypes in language or art. Active seniors are offended by rocking-chair representations of their age group, and children resent being portrayed as miniature, but imbecile, adults.

Quotes

As a public relations writer, you will be using many quotations in your releases. If that is what the person said, then you must use it. No. Paraphrase the quote to weave it into the story in which you may incorporate partial quotes.

Just stringing quotes together makes for formidable reading.

Edit your copy mercilessly. You can do this better if you put it away for a day and go back to it. Get others to read it and offer critiques. The checklist in Table 6.1 provides a guide for assessing drafts of writing.

Internet Language Use

Although Chapter 8 provides a discussion of writing for social media and converged traditional media, something needs to be said here about the stylistic mix of participatory media. Blogs come from individuals, not institutions, although the authors of some blogs may be officers in organizations that are reaching out to their publics in a nontraditional way. Blogs usually invite feedback, so the result is often conversational, rather than expository.

T A B L E 6 . 1	*Writing Checklist*

1. Is the message clear? Have you said exactly what you want to say?

2. Have you identified important publics? Does your writing speak to those publics?

3. Is the style of writing appropriate for the intended medium?

4. Are your sentences instantly clear? Are they free from confusing constructions?

5. Are sentences, on average, fairly short? Have you avoided stringing long sentences together?

6. Is your writing concise and free from needless words?

7. Have you used common, concrete words that evoke visual images?

8. Is your language natural? Can your writing be easily read aloud?

9. Is the sentence structure varied?

10. Are most sentences in the active voice?

11. Have you made sufficient use of personal words and sentences?

12. Have you substituted creative language for trite expressions?

13. Is your writing free from bias?

14. Is this your best effort?

Institutions are also positioning themselves in the social media. Some broadcast media specifically say that their audiences can reach them on their website as well as in one or more of the social media sites, such as Twitter. Brevity is a requirement for Twitter with its 140-character limit. Messages there need to be simple and clear as well as brief. Economy and specificity demand appropriate punctuation for clarity, but lean on language with powerful verbs.

Content: Simplifying the Complex

The need for clear and simple writing has never been greater. With email messages flashing through cyberspace and faxes going around the world, your prose will be translated and interpreted in the idiom of another culture, another experience.

If you always remember to use simple language, you'll be able to write clearly about even the most complex ideas. That is important because the world has become exceedingly complex.

In his first paper on the theory of relativity, written in 1905, Albert Einstein penned one of the simplest sentences you'll ever find in a scientific paper. In explaining a point about time and simultaneity, Einstein wrote (in English translation):

> If, for instance, I say, "That train arrives here at 7 o'clock," I mean something like this: "The pointing of the small hand of my watch to 7 and the arrival of the train are simultaneous events."[8]

You can't get much simpler than that.

Einstein treasured simplicity in writing, and though his scientific papers did get technical in places, his public writings were always clear and readable. Einstein could write simply on subjects like relativity because he understood them so completely himself. He could write clearly, without too many technical terms, because he knew his subject well enough to express the ideas in plain language and retain absolute accuracy.

Public relations writers are not likely to be as knowledgeable about any subject as Einstein was about physics. Yet they are still called on to translate complex subjects into understandable language. There is nothing simple about nuclear power, pollution chemistry or petroleum economics. Medicine, urban affairs and social services can be as complex as advanced calculus. Yet such issues are becoming more and more important to the average citizen. Public relations people must be able to explain the implications of government and corporate actions in these areas, as well as to interpret the latest research findings. It's advisable to have authorities check the final drafts to be sure your translations are accurate. It takes special writing skills to simplify the complex without explaining it inaccurately.

Some authorities think it's impossible to explain complex things like scientific research to the general public. Even Rudolf Flesch, the ultimate advocate of simplifying the complex, advises writers not to try to give complete scientific explanations. You can describe the meaning of a discovery, he says, and indicate its importance. But a complete scientific explanation? Flesch wouldn't even try that with his own readability formula:

> Here I would have to get into statistical regression formulas and multiple correlation and whatnot, and nobody who hasn't had a course in statistics would know what I am talking about. . . . There is only one bit of advice I can offer in this business of giving laymen an exact scientific explanation: don't try.[9]

Not everybody agrees with this attitude. William Zinsser says, "a complex subject can be made as accessible to the layman as a simple subject. It's just a question of putting one sentence after another."[10]

In practice, explaining subtle scientific principles to nonscientists isn't often of much use—not because lay readers can't understand, but because most aren't really interested. If a reader is interested in a subject, however, a good writer can explain it. You can even explain statistics to people who haven't had statistics courses, if they are interested enough to follow what might be a fairly lengthy explanation.

Today, in many cases, people aren't merely interested in scientific explanations. They demand them. If your company is building a chemical plant near a town, you'd better be able to explain to the people who live there what that plant will do and how its safety systems will work. You won't get by with saying, "Don't worry—it's safe."

Conflicting scientific advice also gets into the public agenda, leaving people confused about what to believe or to do. With people increasingly concerned about health issues, in 1998, the Harvard School of Public Health and the International Food Information Council Foundation convened an advisory group of experts. Later this was broadened to include nutrition researchers, food scientists, journal editors, university media relations officers, broadcast and print reporters, consumer groups and food industry executives. The result was a set of guidelines to provide a context in which people can evaluate information.[11]

Another solution is to use the same system both internally and externally to develop a document called a position paper. (See Chapter 9.) Such documents should be developed with input from legal, marketing, customer service, operations, public relations and public affairs and consideration of opposing points of view from activist groups and competitors. Position papers then provide a launching pad for all public statements on an issue about a product, service or project.

And if the public doesn't ask technical questions directly, newspaper reporters and electronic journalists will. Today, the mass media deal with more technical subjects in greater detail than ever before. When reporters working on such stories don't understand something themselves, they often go to PR people for explanations. PR writers, frequently trained only in journalism or English and not in the technical fields they must try to interpret, often find themselves at a loss. When an activist group accuses your company of cheating on taxes, how do you explain the complexities of accelerated depreciation and the investment tax credit? How does the public relations person for a factory suspected of polluting the air explain the difference between primary ambient air standards and secondary emission limits? How does the spokesperson for a nuclear plant explain the meaning of "10 picocuries of radioactivity"?

It isn't easy, but these things can be explained. You can simplify the complex, and you can simplify it accurately—but only if, like Einstein, you know your subject.

Know Your Subject

There is an old saying among newspaper editors that a good reporter can cover any story. If the reporter doesn't know much about the subject, he or she can simply call an expert, ask a few questions and then explain it all to readers in words they'll understand. Or so the theory goes.

This adage may have been true once, but it isn't anymore. And it's no truer for PR writers than for reporters. Nevertheless, pamphlets on complex subjects are often written this way. An engineer produces a technical description of some process or machine in words specific to the profession. The copy is given to the PR person, who edits and rewrites to simplify the language but keeps the facts as the engineer wrote them. In theory, the PR person needs to know nothing about the subject; the engineer provides the facts. The PR writer just needs to know how to write clearly.

The problem is that you can't simplify complex writing unless you know what it means. You must understand it thoroughly yourself before you can explain it to somebody else. You must know more about the subject than you'll ever put into print. If you don't, you won't be able to tell when a simplified statement can stand alone or should be qualified. And you won't know the difference between a correct statement and a false one.

Consider this example from a writer trying to describe the dangers of cigarettes in simple terms:

> Opening another front in its war on smoking, the federal government plans to publicize a new peril—carbon monoxide—to prod the cigarette industry to reduce its use of that substance in cigarettes just as it has reduced tar and nicotine.

This sentence is simple enough, but also sheer nonsense. Carbon monoxide is not a substance that exists inside tobacco, waiting to be unleashed. It is a gas created when carbon (in the tobacco) combines with oxygen (from the air) as tobacco burns. The writer simply didn't know much about the subject. The sentence is also nonsense because carbon monoxide is not a "new peril." It's neither new in the sense of being a new phenomenon associated with burning cigarettes nor is it new in the sense of being recently identified as a health hazard by scientific evidence. "Hyping" a story, often with carelessly chosen adjectives, damages credibility.

Source: Mr. Boffo reprinted with permission of Marie Martin.

The same is true of the reporter who attempted to describe nuclear fast breeder reactors:

The fast breeder gets its name . . . because the chain reaction is so much faster than in conventional . . . reactors.

Again, this is a readable simplification of a complex idea. It's also an incorrect simplification. The fast in "fast breeder" doesn't refer to the rate of the chain reaction (which would be measured by the number of atoms splitting per second), but to the speed of neutrons—small subatomic particles that fly around inside reactors and split atoms. In ordinary nuclear power plants, atoms are split mostly by slow neutrons; in fast breeders, speedy neutrons do most of the splitting.

How can you avoid making such mistakes? You simply must research your subject thoroughly before you begin writing. Get help from experts on points you don't understand. Recheck any passage containing statements you're not absolutely sure of.

Finally, don't try to tell readers everything you know. That always takes you to fringe areas, where your knowledge gets a little shaky and errors begin to creep in. Statements perfectly consistent with what you know might be inconsistent with what you *don't* know. Besides, if you tell the readers everything *you* know, you're probably telling them a lot more than *they* want or need to know. Give readers just what they need to get the message.

For example, if you wished to continue the story of carbon monoxide in cigarette smoke, you might be tempted to write something like this:

Carbon monoxide, a molecule that consists of a carbon atom bonded to an oxygen atom, is danger-ous because of its chemical affinity with hemoglobin. Hemoglobin, a complex chemical substance containing iron, serves as a transport mechanism for oxygen in the bloodstream. Because the affin-ity of carbon monoxide with hemoglobin is greater than the affinity of oxygen with hemoglobin, carbon monoxide impairs the ability of hemoglobin to carry oxygen.

This explanation, while essentially accurate, is too long. Unless you're writing for medi-cal students or biochemists, just say that carbon monoxide impairs the ability of the blood to carry oxygen throughout the body. *You* should know all about hemoglobin and oxygen trans-port. But you don't need to tell everybody about it. The more you know about a subject, the easier it will be to simplify, and the less likely you will be to make mistakes.

There is one danger, though, in knowing a lot about a subject. When you have written on the subject for a while, you may find yourself using the jargon of the discipline. This is the fatal flaw in most writing on technical subject matter. If you want the audience to understand what you write, avoid using technical terms. Instead, follow the golden rule of simplifying the complex: Use plain English.

Use Plain English

Most people know plain English when they hear it. It is everyday language, free from the long words and technical terms that plague the prose of scientists, engineers, economists, doctors, lawyers and writers in other specialized disciplines. All professions and trades have special vocabularies that members use when they communicate among themselves. Unfortunately, some members use the same words—the jargon of the field—when they try to communicate with people *outside* the discipline. It doesn't work. To write plain English, you must avoid using words with "insider meanings." It is especially wrong to use such language in a calcu-lated effort to mislead your readers. That is unethical.

Source: "For Better or For Worse" © Lynn Johnston Productions. Dist. By Universal Press Syndicate. Reprinted with permission. All rights reserved.

Source: Scott Adams, reprinted by permission of United Media Syndicate.

Misleading language confused and outraged USA tax-payers when the public wound up "owning" the insurance giant American International Group (AIG) that distributed much of the taxpayers' money as bonuses to executives, which were part of the failing institution's problem. Although staffer Serena Ng did a credible job of simplifying the financial tangle in a front and page two story on Wednesday, March 18, 2009 in *The Wall Street Journal,* it took reading the story more than once to get a grasp of the situation. Here is one reader's much more succinct, yet clear, account:

Before the taxpayer-engaging bonus payout to executives of American International Group (AIG) the insurance company's new "financial products division" attempted to profit from investing in the unfamiliar and speculating out of bounds.

While few of the very savvy on Wall Street were betting that the real estate boom would bust, as it historically had, the insurance giant—now in the mortgage market—risked it all and lost it all.

As the low-rate mortgages offered to over-extended homebuyers were bundled, bought and sold between loan companies, investment banks and financial funds, AIG left itself exposed as the last rung of a weak ladder.

AIG set the corporation up to regain only a fraction of a penny on every dollar of protection they provided in case these mortgage bundles lost too much value. So, when homeowners did default and the economy plummeted, AIG was holding a heavy, but empty, bag.

American taxpayers' anger at AIG was directed toward the insurance company's bets against the economy that proved true, especially since their gambling was completely unregulated by the government.

Summary courtesy of W. M. Newsom, used with permission.

Much of the problem with the AIG situation was the use by AIG of misleading terminology and language. Semanticists refer to misleading language as *doublespeak*. There are at least four kinds, according to William Lutz: Euphemism, jargon, gobbledygook (or bureaucratese) and inflated language.[12] In some cases, doublespeak fails to communicate simply because it is confusing or vague. In other cases, it is deliberately misleading, and therefore unethical and irresponsible. Misunderstanding may occur, but without serious consequences, with jargon and inflated language. Intentional deception is often the motive underlying gobbledygook and euphemism.

Avoid Doublespeak   Euphemisms may mislead deliberately, like the USA. State Department's decision in 1984 to use "unlawful or arbitrary deprivation of life" instead of "killing" in its annual reports on the status of human rights around the world. Some euphemisms are just foolish, such as calling garbage collectors "sanitary engineers." Some euphemisms may be considered useful, to protect sensitivities or to respect cultural taboos.

Within any profession, jargon has its uses. A jargon term may stand for a complicated concept that would take paragraphs to describe in full. Once members of a profession agree on such a term, they can use it freely, because everyone within the discipline knows what it means. But to people not trained in the field, it sounds like gobbledygook. (See Figures 6.1 and 6.2.)

Mind your FDDFSs and ACCs

HONGKONG — If the opening of Hongkong's new airport at Chek Lap Kok was a headache, then reading the official inquiry report is daunting.

The 702-page tome released yesterday was awash in acronyms.

The report used short forms of better-known companies, but also spewed out impossible gobbledygook like H0.KIA-ASP, AMFSRC and FDDFS.

Try this.

Referring to a passenger who had a heart attack and was not taken fast enough to hospital, the commission said steps were being taken to improve efficiency.

"AA and FSD are arranging a direct line to be installed between FSCC and ACC so that, in future, requests for ACC escort vehicle do not have to go through AMFSRC," it said.

— REUTERS

FIGURE   6.1

This warning about the use of abbreviations illustrates how readers not "in the know"can be left uninformed and confused.

Source: From The Straits Times, Singapore, January 23, 1999, p. 28. Reprinted with permission from Reuters.

DOUBLESPEAK QUIZ

1. __ safety-related occurrence
2. __ incomplete success
3. __ fiscal underachievers
4. __ service technician
5. __ non-goal oriented member of society
6. __ single-purpose agricultural structures
7. __ downsizing personnel
8. __ advanced downward adjustments
9. __ collateral damage
10. __ experienced automobile
11. __ media courier
12. __ unauthorized withdrawal
13. __ digital fever computer
14. __ organoleptic analysis
15. __ nail technician
16. __ philosophically disillusioned
17. __ kinetic kill vehicle
18. __ ultimate high-intensity warfare
19. __ social-expression products
20. __ career associate scanning professional

A. to smell something
B. used car
C. pig pens and chicken coops
D. thermometer
E. repairman
F. newspaper delivery person
G. accident
H. failure
I. the poor
J. bum, street person
K. firing employees
L. budget cuts
M. bank robbery
N. civilian casualties during war
O. grocery-store checkout clerk
P. anti-satellite weapon
Q. scared
R. greeting cards
S. manicurist
T. nuclear war

ANSWERS: 1-G, 2-H, 3-I, 4-E, 5-J, 6-C, 7-K, 8-L, 9-N, 10-B, 11-F, 12-M, 13-D, 14-A, 15-S, 16-Q, 17-P, 18-T, 19-R, 20-O.

FIGURE 6.2

Doublespeak Quiz *Test your skill at deciphering by taking this quiz.*

Source: From Richard Lederer, "Gobbledygook: The Quiz," AARP Bulletin, March 2005, p. 46.

Writers must also recognize another type of jargon that may cause problems—common words that have special meanings to the members of a given group. Printers, for example, use words like *flat* and *signature* in an entirely different way than most people. Writers must make sure that readers understand when a common word is being used with a special meaning.

The lack of understanding special terms can be extremely dangerous too. Low literacy in understanding medical terminology or health care instructions can be fatal. Public relations practitioners working in the various health care fields have some serious challenges. Most health materials are written at the 10th grade level or above. Furthermore, few are translated into other languages. People often are too embarrassed to admit they don't know what they are reading or understand the directions or consequences.[13] Pretest all messages with the intended audiences.

Inflated language consists of fancy words used for common concepts, as when members of a given group use long or obscure words instead of short familiar ones that mean the same thing. Specialists, for example, often use technical terms to sound impressive. Consider the following sentence, written by an engineer explaining some of the drawbacks of solar-electric power plants:

> All solar-thermal systems must accept diurnal transients and rapid transients from cloud passage during daily operation.

He was trying to say that it gets dark at night and that clouds sometimes block the sun. The idea isn't any more complicated than that, and there's no reason to make it sound complicated.

Bureaucratese is also called *gobbledygook*. A good bit of it originates with our largest institution—the federal government. In 1981, Malcolm Baldridge, then Secretary of Commerce, decided to purge at least his area. He issued a memo banning certain expressions and discouraging the creation of new ones. He warned commerce staff to steer clear of "bastardized words, nouns and adjectives used as verbs, and passive verbs." Included were these miscues: finalized ("finished" is OK); impact a situation (you're on safe ground if you "control" it or "affect" it); parameters to work within ("specific limits" are acceptable); I share your concern (Who cares? You still have to say "yes" or "no").[14]

Good writers never use doublespeak when common words will do the job as well. Sometimes, though, common words won't do the job as well. If a word that has no plain English equivalent is essential to your subject, you have no choice but to use it. But make sure you explain to your readers what this new term means.

It may be that all you need to do is supply a simple definition when you introduce the word. But usually there's more to simplifying the complex than defining technical terms; in fact, dictionary definitions are frequently as confusing as the terms themselves. And your purpose is not to build the readers' vocabularies but to convey an idea. Often you can get the idea across more clearly by *describing* the new term than by defining it.

Describe, Don't Define   Assume you're writing about the use of the chemical element lithium as an agent for treating psychological depression. It seems like a good idea to begin by defining lithium. So you turn to the dictionary and find: "lithium: a soft, silver-white element of the alkali metal group. Atomic number 3, atomic weight 6.941." This is not a very useful definition. If this is all you tell your readers, they won't really know much more than they did before.

Instead, you could write, "Lithium is a silvery-white metal that is very light; in fact, it's the lightest metal known. It's also very soft and can be cut with a knife. Its name comes from the Greek word *lithos*, meaning 'stone.' " Now your readers will have a picture of lithium in their heads. You've removed some of the mystery behind the name and can go on to discuss the uses of lithium.

For the same reason, it does little good to define *kilowatt-hour* as "the amount of energy consumed when an electrical demand of one kilowatt is maintained for one hour." You're much better off if you describe a kilowatt-hour as the amount of electricity it takes to run a handheld hair dryer for an hour, or as the energy needed to toast three loaves of bread. These are not good scientific definitions of a kilowatt-hour, but they are good descriptions—and they're much more likely to be understood.

Source: Etta Hulme, *Fort Worth Star Telegram,* reprinted by permission through Copyright Clearing House.

Whether you use definitions or descriptions, though, you shouldn't introduce too many new terms. Using technical terms is a luxury to be indulged in sparingly. Don't expect a reader to assimilate several new terms at once. Of course, some writers operate on the "define and proceed" principle. This is a favorite method of textbook writers. They introduce a new term—or five new terms or however many they need—define them and go on with the story, using the new terms freely. The unfortunate students find they must refer to the original definitions every 10 seconds or so to keep track of what they're reading.

Textbook writers don't have much choice, however, because their purpose is often to teach students the vocabulary of a new field. And this goal requires definitions. But public relations writers have a different aim: To communicate a single message. You can't do that if you introduce new terms just to educate the audience. You have to convey the main part of your message in words the audience already understands. In other words, use plain English as much as possible.

If you're writing a medical brochure about *interferon,* a protein substance in the body that helps to fight disease, you must use the term interferon. But you don't need to give your readers a complete lesson in biochemistry. Avoid the temptation to use words like *fibroblasts* or *lipopolysaccharides.* Even if you define these terms, using them will obscure what you're trying to say about interferon.

What if such terms are essential to the discussion? The point is, they're probably not. At least the terms themselves aren't. Fibroblasts might be important, but you can just as easily say "connective tissue cells." Describing such things without naming them will be easier for you and your readers.

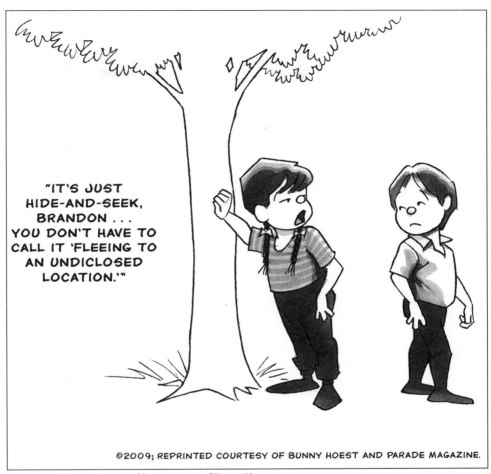

Source: Laugh Parade. Reprinted by permission of Bunny Hoest.

Source: Fired by a Thesaurus Company. Mike Peters, reprinted by permission of The Cartoonist Group.

Of course, you can't describe technical terms without knowing what they mean. So whenever you're writing on a specific technical subject, keep a specialized dictionary on hand. If you're writing about geology, for example, you should have a dictionary of earth science or some comparable reference work at your fingertips.

What if you replace jargons with common words where possible and do a good job of describing any necessary technical terms, and the message is still too complex for the average reader? In that case, you simply must give readers enough background so they will understand. But you have to be careful not to give too much background at once. Take one step at a time.

Take One Step at a Time

You can confuse readers by telling them too much at once. A reader can accept one new fact if you use understandable words, but don't expect to transfer several new thoughts at the same time. The reader's mind will flash "overload" and stop taking in anything. It's like blowing a fuse when you plug too many appliances into the same outlet. The brain, like an electrical circuit, can stand only so much flow.

You have to introduce one new idea at a time. And you must do so in logical order. The first idea should help explain the second, the second the third and so on.

If you start with the simplest idea and proceed one step at a time, you can eventually take the reader to a high degree of sophistication. This is Isaac Asimov's description of how he wrote a book on mathematics:

> It was about elementary arithmetic, to begin with, and it was not until the second chapter that I as much as got into Arabic numerals, and not until the fourth chapter that I got to fractions. However, by the end of the book I was talking about imaginary numbers, hyperimaginary numbers, and transfinite numbers—and that was the real purpose of the book. In going from counting to transfinites, I followed such a careful and gradual plan that it never stopped seeming easy.[15]

Using the one-step-at-a-time approach, you can eventually explain almost anything. The key is to make sure the first step is in the right place. After you've identified the main points and put them in order, look at the first point. Will your audience know what you're talking about? Naturally, that depends on the audience and their level of knowledge about the topic. Knowing where to start, though, depends on a clear definition of all steps. You must determine at the outset what the central points are. Many writers do this well enough, but somewhere between the start and the finish the central ideas get lost. Communicating the complex is bound to fail if only the writer knows what the central ideas are. Make the central points clear to the reader.

Make the Central Points Clear

Whether you're writing on a complex subject or a simple one, the objective is still the same: To convey a message. Messages must be supported with facts, figures, descriptions and explanations. You can't leave out important details. Too often, though, writers let details and descriptions obscure the message. The central point is buried in a paragraph of statistics or turns up at the end of a series of equivocal qualifying phrases. Don't lose track of your purpose. Make sure the main idea stands out.

Usually you do this by stating your main point clearly and forcefully at the outset, leaving the details for later. It is much easier for readers to follow a chain of explanations if they know the point of the story ahead of time.

If you don't make the main point clear, your audience not only won't get the message, but they also won't attach much importance to what you have to say.

When you get sick, you may see a physician because you think the doctor will be familiar enough with your ailment to diagnose and treat it quickly. But if you aren't able to explain the symptoms clearly, your doctor may be stumped, at least at first. You can help your doctor if you prepare for the visit by referring to the *Family Health Manager*.[16] One section of this booklet is about how to get ready for an appointment with your physician. Note in Figure 6.3 the checklist of questions you should prepare to answer for the doctor. Although these questions deal with some complex matters, they are written in plain, simple English almost anyone can understand. That is good writing, because it uses familiar words to describe difficult concepts.

Explain the Unfamiliar with the Familiar

Readers don't easily understand complicated explanations of things they know nothing about. But if you can tie your subject to something within the reader's experience, you can skip several steps of definition and description and get right to the explanation.

Simple analogies can work wonders in getting people to understand why things are the way they are. The energy business is difficult to explain, and especially natural gas because it's usually not visible. When gas utility customers read about a British Thermal Unit (Btu) as a measurement for gas, it's not easy for them to visualize. The explanation in Figure 6.4 helps.

Scientific subjects especially call for explanations in familiar words. A natural science writer helped readers understand a known but seldom experienced natural phenomenon, the northern lights, in this way:

> Scientists today believe that the Aurora Borealis is caused by the "solar wind" particles interacting with the earth's geomagnetic field beyond the upper atmosphere in the area called the magneto sphere. According to Syun-Ichi Akasofu of the University of Alaska's Geophysical Institute, the solar wind generates huge quantities of electricity in the magneto sphere. This energy accelerates particles into the upper atmosphere where they strike atoms of various gases, producing the characteristic colors and staining the sky with dancing light.[17]

Analogies help audiences visualize the unfamiliar. *The Dallas Morning News'* writing coach, Paula LaRocque, cites some succinct examples.

David Stipp of *The Wall Street Journal*:

> These are, to be exact, spotted salamanders. Black, six inches long and spotted with bright yellow polka dots, they resemble baby alligators in overtight clown suits.

And William Grimes, *The New York Times Magazine*:

> It's a quiet site. You can hear the gentle sizzling of high-tension wires from the electrical substation serving the construction works. Hundreds of precast concrete tunnel segments lie baking in the sun—Snack Chips of the Gods.[18]

Helping people see something can also be aided by using concrete words instead of abstractions. Abstractions are vague and open to interpretation. The farther you move away from words that are specific and concrete, the more you leave to the audience's imagination.

Preparing for a Health Care Visit

You'll get a lot more out of your visits to your primary care physician and other health care providers if you plan for them ahead of time — even if you can only manage to arrive at the doctor's office 10 or 15 minutes early, that amount of time to prepare can make a big difference. Be sure to bring your Family Health Manager; it will help you answer the doctor's questions about your own, your children's, or your family's health. And the Medical Visit Checklist will help jog your memory about things you meant to tell or ask the doctor. If you have questions or problems you would like to discuss, write them down and have the list with you during your visit. Don't forget to bring your health plan ID card, and make sure that the doctor's office staff has your correct ID number on your record.

Routine Health Care Visits

Family members usually make routine health care visits for physical examinations, immunizations, and gynecological tests such as Pap smears. Your doctor will give you advice on how often you should schedule these visits.

Nonroutine Health Care Visits

You schedule nonroutine visits when you notice a particular problem — something out of the ordinary that continues to bother you and prompts you to call your doctor. When you call your doctor with your problem, you may find yourself speaking with another health professional first. This valuable assistant to the doctor is trained to listen to your symptoms and decide whether you need to come right in to see the doctor, wait until the doctor can speak to you, or make an appointment. Try to keep the description of your problem as simple as you can, and try to explain problems in the order they occurred.

☐ What is your chief complaint? (Do you have a pain, vomiting, a fever?)

☐ When did your problem begin?

☐ What other problems do you have that relate to the chief complaint? (For example, has your sleep been disturbed or your appetite decreased?)

Use the Medical Visit Checklist as you get ready for nonroutine visits so that you will be prepared to answer the doctor's questions. He or she may need to ask for details about your life-style, including whether or not you use tobacco, alcohol, or illegal drugs. You may need to answer questions about your sexual activity. Be as honest and specific as you can because the diagnosis or treatment your doctor recommends will be affected by the information you share. Your doctor is experienced at listening sympathetically and will keep your information confidential.

FIGURE 6.3

Simplicity in Writing   *Medical terms and issues can be confusing to the average person. This checklist, however, demystifies the questions you may be asked by an attending physician.*

Source: Your Health Care Planner, Steven Krauss, ed. (Boston: Madison Publishing, 1994). Used with permission.

Medical Visit Checklist

To prepare for a nonroutine health care visit, answer the following questions:

A. Describe the problem (chief complaint). What are the symptoms (pain, nausea, burning when you urinate)?

B. Describe the history of the problem.
1. When did the problem start?
2. What brings on the symptoms?
3. What do you think is the cause of the problem?
4. Does anything you do affect the symptoms? (For example, do antacids relieve your indigestion?)
5. Have the symptoms changed? Have they gotten worse or better?

C. If you have pain, answer these questions:
1. Where is it? Can you point to it?
2. Rate the intensity of the pain from 1 to 10.
3. Is the pain continuous or does it come and go? If it comes and goes, how long is each episode?
4. What affects the pain (motion, eating, exercise)?
5. Can you describe the pain? Is it stinging, stabbing, burning, dull, aching, or cramping?
6. Has the pain remained the same or gotten better or worse?
7. Did the pain start suddenly or come on gradually?
8. What do you think caused it?

D. Did you ever have similar pain or symptoms before?
1. When?
2. What happened?
3. Did you see a physician? When? What was the diagnosis? What tests did you have? What medications or treatment did you receive? Did they help?

E. Are you taking any prescription or over-the-counter medication for your problem? What? How much? How often?

F. Describe any medical or alternative treatment (acupuncture, massage, special diet) you are now receiving.

G. If you have seen another health care professional for your problem, be prepared to explain the tests and treatments you received.

FIGURE 6.3 *(continued)*

Counting Energy

We buy gasoline in gallons, coal in pounds, wood in cords and natural gas in cubic feet. Each of these resources has a measurable amount of heat energy stored in it. To compare the energy potential of these different resources, we convert each to a common measure.

A common measure of heat energy is the British thermal unit (Btu). Each Btu is the heat needed to raise the temperature of one pound of water one degree Fahrenheit.

A gallon of gasoline has about 125,000 Btu; a pound of coal, about 11,125 Btu; a cord of wood, about 28 million Btu; and a cubic foot of natural gas, about 1,000 Btu.

Numbers of that size are difficult to understand, especially since we don't think of water by the pound. An easier way to understand the energy value of a Btu is to remember that burning a kitchen match releases about 1 Btu. It takes about 60 Btu to heat the water for a cup of coffee.

FIGURE 6.4

Explaining the Unfamiliar   *"Counting Energy," reprinted with permission from Straight Talk, ONEOK Quarterly, publication of ONEOK, Inc., Fall 2001.*

Use the checklist in Table 6.2 when reviewing a draft of your work on a complex subject.

Make the Message Accessible

Presentation of the message also makes a difference in simplifying material. Some typefaces are easier to read, for example. Most serif type is easier to read than a sans serif because we recognize whole words, not characters, and we tend to scan lines, stopping at intervals. Our eyes catch the tops of the serif type, and we identify the word without even seeing all of the characters. (See Chapter 10.)

In discussing ways to make materials more accessible, Kathleen Tinkel, writing for *Adobe Magazine*, distinguishes between legibility and readability. She says *legibility* refers to the ease of distinguishing one character from another. *Readability* refers to the type as it is set and can include size, spacing, column measure, leading, page layout and other such variables.[19]

Recommendations Tinkel makes include: (1) using natural letterfit and close word spacing; (2) indenting the first line of a paragraph; (3) avoiding low contrast and small sizes if

T A B L E 6 . 2	*Checklist for Simplifying the Complex*

1. Have you researched your subject thoroughly? Do you understand its complexities and the precise meanings of the terms you use?

2. Does your writing stay within the range of your knowledge?

3. Have you told readers only as much as they need to know to understand the point?

4. Have you used plain English as much as possible and avoided unnecessary jargon? Have you substituted common words for technical terms whenever no loss of meaning results?

5. Have you fully described all technical terms you can't avoid?

6. Have you made sure all technical terms used are really necessary to communicate the message?

7. Have you taken the readers one step at a time? Have you started with a point your readers will understand?

8. Have you identified the central points you want to make? Are they made clearly and not obscured by explanation and detail?

9. Have you used familiar ideas to explain unfamiliar concepts?

10. Have you used concrete words rather than abstractions?

11. Have you made the material as accessible as possible?

you think the audience may have impaired vision; (4) not using designs with fine hairlines, colored inks or colored papers if the lighting is likely to be poor.[20]

Another way to improve accessibility is by organizing and trimming materials. Among the most adaptable documents are financial pieces. The Securities and Exchange Commission, under the chairmanship of Arthur Levitt Jr., began trying a new style of prospectus for mutual fund investors. In July 1995, eight mutual funds went from a thick booklet that offered pages of tightly written copy to an 11-point prospectus that fits easily on both sides of one 8.5-by-11-inch piece of paper.[21]

Conclusions

- Remember you are writing for volunteer readers, listeners and viewers.
- Leave readers/listeners with one main thought.
- Write so people will understand what you mean.
- Know your message, your audience and your medium.
- Know exactly what you want to say.
- Tailor your message to your audience.
- Qualities of both the audience and the medium will determine your choice of a medium. In any case, you will have to adapt the style and content of your message to the medium.
- Blogs, social media and other interactive sites have created a more conversational experience that is transactional in its nature.
- The principles of clear writing are readability, naturalness, variety, euphony and human interest.

- Readability depends primarily on the length of words and sentences.
- A conversational style is easiest to read.
- Vary sentence structure and word choice to avoid dullness.
- Write to please the ear, but not at the expense of clarity.
- Use personal words to involve the reader.
- Eliminate clichés and bias.
- Review and edit your writing, using a checklist. Test for readability.
- Complex subjects can be simplified and made understandable, but doing so while maintaining accuracy is not easy.
- It's not enough simply to write short sentences and define technical terms. You must know your subject, as well as follow a number of important principles and rules for simplifying the complex.
- Use plain English, not doublespeak.
- Avoid euphemisms, the jargon of disciplines, gobbledygook (or bureaucratese) and inflated language.
- When you must use technical terms, don't define them and proceed. Describe them so readers will have a clear notion of what you're writing about.
- Know your subject thoroughly, and be aware of what your readers don't know.
- Start at the beginning and proceed one step at a time.
- Know what message you want to convey.
- Identify the most important point and state it clearly. Don't obscure the main idea with clouds of detail.
- If your central point is about something unfamiliar, use familiar ideas to explain it.
- If you follow these rules, along with the general principles of good writing, you should be able to explain anything important enough to deserve explaining.

Exercises

1. Find one book you enjoy reading and another you don't (both nonfiction and on the same subject). Perform a readability test by choosing the first paragraph from 10 pages of each, using a random numbers table to select the pages. (Use an alternate page provided by the table if the page begins with a quoted paragraph. You want to test the writer's work.) Is the more enjoyable book the easier one to read?
2. Analyze an article from *National Geographic* or *Scientific American*. What techniques has the writer used to make the piece both clear and interesting? Also examine devices used to simplify the complex.
3. Write directions for going through the advising and registration process at your school, for someone new to the school. Are your instructions clear? Have you overlooked a step in the process? Could someone successfully register by following your guidelines?

Use InfoTrac® College Edition to access information on topics in this chapter from hundreds of periodicals and scholarly journals such as: *Journal of Public Relations Research, Public Relations Review, Public Relations Journal* and PRSA's *The Strategist (USA); Journal of Public Relations, PRism,* online public relations journal (Australia); *http:www.tictocs.ac.uk* (British).

Grammar, Spelling and Punctuation

Taking grammar, spelling and punctuation for granted can get us into a lot of trouble. One edition of this text actually got into print with the headings in the upper corner of each page in this chapter reading "Grammer." Authors don't handle headings, but the error wasn't caught in the page proofs either. Talk about loss of credibility—that is a good example. Spelling caused a credibility problem for the IRS too when their publication for tax practitioners appeared with "Practioner" on its cover. The "grammer" mistake didn't get any publicity, thank goodness, but the IRS's mistake did. A New York City tax expert called this to the attention of *The Wall Street Journal*, which put the information in its front page "Tax Report" column, along with this question from the tax expert: "How can we rely on what is inside the manual if the outside is incorrect?"[1] The loss of credibility is more serious than the embarrassment.

Of course without the publicity, relatively few people would have observed the original IRS mistake, but what about the following case from the transit system in Dallas, Texas? DART's billboard on one of the most traveled expressways in the Dallas–Fort Worth area, Central Expressway, read: "Don't drive yourself, Crazy." Of course it was supposed to read: "Don't drive yourself crazy." The intended message was: Ride public transportation and avoid the traffic hassles. The unintended result was an insult to motorists, which in turn made DART the butt of many jokes. This story also made the front page of the "Sunday Reader" editorials section of *The Dallas Morning News*.[2]

Computers make it easy for us to check spelling and grammar, but careful reading is necessary too. Editors of a church bulletin were embarrassed when the following message was printed: "The Senior Choir invites any member of the congregation who enjoys sinning to join the Choir." Spell check won't catch that error because sinning is a word and was spelled correctly.

As a public relations writer, you enter the world of professional writing. You join the ranks of skilled wordsmiths. Not only will you be expected to write expertly yourself, but you'll also be expected to edit the writing efforts of others. You'll be expected to know the rules and when to break them in order to communicate.

"Language is for communicating," writes direct-mail expert Luther Brock. "Words are simply a means of expressing one's self and, in our business, of convincing people to do business with us."[3] Writing grammatically correct prose, he points out, isn't always the best way to communicate.

"Unfortunately," writes Brock, "traditionally correct language is dishwater-dull. Why? Because it is not a reflection of the way most people talk. And talk-language just about always outsells grammar-book language."[4] As Brock indicates, the purpose of writing is to get a message across to a reader. In many respects the rules of grammar help achieve that end. But sometimes they get in the way. When they do, the experienced writer may ignore them. That doesn't mean you shouldn't bother to learn the rules or you shouldn't obey them most of the time. But you should keep the rules in perspective. "Rules," says Robert Gunning, "are substitutes for thought."[5] That's true, but they still can be useful. In many cases, it's easier to follow a rule than to waste a lot of time thinking. However, when it comes to making decisions about writing readable prose, rules are no substitute for thought.

Writing expert and syndicated columnist Stephen Wilbers makes the point that writing often calls for deliberate breaking of the rules.[6] He cites at least three cases when, although your computer may advise you to use the active voice, the passive voice is better. One of these is when you intend to emphasize the receiver of the action. The example he uses is: "Millions of people have read *The Hunt for Red October*" (active voice), compared with "*The Hunt for Red October* has been read by millions" (passive voice).[7]

Another example of when the passive is the better voice, Wilbers says, is when you are trying to create coherence between sentences. The illustration he uses is: "We must decide whether to increase our prices. The possibility that we will lose some of our customers should influence our decision." Using the passive voice connects the sentences better: "We must decide whether to increase our prices. Our decision should be influenced by the possibility that we will lose some of our customers."[8]

Sometimes the passive voice is just more diplomatic, Wilbers says. A letter that says "You disregarded the terms of our contract" is likely to create more hostility and less compliance than one that says, "The terms of our contract were disregarded."[9]

Just as "always use the active voice" can be ignored at times, so can other "rules." Take the "like" versus "as" case. One of the main principles of good writing, says Gunning, is to "write like you talk." A lot of English teachers part company with Gunning here, some simply because the rules of grammar dictate that "write as you talk" is the proper way to state the principle. But Gunning responds with three good reasons for using *like* instead of *as*.[10] First, many good writers have used *like* as a conjunction (Norman Mailer for a modern example, and John Keats if you prefer the old-timers). Second, "write as you talk" breaks the rule as it states it. When speaking, people say "write like you talk"—and everybody knows what they mean. That brings us to the third point, which is that "write as you talk" has two possible meanings. It can mean "write the same way you talk" or "write while you are talking." But this is ambiguous, and unintended ambiguity is one of the worst of all possible writing sins.

Ambiguity and Grammar

The main reason grammar exists is to avoid ambiguity. Many grammar rules help us keep our meaning clear. Dangling participles, for example, are condemned by grammarians, and they should be; they can obscure the meaning of the sentence. (Sometimes a dangling participle sounds so silly that the true meaning is obvious, but even in those cases, the sentence is awkward and should be rewritten.)

That Versus *Which*

The common misuse of *that* and *which* is an example of how bad grammar can tangle meaning. Using *that* and *which* correctly is important, for it involves questions of both ambiguity and naturalness. In speaking, *that* comes more naturally. "I picked up the books *that* were on the table; where are the keys *that* I left on the shelf?" In writing, for some mysterious reason, people feel compelled to use *which*. "Attached are the copies *which* I promised to send you."

Rudolf Flesch, in *The Art of Readable Writing*, explains at great length why *that* is better in such cases.[11] His discussion is worth looking up and reading. Not only is *that* the more natural word, it prevents confusion about the meaning of the sentence. In the above examples, the clauses beginning with *that* are restrictive; *which* should not be used to introduce a restrictive clause. When you say, "Bring me the books *that* are on the table," you want *only* the books on the table—not any of the other books nearby. The clause is restrictive. When you say, "Bring the books, *which* are on the table," you're not restricting the books, you're simply telling where they are. The comma is the clue. If the sentence reads correctly without the comma, you should use *that* instead of *which*. (In fact, try to avoid *which* clauses altogether. Clauses with commas slow readers down.)

The desire to tighten copy sometimes tempts writers to eliminate the word *that*. Often this can be done without injury to sense, but you need to watch for three problems that can occur if you strike a *that*. First, when a verb is delayed, readers might have to review the sentence to get the proper meaning. For example: "The registrar revealed the grades of the athletes being disciplined met academic standards." You need a *that* before "the grades" to make the meaning clear. Second, the time element may be rendered ambiguous. For example: "Stockbrokers said last month the decreasing bond and stock prices were a mystery." Either stockbrokers made the statement last month, or they made it recently about last month's mystery. The placement of the missing *that* will clarify which is the case. Third, smoothness may be interrupted because a clause is being used in apposition. For example: "The president's decision is one only the students will understand." A *that* between "one" and "only" makes the sentence much more readable.

Subject–Verb Agreement

Another rule that aids clarity is that the subject and verb in a sentence must agree. Subject-verb agreement helps us avoid confusion over who's doing what. There is a difference, for example, between "Growing vegetables is interesting" and "Growing vegetables are interesting."

Furthermore, merely misidentifying the subject is no excuse to break the rule. A headline in a major newspaper once said, "Workings of the SEC no longer is so mysterious." The subject is workings, not SEC; the verb should be *are* and not *is*. There is no excuse for making the mistake in less obvious cases either, as in "The general, along with his men, are marching tomorrow." The subject here is singular; the additional phrase does not make it plural. The corrected sentence reads "The general, along with his men, is marching tomorrow." If that sounds awkward, simply say "The general and his men are marching tomorrow."

Like any other rule, this one is no substitute for thought. When you write, "The *data* you need are on page 17," you are going out of your way to show that you know there is such a thing as a "datum." Most people would say "The *data* is on page 17," and there's no good reason not to. Your meaning will still be clear.

The plain fact is that in modern American usage *data* can be construed either as a singular collective noun or as a plural. The *AP Stylebook* points out that in a sentence like "The data is sound," *data* clearly refers to a collective unit, and not to the individual bits of information that collectively make up the data. If you want to emphasize the individual entities in a collection of data, of course it is correct (grammatically) to write "the data are."

The *Random House Unabridged Dictionary* recognizes the same distinctions and adds that *data* is almost always treated as a plural in scientific and academic writing. The editors also note that the singular, *datum*, meaning "a piece of information," is rarely found in any type of writing today—even in engineering, where *datum* has a special meaning and the plural used is *datums*.

Another awkward case of subject-verb agreement is the pairing *none is*, which grates on the ear and calls attention to itself. "None of the boats is going out to sea today" sounds silly. Always using a singular verb after none—no matter what the rest of the sentence says—is nonsense. Furthermore, any legitimate dictionary or usage manual says so. More often than not, the sense of *none* is plural. Theodore Bernstein, in *The Careful Writer*, says that the rule to follow is "Consider *none* to be plural unless there is a definite reason to regard it as a singular."[12] For example, when *none* is followed by a prepositional phrase with a singular object, the singular verb sounds better. "None of the cake have been eaten," by contrast, sounds awkward.

Myths of Grammar

Why do most people think *none* is singular and should always be followed by *is* or some other equally out-of-place singular verb? Even the *Oxford English Dictionary* says *none* is usually plural. Well, at some time in the ancient past, a grammar teacher decided that *none* meant "not one" and that it should be singular. That teacher passed it on to a student who became a teacher and passed it on to another student and so on. And all of these teachers were steadfastly devoted to the cause of rules as substitutes for thought. These are the teachers who, as Rudolf Flesch puts it, "tell students from grade school through college that they'd better learn not to write 'it's me' and never split an infinitive; or they'll get shunned by society in later life and never get a decent job."[13]

Some of these grammar "pitfalls" are important; others are merely grammar myths. The old *it's me* or *it's I* question, for example, isn't worth the time it takes to quibble. Almost everybody uses *it's me* these days, and most experts accept it, even though a predicate nominative is supposed to use the subject form of the pronoun. Another contraction you hear is, "aren't I." Literally it is "are not I." This is still not generally accepted.

Also, few good writers would say "between you and I." This is not only grammatically wrong but, worse, it is stilted and unnatural. In this case, the correct form is also the most natural one: "between you and me." The same is true for the common misuses of *myself* when *me* is the right word. "He sent a message to John and myself" is a self-conscious and awkward way of avoiding the use of *me*. *Myself* should be reserved for intensive or reflexive use, as in "I hurt myself" or "I myself will do it."

Split Infinitives

As for split infinitives, every good writer knows that infinitives should sometimes be split. Let the situation be your guide. If avoiding a split infinitive makes a sentence awkward, go ahead and chop the infinitive in two and get on with writing the story. Consider E. B. White's observation in *The Elements of Style*:

> The split infinitive is another trick of rhetoric in which the ear must be quicker than the handbook. Some infinitives seem to improve on being split, just as a stick of round stovewood does. "I cannot bring myself to really like the fellow." The sentence is relaxed, the meaning is clear, the violation is harmless and scarcely perceptible. Put the other way, the sentence becomes stiff, needlessly formal. A matter of ear.[14]

Keep in mind, though, that split infinitives sometimes cause confusion, especially if the insertion of several words turns the split into a gorge. "He wanted to quickly, skillfully and perhaps even artistically complete the project" is widening the split a bit too far. Remember, clarity is the goal.

Sentence-Ending Prepositions

The split infinitive taboo originated with the fact that Latin infinitives are single words and thus can't be split. The same archaic logic led to the myth that you should never end a sentence with a preposition. Some people who remember nothing else at all from their grammar-school days remember this "rule." But in fact, this is just another example of somebody learning grammar from Latin in the Middle Ages and passing it down through the centuries until everybody says it's so but nobody knows why. In Latin, it's very difficult to end a sentence with a preposition. Why allow English to do something denied in Latin?

Fortunately, some noteworthy language experts have ridiculed this rule to the point where few people still follow it. To writers, Winston Churchill's most famous line was not about blood and tears and sweat but the one in which he called the rule against sentence-ending prepositions an impertinence "up with which I will not put." Nowadays, almost all usage manuals repudiate the "rule." As a personal guide, know the "rule," before you decide to ignore it.

Usage Manuals

Once writers realize they are free from the chains imposed by grammar rules, some go off the deep end. If rules are made to be broken, why follow any of them? Well, not all rules should be broken. *Rules should be broken only when, by doing so, you can make the writing clearer, more natural, and easier to understand.* Feel free to dismiss the pedantry of critics who rank split infinitives on the same plane with arson or manslaughter. But do strive to use the language carefully and accurately.

It is no pedantry, for example, to insist that words be used in keeping with their proper meanings. *Allusion* is not the same as *illusion*, for example, and *imply* and *infer* are not inter-changeable. *Parameters* are not *perimeters*, either. Countless words are misused simply because they sound like others. (See Table 7.1.)

Many writers scoff at such criticism, saying, "The reader will know what I mean. Lots of people use the word that way." If you adopt this philosophy, you put yourself in the position of confusing the members of your audience who *do* know the correct meanings of words. The intelligent reader is left to wonder if the writer is using this word correctly, in which case it means something else. Using words imprecisely can lead to such ambiguity. Choose words carefully.

Even some grammar "rules" deserve a little thought before they are rejected or accepted. Any given rule can be good for some situations—possibly even most situations—though bad for others. How can you decide when to follow a rule and when not to? You must decide, of course, but it never hurts to get some advice. Check a few basic reference books. Besides a dictionary and a standard grammar handbook, you should have at least two language-usage manuals that discuss points of grammar and usage in depth. Such manuals analyze many of the tricky usage questions that writers stumble across. See this chapter's bibliography for suggestions.

When you read some of these manuals, you'll find that usage rules aren't as restrictive as you've been taught. You'll be surprised to learn what some language "purists" like Fowler and Follett have to say about split infinitives, for example. You'll also, no doubt, run across subtle but important usage matters that have escaped your attention until now. Cappon's book has a chapter called "Bestiary: A Compendium for the Careful and the Crotchety."

T A B L E 7 . 1	*Commonly Confused Words* Here is a list of pairs of commonly confused words. If you don't understand the differences between the members of each pair, consult a usage manual, the *AP Stylebook* or *Words into Type*.		
absorb, adsorb	assure, ensure	doubtful, dubious	pedal, peddle
accrue, acquire	baited, bated	dual, duel	poison, toxin
adapt, adopt	canvas, canvass	farther, further	pore, pour
adhesion, cohesion	cement, concrete	flaunt, flout	practicable, practical
affect, effect	complement, compliment	fortuitous, fortunate	principal, principle
all ready, already	compose, comprise	grisly, grizzly	rebut, refute
allusion, illusion	continual, continuous	imply, infer	reign, rein
alternately, alternatively	credible, credulous	infect, infest	stationary, stationery
apparently, obviously	deduction, induction	minister, pastor	suspect, suspicious
appraise, apprise	discreet, discrete	naval, navel	whereas, while
arbitrate, mediate	disinterested, uninterested	parameter, perimeter	

Perhaps the most important lesson you'll learn from reading usage manuals is that there is considerable disagreement among the "experts" over what should or should not be allowed. So don't let anybody tell you there is always a right and a wrong where grammar and usage are concerned. Gather some opinions, think about each problem and then make up your own mind. Just be sure that, when you break a rule, you break it for a reason and not because you didn't know. You also need to remember your audience. Materials for international use by English-speaking people need to follow more strictly traditional usage.

Verbs

Where's the action? The action of PR writing is in the verbs: They should keep things moving, capture attention and hold it.

Use active-voice verbs, and avoid using the passive voice. Recast the sentence if you have to. One simple way to put movement into your language is to limit your use of forms of the verb "to be." Consider these examples:

> An honor code is being considered by student government representatives, who want to talk with university faculty about the idea. [Passive]

Source: Johnny Hart, reprinted by permission of Creators Syndicate.

Student government representatives considering an honor code for the university want to talk with faculty about the idea. [Active]

When writing broadcast copy, you should stay out of the past tense. The idea underlying this practice is that all broadcast news should sound as immediate as possible. A new rule on college athletes' eligibility passed yesterday by the NCAA would be written: "College athletes must make higher grades now to stay on the team." The present perfect tense is used most often by broadcasters. It implies immediacy, although the action is over. You just write "has been" instead of "was" and "have been" instead of "were." For instance, "I've been in India" sounds as though you've just returned.

Emotive and Cognitive Meaning

Cognitive meanings are information based. Emotive meanings may be positive or negative or mixed. You must be sensitive to these two different types of meaning. Emotion-charged words are often used in public relations writing, but it is imperative that you know, in advance, the emotion a word is likely to elicit from the audiences it will reach. Negatively charged words are those that evoke bad images, such as prejudicial terms used for ethnic groups. Positively charged words are those that encourage "good feelings," such as "peace," "love," "freedom." Some words may have mixed emotive meanings, and these can be the most dangerous to use. Words like "globalization" have different meanings to people with different value systems.[15]

Spelling

You might expect that spelling would be rather clear-cut, but it isn't. For example, you can spell *benefited* with one *t* or *benefitted* with two. You must decide which one you will use for your organization; you thereby establish the style for that organization's publications. On the other hand, if you are writing for *other* publications, you have to spell words the way *their* style dictates.

With more international communications in English, you have to ask, "Whose English?" Will you use the *s* in spelling *organisations* or the *z* as in usage in the USA? Perhaps some global standardization for English is in sight, since the European Union has chosen English as the preferred language, and it is the major language of the Internet.

Who cares about spelling? Well, the people who hire PR writers for one, so if you want a job, you'll take spelling seriously. There's no excuse for *not* spelling correctly. Just keep a dictionary within arm's length whenever you're writing. If you're not *absolutely certain* that a word is spelled correctly, look it up.

Face it. If your prose is riddled with spelling errors, your readers just might conclude that your facts are also suspect. (They might also conclude that you're not too bright.) Therefore, why should they believe what you've written or even read it at all? It's little consolation to say that most readers won't catch the spelling errors. Then only the educated people will think you're wrong.

Spelling errors do crop up now and again, even in prestigious publications. Even though you make every effort to eradicate mistakes, a spelling error will someday appear in one of your finished products anyway. That's not a reason to be less diligent in your efforts. If you operate with the attitude that "just one error" isn't so bad, you'll end up with many. The old saying that "to err is human" should be applied only as consolation after the fact, not as a license ahead of time to make mistakes.

Sometimes mistakes result not from lack of diligence, but from overconfidence. Some people spell so well that they're sure they can spot any spelling mistakes. Thus they don't look up the words they should. To avoid such overconfidence, good writers and editors should occasionally test themselves on lists of commonly misspelled words. Even good spellers will find some surprises. Test yourself by counting the number of words spelled *correctly* in the list contained in Table 7.2. Word processing systems can check spelling, but if (for example) you have used *there* instead of *their*, the system will not find the error. The system will only find words that are misspelled as nonwords, such as *thier* for *their*. It will miss homophones (words that sound alike but are spelled differently) and misspellings that produce other true words (such as *study* for *sturdy* or *sandbag* for *handbag*). (See Table 7.3.)

The same problem is likely to occur with plurals and possessives in spell-check software. Some grammar software may recognize such distinctions as "the bee's sting" (one bee) or "the bees' sting" (more than one bee). The key to possessives is the apostrophe. With the simple plural, bees, there is no apostrophe, but there is one when you are using a plural possessive. Another area of confusion occurs with the apostrophe when it's used in contractions—*it's*, as just used, for "it is." *Its*, a singular possessive, has no apostrophe. Sometimes *its*, the possessive, as in "The dog buried its bone," is misused for the contraction, as in "Its going to be difficult to find the bone the dog buried." Think of the apostrophe in contractions as standing for the missing letter.

If you answered Table 7.2 correctly without any help, you're a pretty good speller and should have no trouble with the following test. Read the passage and circle the words that are spelled *incorrectly*. Assume that the piece is part of a feature story that is to appear in a newspaper, and follow *AP Stylebook* spelling rules.

T A B L E 7 . 2	*Unassisted Spell-Check*		
How many of these words are correctly spelled?			
badmitton	barbiturates	procede	innoculate
sacreligious	limosine	comittee	pantomine
chaufeur	corollary	comission	inocuous
diarhea	wierd	priviledge	perogative
embarass	cemetary	knowledgable	excell
Farenheit	mispelling	sieze	
flourescent	preceed	satelite	
If you counted two correct, you're right. Only *barbiturates* and *corollary* are spelled correctly.			

T A B L E 7 . 3	*Spell-Checker*

Eye halve a spelling chequer
It came with my pea sea
It plainly marques four my revue
Miss steaks eye kin knot sea.

Eye strike a key and type a word
And weight four it two say
Weather eye am wrong oar write
It shows me strait a weigh.
As soon as a mist ache is maid
It nose bee fore two long
And eye can put the error rite
Its rare lea ever wrong.

Eye have run this poem threw it
I am shore your pleased two no
Its letter perfect awl the weigh
My chequer tolled me sew.

The scientists could not reach a concensus. One physicist argued that his experiments superceded earlier findings.

Beseiged by numerous complaints, the director of the labratory devised a stratagy to accomodate the researchers. He alotted each one 15 minutes to speak. One said everyone had benefitted from the experiments on liquefcation of nitrogen, but he saw no correllation between those results and the experiments on parafin.

"It would take a whole battallion of scientists to solve this dilemna," another scientist said. "We do high calibre work, but when you liquefy a miniscule amount of gas, there's no way to avoid all possible arguements about the results." Another suggested that a questionaire should be drawn up and sent out. "If we could get them all filled out, that would be quite an achievment," he said.

"That's an inovative idea," said the physicist. "I'd like to save my copy of the form as a memento of this occassion."

You should have circled 20 words. If you didn't find them all, a trip to the dictionary (or perhaps the *AP Stylebook*) is in order. By the way, although dictionaries accept *benefitted*, the AP allows *benefited* only. Some dictionaries also accept *liquify*.

Source: "Shoe" © MacNelly. King Features Syndicate.

Word Choice and Meaning

Sometimes misspelling a word interferes with your intended meaning. A report from an organization warned that the scholarship fund was jeopardized because some of the *principle* had been used, instead of just the interest. No. What the writer intended to say was some of the principal, the initially invested amount, had been used. Confusing the two words is fairly common, as is use of the word *attain* when *obtain* is intended. Another common error is the use of "reign in," meaning to contain or control when the correct word is "rein in." Writing coach Paula LaRocque found these examples of misused words:

> Here's a headline on a story about celebrities that refers to "Marquis" names instead of "marquee" names. Another about an athletic field that refers to "sewn" grass. Another that declares, "Frost Belt Unthawing." Unthawing? When something frozen thaws, it unfreezes. So, if it is unthawing is it refreezing?[16]

Writers caught in these mistakes often say, "Oh, well, you know what I mean." No. Not really.

Another error that creates confusion is the use of single quotation marks to emphasize words. A conference paper on the "Going Green" ecology effort referred to 'green' products and 'green' consumers, using the single quotation marks for emphasis. Unfortunately, this error often appears in newspaper headlines. The newspaper headline writers might use the excuse of saving space, but what about using italics? In American English, single quotation marks go inside double quotation marks. The reverse is true in British usage where commas also go outside quotation marks. (See the Global English? section.)

Punctuation

Whereas grammar is mostly a matter of making meanings clear and spelling is basically a matter of convention, punctuation is a little of both. True, proper punctuation is usually just a matter of following the rules. But the underlying purpose of punctuation is to help make the meaning clear, and subtle changes in punctuation can change the meaning of a sentence. For example, the sentence "Woman without her man is an animal" can be punctuated "Woman—without her, man is an animal." Liz Carpenter, former press secretary to Lady Bird Johnson, likes to have people punctuate this sentence as a test for sexism.

Apostrophes are a common source of confusion about meaning. Probably the most common error occurs with the word "it's," the contraction of "it is," with the possessive word "its," with no apostrophe. In this case, "its" indicates possession like the pronouns "his" or "hers" or "theirs." However, possessives such as "Jane's book" or "Joe's pencil" use the apostrophe. Acronyms cause much of the confusion about punctuation. For example, use apostrophes in the case of single letters such as P's and Q's or A's and B's, but only an "s" after multiple letters such as "four VIPs." You create a possessive with "The four VIPs' choice of a restaurant was The Original BBQ."

Most reputable publications follow a fairly rigorous set of punctuation rules and apply them consistently. The virtue of consistency is simply that readers can pay attention to the message without being bothered by changes in the manner of punctuation. Sentences, for example, usually end with periods. Readers know this, and they don't have to think about it. They know that, if a writer ends a sentence with some other mark, it is an intentional act to tell the reader something—as when a question mark is used to indicate a question.

Inconsistent punctuation calls attention to itself. Anything that calls attention to itself takes attention away from the message, and that hinders communication. When you're trying to communicate, there's no excuse for introducing anything that distracts the reader, however slightly.

Sometimes punctuation conventions defy logic, but these conventions are so entrenched that violators expose themselves immediately as amateurs. The prime example involves the use of periods and commas with quotation marks. Whenever a period or comma follows a quotation, it is placed *inside* the closing quotation marks. Always. Without exception (at least in the United States). It doesn't matter whether the quote is a complete sentence or a title or a single word. For example:

John's article, called "The Hands of Time," is well written.

I didn't know he wrote an article called "The Hands of Time."

The rule still applies if single quotes are used inside double quotes:
He said he "wrote an article called 'The Hands of Time.'"

Other punctuation marks, such as question marks and exclamation points, are placed according to the sense of the sentence:

Did he write an article called "The Hands of Time"?
He asked John, "What is the title of your article?"

This may seem trivial, but many public relations writers are their own editors. If you want your material punctuated correctly, you need to know the rules. And in the case of this particular rule, there is nothing to be gained by breaking it. It is followed uniformly (in the United States), and departures from the convention call attention to themselves.

For many other punctuation rules, convention is not as binding. Often, standard "rules" should be broken to make the reading easier or to make the meaning clear. People are taught in school, for example, to place commas before direct quotations, as in

John said, "What's going on here?"

Sometimes the comma is an intrusion, however, and can be dropped with no confusion:

"What did he say?"
He said "Let's go!"

Source: Reprinted by permission of United Media.

Not all rules should be so casually violated. Some are important for keeping the meaning clear; most rules of this type involve the comma.

There are dozens of rules regarding commas, and it doesn't hurt to know them. Most help keep sentences clear and prevent readers from stumbling over tricky passages or linking clauses to wrong elements. In general, comma rules are helpful.

Some writers overdo their use of commas, though, and stick one in wherever they can. Too many commas clog up the works and make for slow reading. The best practice is to use commas only when they are necessary to avoid confusion.

The careful use of commas with nonrestrictive clauses, for example, helps avoid confusion. Restrictive clauses, which are necessary to make the meaning of a sentence clear, are not set off by commas. Consider these examples:

Restrictive clauses, which are needed for clarity, are not set off by commas.

Clauses that are needed for clarity are restrictive.

All restrictive clauses are needed for clarity. Therefore, the "which are needed" clause in the example is merely explanatory and is not essential to the meaning of the sentence. It is a *nonrestrictive* clause and is set off by commas.

Not all clauses are needed for clarity. But the "that are needed" clause is essential to the meaning of the sentence: It *restricts* the types of clauses under consideration. It is therefore a *restrictive* clause and is not set off by commas.

Restrictive and nonrestrictive clauses are also called *essential* and *nonessential* clauses. They don't always use *that* and *which*. *Who* can be restrictive or nonrestrictive, and this fact makes proper punctuation all the more important. Consider these examples from the *AP Stylebook*:

Reporters, who do not read the stylebook, should not criticize their editors.

Reporters who do not read the stylebook should not criticize their editors.

The first sentence says that reporters—all reporters—do not read the stylebook. Therefore, they shouldn't criticize their editors. The second sentence says that some reporters—those who don't read the stylebook—shouldn't criticize their editors. There's a big difference.

Another comma error that can make sentences unclear involves appositives. An appositive is a phrase that stands for a noun and bears the same relationship to the rest of the sentence that the noun does. Here is an example:

Joe Smith, the captain of the football team, signed a contract today.

The appositive following "Joe Smith" is set off by commas. The comma after team is essential. "Joe Smith, the captain of the football team signed a contract today" reads as though someone were telling Joe Smith (whoever he is) that the captain of the football team signed a contract.

Don't set off short titles with commas, however. "Team captain Joe Smith signed a contract" is perfectly correct. "Team captain, Joe Smith, signed a contract" is not. A similar problem sometimes comes up with restrictive appositives, when a descriptive phrase is needed for full meaning. "The American League baseball players, Garret Anderson, Nathan Haynes and Manny Ramirez, are outfielders" is not properly punctuated. This sentence makes them the only players in the American League. Omit the commas after *players* and *Ramirez*, and the sentence is correct. Avoid related mistakes, too, such as the one made by a textbook author who wrote "In his novel, *The Deer*

Park, Norman Mailer describes. . . ." There should be no comma after *novel*; Mailer has written more than one.

Many other punctuation rules are equally important, although it's impossible to cover all of them in a single chapter. Conscientious writers take punctuation seriously, however, and consult such books as the *AP Stylebook* for help on the fine points.

Of course, experts sometimes disagree about proper punctuation. Don't think that every rule should be followed in every instance. But make sure you know the rules. And when you break one, know why.

Global English?

All English is not the same. Not in spelling, not in word meanings, not in punctuation and not, in some instances, even grammar. The question is, which version of English do you use, the British or the American? The answer is, it depends on the medium and/or the public. You use what is accepted and familiar, not necessarily to you. Remember: public, message, medium.

Many publications using the British spellings will have "organisations," not "organizations," for example. In British-language publications, you'll often find "whilst," which is considered "quaint" in the USA. British-language publications are likely to use "venue," whereas American-language publications use "place." Names of things are not the same, as you may know from traveling. An "elevator" is a "lift" in places using British English. British English uses different forms of punctuation too. Where American English uses double quotation marks with other punctuation inside (","), British English uses single quotation marks with other punctuation outside (',).

Fortunately, you can use a computer language system to help. Most computers use American-English spelling, grammar and punctuation, but you can get a British-English system to use when needed. The question may be which system will eventually prevail. Some think it is the American-English system because of technology. Most people who buy computers get the American-English system automatically and have to get the British-English system separately. Time will tell.

Source: "Shoe" © MacNelly. King Features Syndicate.

Source: Dana Summers, reprinted by permission of Tribune Media Services.

To be good public relations writers, you need to be aware of and sensitive to the differences. Fortunately, there's help available, online. At www.tardis.ed.ac.uk, you'll find *The English to American Dictionary Index*. Another source for help is the Association of British Language Schools (ABLS) stylebook and usage guide.

If you are attempting to communicate in another language, be cautious about using the Internet for free online translations. You may not be sending the message you intended. For example, http://www.translate.ru.eng.other.asp offers English, French, German and Spanish. However, if you use a site like this, be sure to translate the supplied translation back into English. English input: *When I go to town to shop, I enjoy taking a long walk in the park before I return home in the afternoon.* Spanish translation: *Cuando voy a la ciudad a hacer compras, disfruto tomando un paseo largo en el parque antes de que yo vuelva a(en) casa por la tarde.* English translation of the Spanish: *When I am going to the city to do buys, I enjoy taking a long walk in the park before I return to (in) house in the evening.* Some words have to be translated in the proper context. A good example is the Polish word *baba*. When a baby says it, the meaning is "grandma," but it can be translated as a derogatory word for "woman."[17]

If you are preparing materials in another language, hire someone fluent in both languages and someone who has recently traveled in the other country where the materials will be used. Language usage changes over time in a country. Also, as you know from experiences with American English and British English, there are significant differences in word choices, spellings and meanings between the two versions of English. This is also true of other languages.

Always Check

At every level of your writing, check to be sure you are saying what you intend to say. With your initial product, reread, read aloud, revise or rewrite completely. When you have what you think is a final copy, then edit it severely. When you have something to send for publication and get back a proof, edit it again carefully (see Table 7.4) for suggestions at each level.

TABLE 7.4	*The Quality Controlling System*	
Quality Controlling for Some Tasks		
Revising	**Ideas**	
	• paragraphs	• change
	• headings	• add
	• bullets	• reorganize/reformat
	• graphics	• eliminate
Editing	**Language**	
	• sentences	• voice
	• words	• tone
	• symbols	• conciseness
		• parallelism
		• modification
		• diction
		• punctuation
		• mechanics
Proofreading	**Hard-copy appearance**	• headings, footers, margins, spacing
		• font consistency
		• common mistakes
		• typos

Source: Reprinted from *ETC: A Review of General Semantics,* Vol. 58(1), Spring 2001, by permission of the author, Philip Vassallo, and the International Society for General Semantics.

Conclusions

- Grammar, spelling and punctuation are important—not as ends in themselves, but as aids to clear communication.
- The public relations writer's chief aim is to communicate, and following the rules of grammar and usage usually facilitates that task.
- Be sensitive to the emotive meanings of words, especially for some of your audiences.
- Correct grammar and punctuation help to eliminate ambiguity.
- Consistent punctuation and spelling help direct the readers' attention to the message, not to the mechanics.

- Occasionally, strict adherence to grammar rules can result in awkward or confusing writing.
- In those cases, public relations writers should ensure clarity even at the expense of traditional grammar rules. But such a step should never be taken lightly. You should know why the rule exists and why it should be broken in a particular situation.
- Conscientious writers take all construction seriously and consult reference books to be sure their decisions are well founded.
- Electronic programs can help you polish your writing but are no substitute for your own competence.
- All English is not the same. While American English is quite commonly used globally because most computers are programmed for it, British English is more familiar to and accepted by a number of global audiences. Be sensitive to language usage in your global communications.
- Check your work at every level: revise, edit, proof.

Exercises

1. Choose the correctly punctuated sentence from each multiple-choice group below. You might want to consult the *AP Stylebook* on some of these. Answers follow.
    1) a. Buy a case of Dr Pepper today.
       b. Buy a case of Dr. Pepper today.
    2) a. I wondered why he asked me, "Where have you been?".
       b. I wondered why he asked me, "Where have you been?"
    3) a. Have you ever asked "What should I do?"?
       b. Have you ever asked "What should I do?"
       c. Have you ever asked "What should I do"?
    4) a. She asked, "Who played the lead role in Hello, Dolly!?".
       b. She asked, "Who played the lead role in Hello, Dolly!?"
       c. She asked, "Who played the lead role in Hello, Dolly!"
    5) a. She asked, "Who wrote the words to 'The Star-Spangled Banner'?"
       b. She asked, "Who wrote the words to 'The Star-Spangled Banner'"?
    6) a. Have you ever exclaimed "My God!"?
       b. Have you ever exclaimed "My, God!"
       c. Have you ever exclaimed "My God!?"
    7) a. First, call your doctor. (If you don't have a family doctor, call the local health clinic.)
       b. First, call your doctor. (If you don't have a family doctor, call the local health clinic).
    8) a. First, call your doctor (if you have one.)
       b. First, call your doctor (if you have one).
    9) a. What should I do? he asked himself.
       b. What should I do, he asked himself.
       c. What should I do, he asked himself?

10) a. "Will you come into my office?" he asked demandingly.
    b. "Will you come into my office," he asked demandingly.

11) a. "Did you see that catch!?," I asked.
    b. "Did you see that catch!," I asked.
    c. "Did you see that catch!" I asked.
    d. None of the above.

12) a. John Smith, author of "What's in a Name?," will arrive soon.
    b. John Smith, author of "What's in a Name?", will arrive soon.
    c. John Smith author of "What's in a Name?" will arrive soon.

13) a. John Smith, state representative from Fort Worth, resigned.
    b. John Smith, state representative from Fort Worth resigned.

14) a. State representative, John Smith, resigned from his job today.
    b. State representative John Smith, resigned from his job today.
    c. State representative John Smith resigned from his job today.

15) a. He didn't shout "Halt, thief!"; I did.
    b. He didn't shout "Halt, thief!;" I did.

16) a. Have you ever said, "Let's go for a walk."?
    b. Have you ever said, "Let's go for a walk"?

17) a. We can go to the beach, if it doesn't rain.
    b. We can go to the beach if it doesn't rain.

18) a. The spinning turbine is attached to a generator, which turns conductors in a magnetic field to generate current.
    b. The spinning turbine is attached to a generator which turns conductors in a magnetic field to generate current.

19) a. A number of activities is available.
    b. A number of activities are available.

20) a. The university has opened it's library to the public.
    b. The university has opened its library to the public.

2. Rewrite the following sentences, eliminating jargon and needless words to make the resulting sentence clear and concise. Suggested revisions follow.

    a. Johnson supported his side of the issue by saying that contemporary revenue athletics, also known as big money sports, forces athletes to cheat in school because they have no time to study.

    b. As in the case with so many of the wars over the course of time, this war was largely a result of previous wars.

    c. If methods of communication had been comparable to those of the present century, there is little doubt that this war would never have begun.

    d. The interaction of petroleum liquid in aqueous media produces a heterogeneous, layered liquid mixture.

    e. Extent of labor and its propensity to fill time is peculiarly elastic; that is, the more time available for the completion of an assigned task, the longer it takes for the assigned task to be completed.

    f. We have encountered our military adversaries and successfully engaged them, taking control of their nautical vehicles.

    g. Whatever there is that needs to be done, this machine is able to accomplish it.

h. Financial statements indicate that the company's financial situation was negatively impacted during the preceding 12 months.

i. After the commission's last meeting, regulations were changed so that the company no longer has to file an application a year in advance.

j. If we use vehicles powered by compressed natural gas (CNG), it is expected that we can help reduce air pollution from cars and trucks to standards well below those required by the Environmental Protection Agency (EPA).

See Appendix C for answers.

Use InfoTrac® College Edition to access information on topics in this chapter from hundreds of periodicals and scholarly journals.

Writing for Traditional Media and Social Media

*T*he Internet has made the flow of digital information a major factor to be considered in the overall delivery of messages. Although the role of different media and the large-scale elimination of media gatekeepers have changed the media mix, there has been no change in the need to understand both the publics of interest to your organization and the strengths and weaknesses of each medium.

Writing for Social Media and Converged Traditional Media

In his speeches, QuickSilver Interactive Group CEO Steve Lee says humans "have come full circle" in our approach to communicating. First, of course, there was human speech, then storytelling and songs, followed by cave drawings and writing. Manuscripts, books and newspapers followed, then magazines, radio and television. Magazines proliferated, with the result that there's "a title for almost everyone." Similarly, cable TV seems to offer "a channel for everyone," and satellite radio makes audio available "whenever and wherever."

Until this point in the evolution of communication, all of the media had two aspects in common: (1) They were one way only—*out*—to one person, to several or to many, and (2) The content was fixed; it couldn't be changed once it was "out there."

Digital communication has changed everything. Internet email, instant messaging (IM), Wikis and texting have made communications personal and ubiquitous. Social media have promoted a return to one-on-one communications, and blogs have returned storytelling to prominence. While most of our communications still are technically one-way, responses can be instantaneous. Some software allows online collaboration, with numerous people making text additions and changes that can be seen by others as they are made.

We're not back to the beginning, but there are similarities. Using technology, we can build communities or "tribes," and share common interests on a personal basis.

Social Media

Want to attract instant attention at a public relations gathering? Just use the words, "social media." You'll have the ears of PR professionals working to effectively use the media preferred by their selected publics. Social media "suggests an emphasis on collaboration and sharing, improved functionality, enhanced organization and categorization, and an approach to the market as an open conversation."[1]

Are social media different? You bet they are! A good way to explain the difference is that when public relations people contact newspapers, radio, television and magazine representatives, they are trying to *push* information out, hoping it will be used. Social media do the opposite; they *pull* people into discussions. Public relations professionals have for decades said they want to develop *relationships* with their organizations' stakeholders (customers, shareholders, employees and so on). Social media offer us opportunities to do exactly that, by beginning and maintaining *conversations*.

Lee says social media are distinguished by "Information content created by people using highly accessible publishing technologies that are intended to facilitate communications, influence interaction with peers and public audiences, typically via the Internet." Social media sites continue to evolve and proliferate around the world. In the USA, some of the most popular sites as of this writing are Facebook, Myspace, Twitter and LinkedIn.[2]

Social media are given major credit for the election of President Barack Obama. "The Obama campaign is the biggest case study of the new communications paradigm and probably the biggest we'll ever see," said Lou Capozzi, chairman emeritus of Publicis Public Relations and Corporate Communications Group. "I call it the conversation age—the forming of opinions through conversations among broad networks of people. Learning how to participate successfully in those conversations is the new critical success factor for communications." Soon after his inauguration, President Obama conducted the first-ever presidential virtual town hall meeting, responding to 104,021 questions that were posted online by 92,937 people.[3]

"Why can't you use Facebook, like everybody else?"

Source: Reprinted by permission of Ward Sutton and CartoonBank, www.cartoonbank.com

"It's a no-brainer that this is going to have a dramatic impact on the PR and marketing professions over the next couple of years as more brands try to replicate his success," commented Mark Hass, CEO of Manning Selvage & Lee. "It fundamentally changes everything."[4]

The point here is, "The Obama campaign has re-focused public relations," said Robert Niles, editor of the *University of Southern California Annenberg Online Journalism Review*. "It illustrates that a powerful PR campaign—and an election is nothing if it isn't a PR campaign—doesn't need to be focused on media relations."[5]

In an effort to dispel some of the myths about using social media, B. L. Ochman wrote in a *BusinessWeek* article:

1. **Social media is cheap, if not free.** While many of the tools come at no cost, effectively incorporating them into a marketing program requires skill, time and money.
2. **Anyone can do it.** Many people claim to be "social media gurus," but hype doesn't compare to experience.
3. **You can make a big splash in a short time.** Social media can drive traffic if people care about your brand—otherwise, be patient.
4. **You can do it all in-house.** To be successful, you need strategy, contacts, tools and experience—"a combination not generally found in in-house teams," writes Ochman.
5. **If you do something great, people will find it.** Until you can drive traffic to your content, no one will know it's there.
6. **You can't measure social media marketing results.** There are several methods that measure the effectiveness of social media, including Google Trends, Twitter search, Google Analytics, BackType and Compete.[6]

Writing for Social Media

Deciding what type of writing is appropriate for social media is akin to writing for more traditional media. That is, you examine the medium, see what's there and adopt a writing style and length that "fit" the medium.

Writing for each is different. For example, some sites like Twitter restrict messages to a very few characters. Despite that, there are many similarities. Brooklyn-based music and culture writer Jesse Jarnow says he uses the same technique when writing for 140-word limit sites as he does for any other piece of journalism. "Don't waste words," he says. "Is every adjective necessary? Could any of the words be more descriptive or accurate? Is it actually 'saying' something?"[7]

Basic to adopting a writing style for social media sites is knowing whether you are writing on behalf of an organization—let's say a *business*—or if it's *personal*. If it's for business, your writing should follow, as much as a site's parameters allow, the style used in writing for other media.

Lee said that from a business PR perspective, *directing traffic to a website* is the principal purpose for the use of social media. "*Control, security* and *anonymity* are major considerations when selecting digital media," he said. He explained that a website provides complete control—you can present exactly what you want and make it available on the Internet. Not true of social media. Although you can say whatever you want, users who see your posts can refute your statements. He added that you need to be aware that whatever you "put out there" on the Internet stays there—perhaps not forever, but for a long time. High school students who send nude photos from their cell phones may be surprised to learn that when they go for job interviews.

Authors of *The Public Relations Writer's Handbook: The Digital Age* summarize writing for digital media in this way: "You may be writing for a company Web site, a blog, a social Web site, a live chat, or the PR war room of a large company facing a public relations crisis. In every case, clear, persuasive written communication, the stock in trade of the public relations writer, is the core skill that can be leveraged by each new technology and technique."[8]

Why should public relations professionals pay attention to social media? Massachusetts-based Paul Gillin, author of *The New Influencers: A Marketer's Guide to the New Social Media*, said, ". . . You don't have a choice. The average age of an evening news viewer now is 60, and there's a segment of the population you have to reach that doesn't use those channels. But it (social media) gives the PR professional a greater chance of success because you're not dealing with the all-or-nothing proposition that was mainstream media."[9]

Reliance on the Internet also has changed the way people get their news. A rapidly increasing percentage of the USA population is switching from TV to the Internet to obtain news. The Pew Research Center for the People and the Press reported, "in December 2008, 40 percent of (survey) respondents said they got most of their news about national and international issues from the Internet, up from just 24 percent in September 2007. Pew said it was the first time since it started surveying that consumers relied more on the Internet for news than on newspapers." The survey indicated that 70 percent of respondents selected TV; 35 percent chose newspapers; 40 percent chose Internet; 18 percent chose radio; 2 percent chose "other" and 2 percent said "Don't know/refused."[10]

Uses of Social Media

Organizations as diverse as corporations, nonprofits and the USA military are using social media. Here are a few examples:

General Motors (GM)   Despite GM's many troubles, Adam Denison, Coordinator of Social Media Communications for the company, explained that the company has had success in social media that "comes from engaging a variety of publics one-on-one." He said that, although the number of people "out there" is huge, he views Facebook, for example, as "a one-to-one medium, not one-to-many." The first step, he said, is "to find the groups most relevant to your organization and start to participate in them" by posting comments, videos, pictures and links. "Next, build a relationship with the group administrators. The phrase 'group administrator' sounds technical, but really, they're similar to editors. When I join a group on behalf of GM, the first thing I do is send a Facebook message introducing myself to the administrator and telling him or her I'm an available resource if they ever need information from GM. This has worked very well."

Denison said he participates in discussions on topics of interest to GM. "Perhaps the best example was a discussion I started on an environmental group site regarding GM's push to diversify our fuel needs. I simply posted a few facts about what we're doing and then asked group members what they thought." He said there has been a huge response.[11]

Motorola   Motorola has given its 70,000 employees in 70 countries social media tools that allow them to publish and share information. According to Web guru Shel Holtz, "Dubbed 'Intranet 2.0,' Motorola's network includes blogs, Wikis, a social bookmarking utility, RSS (Rich Site Summary [or Really Simple Syndication]) feeds and a social search engine that, according to an *Information Week* article, 'improves the quality of searches by injecting results that other users found most valuable.'" Holtz says 95 percent of Motorola employees have used the resources.[12]

Serena Software   "At Serena Software, water-cooler talk has been replaced by Facebook chatter. Nearly everyone in the company, headquartered in Redwood City, Calif., uses the social-network site to hang out with fellow workers, access internal communications, or even challenge the Sydney branch to a movie quiz. That includes the CEO," said Stephen Humphries, staff writer of *The Christian Science Monitor*. Humphries said Serena uses social networks to recruit new hires and market its Web tools, as well as using Facebook as its *defacto* intranet.[13]

Sony   Sony started a blog with the objective of creating a dialog with its fans and foes that has provided a secondary benefit "complementing the company's PR push by creating content that has been picked up by media outlets." As an example, Rick Clancy, Sony's senior vice president for corporate communications and author of Sony Electronics Blog, points to a blog post about the future of Sony's Blu-ray technology, which was picked up by several social media outlets. Other blog posts have turned into stories carried by such mainstream publications as *BusinessWeek* and *The New York Times*. Clancy says "the company is working on a platform that will allow employees to communicate more effectively, share ideas and collaborate on projects." He commented, "There has to be openness and a mutual respect that goes into this."[14]

American Cancer Society   Altogether different objective—but a similar approach—is used by David Neff, Director of Web, Film and Interactive Strategy at the American Cancer Society's High Plains Division that includes six states. Neff said, "We find conversations in progress and join them. We are also starting our own conversations on the [Facebook] site. In addition we're also raising money through the site's Facebook Causes program, which allows certified 501(c)(3) organizations to start benefit groups. The real advantage of Facebook Causes is that people can do what I like to call 'freestyle fundraising,' meaning they can create original event groups to benefit your cause, such as 'Bob's Sunday Brunch to Cure Cancer' or 'Relay for Life of Dallas.' We don't always know the volunteers who start these groups, but our cause certainly benefits from every dollar they raise."

United States Marine Corps   The Marine Corps uses social networking to excite and engage its target 18- to 25-year-old audience. "This generation is not satisfied with hearing a single perspective, so we thought that the best way to tell the story of the Marines was to share multiple perspectives," said Lieutenant Colonel Mike Zeilff of the Marine Corps Recruiting Command. "Using social networks lets us do this. We thought the experiences of other Marines would be the best way to tell what it is like to be a Marine. So we developed a way for them to share their stories on our social networking site and to spread these stories virally across bigger social sites."[15]

Writing for "Traditional" Media

Newspapers are extremely important in public relations' media mix. According to the Newspaper Association of America (NAA), "More than 104 million adults read a print newspaper every day, more than 115 million on Sundays. That's more people than watch the Super Bowl (94 million), American Idol (23 million) or that typically watch the late local news (65 million)."[16]

Newspapers provide PR practitioners an ongoing source for communicating with a wide range of readers who include community leaders, elected officials and affluent readers. So newspapers are an excellent way to reach thought leaders and decision makers.

Let's examine how public relations practitioners provide information for use in these so-called traditional media.

News Releases

First you need to know that news releases differ for newspapers, television and radio. The writing is different, as well as the format.

In terms of length, news releases for newspapers can be longer; those for TV shorter, and those for radio usually the shortest. For all three media, the organization originating the release must be identified, along with information on a person or persons who can be contacted for additional information. The date and location where the release originated need to be identified. The main parts of the news release are the lead, supporting information and, sometimes, a summary description of the originating organization. (See Figure 8.1.)

News releases for television are more apt to be used if there's a visual element involved. The fact that your organization is going to have a meeting of some sort probably won't make the news, unless decision-makers at the meeting will be considering a decision that will affect a large number of people. Public schools are a good example. But a news release about a group protesting a new city ordinance by picketing City Hall stands a good chance of being used because of the possibility of video footage of the protestors and the possibility of a public confrontation.

Providing photos, video and audio can make the release more appealing to media people—assuming that it contains information of interest to a wide swath of the public.

The move toward convergence of social media and "traditional" media has greatly affected how we look at news releases. The Social Media Press Release Template Version 1.5, developed by SHIFT Communications (See Figure 8.2.), provides a guide toward a release that meets the needs of journalists and citizen journalists representing newspapers, television, radio, blogs and other Internet-based sites. It calls for the inclusion of photos, a podcast link, video, quotations, links to related previous coverage, RSS feeds and other information. When those of us who are public relations professionals provide all of these possibilities, we offer media representatives a veritable "cafeteria" of information from which they can choose what they need.

Who Gets News Releases?

Regardless of what your employer or client might think, not everyone wants your story. If you are sending a story by email and not using a distribution service, you might be tempted to send it to a large number of recipients. This is "spamming" and not regarded charitably by most newspeople.

Not only does the Internet make getting the release to the media easier and faster, but there's also more of an opportunity for media exposure, because many media have online sites that are treated and edited differently than their related, traditional sites. Nevertheless, although the news release is probably the most frequently used tool for getting publicity, it also is the most misused. The result is that many news releases are not used at all by media people.

How do they want to receive news releases? A whopping 85 percent said they prefer to receive news releases by email, BUT "Most respondents noted that they really like email as long as it doesn't include attachments." This means, of course, that the news release should be inserted into the email message, making the formatting of news releases much less important than previously. Eleven percent said they prefer regular mail, but only 2 percent said they prefer all other delivery options, including personal delivery.[17]

News Release

Identity and address of organization

ABC Global Communications, Inc.
One Continental Plaza
Anycity, State 97989 USA

Contact for questions and additional information

Contact: Irena Hernandez
(123) 542-4455 Office / (123) 312-6565 Home
(123) 542-4444 Fax / iher@ABCGlobal.worldnet.net

FOR IMMEDIATE RELEASE

Instructions: For immediate release or embargo date and time

Date and location where release originated

Communications executive says international internship experiences a must for communication students in announcing new national competition.

Optional identifying headline

Anycity, State (January 16, 200X)—International working experiences are a must in today's world, according to Jamie Wallace, president and CEO of ABC Global Communications, Inc. (ABC Global). The public relations and advertising company just announced a national internship competition for college students that would place them in ABC Global offices around the world.

Lead

"In a global communication environment, the only way to learn is to be there. That's the reason we have decided to open all 14 of our offices abroad to interns from the USA," Wallace said.

To choose the best candidates for the internships, ABC Global has posted an entry application on its website (www.abcglobalcom.net). ABC Global executive Tom Fields said, "We opened the competition to students in USA colleges and universities only, at least for the time being, because we feel the size of the country limits students' experience with other cultures." Fields will be administrator of the internships.

"We want to choose 50 of the best students from their online applications, fly them in to our corporate headquarters and give them some performance challenges here before we choose those we'll send to our offices abroad," said program administrator Fields. Fields also added that in designing the internships he had been working closely with a national center in Washington, D.C., that has some experience in administering internships.

Supporting information

The National Internship Academy's Deputy Director, Charlene Adams, said the major challenge for an internship is placing the right person in the right position. She added that "bringing the students together and getting to know them personally will help ABC Global place people in successful working relationships."

ABC Global provides public relations and advertising services through its offices in England, Scotland, Wales, Australia, New Zealand, Singapore, India, Belgium, Mexico, Argentina, Brazil, Venezuela, Spain and the Philippines.

Ending indication: ### or - 30 -

###

Ending: "Boilerplate" description of the organization

FIGURE 8.1

Traditional News Release Format   *News releases sent to news media traditionally have been double-spaced. This one is single-spaced, as are most releases that are posted to websites.*

FIGURE 8.2

Social Media Press Release Template   *This template illustrates how a basic news release can be supported by graphics, video, RSS feeds and links to additional information.*

News releases and other information provided by public relations professionals remain the major source of content for journalists. A national study by Cision and The George Washington University Graduate School of Political Management found the following:

- ". . . Submissions from PR Professionals are used by more than 94 percent of editors/journalists, followed by Press Kits."
- "For identifying or developing story ideas, websites are most important, followed by submissions from PR professionals."
- "Social networking sites and podcasts are used least often for editing and reporting compared to other source. . . .
- "Blogs are used by 79 percent of editors/journalists overall, with those 29 or younger (27 percent) and 30 to 49 (26 percent) reporting using blogs "all the time" significantly more often than do those age 50 or older (18 percent)."[18]

Why are news releases rejected? Studies generally cite the following reasons as most significant: Poor writing, incompleteness, inaccuracy, poor timing and little local or no reader interest. No medium can use all the releases it receives. But basically, it gets down to this: Most news releases are rejected because they contain no news. Bad PR.

The first responsibility of a public relations person preparing news releases is to know what news is. If a release doesn't contain news, it won't get used. On the other hand, if it contains valuable news, editors are quite likely to overlook poor writing, typographical errors and other blunders just to get the story. It's essential to know the difference between news and non-news.

What Is News?

Different people have different definitions for news. Textbooks on beginning reporting and articles about the mass media in society construct elaborate definitions of what news is or should be. But for public relations people, no esoteric or philosophical definition is necessary. A practical one will do: News is what newspapers and magazines publish and what radio and TV stations broadcast on their news shows. News is *not* what *you* think it is or what the company president thinks it is. Realizing this will take you a long way toward writing effective news releases.

Writing News Releases

How do you write legitimate news? The answer is simple: If you're writing for print media, prepare the material as you would if you were a reporter working for a newspaper. A news release should be written in the same form and style, following the same punctuation and spelling rules, that the publication you want it to appear in uses.

If you've ever been a reporter, writing a news release should be as easy as writing a straight news story. If you haven't, you need to know something about the methods of writing news.

Approach

Every reporter has a personal method for approaching a story. But all methods should have the same first step: Identify the most important thing about the story. In writing a news release, the first step is identical. You must answer the question: What's the most important thing I have to say? Your answer will determine what you should say in the lead.

Lead   The lead—the first paragraph or perhaps the first two—is the most important part of the release. You can't write a good release without a good lead, and you can't write a good lead until you've answered the question about what's important.

Deciding what's important sometimes takes a little judgment. *Important* must be construed broadly. What you really want to isolate is the most significant and most interesting aspect of your subject. And you have to keep in mind that news is what is happening now.

For example, if the release is about the opening of a new plant, the most important thing is the fact that the plant is *opening*. The action is the news. But is there something especially interesting about the plant itself? Is it the largest plant of its kind? The first? Will it provide a lot of jobs for the local economy? Once you've decided what's important and also what's interesting, you can write a lead.

The most important thing—in this case the action—should form the main part of the lead: "The plant is opening." The interesting thing about the story provides an "angle" for the lead: "The first plant of its kind is opening," according to *X* authority.

Sometimes you don't have to look for the most important aspect of the story. For example, it may be the appearance of someone noteworthy. That's your lead. Of course, that might explain why public relations people planning special events always try to get celebrities to attend. The appearance of a well-known person becomes the focus for the news release.

Using the most interesting angle in the first sentence may cause you some problems in constructing the traditional newspaper lead, in which the who-what-when-where-why-how all appear in the first paragraph. Traditional leads are still the rule for most wire-service stories, because the first paragraph is all some newspapers will use. However, that first sentence can get very long if you try to jam in all the essential elements. The rule is often relaxed, so that only two or three of the traditional elements appear in the first sentence, with the others following in the next sentence or two.

If you're writing a release for a wire service, try to get all of the elements in the first paragraph or, at most, the first two. When writing for dailies in your area, study the papers' styles. Are all the basic questions usually answered in the first paragraph? Or do a paper's staff writers tend more toward the attention-grabbing lead, with the details of time and place following in the next few paragraphs? The style of the papers you write for should determine the style for your releases. You may find it worthwhile to have several versions of a release to accommodate different media. Some newspapers prefer fact sheets rather than news releases. (See Chapter 9 for information on fact sheets.)

Naturally, if your lead sentence contains the most important and most interesting elements of your story, it probably already gives the who and the what. You can sneak in the when, where and why later—but not too much later. The how usually comes last.

Once you've written a lead, read it over to make sure that it states clearly what the release is about and that it grabs the reader's interest. In other words, the lead must give a quick indication of what the story is about and why it is important. And it must be interesting—both to catch the eye of the editor and to get the attention of the newspaper reader.

Angling the Lead   One lead will not suit all of your needs. The news business is not a situation where "one size fits all," not if you expect your copy to be used. Think about the medium and how the news is going to be used. If you are going to an online site, then immediacy and significance are the emphasis. Think about the time delay for the daily newspaper. The story may have been online and perhaps in the broadcast news before it can be printed. You need a fresh emphasis for the lead for the daily newspaper that picks up the story. If you are giving the story to a weekly publication, then there's even more to consider about the emphasis.

What will still be "fresh" when the story is published? You must consider that. Think too about the audience. *The Wall Street Journal*'s audience is not the same as that for *USA Today*. What would each publication's audience be most interested in about your story? That's what the editor is thinking about, and so should you.

A local angle is essential in capturing the local newspaper editor's attention. Most newspapers rely on the wire services for nonlocal news, and a release without a local angle is usually dumped. In fact, some editors cite the lack of a local angle as the single most important reason releases aren't used. Be sure to identify the local angle. Make it clear and get it high in the story, preferably in the lead. If you have no local angle to interest a given newspaper, don't bother sending the release.

Timing is critical if your news is going to a newsletter or to a magazine. You must think not only of the audience and that particular audience's interest in your story, but also when the audience is going to be exposed to the story and what that audience may have learned about the news by then. The way you write the story depends on the editor's perception of its newsworthiness. You have to make it timely and interesting even if, in the case of some publications, there is a long delay, a month or more.

Amplifying the Lead   Once you have a lead that meets all these tests, writing the rest of the release should be easy. Simply amplify each of the elements introduced in the lead, giving all the details. Anticipate the questions that an interested individual might ask about your subject, and answer them in the body of the release.

Use short, concise sentences; short paragraphs; and common, concrete words. Avoid the jargon of your profession. If you must use a technical term, make sure to explain it fully. Above all, avoid editorial comment. Don't try to "sell" something in a news release. A release is not an ad. If a comment is necessary, be sure to enclose it in quotation marks and attribute it to a company executive.

Quotations   In using direct quotations, PR news release writers have a great advantage over reporters: They can *create* quotes. A reporter using quotation marks must report exactly what was said. You, however, can take what you've written to the executive you're supposed to be quoting and ask for approval of the words you've attributed to him or her. Write for time-sensitive use. (See Table 8.1.)

Sometimes you won't know what to create for the quote and will have to go directly to the person to see what he or she wants to say. Often the person will scrawl something quickly on a memo pad or ask you to take something from an official statement already prepared on the subject. Such quotes are almost always awkward and lifeless. You will need to recast the words to make them sound like someone said them in conversation.

Length   Knowing how to write a release is important. But knowing when to end the release is equally important. If a release is too long, an editor may decide there isn't time to read it, and into the trash (digital or physical) it will go.

The essential points usually can be covered in one page. Sometimes an important event will call for two or three pages, however, so if you need that much space to cover the subject, use it. But even then write the release so an editor can chop a few paragraphs off the bottom without damaging the story. That's especially important for releases going to wire services.

Long releases with pages of generally irrelevant material are annoying to journalists. A common example is the release on an executive's promotion, a subject worth only two or three paragraphs. Frequently, however, such releases give pages of company history and information on the company's chief executive, who did nothing more than announce the promotion.

Keep the release brief, at least in most cases. If you really think more information might be needed—statistics or background, for example—attach a fact sheet to the release. A fact sheet lists the basic elements of the institution and the event. (See Chapter 9 for information on fact sheets.)

TABLE 8.1	*News Release Checklist*

1. Is the lead direct and to the point? Does it contain the most important and most interesting aspects of the story?

2. Has the local angle been emphasized?

3. Have who, what, when, where, why and how been answered in the first few paragraphs?

4. Are sentences short, concise? Paragraphs short? Words common and concrete?

5. Has editorial comment been placed in quotation marks and attributed to the appropriate person?

6. Are quotations natural? That is, do they sound as though they could have been spoken?

7. Has newspaper style (AP or other) been followed faithfully throughout the release?

8. Are spelling and punctuation correct?

9. Have all statements of fact been double-checked for accuracy?

10. Has the release been properly prepared in the correct format?

11. Is the release dated? Is the release time indicated?

12. Are names, phone numbers, fax numbers and email addresses for further information included?

13. Has the release been cleared internally?

Ending   It's common practice to use a paragraph summarizing the organization and its operations.

For example, here's the paragraph used by Blockbuster Inc.:

> Blockbuster Inc. is a leading global provider of in-home movie and game entertainment, with over 7,400 stores throughout the Americas, Europe, Asia and Australia. The Company may be accessed worldwide at www.blockbuster.com.

Note that the brief statement provides

- the company's name
- its purpose
- the number and geographic scope of stores and
- its website's URL.

Writing Style

Your most important concern in writing a news release is not length, of course, but getting your message across. To be understood, you must write clearly.

Unfortunately, the writing in most releases is more complex than that in the news stories of a typical daily newspaper. If you write news releases, write as a journalist and write for the editor; *don't* write for your boss. That doesn't mean you should present the facts in such a way that your story makes your company look bad. But it does mean that you leave out *no* pertinent facts, however embarrassing they might be.

When you write a story, it's not enough to conform to newspaper style in level of complexity and in basic story structure. You must follow newspaper style to the finest detail, making sure that every comma and period is in the proper place.

For newspapers, this generally means adhering to the *AP Stylebook*. Most newspapers follow AP style, but many have special style rules that you should know. It's a good practice to ask editors for copies of their stylebooks. You can get a copy of the *AP Stylebook* at a college bookstore, at Amazon.com or by going to the AP online bookstore, http://www. apbookstore.com/

The stylebook will guide you on such matters as when to capitalize, how to abbreviate and what titles to use for specific people. It also describes certain punctuation rules that may differ from common usage. In AP style, for example, there is no comma between a name and Jr. or Sr., as in "Joe Zilch Jr."

AP has adopted *Webster's New World College Dictionary* as the standard guide for spelling. Use the first spelling listed, or the spelling given with a complete definition if a word has more than one entry (like *T-shirt* and *tee shirt*). The *AP Stylebook* lists some exceptions to the dictionary spelling. If a word isn't in *Webster's New World*, check in *Webster's Third New International Dictionary* (and think again about whether you should use the word).

What about grammar? Some writers worry about grammar above all else, combing every line for a possible split infinitive or a *who* that should be a *whom*. Certainly good grammar is important, and awkward, obvious errors like subject-verb disagreements should not be tolerated. But don't worry more about grammar than about communication. Your first concern must be the clarity of the message. If your sentences are clear and understandable, the grammar will take care of itself. (See Chapter 7.)

One more word about style. If you plan to send releases to newspapers other than local dailies—releases about financial news, for example, might go to *The Wall Street Journal*—you should know that these newspapers sometimes have completely different style rules. Some public relations people send the same release to all newspapers, using the style applicable to the majority. You can get away with this, but it never hurts to tailor releases to individual publications.

Electronic Transmission of Releases

Having the correct style is particularly important now that many public relations practitioners are emailing releases to the news media's representatives. The advantage of computer transmission is that it can be opened for editing (or, of course, "killed").

Numerous companies offer Internet-based services for an organization's use in distributing news releases automatically. Digital distribution systems aren't without problems, however. When Consumers Union turned over a news release to such a company for distribution to about 1,000 editors, it learned later that some editors received two, three, or even eight copies of the release. That's more than a little irritating to editors, who raised a storm of complaints. More than 300 letters of apology went to these editors—at the expense of the distribution company, of course—but the damage was done.[19]

Types of Releases

Once you know how to write a release, the next question is: Why and when should you write one? The reason for writing releases depends on the type of organization you write for and what its goals are. Frequently the release is just one of many tools a company uses to get publicity.

So when do you write releases? The rule is simple: When you have news, release it. Certain things call for news releases. Generally these fall into one of several basic categories—announcements, created news, spot news, response situations, features, bad news and special matters.

Announcement Releases   These releases can announce the marketing of a new product, the opening of a new plant, the company's latest financial results or a new company policy.

"Created News" Releases   Often, a mere announcement isn't enough to attract much media attention. A company may therefore try to "dress up" the announcement release by making sure something newsworthy is going on. The company might bring a well-known speaker to a company function, for example, or stage a formal ceremony or other event such as a concert or rally. This gives the news release writer something more interesting or newsworthy to say and an opportunity to draw positive attention to the company.

Spot News Releases   Announcement releases can usually be planned. But sometimes things happen without warning. An electric utility's main power plant can be damaged by a storm, for example, raising the prospect of power shortages or higher costs for replacement power. An explosion can occur in a munitions factory; an airplane can be hijacked. Such occurrences are spot news, and when they happen, a news release is in order. You must fill in the facts as they become available, issue news bulletins and follow with a release incorporating as much information as you can provide. (See Chapter 18, Crisis Communication.) A spot news release often has to be followed with a second release, explaining how the initial events were resolved.

Response Releases   Often news about a company reaches the media from sources other than the public relations department. A consumer group may issue a report critical of the company, for instance. The government may announce an investigation into company pricing practices. A research group may publish a major study on your company's industry. When these things happen, reporters call for a response. Companies with good public relations organizations anticipate these calls and have position papers for reference (see Chapter 9) and response releases ready.

Feature Releases   Not every story in a newspaper involves events that happened yesterday or today. Feature stories about topics of special interest occupy an increasing amount of newspaper space these days. All public relations people can find feature material somewhere in their organizations—something going on in research and development, for example, like a new production process that improves efficiency or helps reduce pollution. Such feature stories can be prepared for newspapers as ordinary news releases. An alternative, if the publication typically uses it, is a narrative style. The feature lends itself well to a "story-telling" approach.

Bad-News Releases   Sometimes events occur that a company would like to keep quiet. The natural tendency in such cases is to issue no news releases at all and hope that the problem will go unnoticed. But more often than not, attempts to keep bad news out of the media backfire. Such stories often involve a company's regulatory agency. Because regulatory agencies are supposed to act in the public's interest, you can be sure the agency will release a report.

Column Notes, Letters, Guest Columns and Photos   Sometimes the information you'd like to see in the newspaper doesn't fit the form of an ordinary news story. That doesn't mean you should forget about it. Most newspapers have special columns or sections that print unusual items, and these are often among the best-read parts of the publication. Individual columnists might make use of readers' information. Or readers might want to write a "guest column." (You might want to write one under the byline of your company's chief executive.)

Such items don't always follow the form of an ordinary news release, but they can accomplish much the same thing. Study the newspapers your organization deals with so you'll know what outlets are available.

Photos are among the most effective publicity tools. Photos must tell a story to be worth using. They can accompany a release as an illustration, or they can stand alone. In either case, they must interest the audience. Sometimes single photos and their captions even qualify as what editors call "wild art"—photos that add reader interest to the page. Captions for photos that illustrate a story carry information that relieves the story of some detail. A caption for "wild art" only tells readers what they are looking at and points out the picture's significance, if any.

Some organizations use digitalized photo databases for images that they may want to use for internal or external distribution on their websites or intranets. This makes images—photos and graphics—available to print and broadcast media.

Government Regulations

You need to be aware that the release of information—especially from a corporation whose stock is publicly traded—falls under federal and state regulations as well as the rules of the stock exchange where the company's stock is traded. The SEC regulates what kind of information about a corporation and its financial affairs can—or *must*—be released and under what conditions.

In an effort to "level the playing field" for investors, the SEC issued its Regulation FD (Fair Disclosure) in October 2000. This regulation makes selective disclosure of information illegal.[20]

The Sarbanes-Oxley Act was signed into law in 2002. It's designed to prevent financial malpractice and accounting scandals such as the Enron debacle and is known as SOX or SOA. It's also known as the Public Company Accounting Reform and Investor Protection Act and is considered one of the most significant changes to United States securities laws since the 1930s.[21]

To conform to these and other regulations, the rule of thumb is to "tell no one until you tell everyone." Once information on a significant transaction or event is disclosed to anyone, regulations require full disclosure, usually in the form of a news release that is widely distributed.

News for Broadcasting

There's something to the adage, "Seeing is believing." Seeing and hearing are influential experiences, even when the information they convey clashes with earlier experiences. As a result, credibility is always at risk in a broadcast world, especially if not much is known about an organization or an individual in the news.

Therefore, the technical aspects of providing information to news media dominate writing for broadcast. You must think of the information in a different way. What portion of the story can you get a person with authority and credibility to say so you can capture it on audiotape? What quote from the story makes a good "sound bite"? Radio stations are interested in the sounds of an event: The voice of the mayor reading a proclamation, the president of the electric company explaining a power outage, the hospital director telling about medical care for tornado victims.

On the other hand, if it wiggles, it's TV news, or so the saying goes. And the remark is only half facetious. What in your story "wiggles" or offers movement and color? How can you capture that video in digital format?

Audio and video are far more likely to be used on radio and TV than is a news release telling what happened and what was said. Postings on a website can capture words, photos and sound. Many news stations encourage audience participation by asking for news with instructions on how to send it onsite by mobile devices. For more standard transmission, CDs and DVDs *can* be used but aren't favored because compatibility can be a problem. If a station refers viewers to its website for additional information on a story it is broadcasting, the digital format makes the information you send more accessible. It is safer is to send the news release in a PDF or JPG format.

Consider your competition. Broadcast stations subscribe to news services that provide written broadcast-style stories and ready-to-air, satellite-fed audio and video for the stories. Additionally, there are packages of whole segments that come ready to air. What chance do you have with your news release unless you take into consideration the elements—audio and video—that constitute broadcast news?

Opportunities for radio new releases improved in 2009 with the economic downturn that caused 70 percent staffing cutbacks in radio and caused 42 percent of radio news reporters to say that they are more reliant on outside sources.[22] Television stations are similarly strapped and often solicit news from viewers. Citizen "journalists" often respond, so remember that you need to be there with your input if any breaking news or a special event concerns your organization. Expectations from the news media are different, though, for professionals such as public relations people.

Facts, Sights and Sounds

Facts are the vital elements of any news story, whether for print media or for broadcast media. Sometimes a formal news release isn't really necessary; the public relations writer can provide the media with a fact sheet, and the reporters can write the story. But with electronic media, facts alone are not enough. Whether you're planning a special event, holding a news conference or dealing with a crisis situation, you must also be aware of sights and sounds. These sights and sounds recorded at a news event are called "actualities."

Announcements and Special Events

For TV, you'll have to stage some activity to record for an advance announcement of your special event. Thus, after holding the first of what is to be an annual event, you'll need visuals for the next year shot during this year's event—video and digital still photos for the news media to see and for your website. One word of caution: When you use last year's pictures as an advance story, be sure you label the pictures carefully. Sometimes editors get too busy to realize that you are sending a picture of something that already happened—and will inadvertently label last year's pictures as this year's. Protect yourself by labeling the pictures clearly and appropriately.

In preparing for an advance story, you should use previous digital documents of the event, preferably with sound. Radio can pull off the sound for its use. For an annual special event, it is a good idea to have some charts and graphs on PowerPoint that show attendance figures and such from the previous year. Be sure to show dates for the upcoming event. Place and dates for the next event of course will be on your website, and you may have some digitized images from the previous year's event there too. Remember that the quality of these is not always suitable for high-definition television, but TV news directors seeing the pictures on your Web page may want that same image, or one close to it, for their own stories. The moral to this is to shoot events with the idea of capturing close to the same images in multiple formats—expensive, but usually worth it.

When you stage an activity to photograph, don't *simulate* the event. You wouldn't want to perpetrate a hoax. Nor would you want to be wrongly accused of doing so. But feel free to shoot preparations for the event; they qualify as legitimate news. For audio, you can use the people involved—dignitaries, if possible—to make the announcements. Have these announcements recorded by technically qualified people so they will be of broadcast quality. As the event gets closer, use interviews with some of the participants. Supply radio and television stations with your audiotapes and videotapes. Don't forget media tours. You can have experts appear on broadcast talk shows too in order to generate interest in an upcoming event.

So much for the advance. For actual coverage of your special event by the news media, find out at least three to six weeks in advance what mechanical equipment you will need to supply. You'll have to check out lighting and sound systems and prepare a list of what activities (of news value) will be available for coverage. When the news media arrive, you should be able to offer (again) all the materials prepared in advance, plus an update of what is happening that day and the next. Mention any changes in or corrections of materials sent previously. Supply these in writing when possible. Table 8.2 illustrates a special-event broadcast news release. Give reporters a copy of a brief story in broadcast style. Attach this release to a copy of the longer story prepared for the print media. In reworking the story or in writing their own to fit the coverage, broadcasters will find the longer release helpful.

It's important at special events to have someone at a central location to answer the telephone and respond intelligently to queries from the news media. That person also needs a complete set of materials on the event, a copy of your itinerary and a mobile with pager. In any case, you need to check in every hour or so regardless.

Remember that you will get only a few seconds, maybe a minute, of coverage. Use that time to direct competing media to different facets of the event. That way they will get better stories and you will get better coverage. Be absolutely sure of all your facts, because there will be no time for correction. The news media are not very forgiving of a public relations source that causes them to broadcast an inaccuracy.

TABLE 8.2	*Format for Broadcast Release for a Special Event*

SPECIAL EVENT LETTERHEAD

Address for Event Sponsor
Phone Number for Event Sponsor
Fax Number for Event Sponsor

Your name, title, phone landline and mobile, fax and email address

Date (and number of release if many are being sent)*

Slug Line (for story identification instead of print release's suggested head)   Time: (in seconds, i.e., :00)

> Set story for 60-space line 12-point font (Times or Times Roman) so copy can be counted and time estimated. That setting will give about four seconds a line. Use triple space on printout so copy can be easily marked and read, although few releases will be read "as is." Keep release to a single page, triple-spaced. When sending a release electronically, use double space because the receiver can convert it to triple space.

> Give announcers a "lead-in" to your release before the lead. Tell people what the special event is. Get them ready for the news.

> Keep your lead to between 16 and 20 words so it will be easy to read. Make the next sentence short to vary the pattern. Think of the listeners trying to follow the story they are only hearing. Think of the announcer and show how to pronounce unusual words or names. Indicate the ending of the story by ###, 30 or End. To be sure about timing, read copy and time reading with a stopwatch.

*Most large organizations number their releases, indicating purposes. For a special event, you need to develop a special series with some reference alpha that tells what the event is or was, like A for Anniversary Celebration; something that incorporates the date, such as 07 for year; and something that separates the media formats, such as B for Broadcast. The number might look like A-1B08. The last release in the series might be A-10B08.

Because broadcasters will be rewriting news scripts frequently during the day, include a print release on the event too so other versions can be created by the station's newswriters. That release would carry a number like A-1P01, with the P for Print. Of course, a cover letter to the news director will explain why the longer release is being sent.

If the release is going to a television station, be sure that you include information about visuals that are available, such as videotape with or without sound.

News Conferences

News conferences are called by public relations directors where some interaction with the news media needs to take place. The situation may be when a major announcement needs to be made by management, or an explanation for an event given, or when a person's time in the area is limited, such as a visiting dignitary or celebrity. The whole point of a news conference is to allow as many questions to be asked as possible. The opportunity to ask questions is especially important if there is a controversy.

There are many ways to hold a news conference. The most obvious one is a live news conference where the news media come to a specific site chosen for convenience or for significance, such as the dedication of a building or memorial of national significance. Often news conferences are held by satellite. This involves considerable planning and expense, but is worth it because of increased participation from media as it doesn't require travel and does allow instant transmission. This is especially important in situations of global significance. A more low-key news conference is one by telephone, something often done by investor relations people to hook up the CEO with a number of securities analysts and economics journalists all at the same time while simultaneously offering listener access to nonparticipants such as shareholders.

However the conference is held, considerable advance planning is necessary. Ordinarily you'll prepare an announcement, giving the reason for the conference, identifying the person (giving background if he or she is a celebrity) and detailing the time, date and place and who to contact (by name, address and phone number) if there are any questions. Most of these announcements are sent to the broadcast media via email. You may use a distribution service or you may have a news conference about financial matters carried by financial wire services. Occasionally your news conference is significant enough that information about it will be carried on general news broadcast wire services.

If you are calling the conference to give information on a problem or to make an unexpected announcement, be sure you have prepared background materials to give to the media people who attend. A package should contain a printed copy of the announcement, biographical material on the person (if appropriate) and background materials addressing the most significant questions. You should also have prepared a "shooting schedule" for pictures. Be sure to have photographers shooting still images and capturing video and sound. You will need these records for your own reference and might also need to supply them to a medium that had mechanical problems.

Remember too that news conferences are not parties for the media. You might want to have coffee or soft drinks on hand, but save the rest for a festive occasion that's not a working situation. Table 8.3 illustrates a representative set of news conference materials. Table 8.4 lists logistical considerations for coverage.

Crises

A crisis, such as a plant fire or hostage situation, is a disorganized combination of a special event and a news conference. The media will need information that even you as an insider will have difficulty getting. Nevertheless, getting and supplying that information is the most important service you can perform. (See Chapter 18.)

Talk Shows

At the national level, public relations people may work directly through the radio or television show's producers, or they may use a national placement agency. These agencies have the contacts, and the reputation with the television producers, for "delivering." What producers don't want is a "no-show," or someone who appears in the studio but really is not prepared to give an interview that pulls audience response, either in ratings or phone calls and emails, if it is a call-in show.

T A B L E 8 . 3	*Reference Materials for Broadcast Media*

- **News release giving basic messages or statements of conference as anticipated.**
  Generally announcements are made at news conferences, but there are responses to questions that of course can't be anticipated.

- **Biographies of all principals involved in news conference.**
  Usually only one or two people are involved in the newsmaking part of the news conference. For example, it may be a major appointment by a government official like the president, governor or mayor, or a university announcement of a new athletic coach.

- **Background information on the situation or the event.**
  For example, the news conference may be to announce an agreement that resolves a conflict. Be sure that the presentation materials are balanced and fair. This might even be a joint news conference, so materials must be shared and coordinated.

- **Who to call for additional information if it is needed when the story is prepared in the newsroom.**
  Be sure email addresses are available, as well as the Web site address.

- **Fact sheet on the event or situation.**
  For events, the details of the event can be given; for appointments, the names and dates of previous holders of the office can be useful to a reporter.

T A B L E 8 . 4	*Logistical Needs of News Media at News Conferences and Speeches*

Broadcasters come with their own equipment bag, but what they need on site are the following:

A good microphone for the speakers and a reliable sound system in a room with good acoustics and lighting.

A mult box with enough sound system connections for the reporters to plug into to capture the audio.

Additional mult extension cords so reporters can connect their recorders and keep them with them instead of having to leave them near the podium.

Industrial extension cords for extra lights and sufficient electrical outlets.

A public address mike on a podium that is large enough to accommodate reporters' mikes.

Telephones with jacks for reporters to file from the scene. (The reporter can feed audio from an audio recorder directly into the phone circuits.)

Internet connections would help those using digital/computer gear.

Plenty of duct tape to tape down all of the wires to keep people from tripping over them. Tape your own wires before the event, but have tape and scissors available for reporters who need to tape their own connections in a hurry.

Pens, pencils and pads of paper are always useful, even though most will be using laptops.

Be sure the doors to the room open wide enough for larger pieces of equipment to be brought in easily, and have technical staff of your own available to help with blown fuses, fuzzy sound systems, contrary mikes and such.

Crews need a place to park, especially if they are bringing a live truck and will broadcast or transmit from the scene.

Easily accessible water fountains and restrooms are always appreciated.

If the show is local, occasionally the public relations person is the talk-show guest, but this really is not greeted with much enthusiasm by the broadcasters. Try to find someone who will capture the attention of not only the broadcaster but also the audience. Shows of this nature are not as fluid as they appear. Generally, they are structured by the host in a brief period before the show is aired.

You'll need to prepare certain materials for such an event. The show's host needs to have a backgrounder or facts sheet on the institution that the individual represents, the event or occasion for the attention and biographical information on the person being interviewed. All of this information must be very brief and in a form the show's host can take on the air—typed triple space on sheets of paper heavy enough not to rattle or in digital form so it can be displayed for the host to read on a remote screen. The guest should have in mind all the information he or she is going to present. To prepare mentally and to keep facts and figures fresh, the guest usually requires briefing sessions the day before and again just before airtime. The guest needs to alert the host to information that should be presented for the benefit of the listening audience. If the talk show is on television, take along materials that can be shown. Remember the wiggle.

News on Call

Some organizations offer broadcast-quality information and actualities (visual or audio) on call either through a special number or a toll-free line.

The information is changed frequently during the day so that broadcast news stories can be updated with fresh actualities.

Although websites continue to be an excellent source of information updates and certainly a good place for gathering background information, the audio, when there is any, like the pictures, may not be of broadcast quality. However, in designing your Web pages, don't forget that broadcast media will be using them, so give phone contact numbers on your news pages and on your home page. The assumption of many website designers is that the contact will be made by computer. With broadcast media, that is less likely if what is needed is an actuality, not just information, although the show's producers can go directly to the site if the broadcast quality is there.

News Releases

Like those for print media, news releases for broadcast media are either advance stories about something soon to occur or stories explaining what has occurred or what is going on. Although no news media personnel will get excited about doing your promotion for you, many will use well-prepared advance stories if the event has enough news value. News releases on upcoming events should be extremely brief for the broadcast media—no more than two or three short paragraphs. However, you should send along your longer print-media version, a fact sheet and (when appropriate) a brochure or printed program. If the event is likely to have regional interest, send a courtesy copy of the news release to the broadcast wire services, just to alert them to an event their reporters might be interested in. Be sure to identify the courtesy copy as such when you deliver or send the release.

If you are sending your materials by email, remember to send a message with the releases, fact sheets and graphics each as separate attachments because the receiver may encounter problems opening the files or downloading the graphics.

A Compelling Headline

What: Don't just tell what is happening; give some descriptions of irresistible visual and/or audio possibilities.

When: Broadcasters live by the clock. Tell precisely when something is occurring, the date, day of the week, time of day for openings/closings and best time to catch the action.

Where: Be very specific about location and access. Give tested directions so no one is confused or lost. Also give your mobile phone contact number just in case someone does get lost *en route*.

Who: Who is sponsoring this event and why and how significant this is to the broadcast audience because that's who matters, not you and your organization.

Contact Information: Your name, email address, organization's physical address and phone numbers including your office, mobile (cell) and home numbers.

FIGURE 8.3

Model Broadcast News Tip Sheet

Electronic transmission of messages, images and sound has changed and continues to change the delivery of information to broadcast media. Direct feeds from satellites are common. Stations can take broadcast-quality interviews by phone. However, the broadcast medium, be it a network or a station, has to want to receive your information. The way you accomplish that is by building a history of credibility and reliability for providing timely and accurate material of broadcast quality.

For stations in your immediate area, it's a good idea to build your reputation through direct in-person contact. You want to develop working professional relationships with broadcast people so they know who you are when you contact them. That's very important now that broadcast stations, especially in metropolitan areas, are security conscious and not open to "drop-in" visits from strangers. Otherwise you literally can't get past the front door. Media advisories and tip sheets help build relationships and pique media interest. (See Figure 8.3.)

Timeliness is a problem for stories about events that have already happened. Nevertheless, the broadcast media will cover most events of any significance—even past events. If you are supplying audio and visual materials, be sure you prepare them to meet media deadlines and mechanical requirements. The quickest is digital. If for some reason, you are delivering material directly to local stations, call the news directors to let them know that the material is coming, and hand-deliver the package. If the event was a speech, attach a complete copy to the brief release. You can file a courtesy copy with the wire service if the speech has regional interest—though, again, the wire services often provide their own coverage.

For television, you can offer graphs and charts to help explain the event; for radio, offer broadcasters a phone interview to flesh out their story and give it a sense of immediacy. In the latter instance, be sure you have all the facts and figures within easy reach for the phone interview. Be aware that your interview will be edited. Still, if you are prepared, editors won't have to cut out dead air—gaps of silence—while you hunt down a fact.

VNRs

Video news releases are increasingly accepted by news directors, especially in the areas of science stories and health and medical news. This may be the only way the broadcast media can get access to the story because of proprietary information in the case of drug companies, the complexity of the material in science research presentations or the need to protect patients' rights in some medical stories.

Writing a video news release means writing a script, just as a news team might write it if the news team had access to the information in advance of the event. Of course, what can happen is that broadcast news teams cover an event with reporters, photographers and technical crews. Then they go back to the station, look at and listen to what they were able to capture and write a script describing what is usable from the audio and video that they got. With staff reductions at both TV and radio, what you may have is a reporter with equipment who will get visuals and sound, add information then send the material directly to the station for broadcast and for the station's website use.

In writing a video news release, the public relations writer has control of the situation. The script is written with the information in place and the visuals and sound indicated. Then the video is photographed and recorded. It is edited to a usable news segment, usually 30 seconds, but it may be longer. The outtakes are kept, and additional footage or a "B" roll usually is shot, as well as some additional actualities as long as the production studio is leased for the VNR.

Remember that your VNRs are likely to be 30 seconds, maybe a minute. A long piece is 3 minutes. If the VNR is a news feature, it could run between 5 and 20 minutes. Although you will be using professional producers, some things you need to watch for in viewing the final piece are suggested by videotape editor Eric Alkire (alkire@worldnet.att.net). Look for useless cutaways and sound breaks, because these interrupt the flow of the story. The story should flow and any break, audio or video, should contribute to, not distract from, the story. Watch for flash frames or muddy audio cuts. Most importantly, Alkire advises, watch objectively and ask if the story gets told and the video is watchable.[23]

Additional suggestions come from Canadian public relations professional David Eisenstadt who warns about being sure that the VNR is really news and not commercial, that the production is simple, not glitzy, so that it fits most stations' formats and that you use sound. Additionally, you need to know whether to send VHS or BETA. Although stations have both, one is usually preferred, usually BETA.[24]

Most broadcasters indicate that they prefer to get the VNR by satellite and want to be notified that it is coming by fax or phone.[25]

Although some news directors still worry about lack of flexibility in adjusting the story to their format, time frame and audience, most have figured out a way to let audiences know that the information comes from a public relations source by a simple credit line. Some VNR productions help by superimposing the words "footage supplied by XXX" over footage of a new product or over a simulation of a scientific breakthrough.

The acknowledgment of the source for VNRs has posed an ethical problem. (See Chapter 2.) However, many VNR producers, other producers and distributors now subscribe to a Video News Release Code of Practice developed in 1992 by the Public Relations Service Council.[26]

Broadcast Writing Style

The basic difference between writing for broadcast media and writing for print media is that copy for the former must appeal to the ear. (In television and video, of course, the visuals must capture the eye.) Copy must capture attention through sound and word symbolism. The words must be clear enough to be understandable the first time through. The listener will not have a chance to review what is said. In radio, the listener can't reread a sentence to understand what it meant and can't go back to the one preceding it to figure out the sequence of ideas. Each offering is a one-time-only presentation. To compensate for the lack of review opportunity, broadcast writers first tell listeners (and viewers) what they are going to tell them, alerting them to the content by calling up frames of reference. Then they present the content. Finally, in the summary, they again tell the listener what the message was. It takes a skillful writer to prepare material in this way without sounding redundant. As the writer follows this sequence, keep the time element in mind. Clarity and brevity are both important.

Because broadcast media are intimate, their style is conversational. Each listener or viewer experiences the broadcast media as an individual and responds personally. The relaxed style means that the leads, or first paragraphs, in broadcast stories, including news stories, are "soft." That is, the listener is introduced to the story before hearing it.

One type of soft lead is called a "throwaway": "Vacationers driving around the country this summer are likely to find lots of detours. The American Automobile Association says road repairs and construction are going on all over the nation." Another soft lead is the "angle" lead that hooks your attention: "Planning to drive your car on your vacation this year? Get ready for lots of detours. The American Automobile Association says road repairs and construction are going on all over the nation." If one news story is related to another, a soft lead may be used to introduce both of them: "Vacationers planning to drive their cars this summer are likely to have some unexpected problems. Road repairs and construction have put detour signs up all over the nation. The longer routes may cause motorists to run out of gas because many small service stations in outlying areas have closed during the last year. New highways bypassing towns have closed stations, and storms are the cause of the road repairs." (The story goes on to say that the American Automobile Association will help car travelers plan trips to find out about detours in advance, and that the major oil companies are offering credit card holders lists of service stations open along interstate, state and rural roads.)

We can make some other generalizations about broadcast writing. Because the tone is conversational, for instance, sentences are sometimes incomplete. We talk that way, so in broadcast journalism, it's acceptable to write that way. Sentence length and structure are also governed by special rules. In broadcast writing, sentences are kept short in deference to both the announcer (who has a limited amount of breath) and the listener (whose attention span shouldn't be taxed). For the same reason, subjects and verbs are kept close together. Normally, sentences should not begin with prepositional phrases; the basic information should be conveyed first. "According to a report from the Mason County Sheriff's office today, vacationers driving through are likely to find fewer service stations than last year." By the time listeners decide that fewer service stations might be important to them, the "Mason County" is lost to all but the most attentive among them.

Broadcast writers should avoid two peculiarities of newspaper style—sometimes called "journalese"—in preparing broadcast copy. One is inverted sentence structure, where the statement precedes the attribution: "'Victims of the Mississippi tornado are all back in permanent housing,' said Scott Smith, director of emergency disaster relief." This sentence illustrates what not to do in writing broadcast copy. Because broadcast audiences may not be attending to the first part of the sentence, information should be presented as it would probably be spoken in conversation: "The director of emergency disaster relief said that all victims of the Mississippi tornado are now back in permanent housing." The name of the director is not important to the story, so his title alone is used. If the story were a long one in which Smith was quoted, his name would be used, but he would be identified in a separate sentence: "Scott Smith is the director of emergency disaster relief."

The second newspaper-style characteristic to avoid in broadcast writing is the identification of subjects by age, job title and such. In newspapers, this information usually follows the name and is set off by commas. But what is efficient in newspaper copy becomes cumbersome when read on the air. Again, the name of an individual is often unimportant; title identification is enough.

Here is a typical print story:

Vacationers traveling by car may be encountering an unusual number of detours this summer, according to James R. Ragland, manager of the Dixon American Automobile Association office.

Storm damage all over the nation has resulted in more than the usual amount of road repair, and the severe winter also put a number of highway projects behind schedule, Ragland said. The result is detours in almost every state.

AAA offices are trying to help motorists plan trips to at least be able to predict delays, Ragland said.

The service is free to AAA members, and there's a nominal charge for nonmembers, according to Ragland. The Dixon AAA office is in the Chamber of Commerce Building at Fifth and Ledbetter.

Here is a broadcast version (30 seconds long) of the same story:

That severe winter the nation had is going to make summer
vacations by car more difficult than usual, the American
Automobile Association says. Triple A is offering travelers plans
marked with all of the detours for road repairs and
construction. Triple A's Dixon manager says the plans are
free to members, but available to nonmembers for a
nominal fee.

An admonition to keep it short but clear comes from broadcaster and academician Dr. Suzanne Huffman: "Most radio news stories on commercial stations are *very* short. As a writer, think in terms of 30 seconds for each story; that's about five sentences long. A story that runs 35 seconds will raise an eyebrow at the editor's desk. . . . Write the bare minimum you need. You have to be clear, but you have to be concise and short."[27]

Physical Preparation

Unlike copy for print media, all broadcast copy is triple-spaced and written on one side of the page. Some broadcast news departments prefer that copy be typed in all caps (capital letters); others prefer the standard combination of upper- and lowercase letters. Most public relations people supplying information to the broadcast news media use caps and lowercase. For radio, select font size and margins to produce a 60-space line, to give an average of 10 words per line.

Most announcers read at a rate of about 15 of these lines per minute. So in radio news, one typed line takes about four seconds to read. A 30-second story is seven to eight lines long. (See the AAA story.)

The audio copy for a TV script goes on the right side of the page, opposite the video instructions. When you are writing for television and using only half the page (the audio side), set your margins to yield about six words to the line, or about 21 lines per minute at an average reading speed—the equivalent of about two seconds per line. Thus, a 30-second TV story is about 15 of these lines.

Much of the format for a broadcast release is similar to that of print copy. Appearing in the upper-left corner of the first page of each story is a slug line—the words identifying the story—the date, the name of the organization submitting the information, your name and phone numbers where you can be reached day or night. On the following pages, all you need are the page number, slug line (story identification) and your last name. The story's end is marked by the traditional "30," and "more" goes at the bottom of each page in the story except the last. Never break a paragraph at the bottom of a page.

To facilitate reading by announcers, don't break words at the end of lines either and don't split sentences between pages. If a word or name is difficult to pronounce, give the proper pronunciation in parentheses beside it *each* time it appears. The announcer should not have to go back and look for your previous instructions. Do not use diacritical markings you find in dictionaries to indicate the proper pronunciation. Use popular phonetics like those the newsmagazines employ (SHEE-fur for Schieffer, for example).

Remember, the audience can't see punctuation marks. These exist only to help the announcer interpret the copy. Don't use them unless they serve this purpose. And don't use colons, semicolons, percentage signs, dollar signs, fractions, ampersands and other exotica. Just use commas, periods, question marks, dots, dashes and quotation marks. Use quotation marks only when repeating the exact words is essential. It is better to rephrase a quote into indirect statements. If you feel that a quote is necessary, precede it with something like, "In his words," or "What she asked for was" or "The statement read."

Use hyphens only when you want the letters to be spelled out individually, as in Y-W-C-A, as opposed to being read as a word, as in *NASA*. Don't use abbreviations unless you want them read on the air as abbreviations. Exceptions are such titles as Dr. and parts of names like *St.* Louis. If you don't know whether to write a word out or abbreviate it, write it out.

Numbers are difficult to follow when they're heard but not seen, so avoid using them as much as possible. Throughout this book, we preach the importance of using AP style. Here is where we'll vary somewhat. If the reporter is used to getting copy from you, then use the *AP Broadcast Manual's* instructions for numerals. It's a bit different from the AP print in that the rule of spelling out numbers one to ten is now one through eleven. AP broadcast style calls for using Arabic numerals for 12 through 999. Above that AP broadcast style calls for using what is more conversational, such as two-thousand dollars but 12-hundred dollars. However, if you are sending copy to broadcasters unfamiliar with you as a news source, use the AP broadcast style, but in parenthesis spell out the numbers. Announcers don't read anything in parenthesis, and it can be marked through in the copy during the editing process or deleted if the copy is going electronically. You must be absolutely sure there is no error in delivering numbers to the news media. It's seldom a risk in print, but can be a real hazard in broadcast copy. Also, to prevent errors, don't use a.m. or p.m. with times of the day; announcers wouldn't read the letters anyway. Write, for example, "this morning" or "tomorrow night." However, because your copy is going to the news media for handling, put dates in parentheses beside the week-day designation—Monday (May 1). When the copy is processed for reading on the air, that information will be omitted. But writing it in will prevent errors. Another expression to avoid when reading numbers is per, as in "miles per hour." Instead, use "miles an hour."

In reporting names and titles, use the title before the name, and avoid beginning a sentence with a name, especially if it is unfamiliar. If the title is long and cumbersome, break it up or shorten it. You generally do not use a person's middle initial in speech, so avoid using middle initials in broadcast copy unless they are important for clarification and identification or unless they are commonly used with the names in question. On second reference use the surname only, except when you are referring to the president of the United States or a member of the clergy. Clergy retain their titles on second reference—Rabbi Brown, for instance.

> *Print version*: Madison A. Clark, bishop coadjutor for the Episcopal Diocese of Dixon, today announced that $50,000 had been raised for the World Famine Relief project. The funds will be sent to agencies designated to purchase and distribute food in Africa, Bishop Clark said. There are three such agencies—the American Red Cross, the National Council of Churches and CARE.

> *Rewritten:* Dixon's Episcopal Diocese has raised $50,000 (fifty thousand dollars) for the World Famine Relief project. The announcement came today from Bishop Madison Clark. Bishop Clark said the money will be sent to three agencies designated to purchase and distribute food in Africa.

Watch for and clarify obscurities. Be very careful about using pronouns. Listeners have trouble following the references. If you are dealing with specialized jargon, translate it. Use words and terms the audience will understand and relate to. If you are writing about little-known groups, explain who they are and what they do. Don't assume the audience will know or understand. And do use contractions, like don't, just as you do in speech. Use the active voice. It gives life and movement to your writing. Keep your verbs in the present tense when possible because broadcast media expect to offer timely information. When your audience's language is not English, provide a translated version of your information.

Structural Considerations

Broadcast story leads differ from print leads, in which the who, what, when, where, why and how are often all crammed into the first paragraph. This burst of information can be confusing for the listener and difficult for the announcer to read. When you are preparing your broadcast story, first alert listeners to what you are going to discuss, getting their attention with something that is important to them. Using a summary statement is a good way to get into the story. Then you can give the essentials. Make your sentences simple; don't use long clauses at the beginning or end or between the subject and verb. As you develop the story, look for ways to connect paragraphs with transitions that allow the story to emerge and flow logically. Keep the listener and the announcer in mind, and think about how each will be able to handle the words you write.

Broadcast wire stories undergo much more reworking than newspaper wire stories, because the broadcast wire serves stations that use news directly from the wire on an hourly basis. One story, repeated hour after hour, can get dull if the audience remains the same—as in offices that have piped-in radio. Research can flesh out a breaking story both to give it depth and to keep the sparse facts from getting monotonous. Broadcast leads vary dramatically from print leads. The lead-in sentence is designed to capture attention. The listener needs to know what the story is about because if it is something that is important to them, they may want to pay more careful attention. Broadcast stories more often follow a narrative format because that's the way we are accustomed to talking and sharing information. Use of the active voice conveys immediacy and importance to the story. Personalizing the story helps too, and more and more newspapers are using this format. Find a person as an example of the issue or effect and start with his or her perspective. Follow with expert information and understandable statistics. Then close with a summary that goes back to the individual used as an illustration, showing the consequences or choices for that person. Remember this when you furnish actualities.

Supplying Pictures and Sound

When you supply actualities in any way other than digitally, you also need to furnish a script. Attach it firmly to the CD/DVD or VNR. Identify the script with exactly the same title that appears on the disk, and add your name, your institution's name and the address and phone numbers where you can be reached day and night. Also give an email address. Broadcasters don't have time to play every submission they get to see what is there. Of course, if they decide the story might be used, they will preview the story, and they are also likely to edit it if they schedule it to run. The station will also write a lead-in to the tape, so it's a good idea to supply additional information—for example, a copy of the news release covering the occasion for making the tape. Lead-ins identify speakers and action without detailing the content of the tape.

As evidence mounts that most people depend primarily on the broadcast media for news, organizations must focus their attention on getting their information into the broadcast media. If one reporter picks up on a story that's broadcast, the chances of it being used by other broadcast media is good.

Digital Delivery and Use

Video content is generally delivered to newsrooms digitally. This includes VNRs and other public relations materials such as Satellite Media Tours (SMTs). All of the materials can be sent digitally, including scripts, videos, graphics and supplemental story content as well as advisories. The delivery is not over the Internet because the results may or may not be of broadcast quality. But other digital news delivery systems do work. Reporters can take the digitally delivered material directly from the station's server to an edit system or videotape recorder.

Advantages of digital delivery are the speed of the system and the ability of the reporters to edit in supplementary material such as "B" roll and more information to update a story and make it unique to the station's newscast. With SMT delivery, much more in-depth material is available to the reporters to flesh out stories they are working on, or for them to develop a feature from the material sent.

Digital material can also be sent to special publics. "Broadcast pubic relations has only recently surfaced as a regularly used term . . . but it has yet to achieve a universal understanding or recognized definition," says Kelli B. Newman. She notes that the varied menu of distribution outlets generated by technology, such as the video iPod, "places a greater priority on content and the strategies used to create it. So, whether webcasting, podcasting, vodcasting, blogging or televising, broadcast public relations delivers the greatest value when defined as a subspecialty of our profession that applies multidimensional content strategies to its productions.[28]

Conclusions

- World Wide Web and email, IM and texting have made digital communications personal and ubiquitous.
- Social media place an emphasis on collaboration and sharing.
- When public relations people contact traditional media representatives, they are trying to *push* information out, hoping it will be used. Social media do the opposite; they *pull* people into discussions.
- Social media offer us opportunities to begin and maintain *relationships*.
- Social media are given major credit for the election of President Barack Obama.
- Learning how to participate successfully in social media conversations is the new critical success factor for communications.
- To decide what type of writing is appropriate for social media, you examine the medium, see what's there and adopt a writing style and length that "fit" the medium.
- Clear, persuasive written communication is the core skill that can be leveraged by each new technology.
- A rapidly increasing percentage of the USA population is switching from TV to the Internet to obtain news.
- Organizations as diverse as corporations, nonprofits and the USA military are using social media.
- Newspapers provide PR practitioners an ongoing source for communicating with a wide range of readers who include community leaders, elected officials and affluent readers.
- News releases differ for newspapers, television and radio. News releases for newspapers can be longer; those for TV shorter, and those for radio usually the shortest.
- The main parts of the news release are the lead, supporting information and, sometimes, a summary description of the originating organization.
- News releases for television are more apt to be used if there's a visual element involved.
- The move toward convergence of social media and "traditional" media has greatly affected how we look at news releases.
- The ideal news release meets the needs of everyone representing newspapers, television, radio, blogs and other Internet-based sites. It calls for the inclusion of photos, a podcast link, video, quotations, links to related previous coverage, RSS (Really Simple Syndication or Rich Site Summary) feeds and other information.
- News releases and other information provided by public relations professionals remain the major source of content for journalists.
- Most journalists want to receive news releases by email.
- Most news releases are rejected because they contain no news or are poorly written, incomplete or inaccurate or have no reader interest.
- If you're writing for print media, prepare the material as you would if you were a reporter working for a newspaper.
- The lead is the most important part of your news release.
- A local angle is important in getting a news editor's attention.
- In amplifying the lead, use short, concise sentences and be sure to cover the who, what, when, where, why and how of the story in the first two paragraphs.

- PR writers can develop quotes for stories and get them approved by the person to whom they are attributed—a luxury newswriters don't have.
- The *AP Stylebook* dictates generally accepted news style, though some media have their own styles.
- News releases are written to communicate announcements, information on special events, spot news, responses to events, features and reactions to bad news.
- Some information should be placed in forms other than straight news releases—for example, column notes, letters, guest columns and photos.
- Photos or graphics and their captions may be sent with a story as illustrations or alone as "wild art." In either case, they are good public relations tools.
- Digital graphics and photos can be sent electronically around the world.
- The decision of where and when to send releases is critical.
- Releases should be prepared in a style and format appropriate to the medium.
- To help communicate public relations messages and to build good media relations, news releases must contain genuine news, must be written in the form and style appropriate for the medium and must be truthful, complete and accurate.
- Release of significant news of corporations whose stock is publicly traded is regulated by the SEC.
- The sights and sounds of events are important to broadcast news.
- Electronic transmission of messages, images and sound is changing the delivery of information to broadcast media, but they still have to want it. To be recognized as a good source, you need to build a reputation for providing timely, accurate, newsworthy material of broadcast quality.
- Digital pictures shown on websites generally are not of broadcast quality but can indicate to broadcast media what types of visuals are available.
- You need to preserve sights and sounds from events in multiple formats for future use by your organization and by news media.
- Special events are the public relations activities (other than crises) most likely to generate coverage by broadcast media, especially television.
- You'll need to prepare a fact sheet and a history of the event for the media's use, and then you must videotape some activity.
- Broadcasters need material written in broadcast style, but because that means the copy will be brief, you should attach the longer print-media release "FYI" (For Your Information).
- Be sure to set up the facilities broadcasters will need to cover your special events.
- Always post someone at a central location to respond to questions, and provide that person with all the facts you have given to the media plus all new, updated information. It helps for that person to have a mobile device to reach you or to access information from the organization's website.
- News conferences are called when someone needs to interact with the news media. In arranging news conferences, be sure to provide the news media with background materials.
- You should "cover" news conferences too and record them digitally.
- A crisis is a disorganized combination of special event and news conference.
- While local talk-show appearances are usually arranged directly with the hosts or their producers by PR people, national appearances are generally arranged through placement firms although some large public relations firms do work directly with national talk-show producers.

- PR people must provide both interviewer and interviewee with appropriate information. The interviewee needs to be rehearsed, and the interviewer should be provided with biographical information and background materials well in advance.
- News on call requires frequent updating for broadcast media to keep stories fresh.
- For broadcast news, you need actualities to give authenticity and to enliven your news.
- Video news releases, or VNRs, are prepared materials ready to air. Be sure to attach a script and contact information.
- Some VNR producers subscribe to a good-practices code to make their materials more acceptable to news directors.
- Broadcast writing style is conversational, and broadcast copywriters must remember that the listener has no opportunity to review or rehear a sentence or word once it has been spoken.
- When you write for broadcast, you have two audiences to consider—the person who will read the copy (the announcer) and the listener or viewer.
- The physical layout and appearance of broadcast copy are designed to help the announcer.
- The structure of broadcast stories is designed to help the listener.
- Broadcast leads differ from print leads in that they don't contain all of the news elements in the story.
- Broadcast news stories are rewritten regularly during the day to keep the material fresh, even when there are no new facts.
- PR people must know how to provide information to the broadcast media that is timely, appropriate for the special qualities of the media and interesting to their audiences.

Exercises

1. Write a news release on a current campus event in print and broadcast style.
2. Write a news release for a specialized publication for the topic, naming the publication and stating its purpose.
3. Write cover letters for both, telling each editor why the story has value for that publication's audience.
4. Find an event from your campus calendar that you think would make an interesting news story. Get information about the event from the planners. Write a media advisory for the event. Write a news release for the student newspaper and then a broadcast version for the student radio station. If you have a television station or stream news on the student publications website, prepare for that editor a revised media advisory that suggests videos for their coverage along with your advance news release on the event.
5. Most universities have visiting celebrities as guest speakers to the campus or to a particular department. Find out information about the appearance of a celebrity at your school and write a news conference announcement. Prepare all materials you would need to have on hand for the conference. Where would you plan to have the conference so the sound and light would be good for the media, the guest would be comfortable and the school would look good in the clips?

6. Universities generate a great deal of research. Look at your university's publication of ongoing research and choose a topic that would make a good video news release. Decide how you would make it timely. Do the necessary additional fact-finding for a video news release and write the script. If this is outside of your academic unit, be sure to tell those you contact that this is a classroom project.

Use InfoTrac® College Edition to access information on topics in this chapter from hundreds of periodicals and scholarly journals.

Media Kits, Media Pitches, Backgrounders and Position Papers

Media Kits

Today many organizations' media kits are digital and available on the organizations' websites. Because a media kit usually has many purposes, it often is also printed on paper.

A good media kit is a basic tool for working with the mass media. Media kits used to be easy to describe: a pocket folder containing information for print and/or broadcast media. Media kit folders have ranged from basic pocket folders from the office supply shelf with a letterhead sticker on the cover to elaborate four-color packages with pockets for videos. Some—especially those introducing new consumer products—are three-dimensional.

Yes, these are "media" kits, not "press" kits. The difference is that public relations practitioners prepare packages of information for all media to use, not just the newspapers or "press."

Traditionally, the contents of the kits have varied based on their use, but the contents are always prepared with the medium in mind. For example, black-and-white glossy photographs that might be useful to print media are not included in broadcast media kits. Sound on CDs that might be in radio news kits are not included in television news kits, which might have videos on DVDs or videotapes.

Cision (formerly, Bacon's Information) reported in March 2009 on a survey of journalists: "One hundred percent of the respondents said they regularly use websites for editing and reporting; 94 percent said they use information from PR professionals; and 87 percent said they regularly refer to press kits."[1]

The advantage of using an organization's website for a media kit is that it can offer news media not only much more material but also much more flexibility. When information becomes outdated, changing the information on the website is fast and quite inexpensive, compared to trashing a supply of printed materials and reprinting.

In a study of online corporate websites, QuickSilver Interactive Group, Inc. found that various companies offer as many as 65 features on their websites. Some of the more popular contents for both Web-based and printed media kits include:

- *Fact Sheet*—gives information about the organization: officers, offices with addresses and phone numbers, a description of what the organization is or makes or does. The fact sheet is the basic "building block" for a media kit. The "standard" fact sheet presents fundamental facts about the organization. These should be readily available, either on a single sheet or in folder form. You probably need more than one kind of fact sheet. A second one would be a historical fact sheet covering landmarks in the organization's development. Special-event fact sheets not only tell others what's going on, but they'll also help you preserve your sanity by organizing information in an easy-to-find-and-use format.
- *About Us*—summary or overview of the organization
- *Annual Report(s)*—most recent year(s)
- *Executives' Biographies*—principals of the organization: officers, founders and others with pictures (head shots), downloadable or reproducible ones for print media, small ones for identification for broadcast media and high-quality ones for magazine use
- *Board of Directors*—names, affiliations and addresses
- *Calendar of Events*—information on coming teleconferences, webcasts and executives' speeches
- *Community Service Programs*—information on charitable and civic activities and policies on contributions
- *Contact Information*—who to contact for media inquiries, customer service and investor relations
- *Downloadable Logos and Photos*—various sizes and forms of organization's logo and photos of typical operations
- *FAQs*—frequently asked questions and answers
- *Financial Information*—earnings releases, financial highlights, stock charts, dividends history
- *History*—background on the organization and historical milestones in its development — when founded and where, when new activities began and so on
- *News Releases*—usually headlines with hyperlinks to the entire release
- *Position Papers*—selected copies of any position papers the organization has prepared on current issues
- *Profile or Backgrounder*—tells about the character of the organization and the nature of what it does, including board committee charters and corporate code of ethics
- *SEC Filings*—information on filings with the Securities and Exchange Commission
- *Publications*—Selected copies of the organization's serial publications such as magazines or newsletters.

See Figure 9.1 for an example of a basic fact sheet that includes "just the facts."

A TEKgroup International survey found that 99 percent of journalists responding said it's important for a company to have an online newsroom. (Fifty-one percent said it's "very important," 36 percent said "important" and 12 percent said "somewhat important.") One journalist commented, "(It's) important to be able to find everything a reporter needs in one place, at any hour, without having to seek assistance." Ninety-seven percent of them said their preferred method of receiving information is to receive email alerts when selected new

Fact Sheet

SOCIAL SECURITY

➤ **In 2009, nearly 51 million Americans will receive $650 billion in Social Security benefits.**

December 2008 Beneficiary Data

o Retired workers	32 million	$37.2 billion	$1,153 average monthly benefit
dependents	2.9 million	$ 1.6 billion	
o Disabled workers	7.4 million	$ 7.9 billion	$1,063 average monthly benefit
dependents	1.8 million	$ .6 billion	
o Survivors	6.5 million	$ 6.3 billion	$1,112 average monthly benefit

➤ **Social Security is the major source of income for most of the elderly.**
   o Nine out of ten individuals age 65 and older receive Social Security benefits.
   o Social Security benefits represent about 40% of the income of the elderly.
   o Among elderly Social Security beneficiaries, 52% of married couples and 72% of unmarried persons
      receive 50% or more of their income from Social Security.
   o Among elderly Social Security beneficiaries, 20% of married couples and about 41% of unmarried
      persons rely on Social Security for 90% or more of their income.

➤ **Social Security provides more than just retirement benefits.**
   o Retired workers and their dependents account for 69% of total benefits paid.
   o Disabled workers and their dependents account for 18% of total benefits paid.
      • About 91 percent of workers age 21-64 in covered employment and their families have protection in the
         event of a long-term disability.
      • Almost 1 in 4 of today's 20 year-olds will become disabled before reaching age 67.
      • 69% of the private sector workforce has no long-term disability insurance.
   o Survivors of deceased workers account for about 13% of total benefits paid.
      • About one in eight of today's 20-year-olds will die before reaching age 67.
      • About 97% of persons aged 20-49 who worked in covered employment in 2008 have survivors
         insurance protection for their young children and the surviving spouse caring for the children.

➤ **An estimated 162 million workers, 94% of all workers, are covered under Social Security.**
   o 52% of the workforce has no private pension coverage.
   o 31% of the workforce has no savings set aside specifically for retirement.

➤ **In 1935, the life expectancy of a 65-year-old was about 12½ years, today it's 18 years.**

➤ **By 2034, there will be almost twice as many older Americans as today – from 38.6 million today to 74
   million.**

➤ **There are currently 3.3 workers for each Social Security beneficiary. By 2034, there will be 2.1
   workers for each beneficiary.**

SSA Press Office   440 Altmeyer Bldg   6401 Security Blvd.   Baltimore, MD 21235   410-965-8904   FAX 410-966-9973

FIGURE 9.1

"Just the Facts" Format   *Fact sheets take various formats, depending upon their purpose. One typical format,
which is a listing of "just the facts" from the USA Social Security Administration, is shown here.*

information is posted to online newsrooms. In the same survey, respondents said it's important to them to be able to access press releases, photos, product releases, executives' biographies, PR contacts by cell phone, archives and company background information.[2]

If you are using hard-copy media kits, then you need to think about how much material you are going to send and how to make it appealing. The most conservative choice is to use a *shell*. The shell for media kits is usually a basic folder that has the name and logo of the organization, and you can have these made up in bulk so they are available when you need them. The only time you would want to have a different shell printed would be for a special event. Then you want the theme of the special event to dominate, although not at the expense of losing the identification of the organization.

Media Kit Use

Media kits are used by organizations for basic information about the organization, special events (preliminary and on-site), news conferences and crises. Usually, the kit has a letter to the user identifying the contents and the people to contact for more information. When kits are mailed, the kit letter is replaced by a cover letter explaining why the kit is being sent, its contents and any other particulars that would be important such as important dates or people who may be contacted.

The key to developing useful media kits is to think of who is going to use them and what that person is likely to need. (See Table 9.1.)

Media kits are not intended to be sent to new members of the board of directors, for example. They are not packages of information for general use by someone who wants to know something about the organization, although selected kit contents might be useful for that purpose. They are for hands-on use by working members of the news media: reporters,

---

T A B L E 9 . 1	*Preparing a Media Kit*

1. Define the purpose for the media kit.

2. Identify the publics you need to reach.

3. Identify the media reaching those publics.

4. Determine which media will receive the kits.

5. Consider how each item in the media kit relates to the purpose for the kit.

6. Consider how the news media recipients will use each item in the kit.

7. For every item included in the kit, ask these questions:

   a. How do you expect the audience of each news medium to use the information?

   b. How does what you are providing the news medium convey that expectation to the medium's audience?

   c. What do you expect audiences of these media to do as a result of receiving this information? How will you measure that? (This question is significantly different from asking if the news media used the media kit or how much of it was used and when. That is easily measured. It's their audience's response that you need to know in order to determine if the kit's e effective.)

editors, news directors and producers. Remember that before you begin stuffing one with copies of ads or sales materials.

Media Kits for Special Events

The use of the kit is particularly important when you are preparing one for a special event. Special-event kits are somewhat different in their contents, which are as follows:

- A *basic fact sheet about the newsmaking event* should detail the event and explain its significance in strictly factual terms. This should be a "stand-alone" sheet that gives a contact's phone and address, because it may become separated from the rest of the material. You need to include all important dates, times, participants and their relationship to the organization and to each other, such as those who work for wholly owned subsidiaries.
- A *historical fact sheet about the event* that tells when it was first held, where, who attended and how many if that is significant. You need to give milestones in the event's history, being sure to make clear why each is significant.
- A *program of events or schedule of activities* should have detailed time data, as that is especially significant to broadcasters. Provide a script if you have one. This is especially useful for the broadcast media but can be important for print photographers too.
- A *complete list of all participants* should explain their relationship to the organization and why they are a part of the event.
- *Biographical information on the principals as well as head shots* of them should be included. The black-and-white prints for newspapers and magazines should be of reproduction quality, and you should indicate when color pictures are available.
- A *straight news story* should give the basic information about the event in an announcement news approach. This should be about a page and a half, double-spaced on a 60-space line for print media and one or two short paragraphs triple-spaced for broadcast media. Be sure to give broadcast media both print and broadcast stories so they have the benefit of the additional information in the longer story. The print media need only the print version.
- A *longer general news story* that ties in the background information may be as long as three double-spaced pages for print media and one full page for broadcast media.
- A *feature story* or two should be included to offer some insight into the more interesting aspects of the special event. There need be no broadcast version of these, but these features should be included in the broadcast kits for information.
- A *page of isolated facts* about the special event and others in the past, if this is an annual event, should be included. These facts often are picked up by broadcasters to use if they cover the event, and sometimes they are incorporated in print copy written by reporters covering the event.
- *Visual materials* can be included, or you can include a sheet that provides small images with URLs that can be used to download the images, along with suggested captions. If the event is a first-time affair, shoot digital images and post them on your Internet site immediately following the event and let media representatives know where they will be. If the event is conducted annually, you can include pictures from the past, but be sure these are properly labeled so they are not misleading. *Do not include any pictures that have been used in advertising.* Also don't include any pictures of participants if they can be

identified unless you have a written release. If you include photos, attach information to the pictures so it can be removed without marring the photos.

- *Information on cooperating organizations* is important for their recognition and support as well as for the news medium. However, you don't just stuff the kit with what cooperating organizations give you. You get the information about the organizations, then prepare information sheets explaining their contribution to the event and their relationship to your organization. For example, an organization may be supplying picnic lunches for volunteers who are taking children on an outing. You need to tell how much food and something about the supplier as well as why that organization is participating in your special event. Use quotes from people in the cooperating organization. If the contribution is significant enough, you may want to do a special news release on one or more of the cooperating organizations. This is especially important for them if your organization is organized as a nonprofit and you have called on profit-making organizations for help in making the event a success. It may be easier for you to get media attention than it is for them, and if you see that they get credit for their support, they will be more willing to participate in the future. Be certain that you clear the information you have prepared with them to be sure it is factually accurate. You don't want your credibility undermined by some participant saying that what you have said about them is inaccurate.

Cover letters for special-event kits should tell the news media why you think the event deserves the attention of each medium, in terms of the interest of that medium's audience in the event. You want to be sure you make coverage easy for them too. Let them know what arrangements are being made, such as the facilities of the media room, and how to schedule an interview with celebrities or other participants.

You'll need to include information about how they gain access to the event, such as how to apply for badges and vehicle passes. You might even want to include information about transportation or eating facilities in the area of the event, if this is important. You could save the information about the immediate area in which the event is held—such as food facilities and so on—for the cover letter that goes with on-site media kits.

On-site cover letters are different. You will need to let the news media know who to contact at all hours of the day and night in case they have problems or questions, and you'll need to let them know how to get others from their news medium in (such as technical crew) and what to do about personal and vehicle passes.

On-site media kits are different too. If you use a hard-copy kit, you'll need a sheet of changes in the front, and you must replace every piece of paper where a change has created an error. Keeping dates on your news releases and all other information elsewhere, such as on fact sheets, makes this easier for you to do. Things get so hectic in a special event though that some people use different-colored paper for different days so there's not a mistake. But this can be a problem with materials like news releases. Obviously, this is why online kits and news releases are less troublesome and also less expensive.

Your on-site kits should have materials arranged in order of importance and have a story for each day of the event or each feature of the event if it is a one-day affair. An example of the latter would be a story on a speaker, a feature on the food for the luncheon or the chef, and perhaps a feature on the planning for the event if there are unusual aspects to that. You can include in on-site kits any promotional brochures about the event that have been used. These often have dates and times that can be a quick reference for the person covering the event. *Do not include these if facts have changed since they were produced.*

Media Kits for News Conferences   When you are preparing a media kit for a news conference, it makes a difference what the occasion for the conference is. News conferences should be called for only two reasons: (1) to provide media access to a celebrity or expert whose time is limited; (2) to offer face-to-face access to a spokesperson for the organization when there is a controversy. The latter will be covered later in this chapter in the section on crisis kits. So if you are preparing a media kit for a news conference in which you are providing access to a celebrity, you need the following materials:

- A *biographical sketch of the celebrity* that is up to date and a recent photo. If there are any restrictions on the use of the photo, you should not include it, because you probably won't be able to control its use.
- *Information about the relationship of the celebrity to your organization,* such as providing entertainment or being a spokesperson in promotions, on issues or on new developments. You need to think of "celebrity" in very broad terms here. The "celebrity" may be a researcher who has done breakthrough research that your organization is able to take advantage of through serving clients in a medical facility or through providing medication or medical procedures. You can provide this information either in a fact sheet or as a backgrounder.
- A *general news story* that is the kind of story someone covering the news conference would write. To do that, of course, you will need to have interviewed the person and asked the kind of questions the news media attending are likely to ask and incorporated the responses in the story.
- A *basic fact sheet about the organization.*

Promotional Media Kits   Promotional media kits are made up differently. These kits often include advertising used in the promotion, quotes from critics or reviewers when appropriate or even reprints of entire newspaper stories (reprinted with permission). It may be that the promotion is part of a larger event such as a national touring performance or exhibit. In that case, many of the materials will be provided by those planning and sponsoring the event, but you will need to add your organization's information to the materials and tailor news and advertising for the media you'll be using.

Media kits that are offered on CDs—other than simple text that can be produced quickly and easily—should be for something special due to the time it takes to produce them. Depending on the organization, it's possible that you could have a basic CD media kit made for the organization. However, such material is easily dated so you need to be sure to provide for periodic updates. It's more likely that you'd create a media kit for a special event or a special observation like a 50-year anniversary.

Some of the materials needed are the same:

- Basic fact sheet
- Historical fact sheet
- Backgrounder

- Biographies of all principals (company officers, speakers, celebrities and others)
- Facts about the situation that can be used as column items, fillers or a story idea
- Visuals that include photos of the principals, pictures of the company or the event or whatever is appropriate to illustrate the purpose of the kit, but carefully chosen and edited with accompanying identification
- News stories
- Features
- Information on any cooperating organizations or perhaps on the site if the event is being held in an unusual place
- A source information directory so reporters or editors can locate names of people to call or to send faxes or email messages. Be sure to include a technology "help" number in case the disk is unreadable.

The CD-based media kit shown in Figures 9.2A and 9.2B. is interactive and includes links to materials on the company's website.

Figure 9.3 shows a more traditional—but nonetheless effective—media kit's fact sheet. This media kit was developed for a news conference and is available on the organization's website.

These suggestions for creating an effective CD are offered by Tony Harrison, owner/publicist/copywriter at COMMposition of Boise, Idaho:

- Make the CD as interactive as possible with a wealth of information.
- Make the CD easy to use by creating easy interfaces with big buttons, large type and readable fonts providing easy navigation from point to point so the users don't get lost offering mini-indexes for different locations so users know what's there without having to go into the location.
- Arrange your images in an easy-to-use order by
  - Scanning photos (or copying digital images) onto CDs if you have a lot of still photography
  - Organizing the images well, so using and choosing the images is easy
  - Creating an image-placement database so that, if a photo or illustration is needed in several places in the CD or needs to be replaced, the change can easily be made
  - Saving (archiving) each step in the process of graphic images so that you can make changes without having to start the process over (for example, an image created in Illustrator, touched up in Photoshop and saved as a PICT file has a typo)
- Update periodically to keep contents current.[3]

Media Kit for a Crisis   You may find that you are using your crisis media kit at a news conference because the confusion caused by crises generally means that at least one news conference is necessary. In the event of a severe, ongoing crisis such as effects of a natural disaster like an earthquake or hurricane, you may be giving daily briefings as well.

With information changing so quickly in a crisis, you will need to keep updating your website. This keeps down the number of direct media contacts you have to handle. It does mean, though, that in addition to your computer at the media center for the crisis communications, you must have a printer and a copier available.

FIGURE 9.2A

Interactive Media Kit   *This interactive media kit, produced on CD, was developed by Christine Martin, Communications Editor, Overwatch Systems Tactical Operations, an operating unit of Textron Systems. Links on the CD access content on the Internet. The CD packet cover is shown here. Used with permission of Overwatch Systems Tactical Operations.*

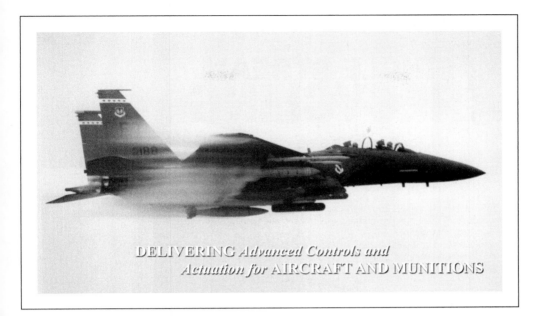

DELIVERING *Advanced Controls and Actuation for* AIRCRAFT AND MUNITIONS

FIGURE 9.2B

Overwatch Systems Media Kit   *The Overwatch Systems media kit on CD contains dozens of images, including corporate executives' photos and many product information sheets. Shown above is the CD's introductory photo.*

Because crises are largely unpredictable, you need to have a supply of basic materials set aside for quick assembly. There won't be time to locate and print these items. You will have the media kit shell, which is a basic folder for the organization. You also should have on hand:

- Basic fact sheet about the organization, with names and titles; addresses of the home office and all branches or subsidiaries (if any); phone numbers, including the numbers of security people and night numbers that override the main control and put the caller through to the person on duty
- Backgrounder on the organization itself—what it is and what it does
- Biographical information on the principals of the organization—officers and board, including long in-depth pieces on the principals, often called "current biographical summaries," which are used for speeches and introductions but in this case may become "standing obits" (material ready for use in case of death)
- Detailed description of all facilities, giving layouts and square footage in each area as well as the number of people who work there and at what times. Some of these may be involved in the crisis
- Information on all the activities of the organization, including products, services, research funded or ongoing, and equipment
- Visual material, including pictures of facilities and principals

It's so Austin. It's so easy.

Single Stream Recycling Fact Sheet

Single Stream...Taking Austin's recycling to the next level!
Single Stream allows customers to mix recyclable paper, plastic and glass in one cart.
This method has many advantages:
- Toss ALL recycling into one cart
- Recycle MORE and more types of items
- Encourages MORE residents to recycle

When does it start?
Beginning October 2008 and extending through the end of the year, crews will deliver blue, 90-gallon recycling carts to City of Austin Solid Waste Services residential customers.

How will it work?
After the new service launches, all your recyclables will go in one cart: paper, cardboard, boxboard, aluminum cans, metal cans, plastic and glass. Crews will collect recycling with automated collection trucks, and recycling collection will occur every other week. Customers will receive complete Single Stream Recycling instructions and a calendar showing their collection schedule with their new recycling cart.

What goes in the recycling cart?
All recyclable items – no sorting!
- Paper: (newspaper, office paper, junk mail, box board like cereal and soft drink boxes, corrugated cardboard)
- Aluminum and metal cans: food cans (labels left on OK), soda cans
- Glass: Jars and bottles
- Rigid plastics: # 1 through # 7, including yogurt and margarine tubs

What cannot be recycled?
- Plastic bags, Styrofoam (cups, egg cartons, take-out containers)

austinrecycles.com

FIGURE 9.3

Single Stream Recycling   *The media kit from the city's Solid Waste Services Department in Austin, Texas contained this "Fact Sheet," as well as a "History of Recycling in Austin," "Single Stream FAQs," "Solid Waste Services—Who We Are, What We Do" and a "Media Advisory" for a media conference and demonstration on how Single Stream Recycling works. Audio and video were available on an enclosed CD, which also contained images of the documents listed above.*

- Historical fact sheet on the institution, giving important milestones in its development
- Statistics on the facilities and the institution, including number of people employed; annual financial statements; major contracts with unions or suppliers; details of lawsuits pending against the institution; information on regulatory or accrediting agencies with some sort of oversight authority over the institution, its products and its services (for instance, the Food and Drug Administration or a hospital's accreditation bureau)

Keeping these materials updated for hasty assembly may be demanding for some organizations, but most have this material available on a fairly current basis from their annual report.

Material to be added includes the following:

- A statement from the crisis spokesperson about the crisis (provided in audio for the broadcast media)
- Information about who to contact for information about the crisis as it continues or moves toward resolution

(Also see Chapter 18 for information on crisis communication.)

Media Credentials

For many events, having media personnel register and receive credentials—usually badges— is essential to maintain security and allow media personnel access where they need it. It's important to define who's eligible to receive media credentials. *The New York Times* reported, "Increasingly, bloggers are penetrating the preserves of the mainstream news media. They have secured seats on campaign planes, at political conventions and in presidential debates, and have become a driving force in news events themselves."[4]

The American Society of Plastic Surgery (ASPS) developed the following guidelines for media eligibility at its 2008 annual scientific meeting:

MEDIA ELIGIBILITY

Media credentials are available to working journalists whose attendance at the meeting may result in print, broadcast or electronic coverage of the ASPS, PSEF or ASMS and its individual members.

ASPS does not issue media credentials to the following: a publication's advertising, marketing, public relations or sales representatives; publishers, editors or reporters from manufacturers; "house organs" or promotional publications; public relations staff of exhibitors or educational institutions; writers creating analyses or reports sold as a commodity to customers; or other individuals who are not actually reporting on the meeting.

Working media representatives may not register as exhibitors.
To obtain media credentials, identification certifying that you are a working member of the news media on assignment to cover the meeting is required. Business cards from established news organizations are sufficient to establish eligibility.[5]

ASPS provided an online form for media registration and provided on-site registration for media representatives in its "press room" at the meeting.

Materials for Media Rooms—Crises and Special Events

The media room in any crisis or special event is an information hub. You need to be sure it is that and not a hubbub. So that staff and reporters are not frustrated, you need to have racks of information available that include all of the materials listed for the kits. In summary, you need:

- Fact sheets, informational and historical
- Backgrounders on the organization and situation
- Annual reports and informational brochures
- Biographical data and photos of organizational principals
- Special facts, such as information on the site, if it's a crisis, or on the event
- Statistics on the organization and/or event
- News releases, dated and numbered
- Quotes from principals, dated and numbered, and any actualities you have of these
- Visuals, with information and identifications attached

What you will be adding to these are *news briefs* on breaking or developing news. You should have a daily summary of new information, something that might be given at a crisis news conference or news briefing and something usually put out each day of a special event to let reporters know what's going on and what has happened that day. Like news releases, these should be dated and numbered so you have a reference later. Unfortunately, some references aren't useful for quick retrieval later. Sometimes, in crisis situations, news releases and news briefs are part of the documentation in a court case. If you have a crisis, you must assume that your organization will be sued. Keep that in mind as you prepare materials. Stick to the facts. Think in advance about what reporters will want to know.

In case of crises, here are some facts reporters are going to want to know (and will find out from other sources if you don't provide the information):

- Numbers of dead and/or injured
- What was damaged and how (descriptive, not dollar amounts)
- Time of crisis events
- Location of all crisis events
- Names of dead and injured (released only after the next of kin are notified)
- Relationship of the casualties to the organization
- Number of people within your organization who were involved and who they are
- Who the spokesperson is and how to get in touch with that person
- What the effects of the crisis are on the organization

This last item is the troublesome question. Don't speculate; just provide facts. Don't sound too upbeat, because you'll appear to be insensitive. Don't be too negative, because your words will affect the morale of employees and the responses of other publics, such as investors and regulators, to the crisis. Keep a written account of everything released, to whom and on what date.

Having basic information on your organization loaded on a "dark" website can be extremely helpful in the event of a crisis. Such a site is developed, but the URL of the site is not made public. As information becomes available, it can be quickly loaded on the site and the URL can be made available to media representatives. This assures that information provided to media is always consistent. (See Chapter 18 on crisis communication.)

Special-event news briefs are generally on more positive news than a crisis, but you need to be sure you have good stories every day for print and broadcast media. Think in advance and plan in advance for good print stories and broadcast coverage. You will need to move around the event interviewing people and getting story material to provide to various media representatives as tip sheets or story ideas. This is your job, not theirs. If you want the event covered, you will have to do the fact-finding and initial story preparation. Again, keep copies and dates and names of the people you've given a story idea to. Remember, feature ideas are given to only one medium at a time. If a journalist seems interested but doesn't use the story in a reasonable period of time, you are free to give the same information to another medium after confirming that the first medium is not likely to use it.

At news conferences for crises and special events, you need to be sure you cover the news conference and capture audio and video of what occurs so you can write a follow-up release afterward. That story will incorporate what actually occurred at the news conference. You send the news conference media kit with this story as a substitute for the earlier news story to news media who were unable to attend the conference. You have to be careful about doing this because in writing the coverage story you don't want to take advantage of good questions asked by media people who were energetic enough to cover the news conference. Nevertheless, you want to get as much mileage as you can out of the news conference.

Media Pitches

A *media pitch* is just what it sounds like—a proposal to a media outlet. It's intended to "sell" a story idea on a specific topic. The media pitch can be in the form of an email, a phone call, a fax or a letter, depending in large measure on how well you know the person for whom the pitch is intended. (See Figure 9.4 for an example.)

The pitch can be for a new product or service, a new use for an existing product, an event or a movie—in other words, just about anything. The media pitch is the accepted way to make media representatives aware of a story idea in a clear and concise format. Each pitch should be targeted to a specific medium and should contain specific, unusual story angles.

Perhaps the most important part of a pitch is to present enough information to demonstrate that the story idea is of interest to their readers, listeners or viewers.

Be Prepared and Be Persistent

Before you send your pitch letter or email, be sure you know the publication or station. Check a media directory, and check with PRSA members or others in the market where it's located.

Todd Brabender, president of Spread The News PR, says that one media pitch isn't enough and that your opportunity for placements "increases with meticulous, media follow-ups and re-pitches." "Based on my professional experience as a PR/Publicity specialist," he said, "I would estimate that media placements occur in the following manner:

25% occur after the 1st–2nd pitch,
50% occur after the 3rd–5th pitch,
25% occur after the 6th–8th pitch."[6]

The Media Relations Maven's
10 Awesome Media Relations Rules
By Margo M. Mateas
The Media Relations Maven

1. Plan the Pitch
Before you pitch, do your homework. Read recent articles. Look up the publication and reporter's profiles in your media directory. Check out its website and editorial calendar. Discover what the media target wants and *then* pitch a story that brings important new information to its audience. Know exactly how your story benefits the publication.

2. Think Like a Reporter
How does this story benefit the publication and its readers? Does it provide real facts, something of interest, something new and timely? If not, throw out the idea and start again! Ask the hard questions. Push back until you have something that will work.

3. Find a Story Angle
A good story serves more than your client or company; it provides interesting and useful information to the public at large. Know what a good story is and how to find it. Dig into the background, philosophy and talents of the organization and people you're pitching. Find the hidden story everyone else has missed.

4. Pick a Section
Have a specific type of story and a particular section in mind when you pitch. *"I thought this would be perfect for your Coastal Getaways section…"* This immediately lets the editor begin to see how your story will fit into the format.

5. *Prepare Your Pitch Bag*
Always have more than one angle or story to pitch in case the first one doesn't pan out. *"Oh, you just assigned a story on new healthcare solutions? How about one on how a new medical device is saving lives?"* Be able to switch tracks mid-conversation so you can explore additional story ideas.

6. Speak in Bullets
Prepare a bulleted "pitch sheet" with key selling points and background information and keep it in front of you when pitching. Keep emails and verbal pitches short, too. Don't waste time dressing up the pitch. Boil it down to its most concise points. Don't bother saying your last name or the name of the product or service: just say what it does and paint a mental picture of its benefits for the editor.

7. Give a Clear Call to Action
First tell the reporter <u>what</u> you're asking for, then tell him <u>why</u> he should do it. "I've got a great profile for your lifestyle section… there's a new museum opening next month…" When scheduling interviews, never ask <u>if</u> a reporter is available, find out <u>when</u> and make it happen. "Is next Tuesday between ten and noon good for you?" Set aside a block of time and get the reporter to commit.

8. It's Never "A Good Time"
Don't apologize for pitching. Just do it well. Don't ask if an editor has time for you. Just call, get to the point and be done with it. If the editor sounds stressed, ask to call back at a better time.

9. They Won't Buy if You Don't Believe
Like any salesperson, you must love what you're selling. You must know what's great about what you're pitching, and believe in it. If you don't love what you're pitching, neither will the reporter. Don't let an editor dismiss you.

10. Become a Valued Resource
Establish relationships, not "drive-by pitches." Give now to get something later. If you hear of a story you know would interest an editor, give it to her, even if you won't get paid for it. It will pay off in coverage later.

Margo Mateas is president of the Public Relations Training Company, a firm that provides media relations and management training. Mateas' methods are used by the world's #1 public relations agency, Fortune 500 companies & more.

FIGURE 9.4

The Media Relations Maven   *One way to let media representatives know about an event or other newsworthy activity is to use a "media pitch." This is an example of an effective email pitch. Telephone contact also can be effective in "pitching"—making media people aware of what you have to offer*

The California Association for Health Services at Home (CAHSAH) encourages its home care provider members to use a series of media "hits" in selling a story idea. It recommends that "Media Hit #1" be made by fax, mail or email. . . . And it says, " . . . Craft your pitch letter to stand out from the crowd." It advises opening with an interesting statement "that motivates the reader to read on. Next, explain why the media should be interested in the pitch. Finally, address your proposal to a particular person, not just 'editor,' in the form of a standard, one-page professional letter."

CAHSAH says the second contact should be by telephone and should focus on how the story will appeal to the reporter's audience. The third contact, it says, should be by mail and should include your organization's media kit. Finally, it recommends following up by telephone to be sure the media contact has all of the information needed to develop the story.[7]

A national study by Cision and The George Washington University Graduate Study of Political Management found that editors and journalists "agreed that email pitches should be more relevant to their beat/area of interest, less promotional, should state benefits for their audiences, have stronger story ideas, cover the five Ws in leads, be better written and have less boilerplate."[8]

If you want to get your story into a magazine, check its editorial calendar—especially if it's a trade or professional publication. The editorial calendar is a tentative list of topics that the publication intends to cover during the next 12 months. By examining a publication's editorial calendar, you should be able to develop story "angles" that will give each magazine or newsletter editor reasons to include your organization in one or more issues. If you have questions about whether your story will "fit" into an issue, call the editor, briefly explain your idea and ask if it sounds as if it will work. A phone call may save both the editor and you considerable time developing a pitch that doesn't have a chance of success. Editorial calendars include submission deadlines, so you need to pitch your article concepts well in advance of those deadlines to allow time for developing the article before the deadline.

Backgrounders and Position Papers

Writing of another kind is critical to public relations planning—the preparation of *backgrounders* or *position papers*. Outside academia, these often are called *white papers*.

The backgrounder is similar to a historical research paper that looks at a situation or problem in the present by considering its origins and its implications for the future. The position paper more closely resembles a research paper that takes a point of view or perspective on a situation and marshals evidence in support of the position taken.

Both can be critical in media relations, particularly in responding to reporters' inquiries. Reporters may ask questions like: "What's your position on [name of act] now before Congress in Washington?" "What's your company's stand on the cause of the pollution in [name of river or area]?" "What does your company believe will be the impact of the new EPA rules?" "I'm doing a story on declining innovation in your industry. Can you give me some information?"

Your organization's executives and spokespeople must be able to respond quickly and knowledgeably to such questions. A "No comment" response is not acceptable. And if an executive promises to call the reporter back, this must be done faithfully. If such queries are not handled with skill and dispatch, the company loses credibility in a hurry. A company's credibility is hard won and easily lost. A thoughtless response can do unlimited damage.

The role of the public relations writer in such instances is to provide either in-depth information on the topic (in the form of a backgrounder) or a clear, definitive company point of view (in the form of a position paper). As the public relations writer, you are the eyes and ears of company spokespeople. You have to arm them with facts—solidly researched and documented, organized in logical fashion, clearly written and easily understandable.

Good public relations departments do not wait until a reporter calls to begin developing basic information for backgrounders and position papers. PR staffers routinely comb media of all types, searching for salient bits of information affecting their company or industry. These bits of information are accumulated and filed for reference. When the task of writing a backgrounder or position paper is assigned, they already have a head start on research.

It's common for backgrounders and position papers to be written and filed away—sometimes on a private intranet—for later use. The hope is that they will not be needed. But if they are, public relations personnel can respond quickly and appropriately to queries from any source.

Preparing backgrounders and position papers is often the first stage in planning a new public relations program. For example, assume that an electric utility is considering a new way of charging for the use of its electricity. The proposal calls for higher rates during the day but very low rates at night and on weekends. The PR department should prepare a backgrounder that describes the history of this time-of-day pricing structure, where such methods have been tried and with what success, the availability and cost of "time" meters and related points. Of course, the backgrounder should also compare this method to the one currently in use and to other methods.

At some point, company management will decide to stay with the present system or go with the time-of-day system. The backgrounder will help management make this decision. If the decision is to adopt the time-of-day system, the backgrounder will be used as the basis for developing and writing a company position paper on the new system. Both the backgrounder and the position paper will contain the information necessary to write news releases, ads, brochures and speeches, as well as articles for the company magazine, newsletter, intranet and Internet sites of all kinds.

Backgrounders tend to be heavy on facts and light on opinion. Position papers are heavy on opinion or interpretation, supported by only a few selected facts. Both can deal with broad or specific questions or issues. However, backgrounders tend to deal with general topics, whereas position papers tend to treat specific issues.

For example, a backgrounder might deal with alternate fuel vehicles (AFVs) to reduce emissions that are contributing to global warming, whereas a position paper would argue for the use of natural gas-fueled vehicles (NGVs) as a solution.

Backgrounders

Backgrounders have many purposes. They serve as an information base for company executives and employees. They provide source materials to copywriters preparing ads, news releases, brochures, speeches or articles for the company magazine, intranets and websites. They may also be used as documents to hand out to reporters or members of the public who inquire about a certain topic. And company executives on the speakers' circuit can use them to bone up on a subject so they can field questions from the audience. Rarely does a backgrounder serve only one of these purposes; keep all of them in mind.

The hallmarks of a good backgrounder are accuracy and comprehensiveness. This means that the topic must be thoroughly researched.

Research   Doing research for a backgrounder often involves using all the research skills, techniques and sources discussed in Chapter 4. You are not being professionally responsible if you leave one bit of salient information unread or ignored in your evaluation. It just might contain the germ of an idea or the fact that makes all of your other material inconsequential or misleading. This can be fatal to the company, because company spokespeople have to rely on you for the information they convey to members of the media or to the public.

Research is a never-ending process. Once a backgrounder is completed, it may become less useful with each passing day because of new information. You should establish the practice of accumulating pertinent information, filing it and updating the backgrounder at regular intervals. Backgrounders that do not include the very latest important information are worthless.

Writing   Writing a backgrounder begins first with a simple statement of the issue and why it is important. Including such a statement may appear trite, but it is necessary to focus your research and writing. It keeps you on the right track. This opening statement should be both precise and concise. Besides helping you in the writing, it tells the reader what to expect in the document.

Once your opening statement is honed to perfection, write the body of the backgrounder. Be sure to provide an adequate, clear history of the issue, a thorough discussion of the current situation and implications for the future.

Background   As the name implies, a backgrounder supplies background and/or helpful information on a topic or issue. (See Figure 9.5.) It often provides a fairly complete historical overview so a reader unfamiliar with the topic can understand how the current situation evolved. You have to answer the question "Why are things the way they are today?" And you can't answer this question without giving details about how things were and how and why they have changed.

The typical backgrounder includes such details as significant historical events, legislative enactments, changes in government and company policy and applicable social conditions. It specifies names, books, documents, articles and reports that played an important part in the development of the issue. In sum, this section of the backgrounder should describe the evolution of the current situation.

Current Situation   Having built a foundation on the past, you should now examine the current situation, including reviewing current public and company policies. Perhaps these points could be extended to include a discussion of alternative policies now under consideration.

The purpose of a backgrounder is to assemble and convey information, not to judge it. Any discussions of policy or alternatives should be presented from an objective, neutral position. Stick to facts. Describe policy options, discuss their good and bad points, but don't judge them.

For example, if the issue is the high cost of home heating and its effects on poor people, one policy to consider might be the use of energy stamps to help poor people pay their utility bills. This idea has its good and bad points. One writer might say

Using energy stamps is a poor way to solve the problem because stamps require a massive, wasteful bureaucracy and excessive government funding.

U.S Food and Drug Administration

Revealing *Trans* Fats

Scientific evidence shows that consumption of saturated fat, *trans* fat, and dietary cholesterol raises low-density lipoprotein (LDL), or "bad" cholesterol, levels, which increases the risk of coronary heart disease (CHD). According to the National Heart, Lung, and Blood Institute of the National Institutes of Health, more than 12.5 million Americans have CHD, and more than 500,000 die each year. That makes CHD one of the leading causes of death in the United States.

The Food and Drug Administration has required that saturated fat and dietary cholesterol be listed on food labels since 1993. With *trans* fat added to the Nutrition Facts panel, you will know for the first time how much of all three—saturated fat, *trans* fat, and cholesterol—are in the foods you choose. Identifying saturated fat, *trans* fat, and cholesterol on the food label gives you information you need to make food choices that help reduce the risk of CHD. This revised label will be of particular interest to people concerned about high blood cholesterol and heart disease.

However, everyone should be aware of the risk posed by consuming too much saturated fat, *trans* fat, and cholesterol. But what is *trans* fat, and how can you limit the amount of this fat in your diet?

What is *Trans* Fat?

Basically, *trans* fat is made when manufacturers add hydrogen to vegetable oil—a process called hydrogenation. Hydrogenation increases the shelf life and flavor stability of foods containing these fats.

Trans fat can be found in vegetable shortenings, some margarines, crackers, cookies, snack foods, and other foods made with or fried in partially hydrogenated oils. Unlike other fats, the majority of *trans* fat is formed when food manufacturers turn liquid oils into solid fats like shortening and hard margarine. A small amount of *trans* fat is found naturally, primarily in dairy products, some meat, and other animal-based foods.

Trans fat, like saturated fat and dietary cholesterol, raises the LDL cholesterol that increases your risk for CHD. Americans consume on average 4 to 5 times as much saturated fat as *trans* fat in their diets. Although saturated fat is the main dietary culprit that raises LDL, *trans* fat and dietary cholesterol also contribute significantly.

See http://www.pueblo.gsa.gov/cic_text/food/reveal-fats/reveal-fats.htm for complete backgrounder.

FIGURE 9.5

Backgrounder: Trans Fats   *Backgrounder: Trans Fats Backgrounders do just what the name indicates: they provide background information for a wide range of publics, including news media representatives. This one, from the USA Food & Drug Administration, is available on FDA's website, http://www.pueblo.gsa.gov/cic_text/food/reveal-fats/reveal-fats.htm.*

Another writer might say

> Using energy stamps is an excellent solution to the problem because stamps could be easily administered by existing government organizations.

Both writers may be justified in their points of view, but this is a backgrounder, not a position paper. Instead of taking a position, write to inform, saying

> Use of energy stamps is one solution to this problem. An energy stamp program would require government funding and a system for administering these funds. Such a program might be administered by existing organizations.

Implications   To this point, we have considered the historical background and the current situation. The next step in writing the backgrounder is to examine the consequences of selecting one policy over another. If the backgrounder does not address such future implications directly, it should at least highlight points that must be considered.

A backgrounder on another aspect of energy policy might deal with state and federal policies that support AFVs. An expectation is that such a paper would put the whole issue into historical perspective by giving first the rationale for needing such policies, second the enactment of various federal policies, primarily by the EPA, and third the policy initiatives by various states. The backgrounder would also be expected to document which policies seem to be most effective, such as the EPA's clean air standards for ozone and fine particulates. The document would bring the situation up to date by explaining the current focus on market-based fuel incentives such as legislative actions that would offer tax incentives.

Identifying the implications of a certain policy includes anticipating developments. The public relations writer has to be aware of the flux of ideas about the issue and which of these may gain or lose support over time. Perhaps a public policy change is being debated now in Washington. Perhaps an extensive government study is under way, the results of which won't be released for a year. Perhaps the topic will be the focus of a convention this year. In all these cases, the issue and its implications are likely to be in the news now and in the future. As a public relations writer, you must be ahead of these developments.

Documentation   You must present full documentation of the information you use in the backgrounder. Before you try to write, as suggested in report writing, get a reliable style manual and study it carefully.

Although a backgrounder does not require the same rigorous scholarship and style required of reports and proposals, a style manual can help you properly cite the material you use in the backgrounder. Use a footnote or endnote system of citation, and include a complete bibliography at the end.

It is important to cite your sources carefully, because people using the backgrounder, whether inside or outside your organization, may want to pursue a specific point more fully. Or if they find a discrepancy between the facts in the backgrounder and those in some other source, they may want to evaluate the sources you have cited. This is especially important when a backgrounder provides the foundation for a position paper.

Position Papers

As the name signifies, a position paper is designed to state an organization's position on an issue. (See Figure 9.6.) The issue may be local, regional, national or international in scope. For example, suppose your company opposes a national health insurance plan under consideration in Congress. The position paper should tell why. Your company may also take a positive position regarding a substitute proposal authored by a representative from the local district. The position paper should explain why it supports the substitute plan.

Like the backgrounder, the position paper requires extensive research. Much of the information you need will be found in the backgrounder, so new research requirements may be minimal. At this stage, however, you will need to solicit the input of management, which must scrutinize salient information, sort out the pros and cons of alternative positions and then make a policy decision. Research on a problem may produce a backgrounder that results in a management decision to offer or support a solution. Then you may be asked to write a position paper.

Once that decision has been made, you can write a thorough position paper representing the organization's point of view. If PR professionals in the company are held in high esteem, management may ask that a proposed position statement be written and used as a basis for discussion. A draft position paper is written with the expectation that it will be approved in principle, modified or rejected. After modifications are completed and approved, a final version is prepared for distribution to management and other publics.

Whenever a new issue surfaces, the public relations department should alert management to the need for a position paper. Recognizing an issue constitutes the first step in writing a position paper.

Stating the Issue   No position paper will have much value if it fails to state the issue clearly. Your job as PR writer demands that you describe the issue fairly and honestly. *Don't* distort the issue to suit your purposes or to make it easier to form—or defend—an opinion. The purpose of a position paper is to address an issue squarely, not evade it.

If you are in the natural gas industry, your position statement will support the use of NGVs and would argue that these provide the most desirable solution to reducing emissions. However, a good position paper would acknowledge that success of NGVs depends on recognition in the marketplace and by state and local governments that society benefits from clean, domestic fuels to the extent that there is continued financial support for private sector initiatives. Furthermore, the NGV position paper would have to recognize current limitations for NGVs, especially such critical ones as fueling and servicing.

Don't dance around an issue; meet it squarely near the beginning of the position paper. One of the most obvious ways of doing this is by providing relevant background information.

Background   If you want your position paper to be comprehensible, you must provide pertinent background information. But remember that a position paper is not a historical analysis; leave that to the backgrounder. Give just enough background to provide a context for your position and to help your readers understand why the subject under discussion has become an issue. The nature of the issue often obviates the need for extensive background information, but be sure to give enough to make the basis for your position intelligible.

Position   Don't keep your readers in suspense. Come to the point immediately. Don't try to build suspense by including elaborate recitations of facts and flashy figures, and don't culminate the paper with an eloquent conclusion.

POSITION STATEMENT | 09

[Originally published in 2004 updated in 2009]

Condoms and HIV prevention

Condom use is a critical element in a comprehensive, effective and sustainable approach to HIV prevention and treatment

Prevention is the mainstay of the response to AIDS. Condoms are an integral and essential part of comprehensive prevention and care programmes, and their promotion must be accelerated. In 2007, an estimated 2.7 million people became newly infected with HIV. About 45% of them were young people from 15 to 24 years old, with young girls at greater risk of infection than boys.

The male latex condom is the single, most efficient, available technology to reduce the sexual transmission of HIV and other sexually transmitted infections.

The search for new preventive technologies such as HIV vaccines and microbicides continues to make progress, but condoms will remain the key preventive tool for many, many years to come. Condoms are a key component of combination prevention strategies individuals can choose at different times in their lives to reduce their risks of sexual exposure to HIV. These include delay of sexual initiation, abstinence, being safer by being faithful to one's partner when both partners are uninfected and consistently faithful, reducing the number of sexual partners, correct and consistent use of condoms[1], and male circumcision.

Conclusive evidence from extensive research among heterosexual couples in which one partner is infected with HIV shows that correct and consistent condom use significantly reduces the risk of HIV transmission from both men to women, and also from women to men[2]. Laboratory studies show that male latex condoms are impermeable to infectious agents contained in genital secretions[3]. To ensure safety and efficacy, condoms must be manufactured to the highest international standards. They must be procured according to the quality assurance procedures established by the WHO, UNFPA and UNAIDS and they should be stored away from direct heat sources. Prevention programmes need to ensure that high-quality condoms are accessible to those who need them, when they need them, and that people have the knowledge and skills to use them correctly.

Condoms must be readily available universally, either free or at low cost, and promoted in ways that help overcome social and personal obstacles to their use. Condom use is more likely when people can access them at no cost or at greatly subsidized prices. Effective condom promotion targets not only the general population, but also people at higher risk of HIV exposure, especially women, young people, sex workers and their clients, injecting drug users and men who have sex with men. UNFPA estimates that the current supply of condoms in low- and middle-income countries falls well short of the number required (the condom 'gap')[4]. Despite the gap, international funding for condom procurement has not increased in recent years. Collective actions at all levels are needed to support efforts of countries, especially those that depend on external assistance for condom procurement, promotion and distribution.

FIGURE 9.6A

Position Paper: Condoms   *A position paper is a close relative of the backgrounder. However, the position paper is intended to clearly present an organization's position on a specific issue. This one presents the World Health Organization (WHO), UNAIDS and UNFPA's position on the use of condoms to prevent HIV and other sexually transmitted infections. It is clear and straightforward—hallmarks of a good position paper.*

Source: http://www.who.int/hiv/pub/condoms/20090318_position_condoms.pdf

HIV prevention education and condom promotion must overcome the challenges of complex gender and cultural factors.

Young girls and women are regularly and repeatedly denied information about, and access to, condoms. Often they do not have the power to negotiate the use of condoms. In many social contexts, men are resistant to the use of condoms. This needs to be recognized in designing condom promotion programmes. Female condoms can provide women with more control in protecting themselves. However, women will remain highly vulnerable to HIV exposure, until men and women share equal decision-making powers in their interpersonal relationships.

Condoms have played a decisive role in HIV prevention efforts in many countries. Condoms have helped to reduce HIV infection rates where AIDS has already taken hold, curtailing the broader spread of HIV in settings where the epidemic is still concentrated in specific populations.

Condoms have also encouraged safer sexual behaviour more generally. Recent analysis of the AIDS epidemic in Uganda has confirmed that increased condom use, in conjunction with delay in age of first sexual intercourse and reduction of sexual partners was an important factor in the decline of HIV prevalence in the 1990s[5]. Thailand's efforts to de-stigmatize condoms and its targeted condom promotion for sex workers and their clients dramatically reduced HIV infections in these populations and helped reduce the spread of the epidemic to the general population. A similar policy in Cambodia has helped stabilize national prevalence, while substantially decreasing prevalence among sex workers. In addition, Brazil's early and vigorous condom promotion among the general population and vulnerable groups has successfully contributed to sustained control of the epidemic.

Increased access to antiretroviral treatment creates the need and the opportunity for accelerated condom promotion.

The success of antiretroviral therapy in industrialized countries in reducing illness and prolonging life can alter the perception of risk associated with HIV[6]. A perception of low-risk and a sense of complacency can lead to unprotected sex through reduced or non-consistent condom use. Promotion of correct and consistent condom use within antiretroviral treatment programmes, and within reproductive health and family planning services, is essential to reduce further opportunities for HIV transmission. Rapid scale-up of HIV testing and counselling is needed to meet the prevention needs of all people, whether they are HIV-positive or negative.

---

[1] *UNAIDS. 2004 Report on the global AIDS epidemic, page.72.*
[2] *Holmes K, Levine R, Weaver M.* Effectiveness of condoms in preventing sexually transmitted infections. *Bulletin of the World Health Organization. Geneva. June 2004.*
[3] *WHO/UNAIDS. Information note on Effectiveness of Condoms in Preventing Sexually Transmitted Infections including HIV. Geneva. August 2001.*
[4] *UNFPA. 2007 report on donor support for contraceptives and condoms for STI/HIV prevention 2007.*
[5] *Singh S, Darroch J.E, Bankole A.* A,B, and C in Uganda: The Roles of Abstinence, Mongamy and Condom Use in HIV Decline. *The Alan Guttmacher Institute. Washington DC. 2003.*
[6] *Gremy I, Beltzer N.* HIV risk and condom use in the adult heterosexual population in France between 1992 and 2001: return to the starting point? *AIDS 2004;18:805-9.*

FIGURE 9.6B *(continued)*

Begin by stating your position, so readers know where you stand. Then support it with facts and figures, logically organized and clearly written. Use examples or metaphors that readers can understand. Use statistics sparingly but include enough of them to support and reinforce your points.

Long lists of numbers might be appropriate in a backgrounder, but in a position paper, they will only clutter up your argument and cloud its sense. Make your point in clear, plain language; then select just the right statistic to support it. If you feel that a lot of statistics should be included as support material, put them in an appendix so they don't overpower the paper. Always provide the sources of your statistics. Readers who spend time with such information place a lot of weight on the authority behind the numbers.

Consider Both Sides   Although a position paper should come down strongly on your side of an issue, don't ignore opposing sides. You are expected to amass as much information as you can in support of your point of view, but don't stack the cards.

"Card-stacking" is a propaganda device whereby all the supporting arguments are given but no opposing points are mentioned. This gives the impression that the favorable evidence is more compelling than it really is. Such a position paper may seem impressive at first glance, but when readers discover other points of view, they will distrust not only this message but also others you send them later.

It is far better to state opposing points of view and try to refute them than to ignore them. This is especially important when the opposition has some good points. Acknowledge the cons, but show why you think these points are outweighed by objective evidence. With this tactic, you will gain respect, even among your foes.

Consider the Public   Although most position papers are written for internal use by management, some are written for distribution to other publics. Even when writing a position paper you believe will only be used internally, you must keep in mind other potential publics.

For example, a position paper may be written for presentation to the board of directors by management in an attempt to explain company policies to stockholders. But Wall Street analysts may ask to see the company's position too. And what about the media's business editors? They may ask for and should be given copies.

This can pose a serious problem for you as a PR writer, because information that makes sense to your management may not make sense to the external publics or to stockholders. It would be ideal, of course, to write one version of the position paper for use by all possible publics, but the nature of the issue may make this impractical. You may have to write more than one version of the same paper. You should not tell a different story in each version; rather, you should tell the same story differently and appropriately. Remember too that different publics may be more concerned with some questions than with others. Alter the emphasis of each version of your position paper accordingly.

Recommendations   It is generally perceived as bad form to be against something without offering an alternative solution. Taking a position means being both against one thing and for something else. If you omit your alternative proposals from your position paper, you will inevitably be asked what you recommend as a suitable substitute for something you oppose.

For example, on the NGV situation, currently there are stringent regulations on the conversion of vehicles from gasoline to alternate fuels (except pure battery electric vehicles). If a bill to reduce these regulations is being proposed and you want to support it, how do you address concerns about safety? Supporting the proposal carries an implicit obligation to help arrive at a resolution of issues posed by opponents.

TABLE 9.2	*10 Awesome Media Relations Rules*

"Pitching," or proposing stories to news media people, requires skills that can be acquired by public relations practitioners. Here are 10 rules that one media relations practitioner uses in her successful business.

The Media Relations Maven's
10 Awesome Media Relations Rules
By Margo M. Mateas
The Media Relations Maven

1. Plan the Pitch

Before you pitch, do your homework. Read recent articles. Look up the publication and reporter's profiles in your media directory. Check out its website and editorial calendar. Discover what the media target wants and *then* pitch a story that brings important new information to its audience. Know exactly how your story benefits the publication.

2. Think Like a Reporter

How does this story benefit the publication and its readers? Does it provide real facts, something of interest, something new and timely? If not, throw out the idea and start again! Ask the hard questions. Push back until you have something that will work.

3. Find a Story Angle

A good story serves more than your client or company; it provides interesting and useful information to the public at large. Know what a good story is and how to find it. Dig into the background, philosophy and talents of the organization and people you're pitching. Find the hidden story everyone else has missed.

4. Pick a Section

Have a specific type of story and a particular section in mind when you pitch. *"I thought this would be perfect for your Coastal Getaways section . . ."* This immediately lets the editor begin to see how your story will fit into the format.

5. Prepare Your Pitch Bag

Always have more than one angle or story to pitch in case the first one doesn't pan out. *"Oh, you just assigned a story on new healthcare solutions? How about one on how a new medical device is saving lives?"* Be able to switch tracks mid-conversation so you can explore additional story ideas.

6. Speak in Bullets

Prepare a bulleted "pitch sheet" with key selling points and background information and keep it in front of you

when pitching. Keep emails and verbal pitches short, too. Don't waste time dressing up the pitch. Boil it down to its most concise points. Don't bother saying your last name or the name of the product or service: just say what it does and paint a mental picture of its benefits for the editor.

7. Give a Clear Call to Action

First tell the reporter what you're asking for, then tell him why he should do it. "I've got a great profile for your lifestyle section . . . there's a new museum opening next month . . ." When scheduling interviews, never ask if a reporter is available, find out when and make it happen. "Is next Tuesday between ten and noon good for you?" Set aside a block of time and get the reporter to commit.

8. It's Never "A Good Time"

Don't apologize for pitching. Just do it well. Don't ask if an editor has time for you. Just call, get to the point and be done with it. If the editor sounds stressed, ask to call back at a better time.

9. They Won't Buy if You Don't Believe

Like any salesperson, you must love what you're selling. You must know what's great about what you're pitching, and believe in it. If you don't love what you're pitching, neither will the reporter. Don't let an editor dismiss you.

10. Become a Valued Resource

Establish relationships, not "drive-by pitches." Give now to get something later. If you hear of a story you know would interest an editor, give it to her, even if you won't get paid for it. It will pay off in coverage later.

Margo Mateas is president of the Public Relations Training Company, a firm that provides media relations and management training. Mateas' methods are used by the world's #1 public relations agency, Fortune 500 companies and more.

Sometimes position papers suggest new policy on an issue or support a recommended but not yet implemented policy. Position papers also can support existing policy in the face of proposed change.

Format

When the writing is completed, determine its format and method of distribution. A backgrounder or position paper intended for internal use may exist only in digital form on the organization's intranet or in the computers of specific spokespersons after being distributed as email attachments. If printed copies are needed, the backgrounder usually is printed on plain or letterhead paper, copied, assembled, stapled and then distributed. Those distributed outside the company may be produced the same way, or they may be published as a printed booklet or monograph, embellished with art, color, design and typography and printed on expensive paper or published on the organization's website.

Some organizations prepare backgrounders for public consumption on special forms. These forms contain a company heading with the word *backgrounder* prominent. Others, particularly those in heavily regulated industries that require a large number of backgrounders or position papers each year, produce punched versions suitable for inclusion in a loose-leaf notebook—much less expensive and more accessible—or put them on their websites.

Many backgrounders and some position papers include charts and illustrations to help explain topics. For formal reports, preparing graphics for either printing or Web use is usually done using computer software, sometimes by a graphic artist. However, you should be fully aware of their content, how they look and where they will appear in the finished report. Locating these visuals close to appropriate text segments makes the information easier to understand.

Special Uses

Although position papers have many uses, especially as frames of reference when questions come from journalists and to orient spokespeople and management personnel, they also have some special uses. An organization that wants to exploit all the avenues for advocating its point of view can use a position paper as the basis for an essay or a commentary to be submitted to the op-ed page in the local newspaper. The position paper should have enough documentation in it to stand alone as the basis of an op-ed piece. If it doesn't, go back to the backgrounder on which the position paper was based. That should give you more than enough information with which to work. Other kinds of documents also can be used as you prepare the op-ed piece, but if a position paper is executed well, there should not be much need to seek and use other information.

Another special area is the use of position papers as the locus for image ads and public service announcements (PSAs) for an organization. Position papers can be of enormous help in positioning or repositioning an organization as it tries to shape and project a consistent image.

Plans for action, as in lobbying for or against something, can spring directly from position papers. If, for example, there's a proposal to cut all government support for AFVs and place the determination totally in the marketplace, the position statement against that policy represents your first line of offense in furthering the cause. Backgrounders may also be of use, but it is the position paper that sets the direction and highlights the major points of contention.

Conclusions

- A media kit is a basic tool for working with the mass media.
- A media kit may be in many forms, including digital versions on websites and on CDs.
- Media kits are prepared especially for the use of particular media. It's not a situation in which one kit will do the job. The way the kit is delivered to the medium usually depends on the situation. It may be mailed if it's something the reporters need in advance. It may be hand-delivered to local media if it's a local event. It may be distributed at a news conference or available in the media room set up for a special event or a crisis.
- Fact sheets for organizations are of two types—functional and historical. The functional ones may be organizational or devoted to special events.
- Fact sheets should always be included in media kits but are also used with other publics such as investors, donors, volunteers and supporters.
- The advantage of a digital media kit on a website is that it offers more material and more flexibility.
- Although the shell for a traditional media kit is something you usually have made up in quantities, you probably will have a special media kit made up for an event, one that promotes the theme of the event. Each media kit has a letter to go with it. The letter is for the person who will be using the kit. If the kit is mailed, it's a cover letter. If the kit is given to a reporter, the letter is inside and generally tells the reporter basic facts and what is in the kit.
- Media kits are used by organizations to convey basic information about the organization, to tell media about special events, to hand out at news conferences and to make available in times of crises.
- Media kit contents vary according to not only the technology of the medium but also the situation for its use. Nevertheless, media kits do have some basic contents: organizational fact sheets, historical fact sheets, biographical material on the organization's principals, a backgrounder and perhaps position papers, serial publications and the annual report if there is one, plus a page of facts about the organization. The kit may or may not have a news release, but ordinarily it does have at least one straight news story related to the occasion for the media kit's use. It may or may not have visuals.
- The key to developing useful media kits is to think of who is going to be using them and what that newsperson is likely to need.
- Media kits for special events in addition to being thematic are likely to have visuals and more news releases, especially features on certain aspects of the event. You want to be sure that you include information on organizations cooperating with you in the event, information that you should clear with them before including it.
- Media kits given out at news conferences are designed especially for that occasion and should provide substantial background information for the reporter, whose time at the news conference is going to be limited.
- Media kits offered on CDs require some of the elements of basic kits, but you need to make the material easily accessible.
- Some media kits distributed at news conferences deal with crises, but generally, the crisis media kit has to be prepared quickly from available materials with a brief summary of the situation and quotes from the principals added. The core of these is regularly

updated, reliable basic information on the organization itself as well as how to get more information.

- The materials in media kits should also be available in media rooms set up to accommodate reporters covering special events and crises. All materials should be dated and numbered or otherwise coded so you can identify the specific piece later. You need to keep a record of what was given to whom with what medium and when, not only for internal tracking but also for later reference. Media kits project an image of the organization, and it's important that you remember that the media kit is speaking for the organization when no one else is there. Be sure it's a good representative of the organization.
- For many events, having media personnel register and receive credentials—usually badges—is essential to maintain security and allow media personnel access where they need it. It's important to define who's eligible to receive media credentials.
- Keep your website updated during a crisis. That helps handle media demands for fresh information. You'll need at the crisis communication center in addition to your computer a printer and a copier to provide hard copies of the updates.
- A *media pitch* is just what it sounds like—a proposal to a media outlet. It's intended to "sell" a story idea on a specific topic.
- The media pitch can be in the form of an email, a phone call, a fax or a letter, depending on how well you know the person for whom the pitch is intended.
- The pitch can be for a new product or service, a new use for an existing product, an event or a movie—in other words, just about anything.
- The media pitch is the accepted way to make media representatives aware of a story idea in a clear and concise format.
- Each pitch should be targeted to a specific medium and should contain specific, unusual story.
- Every organization can count on receiving inquiries about background information and positions on issues. It should prepare for these by producing backgrounders and position papers in advance.
- Backgrounders serve as sources of information for company executives, public relations writers, media personnel, financial analysts, the external publics and a variety of other publics.
- Backgrounders should always provide a historical context, a description of the current situation and a discussion of the implications of the matter under study. This information should be free of opinion.
- Position papers state a position on a topic. They are basically opinions supported by a few facts. They should treat opposing points of view as well as supporting arguments.
- When the company takes a position against something, it should also suggest alternative solutions.
- Backgrounders and position papers—especially backgrounders—should fully acknowledge sources of information used in their preparation.
- Clear writing is a must.
- Position papers can be especially useful as the inspiration and support for essays and commentaries for the op-ed pages of local newspapers.
- Position papers may be used as the locus for image-building ads and PSAs.
- Position papers can set the agenda for action, such as lobbying for or against an issue, task or process.

Exercises

1. Prepare a news release for newspapers from the position paper in Figure 9.6.
2. Write a news release for a specialized publication from the same position paper. Name the publication and state its purpose.
3. Write cover letters for both, telling each editor why the story has value for that publication's audience.
4. Choose a topic that concerns your school, such as the increasing use of drugs, getting term papers off the Internet, other forms of cheating or lack of diversity in the student or faculty population. Do your research and write a backgrounder on the topic.
5. Imagine that you are the public relations director for a city's transportation system, which includes, along with an electric subway system, fleets of gasoline-powered vehicles such as buses as well as special vans for the disabled. The city frequently has air-quality alerts that keep people who are at risk inside. Also, exhaust fumes are killing trees and other vegetation along the freeways. To help reduce emissions, the company has decided to use natural gas-fueled fleet vehicles. Prepare the opening paragraphs of a position paper to support that opinion and, in outline form, indicate what you would include in the rest of the document.
6. The position paper in Figure 9.6 will be subjected to criticism from various publics. List these publics and suggest which areas are open to dispute and/or skepticism.

Use InfoTrac® College Edition to access information on topics in this chapter from hundreds of periodicals and scholarly journals.

Writing for Select Publics

*P*eople who belong to an organization, as either employees or volunteers, or those who closely identify with an organization because of special relationships, whether business or personal, are select publics. The organization controls what, when and how messages are delivered to these groups.

Message Design Concepts

Visual interest is the magnet to messages. Visuals also increase a message's impact and recall. Design is not an additive to persuasion. It is a necessity.

Test your own recall. When you see a three-pointed star in a circle, the name Mercedes probably pops into your head. A "swoosh" sign reminds you immediately of Nike. Along with that recognition of the symbol may also be the slogan: Just do it. Such association isn't accidental. These organizations and many others have mastered the concepts of message design. They know how to shape messages and repeat them often enough that relevant publics take notice and remember.

Message design concepts involve the careful integration of words, images, motion and sounds into a message that easily and clearly conveys an idea to relevant publics. The best of these messages usually are striking in their simplicity. Publics don't need to ponder what they mean. The message comes through even if exposure to it is only momentary. That seems simple enough, but a casual review of messages in the media, including the Internet, suggests that many people don't understand this very well.

The purpose of this chapter is to share with you some broad concepts you can use as you write and design messages for different media. Study and relate them to subsequent chapters in this text. Let's look first at the creative process.

The Creative Process

Some people think of creativity as the time when an individual has a "eureka experience." That does happen sometimes, but if you wait for the light bulb in your head to flash brightly, you may miss a deadline for your client. As a public relations writer, you're expected to produce on demand and present creative ideas to a client's publics. You simply can't wait for the muse to move you. Creativity can be a very personal process, of course, but when you're serving a client, the process is likely to be a group activity that comes only after several steps are taken in concert with others in your organization.

The first step in developing a viable creative concept is to assemble as much relevant information as possible. Review Chapter 4 to refresh yourself about research. You may be expected to gather this information, but it is more likely that other people in your organization will do that.

Who gathers the information is not as important as how well the information is documented. And in the case of contradictory information, which sources of verification seem to be most reliable? These people also may provide interpretations of the information. We recommend that you review Chapter 2 because you, as a writer, are ultimately responsible legally and ethically for what you say. You can't simply say, "They gave me the information and said it was correct."

It is expected and common that you'll have much more information than you actually need. Among other things, this information should clearly describe target publics and their characteristics. The information also should lead to a concise statement of the purpose for messages in a campaign.

You're the writer. You are the person who has to convert this material into messages. So, the second step is to analyze the information in light of the needs of the client. You'll probably do this as a member of a creative team that may involve a creative director, an art director and an account services person. Several brainstorming sessions may be needed about how the information can be used. It is at this stage that no idea, even ones considered to be off the wall, should be left unexamined. After these ideas have been weighed, a few—such as three—are selected for further development.

The third step is to evaluate these ideas from the point of view of how well they communicate the client's purpose as interpreted by target publics. Does one idea convey the purpose of the campaign better than others? Are target publics more likely to respond to another idea? If so, the viability of these ideas may need to be tested for possible results. Even if there is no problem like that, message testing still may be needed when the ideas seem equally compelling. Your role as writer, then, is to write a rough draft copy that can be tested.

You know what the purpose is and who the target publics are. You're now ready for the fourth step—deciding exactly what you want to say. This involves decisions about how you will finally write the message, what format is best to convey it and the overall image you want to project. If no copy tests were done, you begin with a blank sheet of paper or a blank screen. If testing was done, you have the draft copy to begin with, and the task is to rewrite and polish it in light of what these tests revealed.

How you write a message may be influenced also by the media used to deliver it.

Ads don't cross media very well. An ad for a newspaper won't work for its online paper. Same for a magazine ad. Obviously print ads for any medium are not going to work for television. Although the concept should be the same, the message must be crafted to fit each medium.

What is the approach you want to take? Is the overall image friendly, open, selective, confident or what? The combination of words, illustrations, sounds, layout, type, color and so on all combine to project an image. The goal is to select, shape and limit message elements to collectively project a clear image for the client. Four guidelines may help you reach that goal:

1. The verbal part of the message is the most important ingredient. It should control the selection and use of all other elements in the message.
2. Seek a consistent look from one message to the next, from one medium to the next.

3. Simplify everything. Delete all elements that are not related to the central point of the message. These are excesses that clutter the message and could confuse publics.

4. Use as few elements as possible and use only those that contribute directly to the understanding of the message.

Following these guidelines is easier to say than to do. One reason for this is that you must use symbols as substitutes for ideas.

Symbols

In your tool chest of symbols are words, type, color, sound and illustrations of all sorts, including animation, pictures, art, logos, trademarks and graphs of various types. Even when these symbols are used well, many messages may still go awry because receivers of these messages attach their own meanings to them. Those meanings may be unlike what you intended. You must recognize up front that you do not control receivers' meanings. You control only the symbols you use to shape a message. You must select them carefully and craft them with sensitivity to how they may be interpreted.

Words are the basic building blocks of all messages. They are not ideas themselves but are representations of ideas. Words are usually thought of as being concrete or abstract.

Concrete Words   Concrete words are more likely than abstract ones to be interpreted as intended by target publics. The word *table* signifies an object, but modifiers often are needed to give it texture and form. You've seen many tables, so you have an image of what a table generally looks like. The problem is that your image of a table may be unlike the image held by receivers of your message. If you write "The solid walnut, oval table has a soft patina that glows with age, and its four gracefully curved legs are carved intricately," you've painted a picture of a particular table that target publics can "see." Now the table arouses a more precise image. A good writer chooses words carefully to make understanding easier and more complete.

Abstract Words   Abstract words are not as easy to use with the same precision as concrete words. The word *love*, for example, represents an idea, not an object like a table. It represents an abstract idea that can be interpreted in countless ways. Does love mean attraction, genuine affection, sexual relations or something else? Love, like other abstract words, needs descriptors and context to give it clearer meaning. For example, "I love being your spouse because you're also my best friend" defines what love means to the person uttering the statement. And it is likely to be understood and appreciated more fully by the person to whom it is directed.

Good writers make ideas clear. They can put words together so ideas seem to come alive. Their dynamism is arresting and stimulating. That happens only when writers remember to describe, using analogies or metaphors and similar devices that give dimension and substance to the message. Yet, the words they use must be ones that have common meanings to their target publics. Otherwise, misunderstanding and misinformation are unintended outcomes. Except when spoken, words find their primary expression in type.

Type

Type is a series of letter forms that makes a message visible. In this sense, type is one kind of visual communication. The letter forms in a font of type include all of the characters of the alphabet, punctuation marks, numbers and other objects such as quotation marks, ampersands and so forth. Figure 10.1 shows some of the major characteristics of letter forms. There also are several variations to a regular type font, such as italics, boldface and others. When used sparingly, each of these variations can be used to emphasize part of a message. What many people fail to understand is that the correct use of type depends on two key points: legibility and appropriateness.

Legibility   Computers now make many type fonts available by simply clicking a mouse. That means millions of people who select type fonts every day may be unskilled in the proper use of type. They often select fonts that are not very readable. This detracts from a message and may drive away readers of any printed pieces, including website visitors. Some people say that computers have done a lot of harm to the quality of contemporary message design. That may or may not be true. What is true, however, is that the first consideration in selecting type fonts is whether they are legible. If you are unsure about the legibility of a type font, consult an expert in typography.

Legibility is of special concern when you write lengthy text. Copy length presumably is driven by the need to include vital information, but long blocks of text tire readers quickly. If you use type that is even slightly harder to read, you unnecessarily build problems into your message. Be careful. If the type you like most is legible, you then should look at its appropriateness.

Appropriateness   The concept of appropriateness is more slippery than that of legibility. In its simplest sense, appropriateness is concerned with the connotative qualities of a type font. Table 10.1 illustrates four type families. How do you react personally to each of the four fonts? Do they project connotative aspects that may suggest certain kinds of uses? If so, that's the idea of appropriateness.

FIGURE 10.1

Anatomy of a Letter   *Type is measured in points from the top of the highest ascender to the bottom of the lowest descender. The x-height is the height of the body of lowercase letters. Roman type has serifs—extensions at the extremities of characters that make it easy to read. Type without serifs is called sans serif.*

TABLE 10.1	*Four Type Families* These four fonts of type represent four type families. Each has certain characteristics that identify it with a particular family. Look at these examples and consider potential uses for each of these four type groups. Roman and sans serif fonts are what you'll use most often. Cursive and decorative fonts are used only in special situations.

Roman or Serif
This is 30-point Times New Roman.

Sans Serif or Gothic
This is 30-point Avant Garde.

Cursive or Script
This is 30-point Medici Script.

𝔇𝔢𝔠𝔬𝔯𝔞𝔱𝔦𝔳𝔢
This is 30-point Linotext.

If you're writing and designing a proclamation for an official to present during Labor Day ceremonies, you might use a decorative font in the headline or in other ways, such as in initial letters. That would seem appropriate. On the other hand, you may use a cursive or script font if you're writing and designing a formal invitation to a charity ball. That's appropriate, isn't it? And you probably wouldn't use a heavy railroad Gothic for that invitation.

One decision is whether to use a serif or sans serif font. Much depends on the medium, again. Websites use a sans serif because pixels on the computer screen tend to fragment the serif, complicating legibility. Furthermore, what is read on the computer generally gets less time per frame than attention per printed page. If you're designing a 24-page booklet, though, with lots of copy, use one of the most readable roman or serif fonts. Don't just use a sans serif to jam in more copy. Background color matters too, in print and on the screen, and remember that the choice of type has connotative impact.

Type evokes certain feelings in us. It has personality. The clothing you wear says something about you and what image you want to project to others. Dressing for a job interview is different attire than a trip to the fitness center. Like clothing, the type you select can enhance and help clarify your message or it can confuse it. When you write, we assume that you select words very carefully. Use the same care when you select type for its appropriateness.

Type as Art   Although the design of type has always been seen as an art form, the advent of computers has introduced the idea of type as art. With the right software, you can shape a word or several into spirals, waves and other shapes as you wish. In effect, you should treat this digitally altered type like a piece of art. It becomes a visual just like photographs or hand-drawn art. But be cautious about overuse. You can get carried away with this technique and create a visual that is difficult to comprehend. That defeats your purpose.

Logos

A logo is a symbol of an organization, group or person. It is something like your face. Friends know what you look like and can relate your face to your name, much like a logo. A good logo has several purposes. First, it should make a positive impression on us. Second, it should be recognizable. Third, it should have uniqueness that separates it from all other logos, especially competitors', so people can relate the logo to the correct organization, product, cause or issue. Fourth, it should age well. Fifth, it should translate faithfully across media. Taken individually, each criterion seems fairly simple. Taken as a group, however, these criteria are difficult to meet.

Simplicity   The watchword regarding logos is simplicity. Now that many organizations are diversified and some operate across many cultures and political boundaries, logos are even more important. And simplicity is at an even higher premium. The golden arches should mean basically the same thing to publics in Singapore, Caracas, Oslo, Johannesburg, Beijing and New Delhi. If a logo is ambiguous, it fails.

Format   The format of a logo can vary. It might be an abstract symbol or a pictograph. Either should evoke an emotional response. On the other hand, it might be a logotype in which the name of the organization, group or individual is set in type, usually in an uncommon font that is legible and appropriate, such as Sony's logo. Another format is the trademark or descriptive symbol. A trademark can be a name, symbol or a combination used to identify the product of a business. It always should be accompanied by the trademark (™) sign.

Design   If your client is a new company, you begin with a clean slate. If not, you need to know the history of the logo in current use and why a change is contemplated. Organizations that change logos or names, for whatever reason, face an expensive task. And publics don't like changes to things they're accustomed to. Expense and discontent by publics may set the stage for failure, even if the new design is good.

There are five stages of logo design, each built around questions. The first one is research. If it is a new organization, what image does the leadership want to project? If the client has a history, what was the old logo and what did it come to signify to target publics? How closely do relevant publics identify with it? Is it possible that a drastic change might confuse important publics? Why does management want to change the logo? Other questions may arise as you go about researching these questions.

Second, there must be a clear definition of target publics. Who are the people? What are they like? What do they believe? How do they relate to the client? Answers to questions like these often are critical to developing a "feel" for what a good logo might look like. If the logo will be used across cultures or political boundaries, you must be sensitive to potential problems. That makes it difficult to come up with a single logo that works everywhere and under all conditions.

Third, use in different formats may be an issue. Presumably, your original logo design may fit on a letter-size sheet of paper. Will it retain its design integrity if used as a 10-foot-high symbol on the face of the home office or on buildings at global plant sites? Can it be used as a lapel pin and still maintain its design integrity? Will it translate well in all print media, television, film and websites? Will it be distinctive enough to hold its own if used in a promotion with other logos?

Fourth, does the client have enough money and a commitment to use the logo every time as it was designed? That's a critical question that is sometimes overlooked. It is a good idea, even for clients with deep pockets, to design a logo to be executed in a single color. Why? Use of a second or third color in the design may make the logo unrecognizable if it ever appears only in one color. Of course, it may appear in just one color very often, such as in retail ads in newspapers. Costs are a consideration too. The annual cost of using a second color in a logo can be staggering. Design the logo in a single color and add color only on special occasions.

Fifth, a logo should never be designed with the intent of replacing it a year or so from now. The best logos today generally are ones that have been around a long time. Always design with the future in mind. And when you think you have a final design, ask this question: "Will it last?"

Color

Color is an important part of our lives. We encounter color everywhere. It may depress us or make us feel happy. It may suggest springtime freshness or, like odors, drive us away from something. For example, cosmetics packaged in brown often remain on the shelf. And sugar remains there also if it does not have a good bit of blue on the wrapper. Research also suggests that green is a no-no on sugar packages. Why? No one knows exactly, but color does seem to send messages to people. How people interpret color is, of course, entirely subjective. Our memories, experiences and environment apparently influence the associations we make. But there are some broad psychological implications you need to know.

Psychology of Color   No one knows exactly why, but colors seem to stimulate or calm our nervous systems. People tend to associate "warm" colors, like reds, yellows and blends of them, with heat, fire and sun. But "cool" colors, like the blues and greens, are most often related to such things as sky, sea and wilderness.

Our color preferences are complex. They seem to be influenced by emotional behavior, lifestyle, gender, age and our sense of style and fashion. You know, of course, that color in fashion changes frequently, especially as related to the clothing we wear. And it is often the case that color trends in other areas are also seen in the materials organizations prepare for their publics. You need to be aware of these trends and to know the most common emotional reactions people have to colors. For websites and other international exposure, be sensitive to the meaning of certain colors to particular audiences.

Red is a dramatic color that excites not only the bull in the ring but people as well. Red colors stimulate us and are often associated with aggressive behavior, passion, success and impulse. It is fairly common, also, to see some political candidates for major offices wearing their red "power" ties or, in the case of female candidates, blouses. The color orange is a blend of red and yellow. We tend to think of it as a bright, happy and festive color that is not as dramatic as red.

Dark blue colors seem to have calming, relaxing effects. The dark blue of night signifies the end of the day and winding down from a frenetic pace. Blues are also associated with tradition, orderliness and stability. That may explain why so many financial institutions use blues somewhat extensively. Light blues are also associated with cleanliness. On the other hand, purple is thought of as daring, and it is sometimes seen as being royal, elegant and expensive. The violet colors are associated frequently with feelings of intimacy.

But bright yellow seems to raise our blood pressure, although it is often associated with health and well-being. That may explain why you see so much yellow on food packages. Yellow also is thought of as the color of optimism, presumably related to the brightness of a new day.

We tend to associate cool green colors with nature, regeneration and self-preservation. Green is used a lot by organizations and products related to the environment and cleanliness. On the other hand, white is a symbol of purity and innocence, as in bridal dress in Western countries. But in some Eastern societies it is worn at funerals. Black is especially interesting because we tend to think of it as a symbol of mourning. It also can have a sinister connotation, but if it is used in lingerie, it is seen as sexy. It also may be thought of as elegant, as in a "black-tie" occasion.

These color associations are all bound by culture. Look again at how we described white and black. Because we now communicate across cultures routinely, even when we don't intend to, you must be sensitive to the ways colors are perceived in other cultures. That means you need to spend a good bit of time researching the subject because it is too extensive for this chapter.

Qualities of Color Colors have three qualities. One is *hue*. Hue is synonymous with the word color. It is one of the primary colors—yellow, red or blue—or a blend of them. *Value* refers to the level of lightness or darkness in a color. Light blue has a higher color value, for example, than dark blue. *Saturation* refers to the intensity or vividness of color. A full color is saturated. Adding a complement of a color, or gray, lessens the intensity or vividness. Colors of lower intensities are said to be toned down.

Paper Color Paper comes in many colors. Paper stock can enhance or detract from a message in a printed piece. The same holds true of background color on websites. When reproducing color pictures of people, skin tones are the guiding light of good reproduction. That means that you generally must confine your paper selection to whites and eggshell colors. Other colors can make people look unnatural. For example, a picture of people printed on light green paper makes them look sick. On yellows, they appear jaundiced. Test background colors on websites to see how they work, but remember that what you see on the monitor may not be entirely reliable. Be on guard.

Pantone® Color Reproduction of color in printing was for decades an inexact science at best. You had to select from color swatches, much like you do when you go to a paint store when painting your room. Printers had to mix inks with a little dab of this, a little dab of that and so on. Many of them were remarkably gifted at giving people what they wanted.

The process is more precise now because of the use of the Pantone Color Matching System. This is an international color language that lets you specify colors by numbered ink colors. Printers follow these specifications to give you exactly what you ask for. A companion system in use on computers is the Pantone by Letraset Color Markers, available at most art supply stores. These markers are coordinated with Pantone color inks so you can design on a screen and specify colors that match in the printing process. Again, remember that what you see on the monitor may not be exactly what you get.

Color on websites is a special consideration. Consider this from designer Broxon Sears:

> The difference in screen resolution and calibrating causes a difference in how colors are displayed on users' monitors. Web-safe colors are a basic set of 216 colors all browsers display uniformly, regardless of platform. Working only with these colors, you can be sure that art you prepare for the

Web will not dither on a system set to display 256 colors, the minimum number of colors that a system supports, although not always the same set of 256 colors across systems. The difference between the two major systems, Macs and PCs, is 40 colors, so using the 216 colors will assure proper display on either computer.[1]

Photographs and Art

Photographs and art should be selected first because they are appropriate to the message. A well-known brand of watches once ran a large ad that said its watches are for people with inner strength. A photograph of a man filled the top half of the space. The picture was of a professional athlete but looked as if it had been taken during a police booking. All that was needed was a set of numbers across his chest. The athlete's appearance is immaterial. What is important is that no attempt was made to interpret the idea of inner strength or how the athlete reflected it. It remains a puzzle how the picture relates specifically to inner strength.

Deciding that photographs and art are or are not appropriate is a judgment call. But the process is made easier if you have a very clear idea about what the message is supposed to say. The watch ad may have turned out the way it did because its creators were unsure of what they meant by inner strength.

A primary function of visuals is to get the attention of readers or viewers. The picture in the watch ad certainly did that. But the attention was probably negative, at least momentarily. Negative attention can sometimes be useful, but mostly when the purpose of the message is to warn readers or viewers away from something or to encourage them to take protective or evasive action.

Another major function of photographs and art is to impart information. Suppose your client is a jeweler who specializes in diamond wedding rings. You might use a visual that shows a man holding out a diamond to a woman whose face is alive with excitement. The headline says, "The answer is yes." The picture distills the essence of the message because of its appropriateness.

Photographs and art also should never be used merely to dress a presentation. Each should contribute specifically to the purpose of the message. Neither should they be selected simply because they are beautiful nor because you are fond of them.

Infographics

The term *infographics* signifies the use of visual devices intended to communicate complex information quickly and clearly. These devices include charts, diagrams, graphs, tables, maps and lists. You may have endured a lengthy discourse that used a lot of economic data. Even if it was entirely accurate and written simply, it still may have been confusing. Perhaps you got lost in some of the details and had to go back to previous points to iron out uncertainties. In that case, you may have wished the writer had used infographics to explain the text. Several techniques are available, and their use depends on what you're trying to say.

Devices   Among the most common infographic devices are *bar* (horizontal) and *column* (vertical) charts that can visually summarize lots of statistical information. *Pie charts* are usually seen as circles or ovals in which slices or wedges of the pie show data as parts of the whole.

Diagrams can be used to show how a system works, such as the internal combustion engine that powers your car. In the case of an engine, the diagram will be what is known as a *cutaway* that shows internal parts. In other cases, the diagram may be an *organizational chart* that shows lines of authority, or a *systems flowchart* that shows sequential movement.

Illustrated graphics use images—rather than bars, lines or pies—to relate data. The snapshots features used every day by *USA Today* are consistently good examples of this technique. *Tables* are commonly used. And they are easier to design than graphs. Just because tables may contain lots of numbers isn't a reason to view them as anything less than infographics.

With the advent of computers, the availability of all sorts of *maps* on disks has increased the use of maps as informational graphics. If your organization has a plant in Borneo and you want to feature it in the annual report, for example, you can quickly give readers a geographic context in which to understand the message more clearly.

Bulleted or *numbered lists* are also infographic devices. Bullets are appropriate when you need to show related items that are not sequential. Numbered lists should be used when the items have an order.

Guidelines for Good Usage   Check and double-check all facts. Nothing is more distressing to people than to discover an error in fact or in rendering infographics. Make sure you have all the information you need before you begin designing. The design of the graphic should never overwhelm the content, but rather amplify it.

Everything should be labeled clearly. Be as precise as possible. You've probably seen tables of data in which you got lost, temporarily at least, and had difficulty understanding exactly what you were seeing. Remember that your first concern is to communicate the whole message as clearly and easily as possible. Each infographic must help. If it does not, it should be redesigned or not be used.

Sound and Motion

Radio, television, videos, film and the Internet present opportunities to use techniques and symbols uncommon to other media. When used well, these techniques can add measurably to a message. To use them well, however, you must observe certain cautions. Let's look first at sound for radio and audio for computers or television.

Radio and Other Audio

Broadcast news and features are discussed in Chapter 8. So, this section on radio and audio applies only to commercial messages and public service announcements. A message for delivery on radio requires that you resolve several questions. You know, presumably, who your target publics are and the strategy and creative tactics you want to use. You'll begin with a script sheet. The verbal part of the message is confined to the right of the script sheet. The left side has all of the production information.

The key thing to remember is to write the message first. Refine it until you're sure it is exactly what you want to say. Then write production cues on the left. Once these are done, break the message into chunks so what is said corresponds to the production cues. These cues vary a lot depending on elements in the production such as voice, sounds, music, etc. Usually the message is produced in a recording studio in which an announcer reads the script, with music and sound effects. When final production is done, the message is digitally produced for distribution.

Sound effects can be copied from sound libraries. Music can be used from music libraries. Some of it may be in the public domain so you can use it without charge. Much of it, however, is copyrighted, and you'll need to pay a fee to use it. Most permission fees have specific limits and have residual fees. These apply to all creative materials and to artistic talent. You'll need to rely on the station or recording studio that does your production to advise you of the music's copyright status. In some cases, you may need to commission professionals to

"See! Right there, in between all that scrolling data and those splashy graphics, right next to that little station ID thingy ... I think I can actually see the news anchor!"

Source: From Quill Magazine. Used by permission of Alan Vitello.

compose original lyrics and scores to get the particular effect you want. If so, be sure to work out in advance who owns the copyrights to this new material.

You may want to do location sound recording to get the "feel" that you want for your message. That involves a sound crew, a truck, travel, lodging, meals and so on. Expect to pay a lot more than if it is done in a station or recording studio. Most audio is produced digitally.

Television, Video, Film and the Internet

Each of these media uses moving images as well as sound. Designing a message for television begins with the development of a storyboard if it is for an ad or a public service announcement. See Chapter 13 for a sample storyboard. A storyboard shows sequential rough sketches of major scenes. The script appears below or adjacent to each frame of the board so it is easy to connect verbal content to the visual, including animation, for the digital product.

If your message is longer than a traditional spot or PSA, you may construct the message in production script form. Ask your instructor for a copy of a production script in the instructor's manual that goes with this text. This example is a segment of a time-coded film script. Time coding measures the length of each scene, many lasting no more than seconds. Action cues, music and other production information appear down the left side and the narration is on the right, just like a radio script.

Try to maximize a major asset—the ability to show movement. Generally, avoid talking heads because they don't exploit this quality. Movement attracts attention, and it can hold it if the verbal content and sound effects blend well with it. Don't use action for the sake of action. Use it for a purpose. Make it fit what is being said.

Production of these messages usually is assigned to television stations or video production studios. They ordinarily are selected through a bidding process based on the lowest and best bid. The latter point is critical because some production people are better than others at doing some kinds of production. You want to be sure that your message is produced as intended.

Even if your message is short, the costs of production can be high. And the way you build your message may drive the costs even higher. For example, the nature of your message may demand that production be in the field. On-site production is generally a lot more expensive than in studios, if for no other reason than travel, meals, rooms, the production crew, equipment and other expenses. So be sensitive to costs as you develop the message. Your client will appreciate that.

If your production is to be distributed through a website on the Internet, it is a good idea to search sites that have canned video segments you can use. Some segments are free. Others require fees. Look closely at what is available, but don't be surprised if you can't find something that fits your needs perfectly. Prerecorded materials are available, though expensive. Video outlets can provide film and high-quality sequences for almost any project, although you may have to produce project-specific video for use on the site. Websites are less expensive to build than they are to maintain.

A word of caution: because production equipment is so available now, there is a tendency to think that anyone with the technology can produce professional-quality materials. That is not likely. Pay for professional production.

Qualities of Good Message Design

There's no mystery to good message design. Certain qualities should be kept in mind as you work.

Clear Creative Concept

We've already noted that you must have a clear strategy that focuses on the key point you want to communicate to publics. But a clear message concept is not the same thing. It is the creative way you decide to interpret the strategy. It is the tactical way you finally shape the message. It affects all elements in the message.

Suppose your client is a candidate for governor in your state. The candidate's strategy is to make renewable resources an essential part of every campaign message. The question is: How do you interpret renewable resources in a meaningful way to each public?

One message in a series might be built around the candidate's personal view of the importance of conservation. For example, the copy might say "(Name) believes in careful use of resources for sustainability." This can be expanded in the body of the copy and illustrated, perhaps, with the candidate discussing water recycling at a purification plant. Another message might say something like "(Name) believes that people must take personal responsibility for their own behavior." The illustration could develop and support that idea by showing the candidate's family sorting disposables in recycling bins.

The point is that a good creative concept is one that focuses all elements of the message on a specific idea. Not two or three ideas. Just one. Creative interpretations of strategy for a client are limited only by your imagination.

Getting and Holding Attention

A good creative concept gets and holds attention. Getting attention may be fairly easy, but holding attention can be difficult. That's because publics are inundated with information and they're busy. A well-executed concept encourages readers and viewers to pay attention to the whole message, not just a small part of it. This calls for the careful integration of words, visuals and design. Weakness in any of these areas can drive people away.

Understanding Publics

One of the most critical problems in developing a good creative concept is the degree to which you really understand the publics for which a message is intended. Refer to the gubernatorial candidate again. Conservation may, and often does, mean various things to different publics.

For example, are there differences in perceptions of conservation in different lifestyles and among different ethnic groups? If so, what are they? You'd better find out if you don't know. This is where the research information mentioned earlier can be of special use. Will the same message work for all of these groups or must you tailor the message to each group? It depends. You'll be lucky if a single message will work for all.

Publics often discount quickly messages they perceive as not reflecting their beliefs. Unless they are predisposed to the point of the message, they're likely to discount it. The claim that you should know publics goes well beyond semantics. It signifies the degree to which you are limited by your knowledge of their beliefs and behavior. Developing a message without this kind of knowledge guarantees that it will be less successful than expected.

Good Organization

Your message should be organized so that it seems to flow naturally from point to point. When readers or viewers encounter a message that challenges their ability to decipher content, they are likely to move on to another and forget you. You have to give them a reason to volunteer their time to understand what you are saying.

The way you write the message helps with its organization. And the way it is laid out in printed form or presented on a computer screen also gives a sense of organization. Layout—the physical arrangement of elements showing how they are related—that seems haphazard is recognized quickly by publics as disorganized, even if they are unskilled in such matters. They wonder if they should volunteer their time to pay attention to what you say. Many decide not to.

Visual Principles

You should keep in mind a few visual principles as you put together a message. These principles should be applied after you've written the verbal part of a message. They should be applied when you do a layout for a printed piece or a storyboard for television, video or a website. Layout deals with the physical arrangement of elements and how they are related. A storyboard is a series of layouts that shows the sequential development of an animated message.

These visual principles are important for several reasons. The human eye tends to perceive a message by grouping information by similarity, proximity and continuity. Elements that don't fit arouse dissonance, which may prompt questions about the message itself as well as the source of the message. That tends to drive publics away.

People also sometimes "see" messages that are not overt, but only implied. This can be especially devastating if an implication is unintended, because it invites unwanted speculation. It is best not to rely on inference. It is difficult enough to communicate overtly. Why create potential problems by using inference? Some people are more visually acute than others. They "see" much more in a message than do other people. This explains, at least in part, why the meanings they attach to a message may be quite different from interpretations by less visually acute people.

When people look at your message, they filter it through their past experiences. They apply their own values and belief systems to interpret the meaning of a message. Remember, also, that in Western cultures people are taught to view messages from left to right, top to bottom and front to back. People in some other cultures learn to address messages from right to left, bottom to top and back to front. Those points need to be kept in mind if your message is going across cultures.

With those points as background, let's look now at eight visual principles.

Balance

Some people say that balance is the most essential of the visual principles. Perhaps the easiest way to envision this concept is to draw an imaginary vertical line down the center of a sheet of paper. Keep this sheet in mind as we look at two kinds of balance.

Formal   When all of the message elements are equal in visual weight on both sides of that imaginary line, the balance is *formal* or *symmetrical*. Formal balance connotes stability, security, authority, leadership and thoughtfulness. It also may be seen as unexciting, unimaginative and lacking tension or movement. Its primary value is that readers or viewers don't have to work hard to see relationships between message elements.

Informal   Placing elements of unequal visual weights on either side of that imaginary line produces *informal* or *asymmetrical* balance. It offers less stability but it generally is seen as being more interesting and exciting. It seems to require more effort by readers and viewers to perceive the whole message. It can be a little unsettling to some people. A message using informal balance is seen as dynamic, fresh, inviting, casual, creative and friendly.

Visual Weight

Applying the principles of balance depends also on your ability to understand the concept of *visual weight*, which transcends size. For example, a small, dark visual may have as much or more visual weight than one much larger in lighter tones. Black is heavier than white. Intense colors are heavier than those that have been toned down. The point is that you have to think in terms of visual weight and size as well as the distribution of elements on either side of that imaginary line.

Horizontal and Vertical Lines

Horizontal and vertical lines tend to stabilize our visual perception of a message. But diagonal lines seem to create visual or dynamic tension. This contrasts sharply with our normal view of up and down and side to side. A single diagonally shaped visual can alter entirely our perception of a message on a page or on a screen. Does that mean that you should never use diagonals? Of course not. You simply need to remember that diagonals tend to jar readers and viewers. Used with restraint, they can be very effective.

Contrast

There is a saying that opposites attract. Keep that in mind because contrast is a primary way to indicate differences as opposed to similarities. Contrast builds interest and stimulates our attention. Without contrast, a message quickly gets boring. That turns away readers and viewers. You can think of it in another way, too. A photograph without at least a small area of pure black and white keeps us from seeing the full range of grays or colors in it. Contrast helps anchor the eye so it can see a visual more clearly.

Use contrast to exaggerate, emphasize, accent, dramatize, excite and attract attention. One of the easiest ways to call attention to a large visual is to put a small one next to it. You can build contrast into a message by contrasts in size, type, colors or images.

Large, dark type in a headline contrasts with smaller, light type in the text. If a darker image is contrasted with a lighter one, each seems to enhance the other. Remember, too, that dark images will seem closer than ones of equal size but lighter. If you put a dark image in a light space, it appears to be even darker and heavier. You can also build in contrast by content. For example, if you're trying to show the size of a 5-carat diamond, put it next to a familiar object, such as a golf ball or a small pager. Search for ways to build contrast into your message. A message without contrast is boring.

Movement

Return now to that sheet of paper with the imaginary vertical line down the center. Now draw an imaginary line horizontally through the center. That divides the paper into four equal parts. Where the lines intersect is the symmetrical center. Move up the horizontal line about one-fifth of the way from the symmetrical center to the top of the sheet. Put an imaginary X on the vertical line. The area of the X is called the optical center.

The point of this exercise is to illustrate the idea of natural eye movement. When you pick up a blank sheet of paper your eye first looks at the area of the optical center. If there's nothing there to move it in another direction it will move up through the upper left quadrant, then over to the upper right quadrant, then back through the symmetrical center into the lower left quadrant and then into the lower right, where it will then exit from the space. That pattern produces something like a stylized reversed "S."

If this is the way the eye behaves naturally, then it is a good idea to place a key element in the general area of the optical center. That does not guarantee that people will read your message, but it does help get them into the message. Once into the message, arrangement of elements can lead the eye through other patterns. Arrangement of elements creates the illusion of movement and keeps the message from being seen as static and uninteresting.

Several techniques can be used to enhance the sense of movement and rhythm that leads people through a message. People tend to look in the same direction as figures in photographs and art. A guideline to remember about this is to always place these visuals so people always look into a page or screen. If you don't, that's an open invitation for readers or viewers to go elsewhere. Visual elements, including blocks of text placed in certain relationships, can lead people naturally through a message. Contrived devices can also be used, including pointing fingers, arrows, sequential numbers and letters of the alphabet, to lead people from one element to the next.

Harmony

This is a slippery concept. To understand it better, think of a jigsaw puzzle with all of its pieces in place. The message of the puzzle is harmonious because each piece is where it is supposed to be. Good layouts and storyboards have harmony. All of the pieces fit together in what appears to be a natural, cohesive way. They collectively convey a clear message that is enhanced by the type, visuals, color and paper or screen. They "speak" with a single voice.

Unity

This principle is related to harmony, obviously, but it goes beyond that to deal with how all of a message's elements tie together visually. A message with good unity is one where all of its elements are complementary. They enjoy a relationship that is more than spatial. Some of the most common techniques to unify a message include, but are not limited to, the use of borders, screens, background colors and overlapping elements. Overlapping some elements also can help the natural eye movement through a message. Another important technique is to group related small visuals into a single block. Grouping gives them the impact of a larger visual without taking away from the content of each. If they aren't grouped, the message may have a checkerboard look that is generally uninviting.

Proportion

If you stand on the sidewalk in front of the Empire State Building and look straight at the building, you see only a small part of it. If you cross the street and look again, you can see more of it. You may have to go several blocks before you can see the whole building.

The point is that messages in printed, electronic and film forms are read, viewed and scanned up close. People have difficulty seeing the whole of extreme shapes. Visuals with a proportion of height to width approximately three to five or five to three are easier for the eye to see. Must every element fit that exact ratio? No. But it is a good idea not to vary too much from it. Avoid extreme vertical and horizontal shapes.

Another way to look at proportion is to think of the relativity of all the elements. When we see a message, we see several elements, each in relationship to all the others on the printed page or screen. We react automatically to their size, shape, weight, color and so on. Varying the proportions of elements also can add to the contrast in the page or screen and can help to gain attention.

Conclusions

- Skillful message design involves the careful integration of words, images, motion and sounds to convey a message to target publics.
- For public relations writers, creative work is expected to be produced on demand, and it is usually the end result of group activity that involves several steps.
- Writers use symbols to represent and convey ideas.
- Words are the building blocks of all messages. They transcend all other elements in a message.
- Type is the most basic way of expressing ideas. It must be legible and appropriate.
- Computer software can be used to massage type in ways that convert it into art.
- A logo is a symbol of an organization, group or person.
- A good logo is simple, can be used in all sorts of media, is easy to recognize, maintains its design integrity and is durable.
- Color tends to send subtle messages to people, although its perceptual meaning varies from one individual to another and is influenced by culture.
- Different colors have psychological implications.
- Color has three qualities—hue, value and saturation.
- The Pantone Color Matching System is an international color language that allows specification of color by numbers.
- Computer monitors cause colors to be displayed differently; however 216 colors are Web-safe for browsers, regardless of the platform (Mac or PC).
- *Infographics* is a term that signifies the use of visual devices used to convey complex information.

- The most commonly used infographics are bar, column and pie charts, diagrams, graphs, tables, maps and lists.
- Sounds are recorded in studios, taken from sound-effect or music libraries or recorded at on-site locations.
- Copyrights often apply to creations of all kinds and also to talent so permissions must be gained and fees paid initially and usually again for reuse.
- If prerecorded sound or music does not fit, original lyrics and scores can be composed to fit the message, but be sure the contract specifies who holds the copyright.
- Use movement in video messages.
- Prerecorded illustrations and video segments may be downloaded from several Internet sites for free use, but these often don't precisely fit a message.
- A clear creative concept is requisite of good message design, which must get and hold attention.
- A good writer creates messages that publics interpret as being meant for them, not some generalized other.
- Good message design reflects keen organization so that the message emerges naturally and without effort by target publics.
- Visual principles of good message design include balance, visual weight, horizontal and vertical lines, contrast, movement, harmony, unity and proportion.

Exercises

1. Find a printed message that leads your eye easily through the whole message. Find another that your eye has difficulty following through all the elements. Write an analysis in which you compare the two pieces, including recommendations for improving the second example. Attach copies of the pieces to your report, which should not exceed two double-spaced pages.
2. Find a logo that you think is especially good and another that you believe is not very good. Write an analysis in which you compare the two. Be sure to explain what are the good and bad features in both logos. Attach copies of the logos to your report, which should not exceed two double-spaced pages.
3. Several visuals are discussed in this chapter. Find a printed piece that illustrates most or all of these principles. Analyze the piece critically and focus on principles that are not exploited as well as they could have been. Attach a copy of the piece to your report, which should be no more than two double-spaced pages.
4. Find three websites that are well designed and encourage involvement either intellectually or actively or both. Explain in your analysis how these affected you and why you think the design was integral to your interest and involvement.

Use InfoTrac® College Edition to access information on topics in this chapter from hundreds of periodicals and scholarly journals.

Email, Memos and Letters

Email, memos and letters are the frontline pieces in public relations that help build and sustain professional relationships by maintaining a good, relevant and timely flow of information within an organization and with its external publics. It is exciting, of course, to write copy for a showpiece brochure that is a major part of a campaign. It is a professional fact of life, however, that more seasoned writers probably will be assigned such tasks. New writers are assigned what some consider more mundane tasks, such as writing emails, memos and letters.

Public relations professionals write lots of emails, memos and letters in their everyday routine office work. They also write many such pieces for key officers in the organization, because these forms of writing frequently function to persuade in some way. The purpose of this chapter is to give you some basic guidelines to follow when you must write in any of these forms.

Email

"It happened with cigarettes. It happened with red meat. And carbs. And SUVs. And now it's happening with email. The preferred communication channel of millions of Americans is no longer cool," according to *Los Angeles Times* staff writer Leslie Brenner.[1]

Cool or not, email is a required tool of the public relations professional. For example, a PWR New Media survey of newspaper and magazine journalists found that, "Email is clearly the preferred method of receiving releases with a whopping 85% saying that email is how they 'prefer' to receive releases." About 11 percent said they prefer regular mail, but all other delivery options (fax, wire service, RSS feed, in-person delivery) ranked under

2 percent.[2] Created just four decades ago, email now is everywhere—in the office, at home, even on airplanes, cell phones and tiny BlackBerry® devices. In the novel, *Present Value,* the author provides this delightful description: "The Berry must be read, always and everywhere. All over America, lawyers and investment bankers and deal makers were still flying across the country to meet in restaurants and conference rooms, and yet after coming together in person, the first thing they were doing was checking the BlackBerry®. The prospect of an electronic message was more immediate, more vital, more interesting than whatever the poor human being in the room was saying. So the speakers at such meetings found themselves, like priests among penitents, speaking to bowed heads, while the bowed heads prayed to their new god."[3]

Most public relations professionals use email extensively for all aspects of their work. Some receive and send hundreds of email messages each day. Email systems allow a person to send the same message, and attachments, to one, ten or even thousands of people. Many organizations have email systems that allow distribution of a message to selected groups by title—or even to all employees. More than a few people have been embarrassed by selecting "All" by mistake.

Such a mistake was reported by the *Los Angeles Times.* "The email, which began, 'We're thrilled that you've been admitted to UC San Diego, and we're showcasing our beautiful campus on Admit Day,' was sent to the entire freshman applicant pool of more than 46,000 students, instead of just the 18,000 who had been admitted. All 28,000 applicants who had been rejected received an e-mail congratulating them on their acceptance, only to receive another notification admitting there was a mistake."[4]

People seem to pay more attention to email messages and respond to them more quickly than to paper messages. It's easy to figure out why. It's easier and quicker.

Email also has its problems. The major ones are spam, malware and zombies. Sophos, a world leader in IT security and control that helps organizations defend themselves from unwanted digital intrusions, reported that spam "represented 92.3 percent of all email during the first quarter of 2008." Sophos' "Security Threat Report 2009" included the information that malicious email attachments were five times more prevalent at the end of 2008 than at the beginning and that one new spam-related Web page is discovered by Sophos every 15 seconds.[5]

Malicious codes can infect a computer through websites visited, in addition to email. Sophos reports, "The Web is now the primary route by which cybercriminals infect computers. . . . As a consequence, cybercriminals are planting malicious code on innocent websites. This code then simply lies in wait and silently infects visiting computers. The scale of this global criminal operation has reached such proportions that Sophos discovers one new infected Web page every 4.5 seconds – 24 hours a day, 365 days a year. In addition, SophosLabs, our global network of threat analysis centers, is sent some 20,000 new samples of suspect code every single day."[6]

Back to email: You need to understand is that email is not private. Because email messages are owned by the organization where they are created, it's common for them to be subpoenaed in legal cases. If you don't want it on the front page of the newspaper, don't email it. Google "email lawsuit" and you'll get 18.3 *million* responses!

Interoffice or external postal systems can suffer from delays in delivery. But email is instantaneous. This can be an enormous advantage when a major development—especially one that was not anticipated—begins to unfold. Speed counts, and email meets that need.

Time management can be enhanced by email. If you're working and have a question for someone, you can send the query immediately (before you forget it) and that person can respond when convenient. Your message is kept in your "Sent" mailbox for reference. You can also leave messages for people when they are away from their desks—at meetings or on business trips or on vacations. Then they can respond and you'll get the message even if this time you're the one who's not available.

Email is interactive—that is, two-way communication can occur. So a message may be superseded immediately by an exchange of information between senders and receivers. When they use interactive systems, people tend to feel they are listened to more carefully by their supervisors. And they can "talk back" without the risk of a face-to-face confrontation.

Notebook computers and handheld devices have increased the use of email. Suppose you're on deadline with a major writing task and you work at home until 3 A.M. to finish it. You write a short memo to the vice president for corporate communication explaining that, because you finished the project at 3 A.M., you won't be in the office at your regular time. You send the memo and your copy to the office and go to bed. The next morning, you find an email message from the VP saying that the copy looks great and that you should sleep tight.

And email systems make it possible for you to be an integral part of your organization even though you may be working at home or in an airport lounge on the other side of the world. Wireless connections have made emailing from schools, airports and even entire towns more omnipresent and convenient.

With email you can attach digital images as well as text documents and database files. This makes working with news media representatives both fast and convenient, since you can send what the media folks want, and they can receive it immediately, whether they're across the street or on the other side of the world. High-quality images can be huge, so they should be transferred using file transfer protocol (FTP) with email messages to media representatives giving information on where to locate the images.

Companies in crisis situations have found email particularly useful because it allows for a timely interchange of information across not only geographic boundaries, but also those that separate customers and investors from management and even employees from management and each other.

Formats and Content

One version of email, IM, allows a person to interact instantly via an email format with people on a "buddy" or "contact" list, as long as all of the people involved are online. IM allows a person to create a private chat room with another individual or group, if all are online.

Short-text messaging service (SMS) allows the user of a cell phone or BlackBerry®-type device to send and receive email. *Encyclopedia Britannica* reported that the volume of text messaging in the United States grew to 14 billion per month in 2008. "Worldwide," the encyclopedia said, "the number of text messages sent each year is approaching one trillion, and the major wireless companies report that users now do more texting than talking on their cell phones."[7]

The consumer research company Nielsen Mobile, which tracked 50,000 individual customer accounts in the second quarter of 2008, found that Americans each sent or received 357 text messages a month, compared with 204 phone calls. That was the second consecutive quarter in which mobile texting significantly surpassed the number of voice calls.[8]

Responding to an email is simple; all you need to do to respond is click the reply button, type in your response and then click "send." The problem is what you say and how you say it. The ease of this technology often works against clarity and accuracy. People tend to write "stream of consciousness" messages and send them unedited. The consequences can be mystifying to the recipients, who try to figure out what you meant from what you sent. Other consequences, such as lawsuits, are more serious.

The spontaneity of the process often encourages intemperate remarks that can result in legal action. The system itself is regarded as a cross between a telephone message and a letter or interoffice memo, so it encourages people to put messages on the screen that they would never put on paper. The result has been some unpleasant legal battles over discrimination or sexual harassment, for example.

Like messages in other media, you need to know exactly what you want the receiver to think, know or do. That strategic approach sharpens the focus of your message. You also need to know how much the reader knows about the subject. If it is a lot, your message can be terse. If it is little or none, your message must be longer because you must provide enough background from which the reader can make a decision.

The process of emailing is so easy that some people tend to forget that it is also writing. That can be disastrous because writing demands a lot more precision than speaking. That fact alone should warn us away from being too casual in the way we write emails.

In the fourth annual Email Addiction Survey conducted by AOL Mail, 68 percent of respondents said emails with spelling and punctuation errors annoyed them. Interestingly, 74 percent said they excuse errors when emails are sent from a mobile device like a BlackBerry® or iPhone®.[9]

"At the end of the day, it's all about your image," added Cherie Kerr, author of *The Bliss or 'Diss' Connection? Email Etiquette for the Business Professional*. "Typos and poor grammar are the equivalent of walking into a room looking unshowered and disheveled. Good writing in an email shows you have both professionalism and class."[10]

Style

Remember that although the message is electronic, the recipient is human and you need to imagine how that person is likely to respond to your message. Begin with an appropriate greeting, one that you might use in face-to-face conversation or on the phone with that person.

You need to be conversational in tone because this is a more spontaneous type of communication, but avoid words that might be acceptable if spoken but sound too harsh or inflammatory in print. They will be in print, on the screen, even if a hard copy isn't made.

Let the person know right away what the message is about so they can begin to follow your thought processes. In the subject line, use short but relevant information that will lead the reader into the message. Make it easy to read by using simple words, short sentences and very brief paragraphs.

Let the recipient know what you expect from them. Use something like, "Please let me know about *xyz*." Or "I'll expect to hear from you this afternoon [or a time and date] about the following: 1. *x*; 2. *y*; 3. *z*." This allows them to respond perhaps immediately by saying something like, "Thanks for your message this morning. I can tell you now about *x* and *y*. Before I answer you about *z*, I need to make some phone calls. I'll get back to you by [date and time]. Good to hear from you."

Used the right way, email can be a very satisfying means of communication. Excessive, inconsiderate or inappropriate use can elevate your blood pressure considerably. See Table 11.1 for some email dos and don'ts.

| **T A B L E   1 1 . 1** | *Dos and Don'ts of Email* Most people think of email as quick, casual, responsive and fun. It is so easy to use, it may be abused. These dos and don'ts may help you to better use business email. |

1. Make hard copies of important documents sent or received. If your hard drive crashes, it takes your email messages with it!

2. Be sure the email address is correct. If incorrect, it may not return to you for hours. The solution is to keep your online address book current.

3. Always write a subject line. This gives addressees an idea of the content in just a few words.

4. Verify frequently that the internal clock on your computer is correct. This helps you and receivers to sort through messages chronologically.

5. Keep the caps lock key in the off position. All caps in emails is the equivalent of shouting.

6. Avoid abbreviations. However, they're acceptable in personal emails.

7. You can express yourself informally in email. But remember that email demands good writing, a level of preciseness that speaking sometimes does not require. Your writing can't duplicate speech.

8. Formal greetings or closings don't work well in email. Be more personal, as in "Hi, Diana." Don't use "Sincerely" or "Respectfully" in closing. Use something like "Cheers" or "All the best."

9. Keep sentences short, averaging no more than about 12 to 15 words. Avoid run-on sentences and conditional clauses. These can be confusing.

10. Remember that email is instant. You don't get a second chance after clicking on the send button. Make sure the message is accurate in fact and correct in grammar, spelling and punctuation. If your email program has a spell checker, be sure it's turned on.

11. Attach only documents to your email that you know can be downloaded by the receiver.

12. Be sensitive to what you say and how it may be interpreted.

13. Email is not private. Don't say anything in email that you don't want your boss to see or that you would not want to see on the front page of a newspaper. Send it another way if your message is private or confidential.

14. Read your incoming email regularly, perhaps at set intervals during the workday.

15. When an email requires action by the receiver and you don't get a timely response, follow up. Don't delay.

16. When sending to a group, ask three questions of yourself: Does each group member need the message? Does each have sufficient background to understand the message? Does each member of the group have operating responsibilities that relate to the message? If no, modify the content or exclude them.

17. Don't use business email systems to send jokes and other nonbusiness matter.

Memos

The word *memo* is the short form of *memorandum,* meaning an informal reminder of something important that has occurred or will occur. Memos are generally used to communicate within the organization. They should seldom be used to communicate with people outside the organization, with the exception of those sent to members of boards, committees and task forces. Messages sent by email and fax often are written in memo format.

Memo Formats

A good memo disseminates information simply. It should begin with a guide to its contents, as shown in Figure 11.1.

If the writer and receiver know each other, the memo style may be even less formal, containing neither last names nor titles. This is especially common when the memo is to someone in the same office or immediate area of operations.

When people have the same mailing address, it is unnecessary to use anything more than a departmental designation. Include addresses below the names if the addresses are different, such as different internal post office box numbers. Of course, if you're using digital or printed letterhead, there's no need to include your address below your name. If you don't use letterhead or if you have stationery that does not include phone numbers and addresses, include your address. The heading for the memo would then look like this:

TO:	John Gill, controller, POB 311
FROM:	Susan McConnell, investor relations, POB 286
DATE:	September 7, 201x
SUBJECT:	Planning conference for 200x annual report

A variant of this format is to use "RE" for "Regarding" instead of the word "SUBJECT." An element that may appear on memos when mailed or sent by fax is information on who is receiving copies of the communication, in addition to the person addressed. The old designation of "cc" stood for "carbon copy." No one uses carbons now, so just use one "c," either lowercase or a capital, or "COPY." This can go below the topic of the memo or at the end of the body of the memo.

Body   The body of a memo differs from the body of a letter by being shorter and by providing more visual cues, such as lists of numbered items.

Memos are designed to communicate salient information quickly and efficiently. Their tone ranges from formal to informal. Memos directed up the chain of command tend to be more formal, whereas those directed down the chain tend to be less formal. The least formal of all are memos that move between people at the same level in the organization. Exceptions to these guidelines turn on personal relationships. For example, an account executive in a public relations company would probably write a fairly formal memo to the president of the agency, unless the president happened to be a fishing partner.

Memos ordinarily have a limited public. They usually are addressed to just one person or to a small group. At times, however, they may be directed to a large public. For example, the president of the company may distribute a memo to all 600 employees simultaneously, stating

XYZ Corporation

Internal Memorandum

Printed memo heading

When a pre-printed memo heading is used in an organization

TO: John Gill, controller

FROM: Susan McConnell, investor relations

DATE: September 7, 201x

SUBJECT: Planning conference for 201x annual report

Basic information

TO = Recipient
FROM = Originator
DATE = Day sent
SUBJECT = Guide to contents

Our first planning session for the 201x annual report will be conducted at 2 p.m. on September 14 in the conference room. Please be prepared to discuss the following:

➤ Annual report design

➤ Production schedule

➤ Photography

➤ Writing responsibilities

Body of memo

Short and to-the-point message containing only necessary information

No signature necessary

Some memos are initialed by the sender beside the name in the "FROM:" area, but the closing and signature used in a business letter are not necessary.

FIGURE 11.1

Memo Format *Formats for memos vary from organization to organization, but this one is typical. Memos are used when those addressed don't have email and when posting on bulletin boards is a good way to communicate— for example, with groups of employees who don't have computers in their workplaces.*

that the company has just recorded its highest annual profits ever. This information, of course, also would be appropriate in the company newsletter and must be released to the media at the same time or earlier, but the memo often is used to share important information quickly with all employees. A common practice is to use email to reach all employees who have email addresses within the organization and to send paper copies to those without email at their work location.

Visual Cues   In addition to having an explanatory salutation, the memo usually contains a number of visual cues that help communicate important information quickly.

The most important stylistic characteristic is the use of common words, short sentences and brief paragraphs. The last is especially important, because a memo is typed single space with double spaces between paragraphs. Each paragraph represents a new but related thought. In effect, each paragraph is a subsequent "take" in the thought processes that organize information related to the content and purpose of the memo.

Other visual cues, often not found in letters, are indented paragraphs (for emphasis), numbered or bulleted items (to accent important matter), fragmented sentences (for emphasis, but be cautious about using these often) and lists of items (often in vertical format rather than serially in a paragraph).

Context   Memo writers tend to assume that, because the person addressed in the memo is a member of the team, he or she knows all the pertinent background information related to the topic at hand. This often is a mistake. If you want to be understood, provide clarifying information that makes what you say comprehensible and leaves little room for misinterpretation. Do not, of course, provide superfluous information.

Establishing a context for your message is especially important if the memo is directed to people with whom you do not work regularly. When in doubt, always provide appropriate background materials. These may not be needed, but it is better to be safe than sorry. (See Table 11.2 for what *not* to do.)

When you do provide background materials, you need to say so. The way you do that is to put at the bottom of the memo the word "Attachments:" or "Enclosures:" followed by a list of everything you're including. List the items vertically and use bullets so it's easier to check them all. Sometimes not all of the enclosures make it into the envelope. The intended recipient needs to know what to expect.

The procedure is a bit different when you're sending a fax. You may need to use a cover page for the fax, which looks like the heading of the fax, but also tells the addressee how many pages to expect.

TO:	Alan Cooper Phone: 313-457-6733 Fax: 313-457-6734
FROM:	Susan Foster Phone: 623-535-6354 Fax: 623-535-7453
DATE:	October 1, 201x
RE:	Artwork for St. Louis Hospital Brochure
PAGES:	6 plus cover

Classifications of Memos

The tone and tempo of a memo depend on its purpose, style and public. There are six general categories of memos: bulletin, essay, informative, action, summary and file.

T A B L E 1 1 . 2	*How to Make Sure No One Reads Your Memo*

1. Hide the Message in a Block of Print

You want your reader to pick up your document, and put it down again. You can get this block effect in several ways.

- Make the document as long as possible. You see how forbidding the one-page memo is. Imagine seeing two pages of it. Imagine them printed on both sides of one sheet.

- Make your paragraphs long. Think of three inches as a minimum length. Write everything single-space.

- Don't leave a blank space between paragraphs. Announce a new paragraph by indenting the first line 1/4 of an inch. Add as many modifiers as you need to make sure the last line in a paragraph extends to the right margin.

- Justify the right margin.

Do this and you'll produce a formidable document. It's one most readers will glance at and immediately set aside.

2. Make the Message Appear Difficult and Irrelevant

Your goal is to lose the reader's interest.

- Send the message "To: File" or "To: Distribution." This is a strong barrier. It tells readers that the document has no relevance to them personally. The longer the distribution list at the end, the clearer the message.

- Use the "Subject" announcement to turn off the reader. It should make your topic seem dull or complex. (The word "theory" is especially useful here.)

    There must be no hint that the topic has any immediate importance.

- People who read beyond the subject-heading are a threat. You have to stop them with the first sentence of the text. This sentence *must* contain 30–50 words. It will help if a dozen of these words separate the subject and the verb.

    The first sentence should discuss a single detail of the report. There must be no suggestion of a summary or a conclusion.

- Use the second sentence as a fail-safe device. Hopefully, no one will do more than glance at it. But that glance must show it says nothing about the purpose of the document. It's a good idea if the second sentence starts with a long dependent clause. Let it begin with "If" or "Although."

Readers who go beyond the second sentence are intrepid and will be hard to stop. But they can be slowed down. You must take steps to frustrate them.

3. Make Individual Sentences Difficult to Read

Again, you should follow the example of the Fort Knox memo. It illustrates all the important techniques. Try them.

- Use a typeface that is hard to read.

    Write with a sans serif font. This is more difficult for many people to read. (A good word processing program will let you choose from scores of fonts, some of them pretty bizarre.)

    WRITE IN ALL CAPS. THIS SLOWS DOWN READING BY 10 PERCENT OR MORE.

    Use 8-point type. The tiny print puts so many words on a crowded page that your reader, on finishing one line, will have difficulty seeing where the next line begins.

- Write crowded sentences.

    Use long, compound-complex sentences. Begin with a participial phrase 15 words long, and end with a "which" clause that is 20 words long. Insert one or two parenthetical sentences in every paragraph. Keep your subject some distance from your verb. Stay with the passive voice.

(continued)

T A B L E 1 1 . 2	*(continued)*

- Use vague jargon that turns off the reader. Rely on abstractions, words ending in "ness," "ity," "tion," "ence," "ship," and "ment." Avoid anything specific, like proper names or sums of money.

  Devise difficult words, like "consortial," and challenging phrases, like "quantum signification." Introduce obscure acronyms, like "B.O.A. optimization." Sprinkle the message with high-sounding cliches, like "pursuant," "in lieu of," "per," "parameter," "closure," and "prioritize." These have deadened reading for years.

- Confuse readers with an unusual division of words. This is a subtle tactic, but quietly effective.

  It bothers most people to see merged forms like "problemsolver" and "costeffective." They are thrown off by words unexpectedly separated, like "fore men" and "counter indicated." They will be frustrated by unusual hyphens, as in "bi-nomial" and "di-agnostic." And you can unsettle them with slashed creations, like "enhance/monitor." Always justify your right margin. This leaves disturbing gaps between words throughout the text.

- Provide a dim copy. Make your readers work to recognize the words on the page.

By now you have the message. If you want your memo to remain unread, you can do wonders. You can offer a block of print, or introduce it with a deadly subject-head, or write awkward sentences full of strange acronyms. You won't need to do this often.

But you will see these forms every day. You'll see reports crowded with pages, and pages crowded with words, and paragraphs crowded with tiny print. You'll see messages written in all-caps or in italics or in the Mos Eisley font. You'll see dot-matrix print too faint to read and dittographed memos which have faded into obscurity. You'll throw away some important announcement because the subject-head read "Patterns of Supernumerary Clarification." And all these documents come from people who genuinely want to be read. Somehow they never learned that effective writing takes more than facts, vocabulary, and prose style. It takes readability.

Source: This table is excerpted from Daniel McDonald's "Achieving the Unreadable Memo" in *Et cetera* (Fall 1992): 280–284. Reprinted with permission of the International Society for General Semantics.

Bulletin Memo   The bulletin memo usually has a sense of urgency. It is generally brief and may be terse in style. It is the "telegram" of the memo world. The bulletin memo gets its name from the bulletins that appear on the wire services notifying editors that something important has happened or is about to happen. Given the nature of its content, such a memo may wind up being posted on a bulletin board, even if it is addressed to just one person.

Essay Memo   An essay memo is usually much more descriptive than a bulletin memo. It is used for "let's talk it over" material or situations. Its content may range from management philosophy to questions of how to get employees to clean up the coffee room after using it. The style is often conversational.

Informative Memo   The informative memo is usually a detailed descriptive piece of writing. An example might be a memo from the account executive to the account group and client. This memo might document actions taken and their results. Or it might recommend programs and describe projected outcomes. The style and tone of these memos are usually fairly formal.

Action Memo   The action memo describes action taken or planned. Such memos, especially those dealing with future actions, often contain places for responses by recipients. For example, there might be a space for the receiver's initials on a section to indicate that he or she accepts responsibility for the initialed action. Or in the case of a supervisor, the initials might indicate approval or disapproval of the planned action.

Action memos sometimes include an element of coercion. This may be the case, for instance, when the author of the memo does not assign or suggest responsibility but seeks volunteers to assume responsibility. Coercion is at work when the implication of the memo is, "If you don't select an area of responsibility, one will be assigned to you." If you're alert to this message, you'll quickly "volunteer" for the area of action that you will do best and enjoy most.

Summary Memo   This is a detailed descriptive memo in essay or outline form. Discussions and actions are collected under appropriate topical headings to facilitate progress during a meeting. The summary memo is used, too, in evaluating the progress of a program. In this case, it reflects an accumulation of information over time and often explains actions taken or planned.

File Memo   As its name implies, a file memo is addressed to the file—not to another person. It simply records information and is stored for reference. Memos of this type are used extensively when the program being planned is complex, when many people are involved in some ongoing action or program or when sharp divisions in points of view arise as to how or whether something should be done. In style and tone, it may be terse, almost cryptic. The purpose, remember, is merely to record information for internal use.

In a sense, a file memo is like a diary. It records names, dates, places and points of information. If serious debate arises over how or whether something should be done, the file memo should identify individuals with their respective points of view, even including verbatim accounts as necessary.

Factors Affecting the Use of Memos

Memos should be personalized. Involve the recipient with your memo by emphasizing "you." This is not only a pleasant way to write, it is also effective.

The way your memo is distributed may affect the attention it receives. Email distribution is the most common way. Routing one paper copy to the people who should read it is another—but much slower and less reliable way. A routing slip is attached and the memo is passed from one person to the next. Each person initials the slip to indicate it has been read and then passes the memo on to the person whose name appears next on the list. Although routing is a common practice, it can be a problem if the content of the memo is timely. People tend to assign a lower priority to a message attached to a routing form than to a message addressed to them personally. So even if you save some paper and copying costs by routing memos, you may wind up paying a high price in lost opportunities.

Posting memos on bulletin boards is a common practice, but this can be even less effective than routing them. The company bulletin board often is filled with messages that remain unread by many people in the organization. If you intend your memo for posting, design it like a poster. Add graphics to gain attention, and treat the content like a bulletin to encourage easy, quick reading.

If your memo is to be distributed to a large number of people in the organization, you have several options. The best approach, of course, is to email the memo to each person. An alternative is to provide supervisors with stacks of copies and rely on them to pass a copy along to each employee. Many supervisors will be careful to distribute the information, but others will not, and communication breakdowns may result.

Some memos are best suited for special methods of distribution. For example, a memo about the company picnic might better be mailed to employees' homes, as you'll want other members of the employee's household to know about the event too.

The setting in which the memo is received may also influence its effectiveness. Obviously, the company picnic is a social event that involves the employee and the employee's family. Therefore, it is appropriate to send the memo announcing it to employees' home addresses. However, a memo calling a meeting of department heads should be emailed or sent to the recipients' respective offices, not to their homes. In general, if the memo is social, send it to the employee's home; if it is business, send it to the employee's work address.

Letters

Even though the use of email has greatly increased, letters still play a significant role in business relationships. The problem is that some letter writers think that because they are going to the trouble to write a letter it must be long. One solicitation letter from a university president to alumni was four full pages. Too long. As a rule, try to keep your letters to one page in a readable size type. To give one-page letter writers more space, many letterhead designers put all addresses, including email, phone and fax information, in a single line along the bottom of the stationery.

Business Letter Format

The typical business letter has six parts: heading, salutation, body, close, signature and reference matter. (See Figure 11.2.)

Heading   The heading has two parts. The first is the identity of the sender. This material is usually printed on the letterhead. The second part is the date, plus the "inside address" containing the name, title and address of the recipient. The heading should always contain these elements, even when you know the person you're writing to quite well. Always document the sender and receiver completely and accurately.

Salutation   In the salutation, you address the person to whom you're writing. This might appear to be simple, but it can cause some problems if you're insensitive to your receiver.

Suppose you're writing a letter from your CEO to Doug Newsom, one of the co-authors of this text, seeking names of people who might be used as public relations consultants. You might address Doug variously as "Dear Mr. Newsom," "Dear Professor Newsom," "Dear Dr. Newsom" or "Dear Doug." The first salutation would be incorrect because Doug's name is Douglas *Ann* Newsom, but she goes by Doug. The second form would be acceptable, because she is a professor. The third form would be correct too, because she does have an earned doctorate. The last form would be correct only if your CEO knows her personally. Two points are illustrated here: Avoid using a gender-specific title if you don't know the person's gender, and do not use a title if you don't know that it is correct.

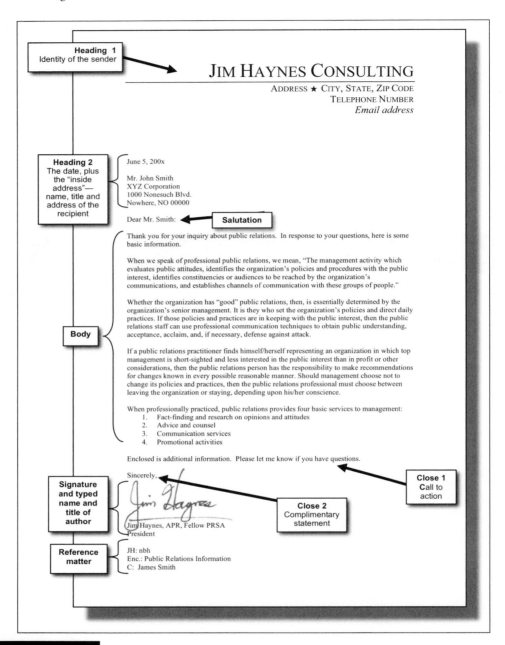

Heading 1
Identity of the sender

JIM HAYNES CONSULTING
ADDRESS ★ CITY, STATE, ZIP CODE
TELEPHONE NUMBER
Email address

Heading 2
The date, plus the "inside address"— name, title and address of the recipient

June 5, 200x

Mr. John Smith
XYZ Corporation
1000 Nonesuch Blvd.
Nowhere, NO 00000

Dear Mr. Smith:

Salutation

Thank you for your inquiry about public relations. In response to your questions, here is some basic information.

When we speak of professional public relations, we mean, "The management activity which evaluates public attitudes, identifies the organization's policies and procedures with the public interest, identifies constituencies or audiences to be reached by the organization's communications, and establishes channels of communication with these groups of people."

Whether the organization has "good" public relations, then, is essentially determined by the organization's senior management. It is they who set the organization's policies and direct daily practices. If those policies and practices are in keeping with the public interest, then the public relations staff can use professional communication techniques to obtain public understanding, acceptance, acclaim, and, if necessary, defense against attack.

If a public relations practitioner finds himself/herself representing an organization in which top management is short-sighted and less interested in the public interest than in profit or other considerations, then the public relations person has the responsibility to make recommendations for changes known in every possible reasonable manner. Should management choose not to change its policies and practices, then the public relations professional must choose between leaving the organization or staying, depending upon his/her conscience.

When professionally practiced, public relations provides four basic services to management:
1. Fact-finding and research on opinions and attitudes
2. Advice and counsel
3. Communication services
4. Promotional activities

Body

Enclosed is additional information. Please let me know if you have questions.

Sincerely,

Close 1
Call to action

Close 2
Complimentary statement

Signature and typed name and title of author

Jim Haynes, APR, Fellow PRSA
President

Reference matter

JH: nbh
Enc.: Public Relations Information
C: James Smith

FIGURE 11.2

Letter Format   *The parts of a typical business letter are shown here. When no letterhead is available, the sender's address; city, state and zip code; and the date are placed above the "inside address" of the recipient. This example shows a block format in which every line is flush with the left margin. Using an indented format, the date (and the sender's address; city, state and zip code when those are typed) appears indented halfway across the page, and the complimentary statement, signature and typed name and title are indented in the same way.*

If you're writing a promotional letter to send to hundreds of clients and it will not be personalized by name, use a salutation like "Dear Customer," "Dear Client" or "Dear Colleague." Even though these salutations are impersonal, they are better than ones that might be genuinely offensive.

Body   The level of formality in the tone depends on the relationship between the writer and the recipient of the letter. If a personal relationship exists, the letter may have a casual salutation and a conversational tone. In general, the tone of the body will be more formal if the letter is addressed to a person whose status is higher than that of the writer; it will be more informal if the writer's status is higher than the recipient's.

Close   The close of a business letter contains two elements. One is a call to action (if that is the purpose of the letter) or an offer of further help. The other is a complimentary statement that appears above the signature. Most business letters close with a simple "Sincerely" above the signature block. Business letters to and from friends outside the company sometimes close with "Best regards," "Cordially yours" or simply "Cordially." Letters between strangers are more likely to have a more formal close, such as "Respectfully yours" or "Respectfully." Whatever the form used, only the first letter of the close is capitalized.

Signature   The name of the writer should always be typed; the handwritten signature will appear just above it. The signer's title should also be typed immediately below the name if the title is not printed on the letterhead.

When the recipient is a friend, the signer might inscribe only his or her first name. If little or no personal relationship exists between the writer and the receiver, then the full signature is required.

Reference Matter   All business letters prepared by a person other than the sender should contain symbols below the signature block that look like this:

BC: rlb

The capitalized letters are the initials of the writer and the small letters are the initials of the person who keyboarded the letter. If the writer also keyboarded the letter, do not include any initials.

The next element in the reference material is a notation about enclosures, if any, that go with the letter. The notation reads like this:

Enc.: [name of enclosure(s)]

This note serves both as a form of documentation by the sender of the message and a flag to the receiver that material is enclosed.

The third element in the reference material designates other people (if any) who are to receive a copy of the letter. The designation reads like this:

C: [names of people who also receive copies]

You may use "bc," which stands for "blind copy." Use this when you want to share information with another without letting those who received official copies know about it. The "bc" should appear on your copy and on copies sent to recipients of the blind copies to alert them that they are being notified confidentially.

Types of Letters

Public relations writers generally find themselves writing six types of letters: information, solicitation, promotion, transmittal, cover and response.

Information   Naturally, these letters inform. They let people know about an event coming up, a decision made or an action taken. A letter of recommendation for a person would also be of this type. They are straightforward and try to anticipate and respond to any questions the reader might have. Although these letters might require an acknowledgment, they seldom require a response.

Solicitation   Letters making any kind of request can be considered a solicitation. Nonprofit organizations often write letters asking for contributions or pledges of support of one kind or another. Politicians ask for your support and your vote. These letters should be careful to suggest some sort of reward, usually intrinsic, for that support. Letters from an environmental group may ask you to "Save the Rain Forest." The question is "Why?" The letter will probably tell you that many of the new medicines that could save your life are being discovered in the rain forest.

Promotion   Causes or events are promoted in letters that encourage the recipient's acceptance and participation. There should be an emotional appeal in the letter but also a specific call to action. By using subheads, italics, boldface, underlining and indents, you can help the reader to spot these two important elements in your message.

Transmittal   Use letters of transmittal when you're sending a number of materials to someone, like a client. The letter reminds the receiver of what's being sent and why. Sometimes it's appropriate to tell the person to call after receiving the materials, especially if there are any questions or concerns. This letter should have a paragraph that lists the contents, separating items with indented bullets, with at least the titles in boldface. You want to make it easy for the person to look at the letter, see what should be included in the package and quickly determine if everything listed is indeed included.

Cover   Some people confuse cover letters with letters of transmittal. The cover letter is a very brief note in letter format that simply tells the recipient what is being sent, why and what the recipient might be interested in doing with it.

Response   The most important form of response letter is the "Thank You." You should thank people for doing or saying something to support you or your organization. It's amazing how many people think to ask but forget to thank. You can build strong relationships by being gracious and thoughtful.

Responses can be intended for private or public use. Response letters usually are written to react to something that has occurred, which may be something said or written. *Private response* letters are written to *individuals* with the anticipation that the letter will not be made public. However, it's always possible that the recipient will make the letter public. Therefore, it's better to write all letters with the anticipation that the contents may be made public.

Some letters are written for public use, and often these are sent to news media to be published or broadcast. Some are written to correct or to put something in perspective. Others are observations or comments. You can find these in newspaper and magazine "letters to the editor" columns and hear them on radio and on television, where a brief version of the contents often is scrolled for the viewer. The important point to remember about public letters is to be direct and concise. The editor of the medium is not going to give you much time or space. Think in terms of sound bites even when you're writing for print.

Choose your words carefully, because the tone of the expression conveys both mood and character. Be persuasive in your choice, because you want to have an impact. You may be writing to change an opinion that a previous presentation in the media has created, or you may be attempting to correct an error that has been made by a medium. Be clear. These letters get a quick scan. You need to be sure your point is not missed.

Some broadcast media allow verbal responses called in to be taped. If you plan to make such a call, write the response first. Read it into a tape recorder and play it back. You should say what you have to say in 15 seconds or maybe 20. No more. It won't be used if it isn't succinct. Try your response on some others who are hearing it for the first time without seeing the written piece. Test for tone and clarity. Many public relations writers will have to get response letters cleared by multiple levels of management. You will have to be persistent to prevent distortion of the message. Be cautious about using humor or sarcasm. These can be easily misunderstood or taken for arrogance.

Conclusions

- Email now is everywhere—in the office, at home, even on airplanes, cell phones and tiny BlackBerry® devices.
- When email is a major part of an organization's communication structure, it decreases response time during a crisis.
- Email facilitates distance communication because messages can be sent to and from anywhere in the world through cyberspace.
- One difficulty is that, because email messages are so spontaneous, writers tend to be careless about content.
- The spontaneity also encourages intemperate remarks that can result in lawsuits.
- Organize email messages carefully, use simple language and tell the recipient what you expect from them by way of a response or some sort of action.
- IM allows two or more people to connect and post messages that all members of the IM group can see, identified by screen names.
- SMS allows a cell phone user to send and receive email.
- Memos usually are for internal communication, an exception being messages sent by email and fax, which employ the memo format.
- The form of address on the memo or fax is critical to getting a good response.
- Memos can be classified in six ways: bulletin, essay, informative, action, summary and file.
- Memos are most effective when addressed to individuals. Effectiveness decreases when they are sent *en masse* or are posted.

- Letters remain an important means of communication, especially for formal correspondence within the organization and for external communication.
- A letter has six principal parts: heading, salutation, body, close, signature and reference matter.
- Letters can be categorized as: information, solicitation, promotion, transmittal, cover and response.

Exercises

1. You are a public relations writer at the headquarters of a hotel chain that operates a major hotel immediately across the street from the World Trade Center site where buildings were destroyed in the 9/11 disaster. Now construction of major new buildings is underway. Contractors are behind schedule and are working from 6:00 A.M. until 2:00 A.M. Noise levels inside many hotel rooms have increased. Prepare a letter for hotel guests who have reservations for next week. Explain the reason for the noise levels, and offer to provide ear plugs, a CD containing sea wave and other gentle sounds to overcome the construction noise.

2. Draft a memo for bulletin boards that tells students in your department when the next grammar, spelling, punctuation and keyboard proficiency (typing) tests will be given. Be sure to tell them how to sign up for these tests and how to prepare for them. Let them know if these are prerequisites for taking certain skills classes. Don't forget to address the problem of transfer students who may have had tests like these before. Consult your department's policy on giving the tests.

Use InfoTrac® College Edition to access information on topics in this chapter from hundreds of periodicals and scholarly journals.

Reports and Proposals

Remember those book reports from your high school English classes? The reports that public relations people write are not so different. The author examines what might be a complex set of facts, then puts fingers to keyboard to distill the information into a one-of-a-kind summary.

And do you remember when you said you wanted to drive on public streets the first time? That was a proposal—a suggestion, stating something for consideration.

Reports and Proposals Compared

They may look alike, which can be confusing, but reports and proposals are very different. Their differences become apparent in their purposes. A report summarizes information on some topic. A proposal details a plan of action to be considered.

You might say that a report is a summary of the status of something. Suppose you're on the management team of a food processing company and marketer. The company has endured a slight decline in market share and profitability the last two years, because it has not adopted some new technologies that competitors are using to produce products at lower costs. The chief financial officer was asked to prepare a report that evaluates the economics of these new technologies. That report, contained in a 48-page booklet, is before the team now, having been distributed to members a week earlier so they could study it in detail.

After lengthy discussion, the team asked the director of manufacturing to prepare a proposal that describes in detail what the company must do to acquire these technologies, its costs and a timeline that projects when the new technologies could become operational. It should be clear that when the report is presented it will deal with a planned, recommended course of action. It is then that the management team must make a go or no-go decision to take the proposal to its board of directors for ratification and implementation.

The requirements for organizing and writing reports and proposals are similar enough for both to be considered together. As used here, the terms *report* and *proposal* refer to extensive documents that are researched, written and presented much like a traditional scholarly research paper or the manuscript for a monograph or book.

In fact, if you must write a report or proposal of this type, the first thing you should do is get a copy of a style manual such as Kate L. Turabian's *A Manual for Writers of Term Papers, Theses and Dissertations*. A style manual will save you innumerable hours of research time by showing you, as you begin to research the project, what information you need to gather and how to credit it.

Organization of Reports and Proposals

After your research on the topic is completed, you're ready to begin to organize and write your report or proposal. This requires special skills and attention to details, because a finished project often has as many as seven major sections: letter, front matter, executive summary, body, references, bibliography and appendixes. In a proposal, there's also a proposed budget and timeline.

Letter   A letter of documentation should always accompany a report or a proposal. Sometimes a letter of transmittal should also be included if there are many enclosures.

A letter of documentation, sometimes called a *cover letter,* addresses the person or people who will consider the report or proposal. It usually describes both the content of the report and the people who did the research, planning, writing and illustrating. The letter may close with a brief summary of findings or recommendations, and it may call attention to any conditions affecting adoption or rejection. Finally, it should indicate where to locate the person who signed the letter. A letter of documentation is sometimes made a part of the report, in which case it should be inserted immediately following the front matter.

A letter of transmittal is needed when a person or group has been authorized to write a report or proposal. It should seek to establish the credibility of the report or proposal. The letter should note who gave the authorization and when, as well as summarize results or recommendations. It may include a list of acknowledgments of special help or meritorious work by individuals who contributed to the project. Such a letter allows you to include information that may not belong in the body of the document but nonetheless provides additional insights into what is there.

Skillfully written letters of documentation and transmittal prepare readers of the document for what follows.

Front Matter   The front matter in a report or proposal is organized in the same general way as the front matter of this book. It consists of a cover page, a table of contents and a list of tables, figures and illustrations. These pages are numbered serially with small Roman numerals (i, ii, iii, iv, v and so on). Although the cover page is counted in this series of numbers, no number appears on the cover page.

Executive Summary   When an executive summary or synopsis is used, it appears at the end of the front matter and before the body of the report or proposal. Usually only a page or two in length, it is a concisely written digest of the content of the document. Its purpose is to give the reader a clear picture of what is in the document. In the business world, *executive summary* is the term most often used, and you'll be expected to use it when your employer asks you to write a report or proposal.

Body   The body of the report or proposal follows the executive summary. It consists of three basic parts: introduction, body and conclusions.

The introduction should review the background of the problem being studied, the scope of the study and the methods used in the study. It should also explain why the study is important, what special problems (if any) were encountered in the course of research and how these were resolved. The last point is especially important because it prepares the reader for any limitations of the study. In a proposal, the introduction might review the activities that have preceded the submission of the proposal—meetings, the request for the proposal and, sometimes, the proposing organization's capabilities and competencies related to the work to be accomplished. Often a proposal is written in response to a request for proposal (RFP) and must follow the guidelines for content specified in the RFP.

The body of a proposal often focuses on the objective and goals to be met if the proposal is accepted, along with the activities to be undertaken. A timeline for the activities, along with a budget and information on the people who will be undertaking the activities, also is common.

The body of a report should be built around a single, simple statement. Called a *thesis statement* or *hypothesis,* it unifies the entire report and helps you address the issue point by logical point. Develop each point and support it with pertinent facts. Use headings and subheads to guide the reader through the body of the report.

Conclusions should follow naturally from any summary findings in the report or proposal. Sometimes recommendations will stem from your conclusions. Conclusions and recommendations should be stated clearly. This may take courage, because you may conclude or recommend something that your readers would prefer to ignore. Clarity is necessary because a report or proposal that invites many interpretations is not very useful to anyone.

References   In a report or proposal of this type, you must properly cite the source of every piece of information that is not common knowledge to your public. This means using footnotes or endnotes, with complete bibliographic citations, so anyone can locate and read the original materials. In this respect, proposals and reports are exactly like scholarly research papers.

Bibliography   In addition to supplying footnotes or endnotes, you must include a full bibliography. The bibliography, of course, includes all of the basic sources cited in the footnotes or endnotes, but it also includes sources you reviewed but did not specifically cite in the body of the paper. Thus the bibliography identifies the full range of works you consulted, whether or not you eventually cited them.

Appendixes   An appendix contains any charts, tables, illustrations, maps, copies of questionnaires and other exhibits that could not be woven into the body of the paper. As a general rule, the only items of this type that should appear in the body are simple tables and charts illustrating specific points. More complex material goes in the appendixes. Be certain, however, that you interpret the complex materials sufficiently to make them understandable. Each appendix should be labeled separately—Appendix A, B and so on.

Readability and Applicability

A reader of your report or proposal should be able to conclude something from what you have written. Two factors will influence this outcome: readability and applicability.

Readability   If your report or proposal is in a specialized field, your reader expects to see jargon common to that field used in your document. But this is not a license to use jargon without restraint. On the contrary, you should write in plain English with just enough jargon to establish your credibility with the reader.

Jargon invariably makes your writing more difficult to understand. Try Gunning's Fog Index (http://simbon.madpage.com/Fog/) on some samples of writing in your report. Then go back and do some severe editing to make it clearer and easier to understand.

Unless you're an extraordinarily gifted and lucky writer, you will not be able to write a good report or proposal in the first draft. You will probably have to write the whole report at least twice. You may have to rewrite several times. In this sense, the art of good report and proposal writing is rewriting.

If time allows, you're sure to improve the readability of your report by writing a draft and then putting it aside for a week or more. When you pick up the document and read it cold, trouble spots will jump out at you. Fix them immediately and do the reorganizing and rewriting necessary to clarify the draft. And don't forget that headings, subheads, indented segments, underlining and other visuals, including tables, charts and graphs can improve understanding.

All these points apply to both reports and proposals, but one consideration applies to proposals alone. In a sense, proposals resemble ad copy. They are meant to persuade—to sell ideas. So showmanship with words counts more in proposals than in reports.

Applicability   When you complete a report, you will want your readers to accept the document as meaningful and significant enough to prompt a course of action. You'll want your readers to say, "This is important. We should do something." When you submit a proposal, you'll be trying to evoke this response: "This is a really good idea. Let's go with it." You will elicit such judgments only if the reader finds what you have written to be clear, reliable and justified. Additionally, what you present should be singularly relevant to the situation. And any action you call for must appear easy to accomplish.

Annual Reports

First you need to know that a corporation whose stock is publicly traded is required to prepare not one but *two* annual reports. One is the SEC Form 10-K annual report to the Securities and Exchange Commission.

SEC Form 10-K   The SEC Form 10-K is prepared in a format decreed by the SEC that is plain—no graphics, no photos, no color, just black type on white paper. Because it is a legal document, it usually is prepared by accountants and attorneys, and it must be transmitted electronically to the SEC.

As a result of corporate scandals involving fraud at companies including Enron, World-Com, Global Crossing, Arthur Andersen and others, the then President George W. Bush signed into law the Sarbanes-Oxley Act of 2002 (SOX). On its website, the international accounting and consulting firm PricewaterhouseCoopers says, "Without a doubt, the Sarbanes-Oxley Act is the single most important piece of legislation affecting corporate governance, financial disclosure and the practice of public accounting since the USA securities laws of the early 1930s."[1]

The Act mandated a number of reforms to enhance corporate and management responsibility, enhance financial disclosures and combat corporate and accounting fraud and created the "Public Company Accounting Oversight Board," also known as the PCAOB, to oversee the activities of the auditing profession. In signing the bill, President Bush said, "This new law sends very clear messages that all concerned must heed. This law says to every dishonest corporate leader: you will be exposed and punished; the era of low standards and false profits is over; no boardroom in America is above or beyond the law."[2]

Because SOX requires increased disclosure and reporting—public companies now must provide shareholders much of the information contained in a corporation's SEC Form 10-K—many companies now provide the Form 10-K to shareholders. More than half "wrap" their annual report to shareholders around the 10-K. Some "wraps" are limited to the cover; others have pages devoted to explaining the company's operations and include four-color photos. A survey by the National Investor Relations Institute (NIRI) indicates that only 32 percent still use a traditional annual report format. "Ninety percent of the firms that have moved to a 10-K wrap cited cost-cutting pressures and 63% mentioned ease of production as reasons for adopting the abbreviated format."[3]

The SEC's website says, "The annual report to shareholders is the principal document used by most public companies to disclose corporate information to their shareholders. It is usually a state-of-the-company report, including an opening letter from the Chief Executive Officer, financial data, results of continuing operations, market segment information, new product plans, subsidiary activities and research and development activities on future programs. The Form 10-K, which must be filed with the SEC, typically contains more detailed information about the company's financial condition than the annual report."[4]

Annual Report to Shareholders   The annual report to shareholders is a principal public relations responsibility and is printed on paper. In addition, it usually is available on the organization's website. Some annual reports to shareholders may look like magazines, but the similarity is mostly superficial. Annual reports are publications required of publicly held companies as a way of documenting fiscal soundness and chronicling the year's events. Many privately held companies and nonprofit organizations also produce annual reports, although they aren't required to. Whether public, private or nonprofit, many annual reports seem to have one thing in common—obscure language.

Here's one sentence from a real report—a good example of how *not* to write: "Net Profits from the sale or disposition of a Partnership property are allocated: first, prior to giving effect to any distributions of Sale Proceeds from the transaction, to the General Partner and the

Limited Partners with negative balances in their capital accounts pro rata in proportion to such respective negative balances, to the extent of the total of such negative balances; second, to the General Partner, in an amount necessary to make the balance in its capital account equal to the amount of Sale Proceeds to be distributed to the General Partner with respect to the sale or disposition of such property and third, the balance, if any, to the Limited Partners."

Some obscurity may come from meeting regulatory requirements of publicly held companies, but that does not justify it in the annual reports of private and nonprofit organizations. Indeed, the SEC itself encourages simple writing. It has published a handbook, *A Plain English Handbook—How to Create Clear SEC Disclosure Documents.* The handbook is available free on the SEC website at http://sec.gov/pdf/handbook.pdf. It contains details on the following writing tips:

- Use the active voice with strong verbs.
- Don't ban the passive voice, use it sparingly.
- Try personal pronouns.
- Omit superfluous words.
- Write in the "positive."
- Use short sentences.
- Replace jargon and legalese with short, common words.
- Keep the subject, verb and object close together.[5]

Until 2006, all USA corporations were required to send paper annual reports to shareholders at least 20 days prior to the annual meeting of the company's shareholders. In 2006, the New York Stock Exchange (NYSE) changed its rules, dropping the requirement for delivering paper annual reports to shareholders. Instead, NYSE-listed companies must post copies of their Form 10-K on their websites when they file the form with the SEC and at the same time distribute a news release announcing the filing. "This rule change does not affect the SEC's current requirement that an annual meeting proxy statement be accompanied or preceded by an annual report. Therefore, USA companies and other companies that are subject to USA proxy regulations still must deliver paper copies of their annual reports to shareholders"[6] and issue news releases announcing the filings.

Rule 14c-4—a part of the Securities Exchange Act of 1934 and still in effect—requires that information in the annual report to shareholders "in roman type at least as large and as legible as 10-point modern type except that to the extent necessary for convenient presentation, financial statements and other tabular data, but not the notes thereto, may be in roman type at least as large and as legible as 8-point modern type. All such type shall be leaded at least 2 points."[7]

Most corporations make their annual reports available on their corporate websites. In addition to annual reports, companies usually provide the following information on the Internet:

- Audios of conference calls
- Biographies of senior management
- Calendar of events
- Contact information
- Corporate governance information
- Dividend history
- Fact sheet or corporate profile

- Historical stock price information
- Information on products and services
- News releases other than earnings
- Quarterly earnings releases
- SEC filings such as the 10K or 10Q
- Stock prices and charts
- Stock transfer agent information
- Webcasts

Clarity Versus Accuracy

If a more readable report is more popular, why don't more organizations produce them? Evidently, readability is related to truth, truth is often equated with fact, and fact sometimes does not make a company look good. Because management has to have new capital to work with—and that means attracting new investors to the company's stock—writers of annual reports sometimes resort to obfuscation. That is, they fog up the report with writing that may be entirely truthful but is nonetheless so murky that hardly anyone understands what it says. On this point, a federal judge once said, "What has developed is a literary art form calculated to communicate as little of the essential information as possible while exuding an air of total candor."

There are other reasons, of course, why annual report writing is so bad. Some company executives demand formality in writing because they believe this makes their divisions look more important. Some company presidents, for example, wouldn't think of writing a letter that just anybody could understand. Furthermore, some presidents who know nothing about writing insist on writing their own letters without the help (or subsequent editing) of a seasoned public relations writer. To do otherwise would imply that they did not know how to write.

Another reason the writing in some annual reports is so bad is that it has to be cleared at many levels in the company before it is finally approved. Everybody wants to add, delete or change words. "The legal department, the accounting department, and all the others tend to put in a few more terms or qualifications, just to show, if nothing else, that they are on the job," says Robert Gunning, an expert on clear writing.[8]

Once you are in an organization and have turned out an annual report or two, you'll probably begin to anticipate such changes and start writing gobbledygook to begin with. But this won't help, because the same people who made changes before will make them again. So it's best to resist the temptation to join the crowd, and instead to write simply, directly and clearly, as usual. Remember, the annual report is a public document, intended to communicate the status of the company to the public. Says Gunning, "Many writers fool themselves into believing they are writing for the public when they are actually writing to impress the boss."[9] He says that no accountant would fake the net income figure just to make the boss feel better. Yet writers often do the equivalent in annual reports. The result is that annual reports end up containing long words, long sentences and long paragraphs, many of which are not needed at all.

Say It Right and Simply   Some executives will scream when you start shortening sentences and cutting out vague words. "You need those words to be accurate," they say. "It won't be correct if you say it any other way." You must recognize, too, that they may be right. Listen to them because they are experts in their fields, although they may not be expert writers. The point is not to say it right or to say it simply, but to *say it right and simply*.

You will quickly find that it is not always easy to say it right and simply. You may have to spend an inordinate amount of time with a sentence or paragraph to make it both right and simple. The fog that billows through some annual report writing is not produced by adherence to the dictates of strict accuracy but by the inclusion of details and qualifications that don't bear on the main point of the sentence or paragraph. If a detail or qualification alters the point, include it. If it does not, delete it and make it the primary occupant of another sentence or paragraph.

The key point here was stated clearly many years ago by USA Supreme Court Justice Benjamin Cardozo: "There is an accuracy that defeats itself by the overemphasis of details . . . The sentence may be so overloaded with all its possible qualifications that it may tumble down of its own weight."[10]

Comprehension   Vague words are also known as "glittering generalities." They are usually very abstract and impressive, but they don't communicate much. As a professional writer, you must be dedicated not only to truth but also to making your copy understandable. Comprehension increases in direct proportion to your use of simple, concrete words. Remember, you are writing to communicate, not to obfuscate. Annual reports that are not clearly written breed distrust.

In the following example, a company is having trouble selling some worthless land it owns in the West. But thanks to a deal made with another company, it may be able to dump its real estate soon. How did this relatively simple fact get reported in the annual report?

> We were less successful than we had hoped last year in achieving our goal of disposing of the properties of our land division, located principally in the western part of the United States. While conditions in real estate were difficult, we did conclude an important joint venture with [name of other company], which we expect will facilitate the disposal of our real estate assets.

Is it any wonder that people find fault with the writing in annual reports? The situation is changing though as government regulators are getting serious about requiring companies not only to tell the truth in annual reports but also to tell it plainly. The problem now may be that there's often not enough information, unless you ask for the 10-K.

It is easier to point out what is wrong with the writing in annual reports than to explain how to do it right. The first step, however, is to follow the principles of good writing. But even this is not enough; for your annual report writing to be successful, you must do it with a purpose. This means that you must proceed from a carefully drawn plan. One does not write an annual report on the basis of whimsy; rather, one approaches it as an important undertaking. The annual report is costly, time-consuming, sensitive and important. It makes sense to do such an important task right.

Planning the Report

Although our main concern here is writing, in writing an annual report you should never forget that the report is a publication—much like a magazine, in fact. It takes careful planning to produce a unified product. Art, design and writing must all mesh if communication is to be effective. Before you decide on format, choose type or begin to write, you must establish the report's purpose.

Purpose   The fundamental purpose of most annual reports is to provide investors with financial data and a description of the company's operations. But annual reports can do much more than this, and good ones do. Not only can the report tell the company story to investors, it also can present the company's views to many other publics—the media, community leaders, employees, prospective employees and financial analysts, for example.

Thus the first step in annual report planning is answering these questions: What should the report accomplish? Do you want to comfort investors, sell stock or paint a glowing picture of the company in order to attract new customers or employees? Is the purpose merely to maintain good employee or investor relations? Will the report be used to convey the company's point of view on key issues to community or industry leaders and to the media?

Obviously, the purpose is closely related to target publics. Whatever you want to say, you must know who will be reading the report so you can tailor your message to them. Step two of annual report planning, then, is to define your publics.

Publics   Stockholders are rarely the only public for annual reports, and they may not be the most important. Some companies—for example, those owned by holding companies—don't sell stock directly to the public. Annual reports for these companies might be directed to entirely different groups—perhaps to employees or legislators. The readership of annual reports is even broader now than before because many are available online. After the SEC required electronic filing, many companies decided to make the information generally available electronically because many brokers, analysts and financial editors would also be interested.

As with any piece of writing, then, it is important that you first define your readers. If there are two or more significant publics, you must also establish their relative importance. That means you must set some priorities. For example, if you are writing the annual report for a company in a heavily regulated industry, logically you will be concerned with both stockholders and regulators. But these are only two entries on what might be a fairly lengthy list (presented alphabetically):

Bankers	Legislators
Brokers	Potential customers
Community leaders	Potential employees
Consumer advocates	Potential stockholders
Customers	Regulators
Editorial writers	Reporters and business editors
Educators	Stockbrokers
Employees or members	Stockholders
Financial analysts	Suppliers

The list could be extended by several additional publics. However, you get the point that your annual report might be directed to several groups. And depending on the type of company and its industrial field, the list may include some of the preceding or a completely different list. It all depends on the purpose behind the report.

Don't start writing until you have listed all your possible publics. Then establish some priorities. The publics are not equally important. If you have difficulty establishing priorities, enlist the help of company management. Construct a short questionnaire that lists the options and a scale of importance for each. Company executives who know the relative importance of these publics can be of great help. Once you have clearly identified your major publics, you should direct your report to them.

Even if you identify and direct your report to only one public, remember that others may also read it, including competitors. If you are writing for stockholders, for example, remember that some stockholders may also be employees. If so, you will not improve employee relations by stressing how well your company is holding the line on costs by paying low wages.

Writing the Report

Once the purpose is set and publics have been identified, you can begin compiling information to use in the report. The first concern at this stage is content: What should the report say?

Determining Content   Determining content is probably the biggest problem in writing an annual report. In probably no other writing task is determining content so difficult. An individual writer composing a piece on a single topic merely gathers information, decides what to say and then says it. As an annual report writer, however, you will have to please many people before the report ever reaches its intended publics, and you are likely to run into some difficulty in trying to write material that is truthful, clear and acceptable to all.

Fortunately, there are some guidelines regarding content. For instance, government rules specify certain items that must be included. Among the essentials either required by law or generally demanded by the investment community are these:

Financial highlights
Financial summary
Letter from the chief executive officer
Corporate description
Narrative section describing operations
Balance sheet and income statements
Statement of sources and use of funds
Notes to financial statements
Auditor's report
Chief executive officer and chief financial officer's certification of financial statements
Ten-year statistical summary

Most of these essentials are simply tables of numbers, and they won't be of immediate concern to you as the writer, but their content may provide important clues to points you should emphasize in the narrative portion of the report. Accountants supply the numbers; writers supply the words. Providing the words usually means writing the chief executive's letter and the narrative section of the report.

CEO's Letter   When preparing the chief executive's letter to shareholders, you must first meet with that person to find out how the letter is to be written. Sometimes the executive will write a letter and turn it over to you for editing or rewriting. Sometimes it works the other way around. And sometimes the writer interviews the executive and then prepares a letter based on the executive's responses. Above all, the letter should "sound" like the chief executive. Any of these procedures is acceptable as long as a good letter is the result.

But what makes a good letter? There's no agreement on this—or even on what the letter should contain. Some simply summarize the year's financial results. Others may ignore money matters and talk about social problems facing the company and its industry. Still others may combine financial material and social commentary in a lengthy treatise designed to convince everybody that things are better than they seem.

Annual reports that are rated highest by financial analysts usually contain letters that adhere to a few basic principles. First, the best letters don't delve deeply into financial matters. Letters crowded with statistics are difficult to read. Except in brief mentions of key financial results, the numbers are best left for the tables and charts in the body of the report. Second, an incisive, concise letter is preferable to a lengthy dissertation that attempts to cover the minute areas of operation. Third, analysts expect the executive's letter to be devoted primarily to results of the previous year and expectations for the coming year or two. In this regard, the letter should include a discussion of future problems as well as anticipated successes.

Whatever the focus of the letter, it sets the stage for the narrative of the report, where the company's operations are described in detail.

Narrative   The body of the annual report is where you tell the company's story. This section contains a general description of the company or institution; its location, purposes, products and services; and its related activities. The narrative reports the company's results of the previous year and its plans for the future, even if these are mentioned in the executive's letter. The narrative must disclose and discuss events, management decisions, sales, mergers and conditions that have had significant effects on the company's operation.

At the same time, the narrative must also achieve the communication objectives set for it during the planning process. If the report's purpose is to get people to buy stock, the narrative must give reasons why the company's stock is a good deal. You can do this best not by talking dollars and cents but by describing the company's position in the industry, its management philosophy and its foresight and record of success.

The narrative of most annual reports also covers such topics as plans for expansion, research and development programs and the nature of the company's customers or markets. But merely presenting such basics isn't enough. Financial analysts want information on the problems facing the company and its industry, and a discussion of current economic conditions and their impact.

Analysts become specialists in certain industries and then carefully follow selected companies in those fields. You can't make your company look financially healthy if the numbers show that it isn't. What you must do is treat problems candidly but emphasize what the company plans to do to solve them. If the plans are sound, your candor may sell lots of stock. Even if it does not, you'll certainly earn credibility for your company in the financial community.

Discuss the status of the natural resources (if any) your company depends on, including the possibility of shortages and how the company will cope with them. Describe the marketing, advertising and public relations strategies that have been designed to communicate your company's goals and objectives. Tell how the company is responding to demands for greater corporate responsibility. All these matters are just as relevant in annual reports as the bottom-line figures of the income statement.

It is inevitable, of course, that even if you are determined to include all these things, you will have to fight the space battle. Something may have to be left out. How do you determine what can be deleted? First, check with the corporate attorney to identify items that must be included by law. As examples, the company may be involved in significant legal action or in some major financial transactions. Next, identify the items that most stockholders and analysts expect to see in any annual report. These include industry trends, financing, capital expenditures, consolidations, research, marketing and energy supply.

Selecting specific events to include in these categories is more difficult, however. One approach is to ask the executives in charge of company divisions which events and actions of the past year were the most important. This personal-interview technique is quite common. In fact, some annual reports simply use verbatim interviews with division heads, in a question-and-answer format. If you do this well, the technique can provide the necessary information whether or not you use that format in the report. Just keep in mind that the purpose of most interviews is to provide raw information that you need to sift and shape for your readers.

Another way to gather information from company executives is to use a written questionnaire. A simple survey can often help you get the information you need to gauge the relative importance of different topics—and thereby help you decide what to leave out. The simplest questionnaire merely asks executives to rate the importance of a few key areas. Such a form might look like the one in Table 12.1. To meet the needs of a given situation, you could add or leave out categories. In addition, you might leave space for comments or observations about the problems or successes a respondent designates as most important. A more extensive questionnaire might be called for if you want more detailed information. A series of short-answer questions like those in Table 12.2 could bring more useful responses.

TABLE 12.1   *Simple Structured Questionnaire*

In column A, rank the areas in which the company has achieved the greatest successes during the past year (1 = greatest success). In column B, rank the areas in which the company has experienced the greatest problems in the past year (1 = greatest problem).

A		B
_____ Community relations		_____
_____ Competition		_____
_____ Customer service		_____
_____ Employee relations		_____
_____ Energy supply		_____
_____ Government relations		_____
_____ Tax and regulations		_____
_____ Marketing and sales		_____
_____ Media relations		_____
_____ New product development		_____
_____ Stockholder/investor relations		_____
_____ Other: _____		_____

TABLE 12.2	*Annual Report Questionnaire for Executives*

1. Inside the company, what do you think was the most significant event of the past year?

2. What external event of the past year do you think had the most significant impact on the company?

3. What do you believe was the most significant accomplishment of your division of the company during the past year?

4. What do you believe is the most significant problem facing the company as a whole?

5. What was the most important event or development in your division of the company during the past year?

6. What do you believe was the most significant accomplishment of the company as a whole during the past year?

7. What do you believe is the most important problem facing your division of the company?

8. What event of the past year had the most significant impact on the company's industry?

9. What do you believe is the most important problem facing the company's industry?

10. What are the most significant things the company is doing to deal with companywide, divisional and industry problems?

Source: Adapted from a questionnaire by permission of Armstrong World Industries, Inc., Lancaster, Pa.

Responses to questionnaires like these will help you choose topics to include in the annual report. But you should never rely solely on such surveys. If your own research shows that something else is important and should be in the annual report, don't leave it out just because it didn't appear on the survey forms. Put it in and be prepared to explain why you included it.

Double-Checking the Narrative   Once you're in the throes of writing the narrative, the following points may prove useful. The SEC is concerned particularly with three areas: results of operations, liquidity of assets and capital resources. You must couch your discussion in the context of the three years of financial information required by the SEC. You can't simply list material items, unusual occurrences or infrequent transactions. You must discuss them in sufficient detail so that your least knowledgeable readers can understand them. The SEC provides no boilerplate solutions on how to write the narrative, but it doesn't want a line-by-line discussion of the financial statement. However, if a line item represents a significant change, that item should be discussed in detail. You are expected to find a way to characterize the company's business experience of the last year. The narrative is also expected to talk about trends and uncertainties. This expectation calls for you to peer into a crystal ball, however dark, so be cautious and choose your words carefully. Remember that you and your organization must live with those words.

Theme   Once you have settled on the content, the next step is to put it together in a cohesive way. You want the company to appear to be well managed, well organized and unified. The annual report should mirror these qualities from cover to cover.

The most common way to ensure cohesiveness is to find a theme. A theme is an organizing principle that provides a creative peg on which you can hang content. It helps you position content so that it flows naturally. Although each element should be sufficiently strong to stand alone, when all elements are taken together they should have super-additive qualities that yield a sum much greater than the individual parts.

For example, you might build an effective theme out of a significant event in the life of the company that occurred during the past year or that is on the horizon. Or you might find a theme in some major event or development that affects the entire industry, not just your company. A new product or service could supply a theme, especially if it signifies that the company is moving in a new direction. A good theme is one that provides a context for content. It should never overpower content, and it should never call attention to itself.

Prudence, however, shouldn't interfere with developing good, creative themes. Sara Lee built its annual report around paper dolls. That theme is much less sober than those usually seen in annual reports. Scissors, pages of paper dolls and an invitation to order paper doll books went with the annual report to investors. Paper dolls decorated the cover. They also were on inside pages to represent the company's business lines—packaged meats and bakery, coffee and grocery, personal products and household and personal care. The response to this unusual theme was so good that Sara Lee printed more than 10,000 paper doll books. Some investors even bought stock for children and grandchildren. They equated this creative strategy with a management style that signifies a good investment.[11]

Style With purpose, content and theme defined, you can begin to write. That means dealing with the question of what style of writing to use in the report. Degree of formality is often the first question of style to be answered.

Many annual report writers and most corporate executives might object to the informal style generally advocated by readability experts like Flesch and Gunning. Such objections are often based on the belief that an annual report is a very serious document and that informality is therefore inappropriate. It is true that the style should be appropriate to the document and to its readers. However, neither the document nor the readers should be the sole determinants of style.

Style is part of what you say—content and purpose. If your company wants to portray itself as a friendly, informal, neighborhood company eager to do business with just plain folk, then a stuffy style is as inappropriate for the annual report as it would be for a commercial on television. But a company that wants to be viewed as formal and sophisticated may use a refined writing style in its annual report, with contractions and humor kept at a minimum or prohibited altogether.

A formal style is no excuse for foggy writing, however. The annual report must be readable and comprehensible, whatever the style. No company wants to be viewed as incoherent and confusing. And no company wants to give the impression that the person representing the company in print is incapable of thinking clearly enough to write understandable prose. Many astute observers note that in one way or another fuzzy writing is usually a sign of fuzzy thinking. You should keep that point in mind—and it might help if you also passed that word to the legal staff.

The fact is that the final wording of the annual report is frequently the result of a clash between writer and lawyer and sometimes the chief financial officer, usually a CPA. Attorneys should have the last word in matters of law, but too often, attorneys are given the last word, period—even regarding writing style. And that can be bad news for simple writing. Gunning writes, "If a man draws a document that only he can interpret," "he has built himself a degree of security. He must be retained to interpret it."[12]

In general, neither attorneys nor accountants would lose their jobs if their writing was not understandable. Most don't intentionally confuse things, but many are not good writers. They are not trained as writers. So when it comes to issues of style, the professional writer must have the last word.

Timing   Clearly, an annual report is a major project for any company, and it is critical that the report be issued on time. That means setting and meeting deadlines over a long period. It is not unusual for the production of an annual report, from its inception at the planning stage until its delivery to its readers, to take six or seven months. One reason it takes so long to produce a good annual report is that the writer has to await the final version of the financial data following the close of the fiscal year before wrapping up the final details. Then the final report has to be approved at many levels in the organization.

There is no foolproof method of scheduling and producing an annual report. However, review the approximate schedule in Table 12.3 of a typical annual report of a company whose regulatory agencies require copies no later than March 31 of each year. This timetable will not work for every company or institution, but it will serve as a rough guideline for most situations.

TABLE 12.3	*Annual Report Timetable*

This is a sample production timetable for the annual report of a company whose regulatory agencies require a copy of the report by March 31.

September: Begin preliminary planning.

October: Send questionnaires to company executives. Compile research from company publications and other sources on events of the year.

November: Interview executives. Decide on theme and approach. Begin development of publication design options. Collect photographs and assign additional needed photographs to the photographer. Begin production of charts, graphs and other artwork.

December: Begin writing preliminary draft of chief executive's letter and narrative. Decide on publication design. Complete photographs, graphs and artwork, except for financial charts. Determine approach for Web site version of publication.

January: Circulate draft of narrative for review by various company departments. Begin publication production art. Revise draft of chief executive's letter and narrative as required.

February: Circulate final draft of letter and narrative for approval by executives, lawyers, auditors and other company departments as appropriate. Make final corrections. Complete production art on narrative, letter and financial tables (if available). Deliver disk of production art to printer by end of the month. Begin production of online version of report.

March: Review proofs provided by printer. Make final corrections to print and Web site versions. Distribute printed copies to regulatory agencies with required forms and to stockholders and appropriate distribution lists.

Source: Adapted from a timetable by permission of Armstrong World Industries, Inc., Lancaster, Pa.

Conclusions

- Reports and proposals may be done much like scholarly research papers.
- Reports and proposals can have as many as seven parts: letter, front matter, executive summary, body, references, bibliography and appendixes. Proposals also have budgets and timelines.
- Jargon is expected by readers in specialized fields but it should be used with restraint.
- Style and visual elements should be used in reports and proposals to improve readability, understanding and acceptance.
- Your reader should come away with a clear sense of the problems studied and your proposed solutions.
- Your suggestions should also serve as a call to action that appears to be doable.
- Some annual reports are getting briefer and some companies are working to make them more clear and more creative.
- Foggy writing may be caused by a conflict between telling the truth and looking good.
- Writing in annual reports should be clear and simple.
- Preparation of good annual reports includes careful planning, definition of purpose and identification of important publics.
- Some major divisions of content of annual reports are the chief executive's letter, which sets the stage for the entire report; the narrative description of the company's operations for the last year; expectations for the future; and financial summaries.
- Writing style may range from informal to formal, but should reflect the purpose behind the report.
- Production of an annual report is usually spread over several months. This is due, at least in part, to the fact that content has to be cleared through so many levels in the organization.

Exercises

1. Now that you work for a public relations firm, you are involved in working with a small group that's responsible for proposals that are presented to prospective clients. As she was leaving for the airport, Anita Strong, your supervisor, dropped on your desk a very thin file with the label "O. Joyitz Funn Manufacturing Systems (OJF)." OJF is interested in retaining a PR firm to help with media relations and occasional special events. Strong asked you to outline the contents of your firm's proposal to OJF. Review Chapter 6, then draft an email message to Strong containing the outline.

2. You are the vice president of communication at O. Joyitz Funn Manufacturing Systems. OJF is a major producer of plastic toys. The research and development department has recently created and successfully tested a new toy. Tests seem to suggest that the new toy, called "Rotzie," will be a huge seller. OJF is frantically working on a plant expansion to help accommodate the demand it expects when Rotzie is introduced. You are equally busy getting communication plans ready for a formal announcement two months from today. Although some employees are aware of Rotzie, most of them have no clue as to

how its potential sales will affect them or OJF. You know that you must put together news releases for local and national media as well as trade journals, and prepare speeches, brochures, sales literature and other things. But right now, you're pondering how to approach a feature story about Rotzie for the OJF employee magazine and the leading toy trade journal. Should the approach be the same for both? Why? Why not? Explain your decision.

3. Get a copy of an annual report from a publicly held company and another from a nonprofit foundation, either on paper or from Internet sites. Do a written comparative analysis of:

   a. Purpose
   b. Publics
   c. Content
   d. Style

4. Get an annual report from a publicly held company and do an analysis of the writing. In your analysis, look especially at:

   a. Purpose
   b. Readers
   c. Content
   d. Style

   Your report should be no longer than two double-spaced pages. Attach a copy of the annual report to your analysis.

Use InfoTrac® College Edition to access information on topics in this chapter from hundreds of periodicals and scholarly journals.

Writing Advertising Copy

Advertising is ubiquitous. When you retrieve your email, ads pop up everywhere. Ads are even in the social media you use. Corporate members of social media are there too, as part of the medium's constituency to interact with that medium's public and reinforce the organization's identity. You drive down streets lined with signs and billboards. The radio station you are tuned into while driving is likely to have commercials unless it is a public station and then you hear about sponsors. Television program content is sometimes difficult to isolate from commercials, and in some cases, the content itself is commercial.

So, everyone knows what an ad looks like, you might think. Wrong. Sometimes you have to look carefully. Product advertising and promotional pieces often blend into a confusing composite.

Generally advertising agencies prepare the direct sales ads for products and services. Promotional pieces may be done by ad agencies or by PR companies. But as a PR writer, you are in the business of selling ideas. The result may look like editorials or features, or exactly like advertising.

Ads that promote ideas run the gamut in terms of content. Some, like the ad in Figure 13.1, address public policy issues. In this case, the IBM ad notes that electronics are what makes it possible to work globally, smarter and "greener." Sometimes ads like this are called *advertorials*. If they are presented in electronic media, they are often called *infomercials*. Other ads, as in Figure 13.2, simply present organizations as good corporate citizens. Such ads are often called *institutional, identity* or *corporate-image ads*. Figure 13.3 presents Albuquerque, New Mexico, in a light that often is not associated with the state, not just to attract travelers, but also to improve the image of the city and the state.

Corporate sponsorship of nonprofit organizations is another way of enhancing corporate identity by association. Look for the logos of multiple sponsors, common in special events.

A mandate for change is a mandate for smart.

The world is ready for change – that much is clear.

For leaders of all kinds, this moment presents a rare opportunity. Our planet is not just getting smaller and flatter. It is also becoming smarter. And that means we have the potential to change the way the world literally works.

Computational power is now being put into things we wouldn't recognize as computers – cars, appliances, cameras, roadways…even pharmaceuticals and livestock. We are interconnecting all of this through the Internet, which has come of age. And we are applying powerful new systems and sophisticated analytics to turn oceans of data into insight, knowledge and intelligence.

Consider the changes already under way.

Smart traffic systems are helping to reduce gridlock by 20%, cutting pollution and increasing ridership on public transit.

Smart food systems based on RFID technology embedded into supply chains are monitoring meat, poultry and other items from the farm to the super-market shelf.

Smart healthcare systems are helping to lower the cost of therapy by as much as 90%.

Police departments are correlating street-level information from myriad observations and devices to identify crime patterns – helping prevent crime, rather than simply punishing it.

The list is long, and the transformation is just beginning. Its benefits will be reaped not only by large enterprises, but also by mid-sized and small companies – the engines of economic growth everywhere – and by individuals and communities around the world.

Imagine how a smarter planet will transform *all* the things we seek. The ways we pursue economic growth, societal progress, environmental sustainability and cures for disease. The way we interact with each other and with the world.

The opportunity is before us, and the moment will not last forever. Will we seize it? As we look to stimulate our economies and rebuild our infrastructure, will we simply repair what's broken? Or will we prepare for a smarter future?

Join us at **ibm.com**/think

IBM, the IBM logo and ibm.com are trademarks of International Business Machines Corporation, registered in many jurisdictions worldwide. A current list of IBM trademarks is available on the Web at "Copyright and trademark information" at www.ibm.com/legal/copytrade.shtml.

THINK IBM

FIGURE 13.1

Electronics Make Possible Working Smarter and Greener in a Global Society   *Ads attempting to influence public policy may originate with either nonprofit or profit making organizations. Here IBM's ad picks up on the concept of change and how electronics have changed and will continue to change the world.*

Source: Used with permission of IBM.

FIGURE 13.2

Waste Management Is Part of the Green Movement   *Waste Management's image ad reinforces the company's dedication to conservation not only with the message on its trucks, but also in the copy for this ad that carries a message, its slogan "From everyday collection to environmental protection" and its environmental link ThinkGreen.com.*

Source: Used with permission of Waste Management.

WOW! It's a Mountain, Imagine That in Albuquerque, New Mexico   *With exciting colors and sound the "It's A Trip" branch of the city's tourism office manages to entice travelers as well as present an image of the city that may be unexpected.*

Source: Used with permission of the Albuquerque Convention and Visitors Bureau and McKee Wallwork Advertising Agency.

Ads mistaken for features look just like their editorial counterpart. They have a story and art, often both pictures and graphics. The difference is that the ads are paid for, and although they are clearly designated as advertising, readers often don't notice that they are not editorial copy. These seem to appear less frequently now, probably due to FTC enforcement on identifying such content as advertising.

If you are in charge of a special event you may have a whole section inserted in a newspaper or magazine. These inserts also look like editorial material except for their dedication to a single topic. Furthermore, many websites are promotional and thus advertising but often perceived to be editorial.

Two other types of ads you'll be doing are house ads, as in Figure 13.4, in which *The Wall Street Journal* is calling attention to its special section, or public service ads for nonprofit organizations or their subsidiaries, such as Figure 13.5 from *Preservation Magazine*. No money is exchanged in the placement of these pieces, but the two qualify in every other way as advertising. House ads are advertising messages that appear in a company's own publications. They may be informational or persuasive such as urge employees to buy savings bonds or give blood or not to litter. Regardless of the sources or special purposes, ads always try to persuade.

Public service ads are ads that are carried at no charge in the print and broadcast media. When they appear on radio and television, public service ads are called public service announcements (PSAs). United Way, the American Heart Association, United Nations International Children's Fund (UNICEF) and a wide variety of similar organizations and causes benefit from such ads. (See Figure 13.6, a storyboard for AIDS, with Figure 13.7, the format for a storyboard. Figure 13.8 is a radio PSA script.)

The US Government is also involved in public service announcements and campaigns, as Figure 13.9 from the USA's Department of Defense illustrates. PSAs also appear on the Internet. Global crises such as earthquakes, floods and droughts generate online appeals for help.

Advertising as a Persuasive Force

Many people believe that advertising has the power to make people buy things they neither need nor want. If this were true, it would follow that advertising could be used by public relations professionals to make publics accept ideas they might otherwise reject. But advertisers will quickly tell you that advertising does not work that way.

Advertisers know that the power of advertising is limited to persuasion. It cannot coerce. Used skillfully, advertising may stimulate in an audience a predisposition to buy a product, use a service or accept an idea. Advertising has proved itself to be economically efficient at persuasion, because it works on the principle that you attract more bees with honey than with vinegar.

Appeal

The key element in a successful ad is the relevance of the appeal it has for the receiver of the message. This appeal should be as direct as possible. In writing ads, don't leave the appeal to inference. Spell it out. An appeal can be emotional, rational or a combination of the two.

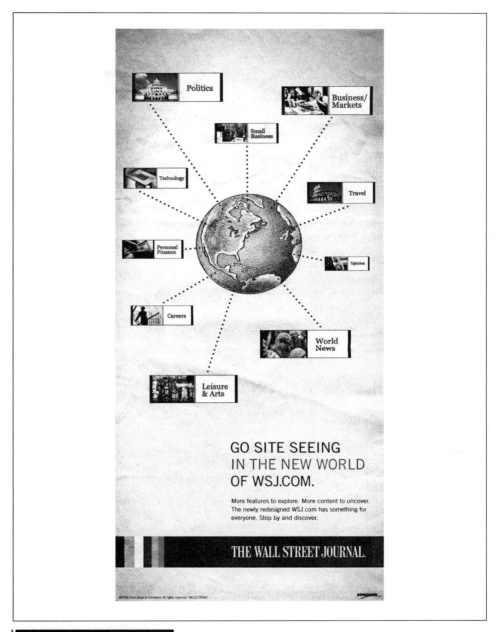

FIGURE 13.4

A House Ad in *The Wall Street Journal* Calls Attention to a Special Section   *Knowing that many readers have special parts of the paper they attend, to the exclusion of others,* The Wall Street Journal *has a house ad to call attention to its special section.*

Source: Used with permission of *The Wall Street Journal.*

Public Service TV Storyboard for Television   *This 10-second PSA, done by Brogan Partners of Birmingham, Michigan, for the Michigan Department of Health, AIDS Prevention Program, delivers a message like a karate punch—swift and hard. It uses finished art—hence, it is called a presentation storyboard—to show the sequential development of nonverbal and verbal content. (V/O means voice-over.)*

Source: Reprinted by permission of Brogan Partners.

Emotional appeals tug at the heart. They suggest that the receiver can benefit—become happier, healthier, sexier, more attractive, more successful or richer in any number of other qualities if he or she behaves in a specific way. The number of emotional appeals open to the ad writer seems to be infinite.

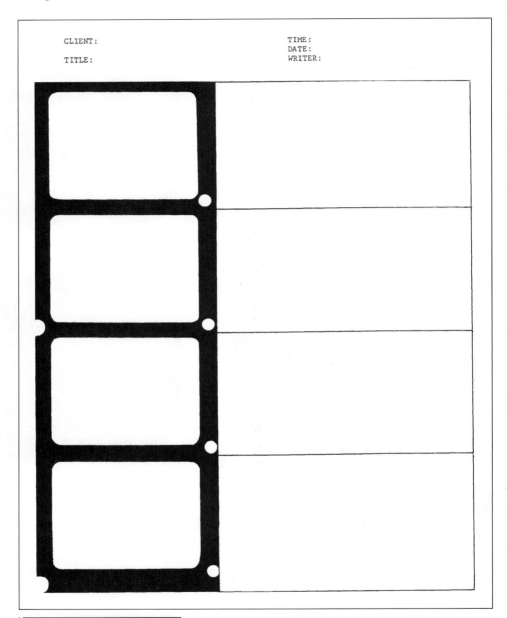

CLIENT:

TITLE:

TIME:
DATE:
WRITER:

FIGURE 13.7

Blank TV Script Sheet *This blank television script sheet may be helpful to writers as they try to conceptualize how words and visuals fit together to form a cohesive, effective message. Review the message in Figure 13.8 to see how well it fits this model.*

Rational appeals, on the other hand, appeal to the receiver's reason. Such appeals are likely to be based on economy, durability, profit, efficiency and performance, among others.

Combination appeals use emotion first to get people to pay attention and then use rational appeals once the receivers are interested in the copy. The copy will usually close by returning to an appeal to the heart.

One reason to use a media mix is the quality of attention these appeals get in various media. A television or magazine ad is likely to get undivided attention, once it is captured. This is usually the case too with other print media, including newspapers, but less true of radio advertising because attention to radio advertising is often divided by driving demands, passengers or mobile phone use. In the case of online advertising, whether it be websites or social media, there are too many distractions due to moving images and a crowded competitive field.

Positioning

A particular appeal works in concert with the marketing idea of "positioning the product." The writer expresses the appeal creatively in an attempt to carve out a special niche for the advertiser in the minds of the public. For example, Hertz has been the dominant rental car company for decades, with Avis in a distant second position. At some point, Avis decided to capitalize on its number two position and appeal to the public's inclination to root for the underdog. In this way, the "We Try Harder" idea was born.

Viewed rationally, a Lexus is a Lexus, whether it has the Hertz logo or the Avis logo on it. If there is no significant difference in the rental fees and services offered by the two companies, why should you rent a Lexus from Avis rather than from Hertz? There is no rational reason. Avis makes an emotional appeal to the prospective customer by positioning itself in the public's mind as number two. Everybody knows that number two has to try harder to be number one. Therefore, the suggestion is, you should rent from Avis, because Avis tries harder. When employees bought the company, the slogan was modified to say "Owners Try Harder."

This principle of positioning was aptly applied when a major city wanted to pass an enormous bond program to rebuild and improve an extensive portion of one of its oldest freeways. Each time they were asked, voters denied the bonds. On its last try, the city launched a "safety bond" program to finance the project. Positioning it as a safety project focused attention on its benefit rather than on its cost. The issue passed by a comfortable margin. Cause-related nonprofit organizations can learn from this to focus on the solutions, not on the problems.

Slogans matter. Slogans reinforce branding because they aid identification. One mistake often made is changing a slogan because the management is tired of it. A slogan encourages employees and keeps everyone in the organization focused on the mission. Slogans comfort customers and give them a reason to choose the product, service or organization. Even children recognize a slogan their parents, and probably grandparents, grew up with: "Melts in your mouth. Not in your hand." The two Ms "Melt and Mouth" reinforce the product's name: M&M.

Postitioning is fundamental to **branding** for an institution. Branding is an effort to create instant identification of the organization and association with what it does and is. In that respect, the repetitive appearance of the brand in the news media appears to enhance brand value, more probably it is brand recognition. Media appearance, though, can be in news or advertising, and this complicates measurements of effect.

"FREIGHT TRAIN" :30 SECONDS

MUSIC: *Ominous and Foreboding Music*

SFX: *Distant Train Horn*

MALE V/O: *"It's coming again."*
                    "In seconds it will be here."
                    "Your heart pounds."
                    "You can't breathe."
                    "You're terrified."

SFX: *Train Horn Getting Louder and Swiftly Closing In*

MALE V/O: *"You're sure you're about to die."*

SFX: *Pounding Heartbeat*

FEMALE ANNCR:

For people with Panic Disorder, this is how it feels to have a panic attack. Find out how you can get help. Call 1-800-64-PANIC. 1-800-64-PANIC. Panic Disorder. It's real. It's treatable. A public service message from this station and the National Institute of Mental Health.

FADE OUT

FIGURE 13.8

Public Service Announcement Radio   *The National Institute of Mental Health Panic Disorder Education Program produced its "Freight Train" PSA in 30- and 60-second versions. The two are identical up to the segment in which a female announcer reads the copy. SFX refers to sound effect.*

Source: NIMH Panic Disorder Education Program, Radio Public Service Announcements, Spring/Summer 1994. Used with permission.

Advertising is always favorable because the message is controlled, and it enforces recognition due to planned exposure—purchased time or space. Exposure in the news media on the editorial side can put the brand in a positive or negative light. As an example, American International Group (AIG) has extensive advertising exposure through its corporate advertising and advertising by its various subgroups or companies. Institutional coverage during the 2008 global financial crisis was not positive. The negative recognition significantly tarnished the brand, for the basic company and all of its subsidiaries.

Behavior

Understanding what people think and do in different parts of society is critical to developing credible advertising. Good advertising writers understand that there may be a little bit (and perhaps a lot) of snob in all of us, because we like to relate to others and have others relate to us.

"FREIGHT TRAIN" :60 SECONDS

MUSIC: *Ominous and Foreboding Music*

SFX: *Distant Train Horn*

MALE V/O: *"It's coming again."*
                    "In seconds it will be here."
                    "Your heart pounds."
                    "You can't breathe."
                    "You're terrified."

SFX: *Train Horn Getting Louder and Swiftly Closing In*

MALE V/O: *"You're sure you're about to die."*

SFX: *Pounding Heartbeat*

FEMALE ANNCR:

This is how it feels to have a panic attack. And for millions of Americans with Panic Disorder, attacks happen over and over again. They come out of the blue. They don't last long. But they can change your life. Trips to the emergency room and medical tests may show nothing's wrong. But you know there is.

If you think you have Panic Disorder, find out how you can get help. Call 1-800-64-PANIC. 1-800-64-PANIC. Panic Disorder. It's real. It's treatable.

A public service message from this station and the National Institute of Mental Health.

FADE OUT

FIGURE 13.8 *(continued)*

Behaviorists spend a lot of time trying to understand our reference groups—organizations to which we belong or want to belong. We all want the comfort of belonging, of being accepted. For this reason, friends and family are important to us, and we seek their approval.

A proliferation of social media has resulted in an acceleration of the spread of information and the reinforcement of opinions, both positive and negative about an organization's products, services, actions, consumer experiences and such. The result is the emergence of unanticipated and previously unidentified leaders.

We are all influenced by opinion leaders, but not the same ones. Different segments of society have different opinion leaders, and each of us reacts to those leaders differently based on our experiences, education and our own personality. For example, authoritarian types are more vulnerable to leaders who have status and authority.

If you are getting the idea that people don't respond rationally to a lot of advertising copy, you are right. Most of the decisions we make are based on emotion, not reason. That is why good advertising copy is a complex blend of information (facts) and appeal (emotion).

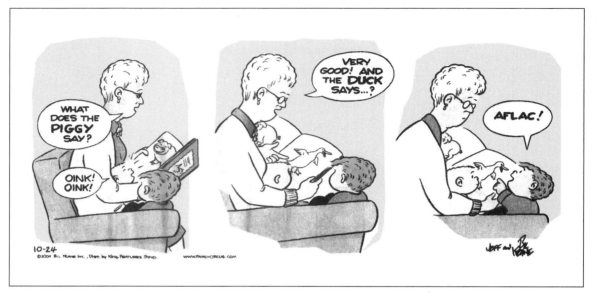

The Family Circus, by Bil Keane, "What does the Piggy say? 10/24/04 Bil Keane, Inc. Reprinted courtesy of Bunny Hoest, Wm. Hoest Enterprises.

Basic Guidelines for Writing Advertising Copy

Advertising copywriters are often believed to have a great deal more creative freedom than most other writers because they work under few artificial restraints. For example, you might view writing a news release as less creative than writing copy for an ad, because in the former case you must conform to newswriting style. But there are rules and restraints on ad copywriting too.

Purpose

To begin with, you must have a clear understanding of what you want to accomplish with the ad. Do you want your public to support the bond issue? Do you want shareholders to vote for the recapitalization of the company? You must know the single (never multiple) specific purpose for the ad. And everything you put in the ad should contribute to that purpose. In editing the ad, delete as excess baggage any word, phrase, sentence, paragraph or visual that does not specifically further the purpose. The receiver should not have to wrestle with excess baggage in discerning the message you are trying to communicate.

Objective Facts

You'll be able to select a specific purpose for the ad only after carefully and thoroughly reviewing all the pertinent facts about the issue. You should review these facts not only from your side's point of view but also from that of your opposition. In fact, the latter review is just as important as the former. And both reviews have to be done with objectivity. Only then can you make an informed judgment about the strengths and weaknesses of your position and those of your competition. And only then should you attempt to derive a purpose calculated to capitalize on one of your strengths or to attack one of the opposition's weaknesses.

Multiple publics always are involved in each effort, so you have to prioritize publics and evaluate desirable outcomes for each. Without a clear behavioral goal for each public involved, you have no way of evaluating the results of your effort.

The Publics

You should review the facts and select a purpose for the ad with a full awareness of the uniqueness of your publics. You need to know their wants, needs and values. This is where demographic and psychographic information assumes great importance. Although no public is homogeneous, you must consider some basic characteristics.

If the members of your public are blue collar, average less than a median income, have a ninth-grade education and suffer from a high rate of unemployment, you may have difficulty in persuading them to support a large bond program to build a junior college in the community. This doesn't mean you won't be successful in gaining their support, but it does mean that you will have to write credible messages that clearly demonstrate the rewards such support will bring.

Publics examine every message for how it may affect them personally. In a diverse society, you need to know the consistency and conflicts of value systems. Furthermore, many of these publics are interactive and share messages and opinions about them. You have to keep in mind that we have a global marketplace of ideas as well as products and services, including media that potentially reach across borders and time zones.

Media

Before you write the copy, you must know which medium or media you are writing for. One of your first concerns, of course, is to meet the technical requirements of the medium.

An ad prepared for a newspaper may not meet the requirements of a magazine, and it certainly won't meet those of radio or television or the Internet. If you are writing ads for a medium with which you are unfamiliar, first check the technical requirements in the most recent issue of *Standard Rate and Data Service (SRDS). SRDS* will also provide you with deadline information, a list of key personnel and other data. *SRDS* is one of the bibles of the advertising business.

Beyond technical issues, you need to know a lot about the medium you will use. How credible is it? How evocative is it? How do people react to it? What audience does it reach? What audience does it seek? What is its editorial slant? What have other advertisers experienced who have used it in similar situations? These are important questions, and you must know—not guess at—the answers. In some cases, you may have to rely on word-of-mouth, but in other cases, you will be able to gather a lot of information from the medium itself simply by writing or calling.

The Creative Approach

Never try to develop a creative approach or write a line of copy until after you have made the decisions specified above. These decision areas are parts of what advertising professionals call a *copy platform.* A copy platform is a succinct document that spells out pertinent information about the public and contains a simple statement of creative strategy. A creative-strategy statement for a little-known candidate running for senator against an incumbent might read like this:

> To convince voters that Mr. X will represent the views of eastern Kentuckians better than Ms. Y.

This statement clearly expresses your purpose (strategy). The question then becomes: How will I do it? That's where creativity comes in.

Let's suppose that Ms. Y is noted for being absent from the Senate floor when important bills that may affect eastern Kentuckians are up for a vote. You could construct a series of ads in which Mr. X pledges to be in the Senate chamber during every important vote. The voters would probably want to hear this message, though they might consider the claim to be mere political rhetoric.

You could take the offensive and attack Ms. Y by showing an empty chair during a roll call. You could then support the point with a table, showing not only the bills on which Ms. Y did not cast votes but also the number and dates of her absences. In other words, you could provide a lot of solid, verifiable, convincing information that Ms. Y is not doing the job properly. Still another approach might be to show Mr. X, dressed in hunting garb and following some hunting hounds on the scent. Mr. X would look up and explain that he and his "dawgs" were looking for Ms. Y. An obvious close would be a superimposed message like this:

> Where *is* Ms. Y? Vote for Mr. X. You will always find him in the Senate.

Of these three approaches, the first is mundane. It is low on persuasiveness because there is nothing unique about its claim. The ad neither excites the emotions nor challenges the reason. The second ad is more creative, and it contains lots of convincing and damning information about Ms. Y. It is more likely to be persuasive. But the third approach, which is obviously best executed for television, is not only more creative but it is also dramatically persuasive. How could a voter see that ad and remain free of resentment toward Ms. Y? And as resentment builds, voters will be more easily persuaded to vote for Mr. X. Emotion is the essence of good creativity in advertising.

Another strategic consideration is what is called a "push" or "pull" tactic. Media selection generally is considered a "push" tactic—placing an ad where it will be exposed to the publics you want to reach. This is a downward message system to the consumer. Pull is an upward message from the consumer, stimulated by a number of tactics creating interest or demand from the consumer. The "pull" tactic is more subtle in that you have to provide for ways for recipients to reach you and encourage that tug.

Prescription drug ads that invite people to ask their doctors about the product are the most obvious. Pull is most subtle in blog links and in social networks. Pull by mentions, promotions, product placement and such are more likely devices that involve public relations writers.

Visualization

As you read the discussion on creative approaches, it may have occurred to you that creative strategy in advertising involves visual as well as verbal thinking. If so, you caught on to an essential difference between writing news copy and writing advertising copy. A good advertising copywriter always thinks in visual as well as verbal terms. The reason the hunting scene just described is so dramatic is that the visual element graphically characterizes the verbal message. In the best advertising copy, verbal and visual content harmonize perfectly so that each complements and extends the message of the other. See how visuals take the reader through the message in Figure 13.6.

Language

It is axiomatic that, if you want to communicate with someone, you must use language that the other person will understand. Language has certain rules, and if they are not generally observed, communication may be impossible or the result unwanted. Thus the common rules of grammar and syntax are the standard in advertising, as they are in other forms of writing. You can break a grammar rule for a purpose—to achieve a specific effect not possible with traditional rules—but doing so should be the exception, not the rule.

Always choose the simple over the complex word. Your public might be able to read and comprehend at the college-graduate level, but people generally prefer to read copy that is two to four grade levels below their ability. And if you have any doubt about the educational level of your audience, you should gear your writing to about three grade levels lower than you believe it to be.

With increasing numbers of Spanish-speakers in the USA, decisions about using Spanish in advertising have copywriters in a quandary. Some attempts have been made to put the ad copy, whatever the medium, all in Spanish. Sometimes a mix of Spanish and English is used—Spanglish, it sometimes is called. People who speak and read Spanish only are more comfortable with Spanish, especially if the copy is dealing with a complex subject. However, many Spanish speakers are just as comfortable with a mix of English and Spanish. Knowing which your priority publics prefer, and in what circumstances, is essential.

Language choices always matter, even in English. Obviously, if you are writing an idea ad for your company that will appear in a highly specialized professional journal, you should use language appropriate to that public. This may mean using some professional jargon. If your ad is to appear in a general mass medium, however, simplify the language and avoid jargon.

Not only should you use simple words, you should also use short phrases, sentences and paragraphs. Sentences should average no longer than 12 to 15 words. Paragraphs should average about three to five sentences. Following these guidelines will improve your writing's readability.

Repetition

Do you recall the outcome of Pavlov's experiment with his dogs? As the number of repetitions mounted, the dogs began to associate the meat powder with the sound of the tuning fork. When the repetitions were plotted on a graph, a learning curve took shape. Finally, the curve leveled; that is, after a while additional repetitions did not cause the learning curve to go higher. Thus repetition is an essential principle of learning. You can apply this principle to your message in two basic ways.

The repetition principle applies first to the actual writing of copy. The general rule is that you should repeat the essential point of your message at least three times in your ad. This does not mean that you have to repeat it verbatim, but only that you must repeat the idea. This is absolutely crucial in broadcast messages, because they are so fleeting.

The principle of repetition also applies to how frequently you repeat the message to your public and in what time frame. Generally, if you are introducing a new program or idea, you will have to present your message fairly frequently during the early stages of your program. As your audience becomes familiar with what you are promoting, you can reduce the number of presentations and space them out, while still maintaining a reasonable level of awareness.

When your campaign ends, the public will begin to forget at approximately the same rate at which it learned. Still, the public's awareness about what you said will not drop back to zero. Hence, it will take less effort in a subsequent campaign to raise public awareness to former levels. This is a good argument for sustained programming, of course, because it suggests that sustaining awareness is more efficient than building it.

These general guidelines apply across all media and in all copywriting situations, so we'll consider writing public service announcements first.

Public Service Announcements

Public service announcements are advertising messages from nonprofit organizations that appear in media-donated time or space. Occasionally, a medium will give the nonprofit organization a "statement" that shows the commercial value of the donation. PSAs are different from situations where a commercial institution surrenders some of its contracted for time or space to a message from a nonprofit organization. When that occurs, the ad usually has a line in it that indicates the donor of the time or space.

PSAs for print media usually appear in the back of magazines or in "fill spaces" of newspapers where a paid-for ad didn't fit or the space, always small, simply was unsold and not desirable for an "in-house" ad. In broadcast media, the traffic manager for the station logs PSAs into unsold time that is not desirable for the station's own promos, promotional announcements.

What that means for the copywriter is that you must prepare public service ads of all shapes and sizes in a digital format so these are available for any open space, vertical or horizonal, color or black and white—usually color that fits just as well if seen only in black and white. Online spaces are less likely to be available, but occasionally are. If you, as a public relations writer, prepare much advertising for broadcast media, it is likely to consist mostly of PSAs.

Whatever the medium, there are some constants to consider. To do PSAs well, you must decide first whether your primary purpose is to *inform* or to *persuade*. If it is mostly to inform, you'll need to amass lots of information, sift it wisely and use it selectively. You must be able to say a lot in a little time or space. If the purpose is to persuade, you'll still need information, but you'll put more emphasis on its interpretation. And you'll arrange it so it has the maximum persuasive impact.

A variation on these two purposes is a "positioning" PSA. Think of the safety bond program described earlier. That was essentially an exercise in positioning or focusing people's attention on safety rather than cost. A positioning PSA seeks to position an idea in some unique way against all other related ideas. Effective positioning can have a significant impact on what people understand, accept, reject or feel about something. It also may influence what they recall and how they associate it with other relevant information.

Whatever your purpose, PSAs for nonprofit organizations can be created on elaborately produced CDs or DVDs. Many organizations' national headquarters provide their own PSAs in these forms, and they usually leave room for a tag line to be added at the local level. More often, however, PSAs are produced locally for local agencies. PSA scriptwriters try to keep things simple. (Refer to Figure 13.6 and see Figure 13.9.)

For television PSAs, you'll need video footage to be edited as the visual for the PSA. A station announcer or a local personality may volunteer services to do the audio. If the volunteer is a local personality, you should write the script to match as closely as possible that personality's style of speaking. Because all of this is recorded, there is some assurance of quality control, and it must be presented in broadcast quality.

On radio, it is possible, although unlikely, that your PSA script given to a local station will be read live by an announcer. You should realize how little control you really have over whether or not your message will be broadcast at all and no control over its presentation. Your best assurance is to write an infallible script and it is always safer to *under*-write—that is, use fewer words.

Writing Advertising Copy for Electronic Media—Television, Radio, Online

Brevity, clear style and sharp technique are the hallmarks of good electronic copywriting. Because an audience's attention is easily distracted, your copy must be simple, direct and provocative. Avoid clichés and slang. Be careful to make smooth transitions from one point to the next. Personalize the message by emphasizing "you" at every opportunity. People are more likely to respond personally to a message if they think it is directed to them. So try to write your copy as if it were a personal conversation between you and a friend.

Avoid exaggerated claims; don't make any claims that you wouldn't make to your closest friend. Your persuasive appeal must be distinctive so that your audience will remember it when they see or hear it again.

You must capture the attention of your audience in the first few seconds or you will lose it completely. Be sure to register the name of the company or organization, and let the audience know what you want it to do. A sense of urgency may help move the audience to action.

With broadcast media, TV and radio, time frames vary by medium and even among stations. Generally, though, you will usually write for periods lasting 10 seconds (25 words), 20 seconds (45 words), 30 seconds (65 words) or 60 seconds (125 words). Word count is approximate. Count it! The actual word limits may vary a little from radio to television to film, but in any case ,you have to tell a complete story in just a few well-chosen words. This is seldom easy.

Radio and television have different technical capabilities, of course, but some styles of message presentation are common to all three media. One is the "slice of life," which is a mini-drama that presents a situation anyone might experience. It provides the context for the message.

Another is the jingle approach, in which music and words are combined to make the message memorable, identifiable and entertaining. A humorous approach is appropriate in either of these media. This may include anything from a cartoon or a mini-sitcom (situation comedy), for television, or to a joke, usually radio only. The difficulty with humor is in finding universal themes that will not go stale quickly. And remember, never make your audience the victim of the humor.

Another technique is the interview. Here an announcer talks with representative members of your public. Still another approach is the testimonial. If you use a testimonial approach, however, be sure to establish the credibility of the people testifying. Otherwise, the audience will tune out your message.

You can use sound effects with any or all of these approaches. And you can combine the techniques themselves in some fashion.

Television and film have the additional benefit of permitting visual demonstration. This may be done through live action, animation or a combination of the two. In writing for television or film, consider the visual aspect carefully.

Your choice of a copy approach will depend above all on your resources—that is, money and facilities. Be prepared for the frustration that comes when you have to reject a creative idea because you can't afford to realize it. As you consider various techniques, you may want to review what others have done in similar situations. You won't want to copy from them, but you should not hesitate to adapt ideas that have worked for others.

Copywriting for TV

When writing copy for television, imagine how your ad will look as well as how it will sound. This will help make the message stronger and more persuasive. Remember that you have to think visually and verbally.

Divide your paper down the middle so that you have two equal columns. Label the left column "description" and the right column "script." In the right column, begin to write the words you want your public to hear. Concentrate on the single, basic idea of the message, and remember to promise your public some reward—a benefit that is both explained and supported.

Now go back and polish what you have written. Pare away unneeded words, phrases and sentences. Get the verbal message into what you consider finished form. Then have someone read the script aloud to you. Make sure the reader doesn't study the message beforehand, but reads it "cold." Listening to your copy being read aloud by someone else will help you to spot parts that need to be corrected, eliminated or rearranged.

Now repeat the process, this time working down the left side and describing the visuals that are to accompany the verbal message. Make certain that the visual images match and interpret their verbal counterparts. In some cases, you may be working from a prepared television script sheet.

Remember that one of television's strengths is action. Avoid static scenes. If the image does not move, the audience will shift its attention to something more interesting. You must pay attention to the visual, but don't become so carried away with it that you forget the message you want to convey.

In television, it is common to carry the preparation process a step further and create a storyboard. Figures 13.6 and 13.7 illustrate this idea. The storyboard depicts graphically what you have described down the left side of your script sheet. Although an artist is often assigned the job of making a storyboard, many copywriters find it is helpful to make their own, using stick figures to properly sequence the visuals. They often write their copy under each frame so they can better judge its unity. Internet ads must be carefully planned also, as these involve color, movement and sound.

Copywriting for Radio

Approach copywriting for radio as you would that for television—by dividing your paper and labeling the columns to make a script sheet. That is simple enough, but writing really good radio copy is more difficult than writing for television. In television, you have visual images to help you convey your message. In radio, you have only the visual theater of the mind. Although this is a vast territory, it is one in which many copywriters get lost.

Begin your copy in the right-hand column. You'll have to search especially hard for just the right words to evoke the images you want to paint in the public's collective mind. That is, you'll have to imagine exactly what you want the public to see. Language can be your best ally or your worst enemy. It will be the latter if you use uncommon words, especially those that have regional or local usages. Be wary of these. Also be cautious about using dialects.

Once you have written the message in the right-hand column, have someone read it "cold" so you can listen for semantic traps. Verify that the mental images you evoke unfold in a logical, easy-to-follow sequence, or you'll lose your listeners. You'll need to build excitement and drama, but be sure to drive home the message by repeating it at least three times in the script.

With the verbal content completed, work in the left-hand column providing complete cues regarding music, volume changes, announcers, sound effects and similar production concerns. Check your descriptions against the verbal messages in the right-hand column to make sure they match. (See Figure 13.8 for a radio PSA script.)

Sometimes in small local markets, radio scripts are read live by announcers. If you distribute your copy to stations in script form to be read live, make sure the words are simple to pronounce and flow smoothly, so the announcers will not foul up the announcement by mispronouncing them. Placing the wrong inflection on a word or phrase can distort the message by giving copy elements the wrong emphasis. The safest step is to prerecord your spots.

Online PSAs

Most large nonprofit organizations have a selection of PSAs for print, television and radio on their websites, available for use. These PSAs may be uploaded to social network sites, and can be converted to a TinyURL to save space.

The American Kennel Club (www.akc.org/press_center/psa.cfm) offers a selection of TV PSAs and Print PSAs, using different approaches or themes. The organization also ties in with commercial organizations, such as films. The site shows color photos representing the theme and offers download of the PSA in different formats and times. The site also has some AKC TV commercials listed, but not available for downloading.

Government organizations at all levels are nonprofit and depend on free time or space. To make access easy, the nonprofits put print, television and radio announcements on a website. The USA Department of Defense launched a campaign to combat an increasingly bad image from news reports about harassment of women in uniform—Sexual Assault Prevention and Response Office (SAPRO) website. DoD representatives called attention to the campaign with news releases about it and with appearances on talk shows. (See Figure 13.9 go to their home page where you can see the campaign and all materials: http://www.sapr.mil/HomePage.aspx?Topic=ResourcesReports&PageName=ReportLinks.htm.)

Centers for Disease Control and Prevention
Your Online Source for Credible Health Information

Novel H1N1 Flu (Swine Flu)

Keep 'em home!   CDC
www.cdc.gov/h1n1flu

On this Page

- Buttons & Badges (#Buttons)
- CDC-INFO (#CDCINFO)
- eCards (#eCards)
- Image Sharing (#ImageSharing)
- Micro-blogs (Twitter) (#Microblogs)
- Mobile (#Mobile)
- Online Videos (#OnlineVideos)
- Podcasts (#Podcasts)
- RSS Feeds (#RSS)
- Social Networking Sites (#SocialNetworking)
- Text Messaging Pilot (#TextingPilot)
- Widgets (#Widgets)
- More Information (#More)

Overview

Since April 2009, the Centers for Disease Control and Prevention (CDC) and the U.S. Department of Health and Human Services (HHS) have been working together to provide consumers and partners with social media tools that provide information about the ongoing 2009 novel influenza A (H1N1) outbreak. Widgets, mobile information, online videos and other tools reinforce and personalize messages, reach new audiences, and build a communication infrastructure based on open information exchange. Visit the CDC.gov 2009 H1N1 Flu (http://www.cdc.gov/h1n1flu/) and Flu.gov ✈ (http://www.pandemicflu.gov/) Web sites for information on novel H1N1 flu.do

Novel H1N1 Flu Social Media Tools

To encourage information sharing, collaboration, and interactivity, CDC provides social media tools. Widgets, mobile information, online videos and the like reinforce and personalize messages, reach new audiences, and build a communication infrastructure based on open information exchange.

Sign up for email updates (http://www.cdc.gov/emailupdates/index.html) to receive announcements of new products we add to this page.

Buttons and Badges

Add a button to your Web site. Let your Web site visitors know how to stop the spread of novel H1N1 flu and where to get more information about novel H1N1 flu.

- Choose a novel H1N1 flu Button in English (/SocialMedia/Campaigns/H1N1/Buttons.html)
- Choose a novel H1N1 flu Button en Español (/spanish/mediossociales/H1N1/botones.html)

http://www.cdc.gov/SocialMedia/Campaigns/H1N1/   10/28/2009

FIGURE 13.9

Social Media Message Location: *Going to publics, rather than counting on their coming to your website, is the CDC's strategy for getting a thorough distribution of H1N1 flu information. Note the scope and variety of messages available electronically.*

Source: Centers for Disease Control and Prevention sources for online messages.

Broadcast Production Relationships

Your role as writer may not end with the completion of a script. You may find yourself involved in a working relationship with production professionals. If you're in an agency, someone in account services will likely assume the role of liaison with production specialists. If not, or if you're not in an agency, you may be called on to coordinate production of your script with these people. You need not be a production expert to do this.

Key Players   There are certain specialists who are critical to the successful production of your video or audio script. You must clearly understand their functions and establish good working relationships with them. Good relationships are built on mutual professionalism, respect and attention to detail. Who are these people, and what do they do?

Executive Producer   This person is in charge of one or more projects or programs. The executive producer coordinates with clients, station or corporate management, advertising and public relations agencies, investors and talent (and their agents, if they have them) and approves and manages the production budget. This person's word is final. Get to know him or her well. If problems arise, the executive producer can be your best ally or worst enemy.

Producer   The producer is the person who will directly supervise the production of your script. He or she has direct supervision of all the production personnel working on your script and coordinates all of the technical and nontechnical elements. In larger operations, there may be *associate producers* (APs) who share some of the producer's responsibilities. In small production houses or stations, the producer may also double as a writer and/or director.

Studio and Field Producers   In large operations, producers may have different assignments. Studio producers supervise only studio productions. Field producers are assigned to on-location, out-of-studio field productions.

Director   This is the key person to direct all talent in the production and technical operations. The director is also the key to transforming your script into effective video and/or audio messages. In smaller production houses or stations, the director may also serve as the producer.

Bidding   When your script is approved by the client, it will probably be put out for bids. Invitations to bid can vary extensively in their complexity. Depending on the nature and length of your script, bids may be sought from video production houses, audio production houses, film production houses, television station studios or radio station studios.

If you're lucky, the winning bidder will be close by, so that eye contact with a minimum of telephone discussions and travel is possible and desirable. But the winning bid may come from a distant source, making substantial travel more likely. In that context, it is more difficult to build and sustain good working relationships with production specialists. But getting what you want is the point, not the difficulty of getting it. Simply remember that professionalism, respect and attention to details are critical.

Copywriting for Print Media

Some general guidelines apply to ad copywriting for the print media. These guidelines turn on the concepts of attention, interest, desire, credibility and action, sometimes referred to as AIDCA. Let's look at each of these concepts separately.

Attention

It is axiomatic that, to communicate a message to a public, you must first command attention. Two elements of a print ad perform the attention-getting function: the headline and the visual design. Although some argue the point, most great copywriters believe that the headline is the single most important element in an ad, period. The headline is the element most often responsible for stopping readers and luring them into the ad. A terrific visual may do this too, but it is the headline that makes the greatest and the most lasting impact. Of course, the visual elements should be harmonious with the headline and its content. A good headline offers a promise to the reader. More often than not, it spells out a benefit to the reader as well. And it does this provocatively so that the reader will pay attention.

The visual, in addition to gaining attention, helps to amplify the content of the headline. Thus the headline and the visual express the same message in different ways. Remember the principle of repetition mentioned earlier in this chapter? Showing the message is a way of repeating what the headline says. Whether verbally or visually, however, the message must convey—powerfully but simply—some benefit to the reader. Ads with the greatest attention-getting value are those that speak to the reader's self-interest.

The use of color can help gain attention. When you buy advertising space, however, remember that the use of color costs extra. This may affect your budget, so check the costs before you commit yourself to using color. Though color generally increases attention, it does not necessarily increase readership or retention of your message. Since the art will go digitally, be sure you consider the color choices in reproduction. (Refer to Chapter 10 on design.)

Interest

Remember that, by offering a benefit, the headline stops the reader. Thus the next phase is to heighten the reader's interest. You can do this by making sure that the first sentence or paragraph of the copy flows naturally from the headline and expands on the headline's promise. For example, suppose your company is launching a recapitalization program against the backdrop of the global recession. The success of this program will depend on whether a majority of stockholders support the program. Many stockholders, if not most, don't really understand recapitalization, and are suspicious of it from the recession experience, in any event, so they are not necessarily apt to return a ballot. Your task is to make the program appealing enough so that they will want to find out more about the benefits to them of supporting the issue. An attention-getting headline in this case might be:

HOW TO INCREASE YOUR INVESTMENT IN [NAME OF COMPANY] BY 36%

That headline would attract the attention of any investor. The task now is to get the reader to understand the how-to. That becomes the function of your copy, especially the first sentence or first paragraph. This must tie in directly to the headline itself. Thus the first paragraph of your copy might read:

> Each of your shares in [name of company] will increase from $50 to $68 if you support the recapitalization program recommended by the board of directors.

If you owned stock in this company and you received this message, you would pay attention to it, because you would recognize how much money you could make by merely marking a "yes" on your ballot. The headline and first paragraph would speak your language. It would clearly be in your self-interest to pay attention to what the company was saying to you. That is the essence of "interest" in good advertising copy.

Desire

Once you have developed self-interest, the next step is to talk about why the idea is desirable. You can do this by filling in details of the plan in subsequent paragraphs: Describe what the plan is, why it is needed, how it will benefit the company and its shareholders and when it will go into effect, and supply other supporting bits of information. This part of the copy promotes the idea that the suggested action is a desirable thing to do.

Credibility

Even if your message is provocative, your public may not believe it. The cardinal rule in this regard is to be as specific as you can. Note the specifics in the preceding headline. The line did not say "about 36%"; it said "36%" specifically. And the first paragraph of the copy did not equivocate on the dollar increase per share. It was very specific: "from $50 to $68." There is no room in this instance for misunderstanding the message. Never leave to inference what you want the reader to know. All your copy should reflect that same degree of specificity. If you hedge your claim, the reader will spot it immediately and begin to discount what you say. So be specific, concrete and direct. You will more likely be believed, even if the reader decides against your point of view.

It also pays to remember that truth is sometimes stranger than fiction and more difficult to believe. This can be a major problem when you are asking readers to accept something that defies common experience—even if it is entirely truthful.

Action

Action is the "bottom line" in advertising. You are paying to present your message. Therefore, it makes sense for you to ask recipients of the messages to do something.

Much of the advertising money spent in traditional media has moved to other venues. Online formats have captured some of the expenditures, and those ads often demand immediate response. The same is true of many television ads for products offered only to those who call in or go online.

Immediate action usually is not as important in some idea ads (especially ones that simply want to convey a positive image of the company) as it is for product ads. Some idea ads, though, such as in the preceding one, you do want action—in this case, support of the recapitalization program. It would be at least a partial waste of the company's money if you did not ask for something specific. You might close the ad with online contact information or a phone number. That kind of close to the ad would leave no doubt as to what course of action you want the reader to take. Of course, that means that you also have to prepare a response to the inquiry in any medium it might arrive.

Now that we have reviewed these points about copywriting, let's look at each medium separately.

Copywriting for Newspapers

Newspaper advertising falls into two categories: display and classified. Display advertising is the advertising that does not appear in the classified portion of the newspaper.

For *display advertising*, words and visuals must provide a unified message, as audio and video do in television commercials. Newspapers are read hurriedly and have a fairly brief life. So it's a waste to use words and visuals just because they look or sound good. If they don't have a purpose in the ad, they should be deleted. Readers won't read "fat" ads, because they don't have the time. Although newspapers are known as a mass rather than a class (or selective) medium, they can saturate a specific *geographic* market more thoroughly than magazines, radio or television. And even though a newspaper is mass in appeal, some segmentation of audiences typically occurs through features and special sections, such as the sports or business section. Some neighborhood publications and shopper papers have a great deal of small display ads that demand creativity and brevity. The advantage is that these ads that do attract attention are often clipped and kept as action reminders. That is true also for some display advertising, especially for higher priced items.

Display   Display advertising is especially good at promoting an immediate demand for products or services or achieving the acceptance of ideas. It works if you have a unified concept to convey designed along the lines of the earlier AIDCA discussion. The size of the space you buy will determine the proportions and sizes of the headline, copy, visuals, logos and other elements of the ad.

How much space to buy is a critical decision, for it determines how much competition for readers' attention there will be on the page where your ad appears. If you buy a full page, there will be no competing message on the page. If you buy a half page, there are likely to be two or three other competing messages—in addition to the editorial matter—all clamoring for the reader's attention. The smaller the space you buy, the greater the competition for attention on the page. Newspapers carry a mix of local and national advertising.

Newspaper ads for local companies are addressed to local readers. A good copywriter takes advantage of the research information about both the medium and its market and tries to tailor a message that will "fit" the market. Of course, national advertisers who use newspapers ordinarily can't tailor their ads to this degree. They might run the same ad simultaneously in newspapers all across the country. Remember, though: If you have the opportunity, write your ad with the local market in mind.

Classified   Most classified advertising sections contain excellent examples of creativity in the use of a limited number of words. Classifieds are also big business on the Internet. Ads in these sections are varied. Classified ads are used extensively by real estate agencies and transportation- and recreation-related companies. A professional copywriter for an agency is likely to prepare hundreds of classified ads for clients. The technique employed here is simply to determine how many words you can get into a specific space. Deduct from this count the number of words that you *must* include—such as the company's name, address and telephone number—and compose your message with the number of words left. Read the classified columns before you begin writing, to help you appreciate the ingenuity of others and to learn the accepted abbreviations in that market. In the process, you'll also find out what your competitors are doing.

Copywriting for Magazines

Magazine audiences are highly specialized. Specific magazines appeal to particular types of people, regardless of where they live. Magazine advertising copy should exploit this specificity in magazine audiences. Both demographic and psychographic information are relevant here.

Although magazine readers do not necessarily devote immense amounts of time to reading magazines at a single sitting, they usually put them aside for rereading as their time and interests dictate. When writing ad copy for a particular magazine, you may want to get in touch with the sales-promotion department for specialized information on the readership.

In writing your magazine ad, you should know its size and placement before you actually begin. Magazine space is ordinarily sold by the page or by the fraction or multiple of a page. It is possible to buy a special position for your ad, but you'll have to pay a premium for it, and that can run up the cost in a hurry. Be aware that most magazines allow, and even expect, a higher level of reproduction quality than newspapers exhibit, especially in the use of color and highly creative visual materials.

Look at several issues of the specific magazine your ad will appear in before you begin writing, so you can get a feel for its character and the tone of its advertising content. Then check the editorial bent of the magazine. These inspections may cue you to use or avoid a particular approach. Some magazines, like newspapers, are online. Look at the online editions to see how ads are included and how much presence they command.

Like those in newspaper ads, the verbal and visual elements in magazine ads should be complementary, not disjointed.

Public Service Ads   Both newspapers and magazines run public service ads for nonprofit organizations and causes. If you are preparing one of these ads for use by these media, observe all the rules that apply to ads you would buy. Remember, you are asking these media to give your message a free ride. If you want your ad run, play by the rules. Be as helpful as you can. You're not buying. You're asking—and hoping.

House Ads   Newspapers and magazines run house ads on a space-available basis. Although no money exchanges hands, the promotion department of the medium is often given a budget for this purpose. It is then the department's responsibility to prepare various house ads and to have them available to run on demand. Some house ads, however, are scheduled as if they were paid ads. These usually promote the magazine or newspaper as a good medium in which companies can reach a market or an audience. Or they may promote subscriptions (particularly in newspapers) or the use of the classified ad section. Even though these are house ads, they are written and prepared just as other ads are.

Copywriting for Web Pages

News and advertising professionals in traditional media have a history of separating news, entertainment and advertising. That does not hold true for the Internet. Commercial messages, known as banner ads, pop up in some of the most unexpected places. In other cases, they are integrated into the news or entertainment program content so that it is seamless. Separation generally does not exist on the Internet. As one example among many, CNN's travel page blends travel articles with reservation services and promotions from a sponsoring travel agency. And such sites as Amazon.com present promotional pieces thinly disguised as book reviews. Many of the Internet search services now put all sorts of links to advertisers above and to the side of actual search results.

Most ads on the Internet don't resemble what we see in other media. They are stripped-down, quick bursts of information with a simple message and a visual. And because of the blending of content, in many cases it is difficult to know what is an ad and what is not. Writing advertising for some web uses is somewhat like writing for an outdoor poster. It is short—often less than 10 words. But if the message is integrated into program content, then it may be somewhat lengthy. It also must fit the style and thrust of program content. Hence, building an ad to be integrated limits the creative latitude copywriters ordinarily have. And space for the display of ad messages on computer screens is always limited. Therefore, good copy for websites should avoid overuse of adjectives, adverbs and conditional clauses. We recommend that you review Web page reading habits in Chapter 8 before you attempt to construct an ad for the Internet.

Copywriting for Direct Response and Direct Advertising

The severest test of your ability as a copywriter is whether you can write effective direct-response or direct-advertising copy.

Copy that is designed to promote direct action by the audience is called *direct-response copy*. It is the type of message that urges people to take immediate action such as going to a website, mailing in a coupon, calling an 800 number, entering a sweepstakes or figuratively raising their hands and saying, "Hey, we're interested."

Direct-response copy can appear in most any medium. The key is not the type of medium in which the message appears, but the type of message conveyed. If it urges the audience to do something now, it is direct-response copy. For example, a commercial on television from Publishers Clearing House touts its subscriptions and provides an incentive by offering fabulous sweepstake prizes. All you have to do is to call a toll-free number, but you have to call *now*.

Direct-advertising copy appears in written, printed or processed form and is sent via a controlled method of circulation to individuals. There are three types of direct advertising: direct mail, mail order and unmailed direct advertising.

Direct Mail   This covers all forms of mailed direct advertising, except mail order. It includes letters, postcards, booklets, broadsides, brochures, circulars, catalogs and stuffers, among others.

Mail Order   Mail-order copy is responsible for the entire "selling" job. It may appear in a variety of forms, from catalogs such as L. L. Bean's to a letter urging the recipient to give to the Disabled American Veterans.

Unmailed Direct Advertising Unmailed direct-advertising copy differs from direct mail and mail order only in its method of distribution. It includes promotional pieces that may be delivered to a person's home or may be picked up in a store, showroom, fair or exhibit or at any other site allowing promotional efforts.

All forms of direct-advertising copy are especially difficult to write effectively, because you have to create the medium as well as the message. You don't have the support of a preselected audience from the standard media.

Each message has to stand alone and produce results. In fact, success is carefully measured by the number of responses generated. These can be in any number of forms—for example, coupons, orders or queries—and the response rate measures precisely how much action you have generated with your writing. Once you have designed and written a successful ad that has proved itself, you are not likely to change it very much in the future.

Obviously, the overall design of coupons, order forms and related material has to be very good, so that people can respond easily.

Copywriting for Out-of-Home Media

The term *out-of-home media* refers to a variety of media—outdoor, transit, skywriting and the like. The key feature they share is that readers go to them rather than the other way around. This characteristic imposes severe constraints on what you can say and how you can say it. The average reading time is about five seconds or less, so the number of words is usually 8 to 10 words. Each out-of-home medium is unique, but the general guidelines for outdoor media apply to all.

There are three basic kinds of outdoor billboards: the poster panel, the painted bulletin and the digital display. Poster panels, which are printed on large printing presses, are of two standard sizes: 8 sheets are 5 by 11 feet or 30 sheets, 12 by 25 feet. These are developed by an agency and shipped to the outdoor company that will be putting them up. Painted panels are created on-site, which could be a board, a building, a concrete wall or almost anything else so the size depends on the site. However, most painted signs are 14 by 48 feet. Some of these have extensions, called cutouts, on the top or side. Digital displays have several advantages in that they can be changed easily and are visible even in bad weather.

Many advertisers use poster panels routinely, changing their messages monthly or several times a year, and advertising in many markets simultaneously. Once the cost of designing and producing the panel is absorbed, the costs become incrementally smaller as additional sites or markets are used.

An advertiser will use "paints" only when cultivating one or a very few markets and when the message will not be changed within a year. Usually an advertiser will not use more than two or three painted bulletins, or "paints," in a specific market, depending on the size of the market.

Digital outdoor signs are getting more popular due to their ability to command attention and the fact that they can be changed less expensively, usually, unless it is a very complex showing.

Outdoor advertising—called *outdoor* for short—is remarkably cost-effective when you need to saturate a market with an idea. The price of an outdoor campaign is based on what are called *showings*. A 100-show is a campaign in which enough panels, including some illuminated for night viewing, are set up to provide 100 percent coverage of the mobile market for a 30-day period. Studies show that it is not unusual for a 100-show to produce a high level of message repetitions—an average of 25 or more per month. A 50-show thus would involve half the coverage and repetition of a 100-show.

Copywriting is especially difficult for outdoor. Because your message may be seen for only a few seconds, it has to be especially simple and compelling to register with the viewer. As a general rule, you can't use more than about eight words, including the company's name, and expect the message to punch through. No more than three verbal and visual elements should appear in the message. Hence, you must restrain yourself in both your verbal and visual thinking if you expect to write a good outdoor message.

Simplicity is the hallmark of good outdoor. If your message is complex, don't use outdoor. But if you can reduce your message to just a few words, and if you can employ bold, even garish, visuals, you will be able to do a lot with a little.

Although ads for subways, taxis and similar media have different size specifications, the same guidelines apply to them as to outdoor.

Copywriting for Sales Promotion

Point-of-purchase advertising, samples, contests, advertising specialties and cooperative advertising are sales-promotion pieces, as are coupons, booklets, brochures and mailers. (See Chapter 15 for brochures.)

Point-of-purchase advertising is advertising displayed with a product, service or idea and specifically designed to inspire the customer to buy on impulse. Most point-of-purchase advertising is strong on emotional impact, particularly symbolism, and ties in with other existing promotional materials to create additional recognition. Another promotional device is the sample, a free product sent out along with descriptive literature. The copy accompanying a sample often tries to inspire a sense of obligation in prospective customers by urging them to accept the "gift."

Contests are designed to offer customers something extra and to maintain their awareness of the idea through participation and anticipation. Advertising specialties can be anything with the corporate logo on it, but generally they are useful objects, like ice scrapers for windshields, or things with high visibility that will be remembered.

In cooperative advertising, the retail outlet appeals for direct sales while receiving support from the manufacturer. When the manufacturer's logo appears alongside the retailer's in a local company's advertising for a product or service, this is usually a tip-off that the ad is a cooperative one, with the retailer and manufacturer sharing in the cost of space, time or position.

Conclusions

- Most advertising copy that PR people write involves promoting ideas.
- These idea ads are in print and electronic media and take many forms, some looking like traditional ads or commercials and some looking like editorial matter.
- Advertising uses persuasion. It cannot coerce.

- Successful persuasion is based on the right appeal, proper positioning and an understanding of how people will respond to the appeal.
- Publics examine every message for how it may affect them personally.
- One reason to use a media mix is the quality of attention advertising appeals get in various media.
- Basic requirements for advertising copywriting include an understanding of the ad's purpose, a careful review of the objective facts to be conveyed, an awareness of the public to be addressed and a thoughtful decision as to the media to be used. Internal requirements are a creative approach, visualization, precise language and repetition.
- Visual media are dynamic, so movement must be integrated into messages for these media, and the verbal and visual elements of the ad must be complementary.
- Internet advertising also involves color, movement and sound.
- Copy for radio is written for the ear, not the eye. Words and sounds must be especially well chosen for radio ads so that the public can "see" the message.
- Although newspapers and magazines are static media, messages placed there must be dynamic and move people to act. Stages of audience response that must be addressed in developing these ads include attention, interest, desire, credibility and action. The headline is the most important element.
- Direct-mail messages are difficult to execute effectively because the message must also be the medium.
- The audience goes to out-of-home media, rather than vice versa, so time is short and simplicity in both words and visuals is crucial. The total message is limited to eight to ten words and three elements.
- Writing copy for sales promotions often involves writing for a variety of media and methods. It is a good idea to review the descriptions and illustrations in this chapter before writing any sales-promotion materials.

Exercises

1. Write five different headlines for ads addressed to shareholders, explaining the recapitalization program discussed in this chapter.
2. Select one of the five headlines you have just written, and write three alternative lead sentences or paragraphs for it.
3. Write a double truck ad (two facing pages) for *Business Week* for the following situation: Your client is an industrial park. It has a lot of undeveloped land, plenty of water and power and the resources to build high-tech facilities for companies relocating to your area. In fact, state and local taxes will be waived in perpetuity for any company locating in the state. This is, of course, a big incentive for companies to move to the area. You are free to expand on this information using a local situation.
4. Write a television commercial for the circumstances described in Exercise 3.

Use InfoTrac® College Edition to access information on topics in this chapter from hundreds of periodicals and scholarly journals.

Newsletters

Is the newsletter dead? Has it been replaced by Web 2.0 technologies that allow interactivity? Not by a long shot. Do a Google search on "newsletter" and you'll find more than 700,000,000 sites that mention newsletters and another 202,000,000 that mention enewsletters.

What *is* a newsletter? Dictionary.com defines it as "A periodically published work containing news and announcements on some subject, typically with a small circulation."

Newsletters often are distributed by email or as an email attachment, while enewsletters usually reside on websites. When a new edition of an enewsletter is available, a link to it usually is distributed by email. Some organizations print their newsletters on paper and make them available to employees or members or mail them to homes. Other organizations, including Southwest Airlines, distribute brief daily newsletters that are sent to supervisors throughout their operating areas and are posted on bulletin boards in the respective areas.

A newsletter or magazine often is rated as the single most important benefit of membership in an organization. That's true at PRSA, where a 2008 member survey indicated that the society's 22,000+ members said PRSA's newspaper, *Public Relations Tactics,* and its magazine, *Public Relations Strategist,* were ranked high among products and services.

Subscriber newsletters that are operated as businesses carry valued information to people willing to pay substantially for it, and these newsletters often are monitored by the business press for trends and other news. How has the Internet affected the value attributes of these print media? The answer seems to be *enhancement.*

Some newsletter and enewsletter subscriptions are free; it's just a matter of signing up to be included in the "distribution." Why would an organization do this? Obviously, whether it is commercial or nonprofit, the access to extended audiences is seen as an opportunity.

Because these publications are being delivered both by the USA Postal Service and by the Internet, they pose new writing challenges. Writing for the two is not the same, as you discovered in Chapter 8. Nor can designs move entirely comfortably between the two, as you found out in Chapter 10 on message design concepts.

Most newsletters now carry their website addresses on the printed versions. (And if the newsletter is membership based or subscriber based, the website likely has a home page with a requirement for the member/subscriber to enter a password to get to the information.)

As organizations began to downsize, many public relations people took advantage of their job losses to go into business for themselves. Early on, those were the people most comfortable with the journalistic tactics of public relations and the ones who had mastered desktop publishing. Now the emphasis is on people who are comfortable working in cyberspace and preparing newsletters that are unlikely to appear in a printed form.

The significance of this to public relations writers is that many college graduates find their first jobs in the newsletter industry. The opportunity usually comes because they understand how to gather information, write in a compelling and interesting way and know desktop publishing.

For organizations, the increasing number of professional newsletters requires that they be aware of those newsletters that follow their activities because the coverage is often more objective and critical than they may be comfortable with.

Criteria for Successful Newsletters

Several criteria affect the success of any newsletter:

- It must fill an unmet need.
- It must be able to do things for its audience other media can't, and it must convey information in some unique way so people will pay attention to it.
- It must be distributed in a way that is efficient and regularly reaches its intended audience.
- There must be a person or a staff of people interested in it, skilled enough to produce it and with time committed solely to its production.
- It must be a serial publication (Vol. #, No. #) issued with enough frequency that its contents remain timely in the eyes of its readers.

Even more important is the writer's approach to newsletter content. In its "Memo to Management" online publication, Edelman—named 2009 Agency of the Year by *PRWeek*—said, "Just as some football fans watch *Monday Night Football* with the volume off to escape the incessant blather posing as commentary and insights, employees are watching, but choosing not to listen. They look for visual clues and pay attention to what's going on around them as company information raises questions rather than answering them. To capture employees' attention when the volume is down, we have to adopt a 'discover' approach rather than a 'sell' approach, meaning the most effective communication is when people discover for themselves leadership's strategic intent. In this regard, communications can help employees experience the necessary changes and the benefits of new corporate initiatives needed to drive organizational strategy. Initiatives, in this vein, are owned by employees rather than viewed as an ever changing 'flavor of the month.'"[1]

Filling Unmet Needs

Memos, letters and bulletin boards are commonly used to communicate inside an organization. But as an organization grows, these media sometimes aren't sufficient to carry all the interesting and important information that should be shared. A newsletter can be as large as necessary (within the budget) to carry important information.

It's important for you to understand that one medium just isn't adequate in reaching a large number of people. Within any organization, both demographics and psychographics vary tremendously. Trying to reach even hundreds of people—much less millions—is destined to fail.

AARP, previously known as the American Association of Retired Persons, has 40 million members and offices in all 50 states, the District of Columbia, Puerto Rico and the United States Virgin Islands. It tries to reach each segment of its membership in appropriate and appealing ways. To do that, it publishes the world's largest-circulation magazine, *AARP The Magazine*. Its newspaper, *AARP Bulletin,* is published 10 times a year and online each day. AARP also publishes *Segunda Juventud (Second Youth)*, a bimonthly magazine, and produces radio programs in both Spanish and English—"Prime Time," a public affairs radio program—and two syndicated TV shows, "Inside E Street," a public affairs show, and "My Generation," a magazine-style show. Its award-winning website is aarp.org. Just consider all of the writing jobs within this one huge nonprofit organization! Of course, preparation of news releases, speeches, marketing materials and all sorts of other materials requires additional writers.

A newsletter can reach out and mobilize the self-interest of such vast audiences. Even if an organization has a magazine, it often emphasizes feature material, but a newsletter, as the first part of the name signifies, can focus on information that is current, thus making it more immediately useful to its readers.

Other media, such as newspapers, magazines and television, provide data, but none of them provide the select, in-depth and sharply focused information found in newsletters.

Uniqueness

A successful newsletter is one that conveys information particularly useful and interesting to its audience. Of the two general types—organizational and subscription—the organizational goes to employees of an organization or members of an association. As an employee or as a member of an association, you have special interests related to that involvement. For example, if you fish for bass, you may become a member of a bass fishing club. That club will have a newsletter that informs you regularly about forthcoming fishing tournaments, who is the current leader in club points and related matters. No other medium provides you with such targeted information.

Subscription newsletters also address special interests, both personal and professional. Some of your interests or hobbies may lead you to subscribe to newsletters that give you "inside information." For example, if you invest in the stock market, you may subscribe to at least one market newsletter that keeps you abreast of news relating to the market. If your interest is in precious metals, you may even focus narrowly on a gold and silver market newsletter. As an avid booster of a professional or collegiate sports team, you may get a personal view of that team through a newsletter that goes only to its contributing boosters.

Note that in all these examples and others, although information about the organizations and interests is available from other sources, none can speak to your special interest as directly as a newsletter.

Distribution

All of the effort and expense of putting together a newsletter is wasted unless the newsletter reaches your intended public. If you work for a membership organization such as a professional society or trade association, that's not too difficult. The organization collects information about each member and typically stores the information in a database. Then the mail or email addresses can be used to send each edition of the newsletter to members as well as others whom the organization wants to receive the publication. Even so, you need to be aware that many people change their email addresses frequently.

The organization can ask its members to update profile information through its website, but that activity might not be high among your public's priorities. Because many societies and associations charge annual dues and send paper invoices each year, the dues billing provides an opportunity to update members' addresses, phone numbers and email addresses.

But suppose you're volunteering to help pass a clean-up-the-environment issue in your community. You may have to start "from scratch" to build an email database. Since you can't just pull information from a directory like a phone book, it takes a lot of effort and attention to gather, file and maintain such a list.

If your newsletter is printed on paper, getting it into the hands of its target audience is a key element of success. And it can be quite expensive. If you can't create a mailing list with the right names and addresses and keep it up to date, you can't be successful. Of course, names of people and their addresses are easy to get when distributing a newsletter through interoffice mail. Some organizations save time and money by simply putting quantities of printed newsletters at central locations like lobbies and break rooms where employees can pick them up; others ask mail room personnel to deliver a newsletter to each employee.

If you must create your own list from scratch, be prepared to spend much time and money building it. Maintaining its accuracy over the years also is expensive and time-consuming. So is delivery by the USA Postal Service, even if your newsletter qualifies for a second-class mail permit. Distribution sounds easy, but it often isn't. So be resourceful and persistent in creation and maintenance of an effective distribution system.

Knowledge and Skills

Producing a newsletter that earns the loyalty of its readers is time-consuming work. It also takes specialized knowledge and a combination of skills at writing, editing, designing and visualizing. Many who start newsletters are short on both knowledge and skills, but if they are long on commitment, they learn by doing. That's often the case in small organizations, because there probably isn't someone on the staff who has the academic or professional training needed for the task. Small budgets also may preclude hiring someone with the knowledge and skills needed. Newsletters from big organizations usually aim for and achieve higher professional standards. But it is the restricted, focused coverage of news that makes readers look forward to the next issue.

Frequency

The frequency of a newsletter is governed by three primary issues—budget, timeliness and serialization. Your budget may restrict your frequency as well as the number of pages in your newsletter. There are trade-offs you can make. If you cut the number of pages, you may be able to publish more often and stay within a tight budget. If timeliness is critical, you must publish more often, even if with fewer pages. If the timeliness of newsletter content is not an issue, you may publish less often but with more pages.

Some guidelines are provided by Mark Brownlow in email-marketing-reports.com:

- Any email newsletter that comes out less frequently than once a month is unlikely to make an impression on its readers.
- Very frequent newsletters (more frequent than weekly) or very infrequent newsletters (less frequent than monthly) must offer exceptional value or impact. For infrequent newsletters, exceptional value and impact can make up for infrequency. For frequent newsletters, exceptional value and impact justify the time the reader has to allocate to the emails.
- Your preferred frequency from the perspective of recognition and awareness also depends on how else you are communicating with these email addresses. Take into account other newsletters you may be sending them, or whether you already send them promotional emails. In other words, look at the bigger picture before settling on a frequency.[2]

Perhaps the least understood influence is serialization. For a printed publication to be classified as a newsletter by the USA Postal Service, it must be issued on a regular basis, and each issue must contain volume and issue numbers. A publication issued on an irregular schedule, although it may have every appearance of a newsletter, isn't one unless published at regular intervals. Also, the only way the USA Postal Service will grant a second-class mailing permit is for you to publish it on a regular schedule. If you distribute your newsletter through interoffice mail, there can be some variability in your schedule, but you still need volume and issue numbers. If you use the USA mail, you must keep a rigid publishing schedule. If your newsletter is distributed only by email, this restriction is not an issue.

Format

If your intention is to deliver your newsletter electronically, your format choices relate to the readers' ability to access and read your content. Email is almost always a player. One of the better choices is to distribute an email message containing headlines and perhaps a brief summary of each article, with links to "Read more." This allows you to place the bulk of the content on a website where you can use graphics without affecting the size of the email messages.

If the newsletter is to be delivered on paper, the best format for a specific newsletter often is a curious blend resulting from content, budget and readers' convenience. If the intent is, as in most newsletters, to write tight, edit tighter and present information in almost-bulletin form, an 8.5-by-11-inch page size may be perfectly suitable. Readers who keep backfiles of the newsletter in binders or in cabinets like the convenience of an 8.5-by-11-inch sheet size. Copies of newsletters that routinely get routed from office to office within an organization also seem to work better in an 8.5-by-11-inch page size. If your newsletter routinely runs longer pieces, especially feature material, a larger page size—such as 11-by-17 inches or tabloid—may be more appropriate. If pictures and graphs are important parts of each issue, larger sheet sizes may be needed.

Format also requires that you weigh the relative merits of vertical versus horizontal layout of content. Small sheet sizes can accommodate either vertical or horizontal displays, if they are done skillfully. Nevertheless, horizontal displays of content are usually more attractive in larger sheet sizes. That apparently is a function of the more pleasing proportions produced by the vertical length of a large sheet size, such as 11-by-17 inches.

Unless your budget is generous, money may restrict your choice of formats as well as the extent to which you can afford to use visual materials and color. Four-color printing can hit your budget hard, but is very important if your distribution is large. Of course that drives down the unit cost. It also, as noted previously, influences the frequency of your newsletter and the number of pages per issue.

Word processing programs like Word and WordPerfect provide templates that simplify and speed the production of newsletters. Some templates are part of the program installed on your computer; others are provided without charge online by the software company.

Although it is important to know about the criteria that can make a newsletter successful, it is equally important to know about the types and functions of newsletters.

Types and Functions of Newsletters

The main purpose of newsletters is to communicate regularly with members of a special public. Sharing information sustains the unity of those bound together only by a special interest.

Employee and Member Newsletters

Good managers know that the success of the company or institution rests on the cooperation and support of employees as much as on their own managerial skills. As an organization grows, however, it becomes increasingly difficult to communicate policy or other information on a personal basis. A newsletter may serve this purpose.

An organization's endurance depends on maintaining its membership base and attracting new members. Frequently a newsletter is a periodic reminder of the organization and invites or structures the member's participation in the organization's activities.

In the case of both employees and members, though, the timeliness of newsletter information may suffer from the production and delivery process. There's something to the term *snail mail*. For employees, email systems may be a better delivery system for messages that need immediate attention, and members of organizations often turn to websites for news and updates.

Internal Communication   Newsletters nevertheless are an effective channel of internal communication. (See Figure 14.1.) Their content is carefully selected, written and presented to convey a common experience and a feeling of belonging, and to promote identification and unity with the group. A newsletter shouldn't be the only means of communicating with employees or members. Interpersonal communication is the most preferred and most effective way to communicate. But as an organization grows, other techniques need to supplement the limited amount of time that senior executives can spend with individuals and small groups.

Resource Center
Tools and training for volunteer and service programs

subscribe

Your Resource Connection *e*newsletter

Vol 7, No 7 - AUGUST 2009

● SPOTLIGHT

National Neighborhood Day ~ Sunday, September 20

Rekindle old friendships and establish new bonds with fellow community members on National Neighborhood Day (NND), celebrated across the country each year on the third Sunday in September.

The goal of NND is to reinforce local connections by fortifying relationships — because a unified community is a stronger and healthier one. Use this annual celebration to promote and increase involvement in any number of cohesion-building and civic-minded activities. Neighborhood gatherings can be a simple block party or potluck, or a more complex service project, such as a neighborhood clean-up — whatever is easy and fun to plan and carry out. As a result of your NND event, your community may see an increase in volunteering, collaboration, emergency preparedness, and adult/youth mentoring relationships.

If you're planning an event now, share your ideas so that others can benefit. And be sure to check out the National Neighborhood Day resources site for tools to help you get started and ideas to sustain the momentum throughout the year.

Nonprofit partners for NND include Campus Compact, the National Crime

● RESOURCES

More Than Neighbors: Creating Community

Why not build on the results of Neighborhood Day? Check out the list below for community resources that will help make *every day* Neighborhood Day.

Lending Library

Great Neighborhood Book: A Do-It-Yourself Guide to Placemaking
Conducting Community Forums: Engaging Citizens, Mobilizing Communities
Guide to Creating a Neighborhood Information Exchange: Building Communities by Connecting Local Skills and Knowledge

Effective Practices

Providing childcare to increase participation in neighborhood events
Honoring ordinary heroes through a community service project
Generating a list of 100 ways teens can serve their communities

● ANNOUNCEMENTS

Nonprofit Management Institute, Stanford University Oct. 6–7

How do you shape an effective organization during tough times? If you're like most nonprofit leaders, you are struggling with this challenge. This year's Nonprofit Management Institute program was designed to help you shape and grow your organization while dealing with the current resource constraints. Speakers are world-renowned Stanford Graduate School of Business faculty and leading practitioners in the field, including a session hosted by representatives from the Corporation for National and Community Service.

Stanford SOCIAL INNOVATION REVIEW

Early bird registration deadline is August 27, 2009. More details: www.ssireview. org/npinstitute

Service-Learning Grants Available from State Farm Youth Advisory Board

The State Farm Youth Advisory Board has five million dollars – that's right! – to award service-learning programs in the United States and Canada. If your students are interested in driving change within the community, they can apply to receive grants ranging from $5,000 to $100,000.

To apply for a State Farm Youth Advisory Board grant, visit www.statefarmyab.com/ apply.php. To learn more about service-learning, visit www.servicelearning.org/.

FIGURE 14.1

Newsletter—Resource Center of the Center for National and Community Service

In many organizations, email is used extensively to communicate. If it's the main source for messages, people get turned off with the increased number of emails they receive. A newsletter can consolidate the messages and provide an outlet for announcements and changes.

Personal Touch   Newsletters are often expected to help humanize what may otherwise be viewed as an impersonal relationship. Because of this, a common thread of content runs through newsletters—a focus on accomplishments.

Employee newsletters often focus on work-related accomplishments. For example, an employee may be given special recognition in the company's newsletter for having developed a new materials-handling system that saves the company thousands of dollars annually. The company is obviously better because of the employee's contribution, which is acknowledged among his or her peers in the newsletter. Such recognition also implies that others can get the same kind of treatment if they contribute beyond the normal call of duty.

Employees often are recognized, too, as people worth knowing because of their dedication, skill or accomplishments in areas not related to their jobs. For example, Rose McKenna devotes many hours of volunteer service weekly to the Big Sisters program. Rose is someone you should know, not because she is one of three quality-control supervisors at the plant but because she is who she is. Companies and institutions routinely encourage employees to take an active interest in community affairs because such interests create goodwill toward the company or institution.

Newsletters for organizations also call attention to the accomplishments of the organization, primarily as achieved through its members This kind of recognition encourages others. If it is a nonprofit organization that is primarily driven by volunteerism, the recognition may be critical not only to encourage other volunteers but also to convince potential donors that the organization engages in worthwhile projects.

In their efforts to humanize the company or institution, newsletter writers sometimes use humor. Humor is, of course, a good method of conveying some information. However, unless you have a special gift for writing humor, avoid it, because poor humor can come across as trite. And it can be inadvertently offensive as well. If you use humor now and then, remember that you should never poke fun at anyone other than yourself or the company or institution.

Gary F. Grates, president and global managing director of Edelman Change & Employee Engagement, says "today's employees receive enormous volumes of unsolicited information and are unable to handle it all."

"Just when organizations have made improving relationships with employees a priority, they've encountered an interesting, sobering reality—employees aren't listening. In addition to information overload—or, most likely causing it—is the startling fact uncovered in recent surveys that a low percentage of the workforce, including managers and supervisors, understand the company's strategy, and that leadership is aghast at that fact. This knowledge deficiency among managers is a serious problem, because these are the very people who must drive the strategy." As an example, he said poor communications with workers at General Motors was the main factor in a 54-day strike that cost the company $2 billion.

Grates said that employees are watching but choosing not to listen. "They are inundated with so much information—most of which is irrelevant or conflicting—that it overwhelms and confuses them." The average employee, he said, receives up to 60 faxes and between

500 and 1,500 emails every week and are inundated with news releases, newsletters, brochures, videos, presentations and every other form of communication, much of it unsolicited. "Is it any wonder that managers say they are unable to handle the volume of information they receive?" he asked. "And that they find it a waste of time and distracting from their primary responsibilities?"[3]

"Instead, they look for visual cues and pay attention to what's going on around them. For instance, they may hear or read in a company publication about a new initiative that realigns the way things are done. But then they see leadership or their managers operating in the same manner as they always have. What's the real message for them? Is the company embarking on a new paradigm, or not? 'Probably not,' employees say to one another. The result is widespread cynicism instead of the enthusiasm and commitment that business organizations need in order to grow and thrive."

He continued, "What employees are looking for, in addition to respect for their intelligence, is information that will help them do their jobs better. They want to help the company survive and thrive so that they can keep their jobs, send their children to college, pay their mortgages and feel good about their lives. Yet conventional internal communications is out of sync with that model. Internal communications is not public relations. It is not about touting, advocating and creating noise. It is about listening, hearing and acting. Internal communication is not about being a trumpet, but about being an organization's ears. Internal communication is becoming a management priority where leaders recognize that a real competitive advantage can be gained through an engaged, motivated, knowledgeable, and respected work force."

"What does this mean for senior management and communicators who understand this paradigm? It means they should stop using tired clichés like teamwork, loyalty and empowerment. Instead of acting as though the employees' volume is still on, leadership should focus on what employees are really concerned about: job discretion, respect, privacy, recognition and reward."[4]

Special-Interest Subscriber Newsletters

The term *special interest* describes group relationships bound by a common interest other than as an employee or a member.

The purpose of these newsletters is to communicate information about the special interest that binds the group. Information is thus highly targeted and seldom presents anything not directly related to the interest of the group.

Writing style is often informal and, depending on the field of interest, may involve jargon. For example, a newsletter for personal computer hackers may be filled with computerese. If you are really interested in communicating fully, though, you'll minimize the jargon and stay with simple English. (See Figure 14.2.)

What's significant about special-interest subscriber newsletters is that the information has to be substantive enough that people feel they are getting value for their money. They are paying for information about lifestyles (traveling, health, economics); earning money or investing it; computers (new software and technology updates); hobbies (gardening, scuba diving); collecting (everything from antique glassware to baseball cards); or renovating old real estate (from houses to office buildings). Subscription newsletters offer a lifeline to important information for people concerned with these and other topics.

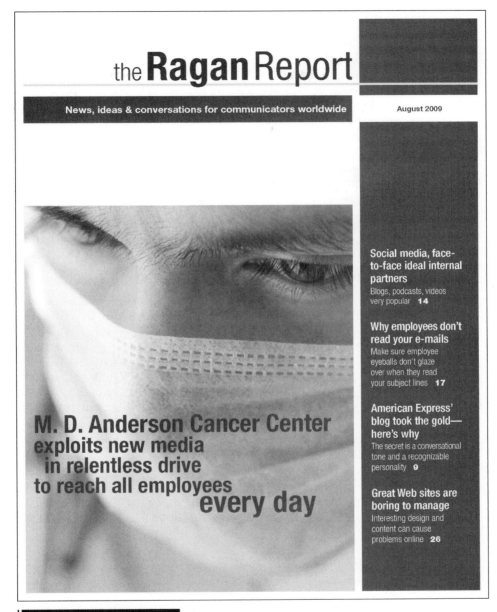

the Ragan Report

News, ideas & conversations for communicators worldwide

August 2009

M. D. Anderson Cancer Center
exploits new media
in relentless drive
to reach all employees
every day

Social media, face-to-face ideal internal partners
Blogs, podcasts, videos very popular **14**

Why employees don't read your e-mails
Make sure employee eyeballs don't glaze over when they read your subject lines **17**

American Express' blog took the gold— here's why
The secret is a conversational tone and a recognizable personality **9**

Great Web sites are boring to manage
Interesting design and content can cause problems online **26**

FIGURE 14.2

Subscription Newsletter   *Many public relations professionals keep up with changes in the field by subscribing to newsletters that follow recent public relations research, trends and people. One such newsletter is The Ragan Report, one of several subscription publications published by Lawrence Ragan Communications, Inc.*

Source: Copyright © 2009 Lawrence Ragan Communications, Inc. Used with permission.

Technical and Content Considerations

There is no best way to prepare a newsletter. The writing style may range from informal to formal, but it is always keenly focused on the interest of the group at hand. Some newsletters are simply prepared on a computer, printed, photocopied, folded and mailed. Others are elaborately designed and printed on fine-quality paper. Budget, of course, is a key factor in determining the appearance and method of reproduction. The important point to remember is that the newsletter's content, not its appearance, counts most. If the content is perceived as important by readers, you have accomplished your purpose. (See Table 14.1.)

Reporting and Writing for Newsletters

Reporting and writing for newsletters are two very different tasks. Reporting deals with getting information. Writing deals with analyzing and packaging information.

Reporting

Getting useful information is the lifeblood of any newsletter. There is no reason for a newsletter if it doesn't have information other media don't have. Otherwise, potential readers may simply yawn away its existence. So reporting is a key element of a good newsletter.

Relying on standard journalistic approaches to fact gathering won't do. You must have an angle that sets your search process apart from others. For example, the *White House Bulletin* began in 1990 with the idea that other media reporting on White House activities were overlooking many important details. Written by an editorial staff of former White House and congressional officials relying on inside sources and wire-service reports, the newsletter is a daily, Internet- and fax-delivered news service for subscribers. In a few years, it has become a mainstay of the Washington press corps as well as government leaders. As it sifts continually for overlooked details, the *White House Bulletin* has scooped national media several times on some major stories.

You can look for a newsletter angle by identifying a gap and trying to fill it. Examples of filling gaps show in these newsletter titles: *Cold Water Oil Spills, Underground Storage Tank Guide, Iranian Assets Litigation Reporter, Back Pain Monitor* and *Anesthesia Malpractice Protector.*

Get It Right or Get Out Every reporter makes mistakes. But mistakes often are deadlier in newsletters than they are in the mass media, because you're dealing with an audience with specialized knowledge. Readers spot mistakes quickly and they are not forgiving. Because of your mistake, they feel that you've broken faith with their trust. Your credibility and the future of your newsletter may go down the drain. That's especially the case if you're reporting for a commercial, profit-making newsletter. Even a decimal point out of place can be disastrous for your readers. You must be right all the time. Impossible? No, it just means that you do what all reporters should do routinely, but often don't—check, double-check and check again.

No-Nonsense News Commercial subscriber newsletters, especially, adhere to a hard-news policy. Fluff, features and humor have no place in these newsletters. However, employee and

T A B L E 1 4 . 1	*Newsletters: What Do People Want to Know?* Newsletter content is more important than appearance. In this article, Jeff Rubin summarizes guidelines for external and internal newsletters.

Newsletters

What Do People Want to Know?
By Jeff Rubin, The Newsletter Guy

Guess what's the most frequent question I'm asked about publishing newsletters? OK. The second most. After people want to know how much it costs, the question I hear the most is, "what should I put in my newsletter?" It's a good question. I know because I see a lot of bad newsletters that contain information I'm not interested in and don't pertain to my business. How do you get the right mix to keep your customers, potential customers and/or employees reading? Here are some of my thoughts.

External Newsletters

These are for your customers and potential customers. What are they interested in? Do you think they'd like to hear about who in your company got married, had a baby or celebrated a birthday, or about how your new product or service can save them time and money and make their businesses more efficient?

Give your readers useful information:

- A few ideas they can implement immediately.
- Updates on trends in your industry which may affect them.
- "How to" information so they can do things themselves (you can't expect your customers to buy EVERYTHING from you).
- General articles that help them save time and money and make their business and personal lives more meaningful.
- A great way to honor a customer is to highlight them in your newsletter. This not only creates good will between you and the customer you're writing about, but shows others that you value your business relationships.

Internal Newsletters

What do employees want to know? A survey conducted by the International Association of Business Communicators yielded the following results:

- Organizational plans for the future—company goals, expansion, etc.
- Job advancement opportunities.
- Job related "how to" information.
- How local, state, world events or changes in the business climate affect their job, their company and their customers.
- Productivity improvement.
- Human Resources policies and practices.
- Staff changes and promotions.
- Benefits information.
- How we're doing vs. the competition.
- Recognition of employees for achievements.
- Human interest stories about employees/customers.
- Personal news (birthdays, marriages, anniversaries, births, etc.).
- News of what's going on in departments/divisions.
- Financial results.
- How profits are used.
- Advertising and promotional plans.
- Company's community involvement.

Jeff Rubin, a former newspaper reporter and editor and instructor at The Learning Annex in San Francisco, is The Newsletter Guy, owner of the Pinole, California-based newsletter publishing firm of the same name (www.thenewsletterguy.com). He's written and designed more than 1,600 company newsletters since starting his business in 1981. He may be reached by phone at (877) 588-1212 or via e-mail at jeff@thenewsletterguy.com.

member newsletters may carry soft news, but if the news is all soft, the newsletter loses its audience. Audiences read newsletters expecting to find current information that is important to them. So go light on soft stuff.

Writing Tips for Newsletters

Newsletter recipients are likely to be fairly cohesive groups. Those receiving a particular newsletter already belong to a club or are employees of a company, or are philosophically aligned with or at least inclined toward a group. Assume but also reinforce readers' areas of shared knowledge and commitment. Use acronyms and other abbreviations accordingly.

As their name implies, newsletters have much in common with newspapers. They are often read for their content and then discarded. The standard rules of grammar, punctuation and spelling apply to newsletters as they do to all other media. However, there are some different emphases.

Crisp, Clear Style   Sentences in newsletters are mostly bare bones—subject-verb-object. Adjectives and adverbs are scarce. Compound clauses and sentences are uncommon. In short, the writing style in newsletters is simply spartan. Much of it might even remind you of what you'd see in a news bulletin. There are two secrets to this type of writing. First, you must know the subject matter very well. That comes from good reporting as described previously. Second, write in your usual fashion but then edit out about half of what you've written. If you allow yourself to get enamored with your prose, you can't be a good newsletter writer. You have to cut and trim until only a polished diamond of information remains. In that sense, editing your copy properly is more difficult in newsletters than it is in most newspapers or magazines.

Five Ws and the H   The who, what, why, when, where and how of standard newswriting also is important in newsletters. But the angle chosen for the newsletter may put the emphasis on one of these in story after story after story. Angle not only influences the focus of your reporting, but it also may shape the way you write a story. If you concentrate on entertainment celebrities, the "who" is paramount in your newsletter. If you focus on back pain, "what" gets emphasized throughout your newsletter.

You also should remember to avoid summary leads. Put the key point into the lead sentence and build the body of the story on that key point only. If there are several key points, make each one a separate story. Use the KISS method—Keep It Short, Simple (see Table 14.2).

Fitting Newsletter Copy and Design

Designing newsletters to display information attractively is important in gaining attention for your message.

Some newsletters may have a great deal of room for copy, if they do not use many, if any, illustrations. The danger is in crowding the piece with too much copy. Headlines, indentations and generous paragraphing help break up the copy in a word-heavy piece. Others tend to use too many illustrations and look cluttered.

TABLE 14.2	*Newsletters—15 Tips On Writing, Editing* A newsletter is the paring knife of communication tools. It seems simple and is easy to take for granted. Handled well, however, it's a highly capable tool.

1. **Keep your strategic audiences in mind, always.**
   What is relevant to them? What is important?

2. **Effective management involves planning and influence.**
   Develop a publication structure, an editorial calendar and written writers' guidelines.

3. **A newsletter must be sustainable.**
   Be realistic about the amount of content you can consistently produce.

4. **Begin with good basics and build on solid ground.**
   The most basic newsletter should have a few lead stories, shorter news items, and a message from your leader. A more developed publication might include features, departments, columns, an editorial, cartoon, in-house news, news tidbits, regional round-ups, etc.

5. **Deadlines are sacred.**
   Build in a safety cushion to allow for unexpected delays.

6. **An editor, like a captain, needs to know where the ship is going.**
   When dealing with writers, negotiate topic, length, treatment and deadline before assigning an article. Include important sources and the key questions which the story will address.

7. **Offer feature writers a byline and an author's note.**
   Writers gain exposure and your publication gains credibility.

8. **Be concerned about how your newsletter reads before you worry about how it looks.**
   Attractive graphics can obscure important content needs. Relevant and well-written content should be able to stand on its own, even as plain text.

9. **If you're doing an emailed newsletter, "clean and simple" spells "effective."**
   Keep it to plain text. Be concise, and put an 'in-this-issue' outline at the top. The footer should have complete 'subscribe' and 'unsubscribe' information. You should archive back issues, with an annotated index, on your website.

10. **Good writing and good editing require direction and hard work.**
    Your copy should sing rather than drone. It should ring when tapped. Write compact copy in the active voice. Edit for clarity, conciseness, jargon, length, correctness. The bottom line is your readership; give them top priority.

11. **Lead with strong items that have broad appeal.**
    Learn from the best daily newspapers—people decide within seconds, whether or not to read. Your editorial or a message from the CEO should have a regular spot after the lead items. In-house or more parochial news should have a regular spot much further in. This gives you the best chance of competing for attention, while those familiar with your newsletter know where to find what they want.

12. **Learn the distinction between simple information and a story.**
    Information comes to life as a story when someone talks about it. Try to cite sources as part of the way you do things.

13. **Any successful newsletter depends on plentiful and reliable sources.**
    Consider an acknowledgment box that lists everyone who contributed to an issue. This will reward people for helping and encourage others to participate.

14. **Look for reader feedback, always.**
    Watch to see how people scan your publication. Talk with a new sampling of readers after each issue. Do a formal readership survey on a regular basis. Track what's happening.

15. **The true test of performance is behavior.**
    You'll know you have an effective publication when your strategic audiences clip and save articles and when people are eager to write for it.

Source: Copyright © 2009 Al Czarnecki, APR – http://www.topstory.ca Used with permission.

Use   The purpose of a newsletter is closely aligned with its use. When you are deciding how to communicate with an audience, you have to determine what you want to accomplish, and then you have **to approa**ch that goal in the way most likely to succeed. If you have a dive shop in the United **States Virgin** Islands, for example, you can excite the imagination and probably stimulate business better with a brochure that presents more pictures than words. On the other hand, if you want to keep in touch with all the Corvette owners in your state, you're better off with a newsletter full of copy about rallies and parts.

How you plan to distribute the newsletter also has a great deal to do with its design. If you intend the newsletter to be a self-mailer, one side will have to carry your return address, the postage and the mailing label. Furthermore, the whole piece will have to meet the specifications of the Postal Service. Always check with the postmaster in the community where the newsletter will be mailed. Postal regulations may seem to be pretty clear, but in practice, they are often subject to local interpretation. It is better to check first than to be sorry later.

With so many organizations becoming international in scope, you may be dealing with postal systems that you don't know anything about. For example, you might inadvertently use USA postage stamps that don't have the numerical value on them for newsletters going abroad. If you read the fine print carefully, those stamps say for USA use only. If you don't read the fine print, your newsletter will not reach the destination country, because that country won't accept postage that doesn't have the value on it. The reason is that it doesn't know whether or not the amount paid is appropriate.

What the receiver is likely to do with the newsletter also has a bearing on the design. Will it wind up on a bulletin board, for example? Some newsletters are designed with that purpose in mind. A copy is sent to the president of a group, who then posts it for others to read. Others may be designed for display in a rack or countertop display unit. In both cases, the display unit has to be designed to call attention to the newsletter, and the newsletter should call attention to itself.

Writing to Fit   When you are writing the copy, you have to prepare the message to say what you think needs to be said in an appropriate way. Then you have to decide how you are going to convey the information on hand in the space available. Some professionals are experienced enough to be able to "write to fit," but most prepare the message and then spend a lot of time trimming it to fit and generally tailoring the message to the medium. A newsletter is somewhat flexible because pages can be added, but that usually costs more money. A better solution is to determine your information hole first and then write the message to fit it.

Writing for Other Cultures   The USA is very culturally diversified, and you can get yourself in trouble within its borders by not being sensitive to mores and taboos. However, the difficulties you can create in the USA are nothing compared to the problems you can cause for yourself abroad if you don't know what is culturally acceptable. Because English has become an internationally accepted language, many newsletters are produced in English and distributed internationally. It is easy to forget that some contents—photographs, for example—are not accepted in some countries, especially those governed by religious and not secular laws. If you have any questions, it's best to ask. Most embassies and consulates are helpful on such matters.

Writing and Designing Newsletters on Desktop Systems

The rules of the game regarding newsletters remain imperative, even if you write, edit, design and produce camera-ready copy on a computer system. That's a point you must understand fully; otherwise, you may wrongly assume that a computer system is the answer to all your prayers.

A desktop system can provide three major benefits to a person engaged in writing, editing, designing and producing matter for duplication or printing:

1. It can speed up the process of getting verbal and nonverbal material into condition for many purposes.
2. It allows you to experiment at little cost (except for time) with formats, graphic treatments, typefaces, type sizes and the like.
3. It enables you to exert more direct control over how things fit and look before you release your work for duplication or printing.

However, a computer can't make you a better writer or designer. Those are uniquely human qualities that no computer has yet been able to simulate. You should use your computer to its maximum advantage, but don't let it mesmerize you. It is a wonderful device that helps you do things you could only dream about without it. But it is still a dumb machine that can only move digitized information through electronic gates. Its behavior is controlled by which gates are open and closed. You open and close gates each time you enter a command. What comes out are your ideas, not your computer's. If your ideas aren't good, your computer can't make them better.

The value of the computer for writing, editing, designing and producing newsletters depends on how you use it. That's what this portion of this chapter is all about: how public relations people can use the computer productively and wisely.

Expediting Editorial Matter

The process of writing, editing and producing finished materials on typewriters was slow and tedious. Manual typewriters were much faster than writing in longhand, and electric typewriters were a little faster still. But both systems required long delays between drafts for hand editing and subsequent retyping.

When using a word processing program on a computer, you are actually using the computer much like a typewriter. A major difference is that your computer has enormous resident storage and useful tools. That's important because, if you're doing a 12-page, 8.5-by-11-inch newsletter every month, you're dealing with a lot of content. You need enough storage to keep all the information at your fingertips, without having to keep track of 50, 60 or more pieces of paper.

Clearly, your computer can speed up your work. And the time you save can be better spent on thinking. If the quality of your work improves, it may be because of this additional thinking time.

Extra time may also result in more *accuracy* in what you write—accuracy in facts, spelling, word choice and grammar. Review Chapter 6 for a more extensive discussion of these points, some of which are repeated here because they bear so directly on the successful use of desktop publishing systems.

Facts   If you're on deadline but you doubt the accuracy of a quote or piece of data, you can check it quickly and make the change instantly in your text, without disturbing other content. This remains true until just seconds before you must release your work for duplication or printing.

Spelling   If you're not gifted at spelling, your computer may save your job. Many good word processing programs include an electronic dictionary of more than 150,000 commonly used words. And these programs usually let you add thousands of other words, especially jargon particular to your needs.

Word Choice   Some programs may also include a *thesaurus*—a dictionary of *synonyms* and *antonyms*—so you can easily review your choice of words. Dictionaries and thesauri also are available on the Internet. But even with a thesaurus, you must remain sensitive to shades of meaning. Just because a synonym or antonym is listed does not mean it will work in a particular situation. You can't simply substitute one word for another, without thinking about them and the context in which they are used.

Homophones   Your computer also is blind to homophones. So when you mean *rein* but spell it *reign,* your computer's dictionary will read *reign* as correct and won't flag it as a misspelled or wrong word. Your computer may be able to flag misspellings like *regn* that are not words at all, but this feature does not relieve you of the need to read and edit your text for content, context and usage. You still must know the difference between *rein* and *reign.*

Grammar   The development of word processing software has reached fairly high levels of sophistication. But software that deals knowingly with grammar and syntax remains pretty crude. Programs can help some writers spot and correct grammatical and syntactical errors. But skilled writers can't get much help. Nevertheless, it is probably wise for every writer to use what is available as a safety net. Even the most skilled writer can't spot dumb mistakes all the time.

Designing

Although efficient word processing was fairly common by the mid-1970s, desktop publishing only began to emerge in the early 1980s. And it was not until the late 1980s that easy-to-use systems at affordable prices began to appear in substantial numbers. The term *desktop publishing* then came into vogue. Although the system certainly fits atop a desk, the operation isn't publishing in the usual sense. A personal computer is used to assemble verbal and nonverbal material into a cohesive unit; and this, if produced on a laser printer, may be used as camera-ready copy for duplication or printing. Here are some popular desktop-publishing software programs:

1. Adobe InDesign: "serious, feature-packed competition to QuarkXPress."
2. QuarkXPress: "a formidable tool in the hands of professionals."
3. Microsoft Publisher: "a major step up from consumer creative printing programs."
4. Adobe PageMaker: "Not quite on a par with InDesign or QuarkXPress, it still delivers professional quality results."

5. Corel Ventura: "Optimized for handling complex, visually-rich documents; integrates well with WordPerfect, CorelDRAW, and Corel Photo-Paint for Windows users."
6. Serif PagePlus: "combines ease-of-use and professional output options, including PDF, with word processing, drawing, and advanced layout and typesetting . . . a strong competitor for Windows users wishing to step away from Microsoft Publisher."
7. Adobe FrameMaker: "provides powerhouse desktop publishing for corporate and technical publishing of complex documents for Web, print, and other distribution methods. Has strong XML capabilities."[5]

Because the software that drives these systems is now easier to use, many people and organizations have been motivated to produce materials in-house that traditionally would have been done by professional designers, typesetters and printers. The results are a mixed bag. Some are superbly done; others are tawdry at best. The reasons for this rainbow of results are many, but a few are vital for you to know as you prepare for a career.

Format A key production issue to settle about newsletters is the question of format. This simply refers to the visual frame within which verbal and nonverbal content is displayed. Is a vertical rectangle, a horizontal rectangle or a square most appropriate? Will the design elements be balanced, unbalanced, modular or free-flowing? One of the features of desktop systems is that you can quickly produce a seemingly endless variety of formats.

This cornucopia of formats can so dazzle the unwary that the next issue of a newsletter may not look at all like the present one or the one before that. Just because you *can* change the format instantly does not mean that you *should*. The best use of a desktop system is to experiment with formats until you create the one that is right for your purpose. Once you have found it, use it consistently. Don't change just for the sake of change. You can create a template of the right format, store it and use it on demand. By using the same format you create a visual identity for your newsletter, one your audience comes to recognize and to trust.

Fit Desktop systems can show you how a story fits into the space assigned to it. This feature simplifies the task of fitting copy to type, because the computer does it for you, instantly. But this does not mean that you should let the desktop system control how much you write. To avoid this trap, observe these steps:

1. Write for content first. Make sure you say what must be said.
2. Then try to fit the content to the space.
3. If it does not fit and you can't excise the surplus without affecting sense or add the deficit without being redundant, change the size of the type or the spacing to fit the content.
4. Never let space rule content.

Visuals The very best systems can't improve the quality that a professional production artist or photographer can achieve. However, when these systems are used by people who have little or no visual sense or artistic skill, the results may be highly undesirable. If the finished product is to be four-color throughout, you can use a system to input information and to provide a basic design for initial approval, but you may want to turn to vendors for the finished work.

Much computer art is clip art. It is generic and general, not organization-specific, and it often is used as "wild art" to dress up a page. It contains little real information. Some software lets you modify clip art to your own needs, but unless you are remarkably deft, your efforts may well be in vain.

Scanners allow you to scan a photograph or printed visuals and create digital images. Digital cameras provide digital images directly to your computer. You also can modify this art, but often with the same results as with clip art. Also available are pencils you can use to draw on an electronic palette. If you can't draw well with pencil on paper, however, don't even try this alternative. No computer can overcome a lack of basic talent.

The mix of desktop publishing for print and for the Internet has created some serious design and content problems for both. It is possible to design a newsletter that can go on the Internet and be printed and mailed, but it requires a great deal of time and talent. Use the separate and different assets of each medium to their fullest.

Conclusions

- Newsletters combine some aspects of newspapers and letters and are issued regularly.
- Newsletters appear in print and on the Internet.
- Newsletters are serial publications that must carry volume and issue numbers.
- To qualify for a second-class mailing permit, printed newsletters must be published on a regular schedule.
- Newsletters represent a growing opportunity for college graduates seeking their first jobs.
- A successful newsletter must meet an unmet need in a distinctive way, be distributed so that it gets into the hands of its intended readers, be issued frequently enough to remain timely and have a person or staff committed to its production.
- The primary purpose of newsletters is to communicate regularly with a special group.
- An employee or member newsletter is one way an organization communicates with people important to its existence.
- These newsletters also seek to humanize the organization with a personal touch.
- The content of subscriber newsletters runs a wide gamut but in all cases offers information of value—worth the cost of the publication.
- Gathering information for a newsletter is much more sharply focused than is reporting for other media.
- Mistakes are deadly in newsletters because readers have specialized knowledge.
- Writing in newsletters is likely to be bare bones—subject, verb and object. Adjectives and adverbs and compound clauses and sentences are less common in newsletters.
- Desktop systems can't make you a better writer or designer of newsletters.
- Word processing and design software has improved dramatically in recent years.
- Desktop systems are cost-effective and efficient for newsletters that need not be produced at the highest levels of quality.

Exercises

1. Find a newsletter for members or employees and another that goes to subscribers. Write an analysis that compares their purposes, content, writing styles and formats.
2. Select a newsletter of your choice. Review the focus of its content. Write an essay describing your perceptions of the readers of that newsletter.
3. Write a story for a newsletter of your choice assuming that the newsletter will be mailed as well as appear on the Internet. How does the dual delivery system affect your writing style, the timeliness of the copy and the number of words you use?

Use InfoTrac® College Edition to access information on topics in this chapter from hundreds of periodicals and scholarly journals.

Brochures

*B*rochure is a term most people are familiar with. The problem is, it doesn't mean the same thing to everyone. This chapter will clarify usage, at least for this text. Public relations people write lots of copy for brochures. But if you ask them to tell you what a brochure is, you'll get a rainbow of explanations. That's because the term can mean booklets, fliers, circulars, leaflets, pamphlets or tracts. The difference between a brochure and these other pieces is sometimes a judgment call, so here are some quick guidelines for you to consider.

When the term *brochure* is used in its narrow sense, it signifies a printed piece of six or more pages, published only once and distributed to special publics for a single purpose. Brochures aren't serial publications like newsletters.

A *booklet* is basically a piece of at least eight pages, stitched on the spine. It often is small enough to fit into a pocket or small purse. *Fliers* and *circulars* are usually single-sheet pieces printed on one side that may be mailed, often in bulk, or distributed directly, like those you may find stuck on your car's windshield in a parking lot.

A *leaflet* is similar but it is usually folded, although not stapled or trimmed. A *pamphlet* is also folded and usually has more pages. A *tract* is a pamphlet or booklet whose content promotes a political or religious point of view.

These differences are pretty nominal. What these pieces have in common is more important, including:

- Message statements are always singular.
- Their purposes are to persuade, inform and educate.
- They are published only once, but multiple printings of some are common, with or without updates.
- They must attract and hold the attention of their own publics.

- Because they aren't parts of other media, they are their own delivery systems.
- They must have clear writing and be visually attractive.

Although the term *brochure* will be used in the remainder of this chapter, the principles will apply to all the types of pieces discussed above. The creation of a brochure is a complex process that includes six basic steps:

1. Clearly define its purpose.
2. Develop an organizing concept for it.
3. Write the content.
4. Design the presentation of information, including format and the use of type, visuals, paper, space and color.
5. Produce the brochure, including the selection of a method of reproduction.
6. Distribute the brochure. This might include posting a digital version on your organization's public Internet site or a private intranet site.

Purpose

The first step is to define the purpose of the brochure. What is it that you really want to accomplish? That sounds simple, and it is. But it can be tricky. That's because people often begin with a general rather than a specific idea of what they want to do. If you force yourself to write a single declarative sentence that describes the purpose, then you can move ahead with relative ease. If you can't reduce the purpose to a simple sentence, you need to think about it some more. You also can define purpose by developing a basic message strategy. A message strategy simply defines the key idea that you want to convey to your publics.

Real estate agents use brochures to show property and to describe the advantages of owning it. Sometimes realtors use a brochure to "sell" the services of the company, rather than specific properties offered by the company. Those reflect very different purposes. Many professional public relations people receive at least one brochure a week describing a seminar that has been designed to help improve their skills—yet a different purpose. Public relations professional groups publish brochures offering members as speakers to interested groups. "Selling" talent is selling a service from which others can benefit. Other brochures may promote membership, affiliation or participation. These serve all different purposes.

Still other brochures sell intangibles, by describing the worth of an idea—for example, those designed to get support (usually financial) for foundations. One mental health foundation sends out brochures "selling" its publications and audiovisual materials at prices that barely cover mailing costs. The foundation "sells" ideas for sound mental health but offers the materials to educate the public about its mission.

Brochures also can be informational and educational in the strict sense. The Hogg Foundation for Mental Health publishes on its website (hogg.utexas.edu) a list of publications and reports on mental health. Most are available online in PDF format, and others are available in print and can be ordered by email. A person seriously interested in the study of mental health issues would find this an invaluable resource.

"It looked a lot bigger in the brochure."

Source: Reprinted by permission of Adey Bryant and CartoonStock.

Informational brochures about subjects like a suicide prevention hot line or accident or crime deterrence are often produced as a community service. A druggist may dispense, along with prescriptions, a brochure on how to prevent poisoning accidents and what to do if an accident occurs. Such informational brochures perform a service and generate goodwill for those who distribute them.

Persuade

Brochures always try to persuade. In that sense, brochures try to "sell" or publicize a product, service or idea. You may find it useful to review Chapter 13, "Writing Advertising Copy," because advertising copy is common to a majority of brochures. Brochure copy, however, is usually much longer and more descriptive.

Your purpose, of course, influences not only the way you write copy for the brochure but also the design you evolve, the visuals you include and, perhaps, the way you reproduce it. If your intent is mostly persuasive, your copy will lean heavily on adjectives, similes and metaphors intended to tug the emotional heartstrings of readers. Although factual information has its place in persuasive efforts, the copy appeal is mostly emotional.

Inform and Educate

If your purpose is primarily to inform or educate, the copy you write will contain lots of factual information, perhaps replete with tables and graphs. This kind of copy appeals to the cognitive behavior of readers. It is a good idea to review the basic persuasive strategies in Chapter 3, one of which is cognitive strategy. This does not suggest that you should use only cognitive strategy in brochures.

But writing copy that informs and educates is more fact-intensive and descriptive than writing copy intended only to persuade. You should remember, however, that even the purest of information can have a persuasive impact. (See Figure 15.1.)

Concept

Once the purpose of a brochure is settled, you're ready to take the second step, which is to define a concept for it. An effective concept is one that helps you to organize words, visuals, color and space so they work well together to tell your story in a way that gets and holds the attention of your readers. How does that work? Begin by referring back to Chapter 13 on advertising copy, especially the portions dealing with creative treatments.

First you need a simple message statement. That statement becomes the basis for a creative concept. The concept has to include some symbolism for conveying the message. Then you need a headline that encapsulates the message. The visual must complement, not compete with, the message. The remaining pages should explain the offer, give the reader response options that are easy to complete and urge the reader to send or to call for further information or to take another action.

A good concept takes a key idea and interprets it, shapes it and, in turn, is shaped by it, and follows through with the production of a fully coordinated message that blends all the elements into a cohesive unit so that the whole is a sum greater than its parts.

Purpose and Object

Although the purpose is to persuade, inform or educate your readers, those broad purposes usually aren't enough to give you the firm direction you need for an effective brochure. You have to combine them with an object or application. Persuasion is usually the dominant purpose of a brochure, but some brochures educate or inform.

The guideline is: Begin with a general purpose—persuasion, information or education—and then extend it to the specific—an object or an application.

The Farmers Insurance Group (FIG), like most insurance companies, was very concerned about the rising number of young people killed or maimed annually in automobile accidents because of driving and drinking. FIG wanted to educate young people about the risks they take when they drink and drive. The general purpose was primarily to educate. The object was to offer advice on how to break the drinking and driving cycle. So the concept evolved into "young drivers at risk." The six-page, 8-by-10-inch color brochure used a magazine design treatment to convey stories about how individuals can make a difference, comments about the rites of passage, the impact of fantasy and a first-person account of how

FIGURE 15.1

Weatherspotter Brochure *This 22-page brochure was produced by the National Weather Service to provide information on severe weather such as tornados, hail and thunderstorms. It is intended to guide weatherspotters—citizens who watch for and report severe weather.*

"A Drunk Driver Changed My Life." The last page carried a signed statement from the chairman of the board and chief operating officer of FIG. Remember to proceed from the general to the specific.

Uniqueness   Not only must you have a well-refined concept for the brochure, but you also want it to stand out from all others that readers may see. You want it to be memorable. That means that you must be concerned with making your brochure different. The struggle to be unusual can lead you into some bad decisions, so be careful.

Cleverness   Inexperienced writers too often depend on cleverness to make a brochure stand out. Being clever is desirable, of course, but cleverness can be a slippery concept. Cleverness may turn out to be terribly trite, as in the case of a brochure for an electronics discount retailer that shouted "You've shopped the rest. Now shop the best."

Genuine cleverness takes something familiar to readers and gives it a *new and different twist*. Suppose you're creating a brochure to "sell" the idea that writing, designing and producing a brochure is really an exercise in packaging information. Talking about packaging information is fairly routine. So you might give it a different twist and call it giving shape to information. Giving shape to information also is more descriptive of what you're actually doing as you prepare a brochure.

Puffery   In their zeal to be unique, writers may stretch the truth. It is true that the FTC allows the use of puffery in language as an essential part of promoting goods, services and ideas. Even if puff words like *best, greatest, lowest, richest* and so on are sanctioned, they often are viewed skeptically by many readers. Readers usually recognize puffery for what it is: truth stretched to the point of unbelief. Puffery can help to create a memorable brochure, but it may be remembered for the wrong reasons.

Suppose the Rose Petal, a chain of 21 high-quality cleaners, has given you the job of developing a small brochure, claiming that the Rose Petal gives customers the cleanest clothes in town. The brochure will be clipped to the plastic bags that cover the cleaned clothing. The story can be told by describing the care Rose Petal's professional staff gives to clothing, including comments about special chemicals they use and so on, but it is best to avoid an exaggerated claim like "cleanest." In the absence of an objective measure, "cleanest" is a red flag that may inhibit credibility.

The guideline to use is: Avoid puffery.

Validity   Puffery aside, you naturally want to put your best foot forward. But your best foot must stand firmly on the accuracy of what you say. You must be careful in collecting information about the subject of the brochure. If you're writing a brochure that encourages prospective clients to lease space in a new office building, make certain, for example, that each office indeed does have its own working thermostat control before you claim that in your copy. If a company rents space and installs computer components that need special temperature control—and there is no thermostat—you can be challenged for misrepresentation in the brochure you produced.

Brochures about financial matters are especially hazardous—investments in particular. You must carefully spell out all the financial considerations and review the copy with both an accountant and an attorney before going into production. The underlying reason in cases like this is the same as with the new office building. People should be assured of getting their money's worth.

A professional organization's foundation offered a brochure detailing for potential contributors the benefits of membership in the foundation. The group's attorney was adamant that the mechanism for providing these benefits be in place before the publication went to press. Colleges and universities now do more careful reviews of their catalogs and brochures after being told by counsel of cases in which institutions were taken to court for promising more than they could deliver. The same caution extends to college and university websites.

Suppose you're promoting contributions to a local philanthropic group and claim that "all your dollars remain in the community." Keeping contributions at home is a powerful appeal to many potential donors, but if you're using a professional fund-raiser, the claim might be perceived as misleading because of the sometimes-inflated commissions that go to fund-raisers.

Brochures that inform and educate are much easier to write than ones intended to create or sustain an image. Image is often nebulous. Informing and educating are more concrete. Accuracy is critical. So is completeness. Now, we're ready for the third step.

Giving Shape to Information

You may not realize it at first, but the overall task in producing a brochure simply is giving shape to information. You do that by what and how you write, and how you illustrate and display it.

Notice that writing is the third basic step in creating a brochure. And you should take that step only after you're thoroughly convinced that the purpose is clear and you have a well-understood concept that helps you to organize and shape the information that goes into the brochure. Before going further, we suggest you review Chapter 10, "Message Design Concepts."

Rules

The rules of good grammar, punctuation and spelling apply to all brochures as they do to other media. Fractured grammar wreaks havoc with the language in a brochure as it does in a news release or a feature story. Reader reaction also may be even more virulent to mistakes in brochures. That's because of the specialized publics of brochures.

Suppose you're 21 years old and in good physical condition, but you find yourself in the office of a urologist. You're there because in the last three days you've had some severe back pain. You wonder if you have a kidney infection or if something is wrong with your back. As you try to relax in the waiting room, you pick up a brochure on kidney diseases. You begin to read it carefully and in the third paragraph you discover a subject-verb disagreement that results in confusion about the number of causes of kidney infections. The earth doesn't open and swallow you, but your anxiety level does go up. You begin to wonder if you can really trust a physician who would produce such writing. Your skepticism may lead you to cancel the appointment and see another physician or, at least, to get a second opinion.

Accuracy

Accuracy is essential. Most brochures have lots of information. To be able to write good brochure copy, you must first be a good reporter. Gather, sort, evaluate and synthesize facts carefully. Check and double-check information you're unsure about. Learn as much about the topic as you can. This is necessary because it is when you are writing about something that stretches your knowledge to its limits that you make mistakes. If you aren't careful, you may not even realize you've made a mistake.

In a sense, when you produce a brochure, you're making a contract with readers. They expect to be able to depend on you. Accuracy is one of the key elements of good brochure copy.

Active Voice

Use the active voice almost always, but there will be times when passive voice seems to better fit the context of what you're saying. So it is permissible to use the passive voice, but a general guideline is to avoid it when you can.

Style

Every piece of writing should conform to a specific style. Your organization may have its own. Use it. If a client has a style that is unique to that organization, you should use that style. If neither your organization nor your client has a standard style, adopt one. If you must adopt one, consult the *Associated Press Stylebook and Briefing on Media Law* for help. AP style is widely used, but often with adaptations. The particular style you use or adopt is not an issue, but being consistent is. That's what style is all about—consistency. Don't use *Mr.* or *Ms.* in one place and not in other places. Such inconsistencies in style nag subconsciously at readers. They may not overtly recognize such glitches in your writing, but they "know" something is wrong. They just can't place it. Adopt a style and use it.

Tone

Good brochure copy has a clear, distinct tone. It may be light or heavy or formal or informal in treatment. The tone should be appropriate to the brochure's purpose and subject matter. It may have a lilting quality or it could be a dirge. It really depends on what you're trying to do. It may walk slowly or run across the reader's consciousness. It might jump, crawl or turn cartwheels. For example, think about writing brochure copy for a funeral home. Death is not easy to talk about. Getting people to *plan* for their own death is a special challenge. You walk slowly, carefully. You might begin by talking about consideration for others who must handle funeral arrangements—physical and financial. Few people want to inflict inconvenience or financial obligations on those they love. Your persuasive appeal and tone have to be personal but not too emotional or sentimental.

Visuals

Thinking visually as you write brochure copy is as important as it is when writing advertising copy. The *process* is exactly the same. Because of space limitations in an ad, however, you may be able to use only one visual. Brochures usually have more space than ads, so you can use more visuals. But it is a mistake to use visuals just because you can. The general rule for using visuals in brochures is: Use a visual to substitute for a paragraph or a section of copy. If you can say it visually, do it. If you can't, then write it.

That raises a question: Do you visualize, then write? No. Write first. Write as much as is necessary to tell the story. Then go back and examine each new idea to see if it can be conveyed visually—by photographic or drawn art. If it can be shown, use a visual. In effect, what you write governs the extent to which you use visuals. And don't forget to use charts and graphs. Done well, they can simplify complex information so it can be understood at a glance.

There are two types of visuals in printed brochures. One is *line art*. This is art with no gradations of tone. For example, a pen-and-ink drawing is all black and white. There are no grays. The other type is *screened* or *halftone art*. Art that must show gradations of tone must be screened. For example, a photograph must be screened before it can be printed. This is done by filtering the picture through a screen that breaks up the image into dots. Screens are designated by their relative coarseness. An 85-line screen means that the screen will break up an image into a dot pattern that has 85 rows of dots vertically and horizontally per square inch. That computes to 7,225 dots per square inch. By comparison, a 200-line screen has 40,000 dots per square inch. This is a much finer screen. Most of the art you'll use in a brochure will likely be screened at about 150 or higher, because coarser screens simply can't reproduce subtle gradations of tone.

Only your imagination and budget limit your sources of visuals. The most common source of visuals is clip art. Clip art can be literally clipped from any printed source (but you can't use it without permission). Clip art can also come from a variety of digital sources. There are many sources that provide clip art—websites, PC- and Macintosh-formatted disks and CDs. You are free to use this art without additional payment or permission. If you have a scanner, you may clip from a printed source, scan it to convert it to a digital format and then edit it to suit your needs, but you must get written permission from the owner of the copyright to use it.

The problem with clip art is that it is rare to find exactly the art needed to convey an idea quickly, precisely and accurately. That's because it was created for some other purpose or it is generic art. The alternative is to hire photographers and production artists to execute the unique art that you want. This is the most expensive method of getting visuals, but it usually is the most satisfactory. When you hire photographers and artists, even though your organization will pay them for their work, they probably will own the copyright for the photos and artwork.

You can save time, trouble and perhaps additional expense by negotiating—before the work is done—permission to use the art and photos for unlimited purposes. Let's say you were responsible for a brochure, and you hired a photographer who took excellent photos. The brochure was printed, and the results were great. Now your boss wants to have the brochure digitized and put on your organization's website. Can you do that without violating the photographer's copyright? The answer probably is no unless you have a signed contract that says your organization has the right to use the photos for purposes other than the printed brochure.

Writing brochure copy is, in a sense, an exercise in integrating words and visuals to their highest degree, more so than even in the best magazines. That's because magazines operate with fixed formats. The format of a brochure is controlled by you, so you have much more flexibility in creating a fully integrated message. In effect, you let the content of what you say dictate the format in which you say it. All of which brings us to the fourth step in producing brochures.

Designing Brochures

The fourth step in creating a brochure is designing. It includes several major elements: format, type, paper, space and color. Each of these elements may be worthy of a complete book. What follows are selected comments intended to give you a general sense of direction. They are not, and can't be, definitive in such limited space.

Format

First of all, a brochure format should complement the content and the method of distribution. Suppose the purpose of a new brochure you're assigned to write for a bank client is to promote the use of the bank's electronic (paperless) banking system. You learn that the brochure will be inserted with monthly statements to customers, so perhaps it's a flyer or a folder. It's probably a good idea not to quibble about the technical definitions. In any event the content of the printed piece will not demand much space, and the brochure must fit into statement envelopes. With those two pieces of information, you can begin to shape the message to a complementary format.

Because an 8.5-by-11-inch sheet of paper will fold to fit easily into a regular business envelope, you can begin with that size of paper. Now you must decide whether it will be done in a flier format (one wide column printed on one side) or in a folded-page format. Because the sheet must be folded to fit into the statement envelope, it makes sense to design the format as a six-page folder where each page measures 3.667-by-8.5 inches.

Consult Figure 15.2 and look at 2A and 2B. The first folding option, 2A, is called a *gatefold*. When folding back page one so you can see the second page, it is much like opening a swinging gate—thus the name. *Accordion fold* is the name applied to 2B because it folds and unfolds like the bellows of an accordion. Folder options 1A and 1B, called four-page folds, do not work well for this project because its page dimensions don't fit into the statement envelope. Folder options 3A, 3B and 3C are referred to as eight-page folds. Folder options 4A and 4B represent standard 12-page folds. Folder options 5A and 5B represent 16-page folds. Folder options 3, 4 and 5 usually are used with much larger paper stocks, like 17-by-22 inches.

A different kind of project might call for something other than a folder-type brochure. For example, if you're doing a recruiting piece for your university, you may end up with a 36-page, 8.5-by-11-inch booklet in full color. If that's the case, you'll work with an 8.5-by-11-inch format and adjust the number of pages to those needed to display the content fully. The key thing to remember about these larger formats is that the number of pages must always be in multiples of 4-, 8-, 12- or 16-page flats. A *flat* is the number of pages on one side of a large uncut sheet of paper stock. Which one you use will depend on the press sizes available from your printer and the number of pages in the brochure. Look at Figure 15.3 for illustrations of the most common flats. Booklets like these usually are stapled along the spine, but some are pasted.

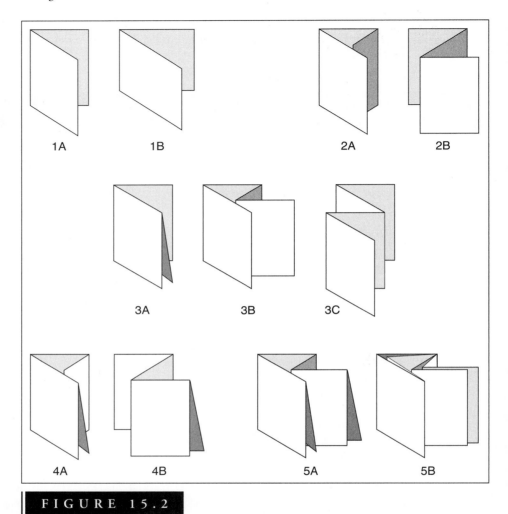

FIGURE 15.2

Brochure Folding Styles   *These are the most common folder options used when producing brochures.*

Using Computer Templates

Computer programs like Word and WordPerfect provide templates that simplify and speed the production of brochures, as well as business cards, certificates, greeting cards, résumés, business letters and even basic annual reports. Some templates are provided online by the software publisher. Microsoft, for example, offers more than 100 templates for brochures, folders and newsletters.

Once you've located a template that you like, you can download it into the word processing software and substitute your headlines, text and photos for the "placeholders" in the template. Then you're ready to print—either on your own printer or at a print shop.

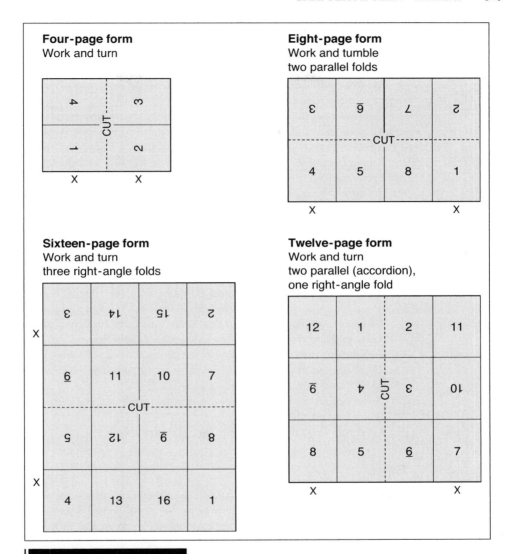

Four-page form
Work and turn

Eight-page form
Work and tumble
two parallel folds

Sixteen-page form
Work and turn
three right-angle folds

Twelve-page form
Work and turn
two parallel (accordion),
one right-angle fold

FIGURE 15.3

Most Common Page Flats for Large Paper Stock   *The actual size of a brochure is determined by its content. Selection of a printing flat is based on the number of pages in a brochure and the size of the printing press on which it will be reproduced. Flats are always done in multiples of 4, 8, 12 or 16 pages.*

Such templates are especially handy for situations where a limited number of folders or brochures is needed and changes are likely to occur fairly often. By printing a few at a time, you can avoid having boxes full of outdated and unusable printed materials. For those smaller printed quantities, some print shops print from digital files that can be sent to them as email attachments. Digital printing eliminates the need to screen color photos.

Type

Review the sections on type in Chapter 10. In addition to the points made there, consider these ideas. Typography is an important design element in brochures. Although you need to stay with traditional text faces in brochures, as you do in newsletters, you have a good bit more flexibility regarding display type.

You will find that the use of decorative or specialty type fonts is much greater in brochures than in newsletters, and even more than in some magazines. However, that isn't a suggestion that you use a myriad of display faces. Choose one and stay with it. If your software offers families of fonts, you can use these family variations to their best advantage in brochures. You also can do special things with type, like using a large initial character (called a *drop cap*) to begin each new section in the brochure. And you can use rules around blocks of type (but don't overdo this) and screens and tint blocks to give variety, yet consistency, to the overall look of the brochure. Here are some typographic guidelines to remember:

1. Use subhead lines to break up long copy blocks. This gives them "air."
2. Put about twice the space above a subhead as below it.
3. Experiment with additional space ("leading") between lines. This also gives air but don't overdo it. Spacing between lines generally should not exceed the point size of the type being spaced. The problem is that some font faces are denser and bolder than others. Only trial and error can lead you to a good, readable design.
4. Avoid using uneven left margins unless fitting copy around art.
5. Don't tilt type at odd angles. If you must tilt it, keep it to no greater than 15 degrees.
6. Don't run type vertically. It kills readability.
7. Select typefaces—text and display—that are legible and appropriate.
8. Avoid sans serif faces for text.
9. Generally, don't try to wrap text around odd shapes.

Paper

The paper stock on which your brochure is printed can add a lot to the impact of your message. If it is printed on inappropriate stock, your message loses some of its impact. Printing stock can be a baffling topic and one far too complex to explain fully here. The best advice is to work closely with a printing expert who can guide you properly. However, there are some basic things about paper that you should know before you talk to a paper authority.

Paper has a *grain*. That means that the fibers run in a specific direction. Knowing about grain is important because paper folds better and cleaner with the grain, and paper is stiffer in the direction of the grain. Paper is also designated by its *basis weight*. Seventy-pound paper is 500 sheets (a ream) of 25-by-38-inch paper. That size, by the way, is the standard for USA book papers, which include coated, text, offset, opaque and so on. The basis weight of typical business letterheads is 20 pounds, meaning 500 sheets of 17-by-22 inches. Cover stocks come from different sizes of basis weights.

Curl refers to the degree to which paper tends to buckle because it has excess moisture. This usually isn't a problem except when you use a cover stock that is coated on one side only. *Paper-ink affinity* refers to the speed with which ink dries on the printed stock. If the paper is very porous, as is newsprint, the ink is absorbed and dries quickly but the images are not as sharply defined as on better stock that dries more slowly. Gas and electric dryers often are used on many paper stocks to speed the drying process.

Paper color can affect color reproduction of lighter tints. Type is generally easier to read on a soft (yellowish) white stock, but four-color process reproduces more accurately on neutral white stock. *Brightness* also can be a factor. It affects contrast, brilliance, snap and sparkle of the printed content. *Opacity* refers to the show-through of printing from the other side of the paper or from a sheet under it. Papers with higher basis weights usually are more opaque than those with lower basis weights. *Smoothness* is a very important quality. If you're printing using a letterpress or gravure process, you need a smooth surface for the best results. Smoothness seems not to matter as much when printing offset. The paper's *ink absorbency* also results in a color appearing to be different on various types of paper.

Paper also is *graded* by its primary uses. Although there are many grades, those that follow are the ones you'll most likely use:

- *Bond* paper is typical business correspondence paper.
- *Coated* stock is what you will likely use when you must have the highest-quality reproduction.
- *Text* paper is noted for its interesting textures and colors. You'll use it mostly for announcements, fliers and brochures.
- *Book* is a grade that is common for trade books and textbooks.
- *Offset* stock is similar to coated and text papers but it is less moisture absorbent to compensate for the extra moisture present in offset printing.
- *Cover* papers have heavier basis weights and are made to complement coated and text papers.

If all of this is baffling, remember the simple rule: When in doubt, consult an expert.

White Space

The term *white space* refers to the unused portion of the total space in your brochure. Good design includes a judicious use of white space because it is, indeed, a design element, just like a piece of art.

The most important decision about the use of white space is how much margin you will use at the top and bottom of a page and on the left and right sides. There are no fixed rules to follow. A rule of thumb you may find useful is that the smaller the page size the smaller the margins can (not must) be. The reverse is also true. For example, if you are working with a page size of 8.5-by-11 inches, you might use three-quarters of an inch margins at the top and left and right sides and one inch at the bottom. Should the bottom margin be wider? Yes, to compensate for the optical center (not the symmetrical center) of the page.

The next most important decision about white space is the line length of your text. Try for an optimal length that is plus or minus one to three picas from the result of the following formula: Text type point size $\times$ 1.5 = line length in picas.

If you're using 12-point type, then the best line length for that size would be from 15 to 21 picas. If you stay within that framework, you'll generally improve the readability of your brochure.

Another decision affecting the use of space is the space between columns of type, or gutter space. A space in points 1.5 times the point size of text type is about the minimum space to consider. For example, 12-point type should have no less than 18 points between columns.

The next consideration is the amount of space you'll use to separate text from artwork. This can vary a good bit, but a general rule is to use the point size of text type as the minimum.

The final major consideration is whether you'll bleed artwork. Bleeding refers to running artwork off the edge of the page. Always stop artwork at the margin or bleed it off the page. Never stop it between the margin and the edge. Bleeding often requires a larger paper size, because the paper must be trimmed into the artwork (and discarded) to provide a sharp edge.

One major rule to remember about white space is: Never trap white space inside the page design. The reader's eye tends to fall into these "white holes," and it is hard to escape them. Always arrange your visuals, heads and copy blocks so there is white space opening to the outside of the design. This avoids the "white holes."

Color

Color enhances the attractiveness of most any publication. Even so, don't use color just to make things look better, because many messages don't need color at all. Using it in those situations is simply a waste of money. But other messages not only need but demand color. If you're creating a brochure for a new luxury hotel, you not only need color but also four-color process to show the decor of the hotel. The same is true if you're trying to raise funds to send underprivileged kids to summer camp in the mountains. How can you really show the thrill of a child catching a trout in the splendor of a mountain stream if you don't use color? So color can be an important element in the success of many brochures.

There are four basic components of color that you need to think about when working with electronic images. First is *pigment*—red, yellow and blue—the primary colors that mix to produce all other colors. The second is *light*—red, green and blue—the color that you see on your computer or TV screen that comes from beaming three light sources at triads of red, green and blue phosphor pixels, which then causes the pixels to glow at different intensities. The third component is *complementary colors*—cyan, magenta and yellow—created by mixing two light sources such as in theater lighting. The fourth component is *print colors*—cyan, magenta, yellow and black—also referred to as process colors or CMYK (the K stands for black), that are mixed in printing to create all other colors.[1]

For electronic colors, the brightness of each pixel is determined by *voltage.* The range is from zero voltage or black to equal voltage or white. The range of brightness is greater than for ink on paper because the brightness of the ink we see depends on the amount of light reflected from the image to our eyes. Different surfaces and different inks affect brightness, as does ambient light. Our eyes have rods that detect black and white, and cones that see color—but not well in low light.[2] You need to know how different colors will show up on the screen because this affects the balance of the design and readability.

There are two broad types of color usage. One is called *spot color.* That's where you use a second color to supplement a basic ink color—usually black. If you use still another color, it will be called the third color. Spot color is fairly inexpensive, and with the creative use of screens and tint blocks, you can get a rainbow of effects for a modest investment. Spot color also is not, in printing terms, close register—that is, it does not have to line up within thousandths of an inch.

The other kind of color is called *four-color process.* Photographic art is screened four separate times with special filters that sequentially block out all colors but yellow, red, blue and black (the primary colors). When they are printed properly one on top of the other, they produce the full range of colors visible to the human eye. Four-color process is close-register printing, meaning that the dot patterns must align precisely or the picture is fuzzy, requiring additional paper and press time for setup. That is why four-color process color is more expensive than spot color. So check your budget carefully.

Reproduction

Unless you are relying on a digital print shop or desktop publishing, you must prepare your brochure for reproduction, meaning you must choose between three types of printing: letterpress, offset or gravure. Each method has its own distinguishing quality and characteristics. Because of rapid technological improvements, differences in the final images produced by these methods are not as noticeable as they were just a few years ago. All three are capable of producing the same copy and art with satisfactory results.

Letterpress

Letterpress printing is the oldest of the three. It reproduces images from raised surfaces, working on the same principle as a rubber stamp. Letterpress is noted for its sharp, crisp printing and slight embossing (because paper is pressed into direct contact with the raised image to be printed).

Well-tooled letterpress printing plates are good for long pressruns into the hundreds of thousands. Quantities of a half million or more will likely require a second set of printing plates. Because there are so many press sizes, letterpress can be an efficient choice, even for small, short-run brochures.

Offset

Offset or offset lithography prints from a flat surface. It works on the principle that oil and water don't mix. The image to be printed is burned into a light-sensitive printing plate and developed with special chemicals. The developing process sensitizes the image so that it will accept ink. The unsensitized area rejects ink. The image is transferred to a rubber blanket that then offsets the image to paper. Thus the printing plate never comes into contact with the paper on which the image is offset or printed.

Offset printing is characterized by soft, smooth transitions of color and tones and slight differences in color balance throughout a pressrun. It is a good method for creating a mood piece, especially if soft contrast in tones is needed. Generally, offset printing is less expensive than letterpress and gravure. It is also easy to work with if you're using a desktop system to produce camera-ready pages.

Gravure

Gravure is a printing system that transfers an image from recessed images on printing plates—the opposite of the raised surface in letterpress. The image is etched into the printing plate so that ink fills the individual dots (wells). A device called a doctor blade moves across the surface and wipes away excess ink, leaving ink in the holes. When paper comes into contact with the printing plate, it lifts the ink from the wells, thus creating an image.

Gravure is known for the finest quality of color reproduction and is often used in high-fashion printed pieces, which many years ago got it mentioned in the song "Easter Parade." It is also known for high-quality printing on a variety of surfaces like transparent and flexible films, cartons and even vinyl floor covering. If you use gravure, get ready for a budget shock, because it is more expensive than letterpress and offset.

Distribution

The way you distribute a brochure may influence its overall design. If it is to be mailed in an envelope, its finished form must conform to the size of the envelope chosen. If it is to be a self-mailer, the back page or panel must be designed with a return address in the upper left corner and a place in the center lower half for the mailing address.

If you're using a postage meter or stamps, postage must be affixed in the upper right corner. If you're using some sort of mail permit, this must be printed in the area where postage normally appears. Check with the post office where the piece will be mailed to be sure that you know and conform to appropriate regulations. In fact, you'd be wise to create a dummy of the brochure and take it to the postmaster for inspection and guidance. It is a lot easier to prevent a mailing problem than to correct one.

Of course, if your brochure will be distributed from racks, as in waiting rooms of physicians, your concern is that the size will fit readily into such display racks and that the paper stock on which the brochure is printed is stiff enough to remain vertical when placed in racks.

Converting your brochure into digital images is an additional option. Once in digital form, the brochure can be loaded onto a website or distributed via email. Here you have several options:

- If your computer has Adobe® Acrobat® software installed and you use desktop publishing software to prepare your brochure, you can produce a digital portable document format (PDF) file by selecting Adobe Acrobat (the complete program; not just the free PDF reader) as your "printer."
- If the brochure was designed by a vendor, that person probably can produce a PDF file, but don't expect that service to be done without charge. As you are preparing your budget before the work is done, ask your vendor to include in the quote preparation of a PDF file.
- Another option is to use a scanner with PDF capabilities to scan the printed brochure and produce a PDF file. The result will be digital images with the same colors as the printed brochure.

If you convert your brochure to a PDF format and distribute it via your website or email, you should provide a link to Adobe's website where a free download of Acrobat Reader® is available.

Keep in mind that if you convert a brochure, annual report or other printed materials to digital format, you must have copyright permission from the owner of artwork, photos and other images in the pieces. Your organization may have commissioned production of the art and photos, but posting digital images on a website may be considered an additional use not covered by the original agreement with the photographer and/or artist. You may be in a poor negotiating position if you failed to purchase the right to use the materials for additional uses with the initial agreements.

Conclusions

- The term *brochure,* used in its narrow sense, means a printed piece of six or more pages, published once and distributed to special publics for a single purpose.
- The term *brochure* is often used to refer to booklets, fliers, circulars, leaflets, pamphlets or tracts.
- Common elements of brochures are: (1) message statements are singular; (2) they attempt to persuade, inform and/or educate; (3) they are published only once; (4) they must attract and hold their own publics; (5) they are their own delivery systems; and (6) they must have clear writing and be visually attractive.
- The general purpose of brochures is to persuade, inform or educate.
- An effective brochure can be developed only from a clear concept.
- An effective concept is one that links a broad purpose to an object or an application.
- A good brochure is distinctive. It seeks cleverness by giving a new or different twist to something that is familiar.
- The best brochures avoid puffery and build credibility by offering only valid information.
- Writing and designing a brochure is the art of giving shape to information.
- The rules of grammar, spelling and punctuation apply to brochures as they do to all other forms of public relations writing.
- Use the active voice. Strive for accuracy, consistent style and appropriate tone.
- Write first. Then design.
- Visuals should be used to substitute, when possible, for what is written, not just to dress up a brochure. For best reproduction of visuals, art must be line art or screened art.
- Good brochure design involves selecting the right format for the information, using type wisely, finding the right paper on which the brochure will be printed, using white space judiciously and using color creatively.
- Word processing computer programs like Word and WordPerfect provide templates that simplify and speed the production of brochures, as well as business cards, certificates, greeting cards, resumes, business letters and even basic annual reports.
- Aside from brochures produced by digital printing and desktop publishing, brochures will be printed by way of letterpress, offset or gravure.
- The method of distribution must be considered at the time the brochure is being planned. Distribution can also affect the choice of paper stock on which it is printed.
- Your brochure can be converted to digital images for loading onto a website or for distribution via email.
- If you convert a brochure, annual report or other printed materials to digital format, you must have copyright permission from the owner of artwork, photos and other images in the pieces.

Exercises

1. Select brochures of your choice from a bank and a hospital (or two other dissimilar organizations). Analyze the two brochures in terms of purpose, concept, writing style, clarity of information and design. Evaluate whether these brochures are attuned to their publics and explain why you believe that is the case.

2. Get a copy of the recruiting brochure from your university. Do a readability analysis of the writing (refer to Chapter 6). Is the readability level appropriate for the intended public? Select three or four consecutive paragraphs and rewrite them to a ninth-grade level.

3. Develop a concept for a brochure to promote the department or field in which you are majoring.

Use InfoTrac® College Edition to access information on topics in this chapter from hundreds of periodicals and scholarly journals.

Magazines

When you think of magazines, you may conjure up an image of the magazines you see on supermarket and bookstore racks. But did you know that thousands and thousands of organizations of all kinds publish their own magazines?

Those magazines usually are published quarterly or monthly. They may be mainly for internal publics or for external publics and occasionally for a mix. An organization may publish a variety of magazines, but each should have a clear and distinct purpose that sets it apart from the others. This chapter focuses on the demands made on the writer of magazines—significant tools of organizational communication.

Even though the contents of Internet and intranet sites have replaced printed publications in many organizations, magazines still can be powerful public relations tools, whether they're published in digital or printed form. They allow greater depth of treatment than most other media, permit more vivid and attractive display and enable writers to compose messages for specific target publics. Printed magazines have a longer life, and they have more "pass-along" readership.

Sometimes the public is internal—when a magazine is published for the employees or members of an organization, for example. Sometimes it is external, like that of *Methodist Health Talk*, published by Methodist Health System, which goes quarterly to 200,000 people in the system's north Texas service area. (see Figures 16.1 and 16.2.)

Methodist Health Talk is one of many nonprofit magazines that "represent a large and stable sector of the overall magazine industry, exceeding the number of for-profit publishers and accounting for more than 7% of advertising revenue. Roughly half of the advertising revenue is earned by 100 organizations. Nonprofit magazines are published by a wide range of organizations, including professional and trade associations, educational and cultural institutions, quasi-governmental agencies, labor unions and charitable groups."[1]

Methodist *health talk:* External magazine with sophisticated distribution techniques

Following are comments from an interview with Kathleen Beathard, APR, Vice President, Public Relations & Marketing, for Methodist Health System about the system's external magazine.

Q: First please give an overview of how the magazine, *Methodist Health Talk,* serves your organization.

A: Methodist Health System uses a quarterly magazine as a primary communications tool to inform the communities it serves about health care topics. The magazine provides information on issues of general public interest as well as specific treatments available within our health care system.

Q: Tell us about your magazine.

A: *Methodist Health Talk* is a quarterly, 12-page, 4-color publication that is one part of Methodist Health System's marketing program. It's printed on paper and also is available on our website, www.methodisthealthsystem.org. One PR Specialist serves as project manager for the magazine, and three staff members write most of the articles. We use an outside photographer for some special feature photography, and we contract with an outside company, Coffey Communications, to create the overall design, provide general health information, as well as printing and mailing the final product.

Q: What is the primary audience for the magazine?

A: Our target audience is insured women, ages 25–54, with household incomes of $50,000 or more in Dallas and surrounding cities—our defined service area.

Q: So you mail the magazine to those who meet those criteria? Do you maintain your own mailing list?

A: For each issue, based on that issue's content, we decide what audience demographics are most appropriate. Then we use an independent vendor to create a mailing list for that issue. We print 200,000 copies each quarter.

Q: Do you distribute the magazine to your employees?

A: Yes. Employees need to be as well informed as our external audiences, because staff members have direct contact with patients, family members and people in their communities. For employees, we make copies available in elevator lobbies and break rooms, and we distribute them at management meetings. We also reach employees through another publication and through email. In addition, we distribute about 10,000 copies of *Methodist Health Talk* through selected community events, and we send packets of copies to our active staff physicians and encourage them to make copies available to their patients.

Q: Do you have a written plan for the magazine?

A: We start with a comprehensive marketing plan, which supports the system's overall goals and objectives. The magazine, along with our other publications and activities, are part of our annual marketing and public relations plan. Our objectives are: (1) to recognize patient successes in ways that accurately share their stories of overcoming health care challenges with assistance from our system; (2) to provide ongoing communication and connection with residents of communities we serve, through information about new or enhanced programs

FIGURE 16.1

A magazine for external publics *A magazine published by an organization for specific constituencies should reflect the personality and culture of the organization and assist in accomplishing its goals and objectives. This magazine, Methodist Health Talk, is published by Methodist Health System for its external publics.*

and services, new and expanded facilities and vital community outreach and clinical initiatives available to serve them, and (3) to increase insured patient volume to Methodist Health System hospitals and health centers.

Q: How are concepts for articles originated?

A: Each year we set production timelines and featured content for each of four upcoming magazine issues, using broad areas of health care topics and our system's services. For each quarterly issue we fine-tune content to incorporate advancements, enhancements, facility expansion, rising trend topics and articles responsive to the ever-changing interests of the communities we serve.

Q: What does content for a typical issue include?

A: We include stories about patients in our key lines of service and specialty areas such as weight loss, cardiology, oncology, neurosurgery, organ transplantation, orthopedics, gastro-intestinal, women's imaging, and ear nose and throat. We also focus on stories featuring Methodist Health System physicians and departments using new treatments and technologies.

Q: Once you have articles researched and written, what's the approval process?

A: Everything we write gets checked by Legal, and I ask our operations vice presidents to check content. We also have an outside professional proofreader do a final check.

Q: How would you describe the writing style of the magazine?

A: We try to write as if we were writing for the lifestyle section of a newspaper. We have some amazing stories to tell, and we have some sensitive areas to deal with. For example, writing about incontinence, cancer, quadriplegia, chronic constipation and many other health issues can be touchy. To make the stories interesting, we need to make them personal—to tell the story of one person and that person's challenges. Some people have no problem helping others by allowing us to print their story, but we might want to use only a first name—or no name at all—in the article. We must conform to federal HIPAA (Health Insurance Portability and Accountability Act) rules and other regulations to protect the privacy of patient information. Our Legal Department helps us assure that we do that.

Q: Where do ideas for stories originate?

A: From many sources. If we want to cover a particular service, we'll seek a way to personalize the article, working with the staff in that service area. Physicians and their staffs often suggest stories about interesting patients, and that's helpful. Often, patients will write letters to their physician or one of our hospital presidents about their positive experience at Methodist. I've even had former patients approach me at community events to share their success stories.

Q: How do you measure the success of the magazine?

A: Measuring effectiveness in health care isn't as simple as counting the number of coupons that customers bring into a store. There *are* no coupons! So we do a number of things. We measure the number of patient referrals physicians receive, and our health system conducts community perception surveys every-other year. Highlighting patient success stories in the magazine often leads readers to make inquiries of our hospital and physicians via phone calls, emails, online visits and community information meetings. Because of the strong positive response to the magazine, the system increased the distribution of copies from 130,000 to 200,000 per quarter to increase visibility. In terms of return on investment, almost 1,500 insured patients per year can be attributed directly to *Methodist Health Talk Magazine,* resulting in about $1.8 million net patient revenue.

FIGURE 16.1 (*continued*)

Source: Methodist Health Talk is published by Methodist Health System. The image of the magazine is used with permission of Methodist Health System.

The Broadcaster: CPS Energy's internal magazine
with 36 employee reporters

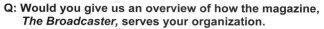

Following are comments from an interview with Bob McCullough, APR, Director, Corporate Communications, and Community Relations; and Pam Maris, Communications Analyst.

Q: Would you give us an overview of how the magazine, *The Broadcaster,* serves your organization.

A: CPS Energy is a publicly owned utility serving about 700,000 electric customers and 320,000 natural gas customers in and around San Antonio. We have approximately 3,600 employees, most of whom work from remote centers scattered throughout the Greater San Antonio area. Our senior management believes that employees are critical in serving the people of our community and that communicating with the work force is essential. So we rely on multiple communication tools, an important one of which is *The Broadcaster.*

Q: Tell us about the magazine.

A: *The Broadcaster* is an 8.5" by 11" four-color publication that is produced six times per year— every other month. It has been published since 1922. Because of a two-month production cycle, *The Broadcaster* is not always our best tool for communicating timely issues, so where we really score is with *recognition*—organizational recognition and individual recognition. That's really important in our company, where longevity is common and there's a family feeling among our employees.

Q: What is the primary audience for the magazine, and how is it distributed?

A: We mail copies to all active employees and retired employees, the company's board members and members of the City Council, because CPS Energy is owned by the City of San Antonio. *The Broadcaster* also is posted on our company's intranet.

Q: How are concepts for articles originated?

A: For each issue our magazine team—our editors, designers, photographer—meet and brainstorm content. The main articles are based on "the talk of the company" at that point in time and also come from the magazine's storyboard.

Q: What does content for a typical issue include?

A: We spotlight our company's major projects and initiatives, specific departments or sections and individuals who are making a difference in our community or have some type of interesting or unusual hobby. We like to have a mix. Some people call the magazine "our family in print," because we not only share what is going on in the work environment but also what is happening in the personal lives of our CPS Energy family. Also, each issue of the magazine includes popular recurring sections such as CPS Energy Scene, which covers employee work-related activities, [service] Anniversaries, Fond Farewell and Family Ties, in which employees share personal information and photos.

FIGURE 16.2

An internal magazine   *The Broadcaster is published for its employees and retirees by CPS Energy, a utility company serving about 700,000 electric customers and 320,000 natural gas customers in and around San Antonio, Texas.*

Q: How would you characterize the writing for the magazine?

A: The major articles are written in feature style, and most other content is written in news style, but more personal and relaxed. Because our work force is made up of employees with varying levels of education (from PhDs to GEDs), we write at the high school level.

Q: How do you gather information about employees and their families?

A: We have area reporters in 33 locations throughout the company who help gather information and photos. Many of them have been reporters for a number of years, so they know the people who work in their areas, and they provide the information for the family-type sections. Also, many of our story ideas come from the work force, including the area reporters.

Q: What is your biggest challenge?

A: Our biggest challenge is to take complicated technical information and make it as understandable as we possibly can. Most people have no idea what it takes to keep the lights burning. They've never been to a power plant; they don't realize the vast quantities of fuel, water and other commodities that are needed, and how we take that vast amount of energy and distribute it through thousands of miles of transmission and distribution lines. We kid around that our company motto should be "nothing we do is simple." So our challenge is to translate all of that – to simplify it so our readers can understand it. Our writers do a great job of interpreting the information and making it simpler.

Q: How do you measure the success of the magazine?

A: Several ways. One way is through surveys. At the end of 2008, we conducted a survey of all employees to help measure how well we are communicating with them. More than 1,080 employees completed the survey. One of the questions posed was, "In general, how well do the following keep you informed about CPS Energy?" On a scale of 1 to 5 with 1 being "Very Well Informed," 55 percent of the respondents rated *The Broadcaster* a 1 or 2. Another question was, "In general, how satisfied are you with the contents in *The Broadcaster*?" More than 40 percent of the respondents selected "Very Satisfied," the highest-rated choice.

Also, employees regularly share positive comments about the magazine and frequently ask for copies of the magazine to share with friends and family members. We get incredible support from senior management, who understand this is one important and well-received communication tool among many.

Q: How would you summarize the purpose of *The Broadcaster*?

A: Our company's core purpose is *benefiting our community by improving the quality of life of the people we serve.* That statement doesn't include anything about gas or anything about electricity; it's all about *people*. We try to share that purpose through all we do in Corporate Communications, including *The Broadcaster*. It emphasizes the fact that we are here for this community. That's reflected in the content of the magazine, recognizing the company's accomplishments as well as individual accomplishments.

Source: *The Broadcaster* is produced by CPS Energy, www.cpsenergy.com. The image of the magazine cover is used by permission of CPS Energy.

FIGURE 16.2 (*continued*)

The five largest such magazines are *AARP The Magazine*, published by the American Association of Retired Persons; *IEEE Spectrum*, published by the Institute of Electrical & Electronics Engineers; *National Geographic*, published by the National Geographic Society; *JAMA: Journal of the American Medical Association*; and *National Dragster*, published by the National Hot Rod Association. Other large nonprofit magazines include those of a diverse group of organizations: *Smithsonian Magazine*, published by the Smithsonian Institution; *Boy's Life*, published by the Boy Scouts of America National Council; *Eos*, published by the American Geophysical Union; and *American Rifleman*, published by the National Rifle Association of America.[2]

By one estimate, more than 10,000 public relations magazines are published in the USA. Many such magazines now are published only on websites to increase their availability and eliminate printing and distribution costs.

The success of such publications is determined in part by format, illustrations, design, editing and proper distribution. But the most important element of any magazine is the writing—its quality, its relevance and its appropriateness for the target readers. The most beautifully designed, illustrated and printed magazine in the world cannot sustain success without well-written articles, because it won't communicate much.

Topics

When you are choosing topics, it pays to look again at the mission statement for this public relations tool. What is it supposed to do? Who are its readers?

Most magazines conduct readership studies, and for budget purposes, a magazine must show a cost-effective benefit as a public relations tool. Because organizational publications compete with mass media for the time and attention of their readers, even if they are "free," you must be sure of their appeal. That means you must give priority to developing good topics for articles. Sometimes your topics will be assigned to you by your superiors, but more than likely, you will be left to your own devices most of the time. Although a good writer can usually make a mundane topic interesting, success can be assured only with a consistent inventory of good article ideas.

Finding Topics   If you know your readers well, certain topics will virtually suggest themselves. Your own flashes of insight may not be sufficient, however, to fill every issue of the magazine you work on. Fortunately, they don't have to be. There are other sources for article ideas. (See Figure 16.3.)

First, however, let's talk more about knowing your readers. As a writer, you need to move about your organization and get to know people from all areas of the operation. You can't know everyone personally, of course, but you should get to know at least a few people in every area. Personnel can be good sources of ideas, and they also can help you gauge the value of your own ideas.

A growing concern these days among employees is the lack of information about where their organizations are headed and the reasons behind these and other decisions. They also want management to listen to them, not just talk down to them. They further believe that, despite claims to the contrary, management does not actually encourage free exchange of information. If this is a correct assessment, your task is greatly simplified. Simply talk to other

101 STORY IDEAS

FOR YOUR PRINTED OR ONLINE PUBLICATION

HISTORIC

1. Anniversaries and other organizational milestones
2. Anniversaries of staff (especially after 15 years)
3. Anniversaries of volunteers with long service records
4. Individuals in the organization making outstanding contributions
5. New building planned
6. Cornerstone-laying
7. 25 or 50-year anniversaries of buildings
8. New achievements in client service
9. New products or services (and their anniversaries)
10. Meeting fundraising goals
11. State and national holidays that can be tied to organization
12. Service awards to the organization or personnel

RESEARCH & ACTIVITY

13. Reports on new experiments, studies, discoveries (or responses to others' experiments)
14. Grant announcements
15. Grant or project achievements or milestones
16. New facilities and programs
17. New research staff or special personnel
18. Response to others' research reports
19. Presentation of papers
20. Publication of books
21. Future programs and milestones
22. Improvements in operating efficiency
23. Patents acquired
24. Procedures developed
25. New uses for old products or services
26. Labor-saving discoveries
27. Employment and other statistics which indicate important trends

PRODUCTS & SERVICES

28. New products
29. New services
30. Improvements in products or services

31. Unusual uses of products
32. Unusual or efficient service use
33. New client groups
34. How, when and where to use organization's products or services
35. Demonstrations
36. Successful bids or awards
37. Efficiency records with clients
38. Comparative tests
39. Quality developments or controls

PROMOTION

40. New channels of distribution or promotion
41. Booths at exhibits, fairs, special showings
42. Speeches
43. Training programs
44. New media use (social media, etc.)
45. Contests
46. New premiums or special deals
47. Success stories (service, product use, employee effort, client success, etc.)
48. Cooperative arrangements with other organizations

FIGURE 16.3

101 Story Ideas   *There's an unlimited supply of possibilities for articles in your magazine or newsletter. Here are 101 of them. Some are "newsy" and more appropriate for a newsletter. Others offer feature story possibilities more suited for a magazine.*

Source: Reprinted with permission of Gladney Flatt of Graphics by Gladney, Dallas, Texas

SLOGANS & ENDORSEMENTS

49. Sponsoring a worthwhile non-profit cause
50. Using quotations from historic figures to "set the tone" in annual reports, product information or literature on services to clients and customers
51. Tie-in with another issue or organization
52. Endorsements by prominent individuals and organizations

PERSONALITIES

53. Interviews with executive staff on important issues or policies
54. Important speeches
55. Visits by famous persons (clients, media stars, noted educators, etc.)
56. New staff members with distinguished records
57. Election of Board members
58. Community service by staff

EMPLOYEES & ACTIVITIES

59. Number of employees on payroll
60. Number of volunteers
61. Personalities with interesting backgrounds, achievements, hobbies
62. Personal accomplishments of individuals within the organization
63. Professional accomplishments
64. Honors, awards, other recognitions
65. Board memberships by employees
66. Training, degrees completed
67. Scholarships to organization employees/families
68. Grants to employees or departments
69. Safety programs and records
70. Donations made as a group
71. Time donations to community groups
72. Retirements, transfers, deaths, etc.
73. Awards banquets, luncheons, parties, picnics

POLICIES

74. Change(s) in policies
75. Change(s) in contract terms
76. State and federal government policies (and responses to these)
77. Community, state and national problems and responses to these
78. Training programs or policies

ORGANIZATIONAL

79. Annual report issued
80. Annual meeting conducted
81. Board meetings, especially on important topics
82. Interim reports
83. Advisory council meetings
84. Forecasts
85. Fundraising events and activities

COMMUNITY ACTIVITIES

86. Participation in community or industry programs
87. Leadership by staff members in community/industry activities
88. Open houses, tours
89. Exhibits, displays
90. News that relates to the organization
91. Assistance to community groups
92. Awards to community or industry groups or individuals

CORPORATE IMAGE/IDENTIFICATION

93. New logo
94. Name for new program
95. New literature, brochure
96. Annual report
97. Information packet
98. Photo file
99. Guest relations program
100. Newsletter(s)
101. Survey findings, industry standing

FIGURE 16.3 (*continued*)

employees throughout the company. Listen carefully. You'll turn up a wealth of topics your readers want to know more about. If you research and write the stories well, your magazine will be greeted with eagerness rather than with a yawn.

But be prepared for the politics of getting some topics approved by management. Many of the things employees want to know are exactly what some managers don't want to talk about. The latter may support you, however, if you prepare them to look at story ideas from strategic points of view.

Doing a story now may defuse a small problem before it becomes large. An organization may gain a lot more support in the long run if it sensitizes employees now to a delicate situation rather than issuing edicts about it later when it may be even more delicate. Yet another strategic consideration is that the pain caused by candor, especially in a crisis, is usually temporary. Candor clears the air quickly, so an organization can get on with its business.

It is becoming common for companies or organizations to perform what is called a *communication audit* or *customer satisfaction study*. This is a systematic evaluation of the effectiveness of the organization's communication programs, including the magazine, if one is issued. The audit zeros in on the strengths and weaknesses in the organization's communication program. Some of these findings become fodder for good magazine articles. Refer to Chapter 4 for more information about communication audits.

Managements sometimes conduct organization wide employee surveys. Survey participants may include readers of the magazine who are customers or who have more than a passing interest in what goes on at the organization. Such surveys may be treasure troves for article ideas.

Public opinion surveys, like those done by the worldwide Gallup Organization, are common sources of ideas. They regularly take the pulse of the American public. You should make it a practice to read, study and save these polls for future reference. Even if the topic of the poll report seems unrelated to your company or industry, later analysis may show otherwise.

Additionally, you must regularly consult both local and national newspapers and a variety of consumer magazines. Save items that strike your interest, even if a specific article idea does not leap out at you. Watch both network and local television news, public affairs broadcasts and special-events programs. Listen to a broad spectrum of local radio stations, and tune in some of the news and commentary programs on public radio.

It should be obvious that you must read the appropriate professional, trade, industrial and scholarly journals. And you should go to meetings of all types. These can range from local service-club meetings to national professional conventions. The point is that you must go.

Any one or all of these may be the source of an idea. And an article idea may come into focus when you least expect it. But the idea you want won't come looking for you. You have to be on the alert all the time. If you're not tuned in, you may not recognize it. The clue may be a word or phrase, even out of context, or a major event. You have to pay attention to what goes on around you.

Form Versus Substance   This chapter began by saying that magazines are good communication tools for organizations. And they are. But are they as good as they can be? No. Who can make them better? Writers. Who are the writers? You. At least, you expect to be. So it is you—not "them"—who will improve company magazines and other publications.

That's not a small challenge, because it seems that everyone interested in the organization is more concerned with the substance of your writing than with your writing skills. That's no license to lessen your attention to proper grammar, syntax and other technical matters. Rather,

Source: Reprinted by permission of Clive Goddard and Cartoon Stock,
www.cartoonstock.com

it is an indication of the trap that some writers fall into: They substitute form for substance.
What you must strive for is both good form *and* substance.

Good substance is defined as what interests readers. There is growing uneasiness among
employees about how they relate to their organizations. Many don't have the depth of personal identification with or loyalty to their organizations that was characteristic some years
ago. They sense they are interchangeable pieces in a chess game being played by management.
They feel frozen out of decisions about which moves to make and why. If they get jumped,
they are summarily removed from the game board.

As a writer, you can help. But you can do this only if you listen carefully to your readers
and are sensitive to their information needs. When you identify those needs, meet them.

Just choosing the right word can make the difference in whether or not you convey your
meaning and—if you do—what the emotional reaction might be. Two studies—one from
Opinion Research Corporation (ORC) and another from Hill & Knowlton (H&K)—call
attention to the different vocabularies of management and employees. In the ORC report, the
findings show that employee-effective words satisfy three criteria:

1. Familiarity: Employees know the word well enough to define it.
2. Understandability: In workers' dictionaries, *capitalism* may be understood differently.
3. Emotional impact: Beyond familiarity and understanding, a word might trigger a different emotional reaction from employees than from management.

A current example might be the word *downsizing*, which management might see as positive (that is, becoming more efficient), but employees probably see as negative (that is, firing a lot of people). The H&K study cited identifies 30 words and 25 phrases that show
how inflated language used by management during a steel strike made matters worse. For
instance, instead of the word *accrue*, simpler words like *pile up* or *collect* would have been

better understood. Similarly, the phrase *exclusive function* should have been translated *sole right*. Both study results came from talking to people to find out what worked for them. Such consultation is important if the publication is to be useful.[3]

Some people think that magazines and other employee publications are perhaps expected to carry too much of the communication load for organizations. That may be true. But it is certainly true that employees place more value on information they get from personal sources than from impersonal ones.

You can't change a magazine or other publication from its impersonal form, but that's no reason for you as a writer to treat your readers impersonally. Talk to them. Listen to them. See things through their eyes. Be them. Then write to them. Focus on the substantive information they want and need. If you do these things well, maybe you can make your magazine a lot better.

Employee Publications

Most organizations have a publication of some sort for employees. Often the employee publication is a full-fledged magazine; sometimes it looks more like a newspaper or newsletter. Often it's in digital form on an intranet or Internet website. But whatever the format, the writing in employee publications should follow most closely the style of magazine articles.

Why? Because whether an employee publication looks like a newsletter, a newspaper or a magazine, it rarely functions as a medium for hard news. Very few are published daily, so an employee publication cannot compete with other information sources available to employees. Informal communication networks among supervisors and secretaries can spread news faster in the organization than can the AP wire. And when important events occur or major decisions are made, they are generally announced at once rather than held for publication in the next month's employee magazine.

According to Carol Kinsey Goman, Ph.D., you can be successful in communicating with employees if you understand these guidelines:

- Emotion is more powerful than logic.
- What employees see is more powerful than what you say.
- Informal communication is more powerful than formal communication.
- Nonverbal communication is more powerful than verbal communication.[4]

Employee publications can be an extremely potent tool of internal public relations, and they should be used to accomplish more than telling of the shop foreman's new baby or the vice president's successful fishing trip. (This is known as the dead-fish-and-live-babies syndrome.) As experienced employee publication editor Don Fabun points out, employee publications today must appeal not only to a telephone operator, but "to an atomic physicist, a systems engineer, a market analyst, and an operations analyst. These latter are not likely to be interested in, or motivated by, bowling scores and a detailed account of the company picnic."[5]

Employee publications can help generate support among employees for corporate goals and objectives. Articles can build employee morale and enhance job satisfaction, thus boosting productivity. Publications can create a broader understanding among employees of the problems a company faces.

How can these goals be accomplished? Mainly by keeping such objectives in mind when you're writing articles for employees, and by following the principles of magazine writing outlined earlier in this chapter. Specifically, you must orient the writing to the reader. Explain the significance of events from the point of view of the employee—not from the point of view of the board of directors. In other words, don't relate verbatim a new company policy as handed down from on high. Explain the policy and tell what it means to the reader. But explain it in an interesting way: Find a good angle, write a good lead and make the article as human and dramatic as possible.

If you take this approach, your company's employee publication can be a valuable asset to the organization. Articles about a company's achievements in research can generate pride among the employees, giving them a good feeling about being part of the company. Articles about the need to save energy or improve safety records can motivate employees to improve their performance in those areas. Articles about the relationship between your company's work and the well-being of the community can give employees a sense of involvement in a socially useful occupation. Articles about the accomplishments of individuals can be an incentive to other workers.

If you write articles on such subjects skillfully, so that employees will read them, you can accomplish much more than you would with a publication written strictly to provide entertainment or to relate social fluff. This does not mean that an employee publication should be a propaganda engine for the views of management. Rather, such a publication should be mutually beneficial to the individual employees and to the organization as a whole.

Association Publications

Members feel very involved in their associations and look forward to receiving the publication that their membership fees entitle them to. Even the government of the USA has associations with membership fees and publications such as the *Smithsonian* from the Smithsonian Institution.

Other associations and societies that have magazines include Public Relations Society of America (PRSA) (see Figure 16.4), the American Chemical Society, the American Association for the Advancement of Science, the American Academy of Family Physicians and various social groups such as college sororities and fraternities. *AARP The Magazine*, has the largest circulation of all USA magazines—three times the circulation of *Reader's Digest's*.[6] Some of the publications carry advertising from external sources and others have only house ads or no advertising at all.

What's important for a public relations writer to remember about them, though, is their high credibility and in-depth reading. Although these publications compete with commercial, newsstand magazines for their audience's attention, they are likely to get it.

Trade and Industry Publications

Most trade and industry publications are of little interest to anyone outside a particular area of business. But for people in the business, these magazines are a major source of information. You can find the *Cattleman* in most cattle raisers' homes or offices and the *Grocer* in most food store owners' and managers' offices.

Although most of these trade and industry publications are the product of associations, they differ somewhat from the lifestyle or interest associations that produce such publications as *National Geographic*. If anything, though, their readers are even more dedicated and more avid. If you go to work for a trade or industry publication, you'll find that the smallest mistake

CREATIVITY · INNOVATION

Want to Lead Creativity?
Why Not Try Something New?

BY JUDITH RICH

Creativity centers on being open to new experiences and aware of what's going on around you and then making connections that help people find new solutions to problems.

For many, however, being open is difficult because of the perceived risk involved in having to relinquish the old. While businesses need to change to move forward, people often associate change with giving something up. In reality, if you don't change, you give up a bigger opportunity — the opportunity to experience something new.

Often, the "old ways" have nowhere to go but downhill, but for fresh ideas to rise in an organization, there needs to be a culture that supports innovation. While many companies claim to have such a culture, only a small percentage of them really do.

In an innovative culture, ideas can function without fear. There are opportunities for ideas to be aided with supportive "plus up" thinking, rather than undercut by subtractive negativity. In such a culture, idea generators are appreciated rather than depreciated. There is no need to resort to the safety of either formulaic or mediocre thinking to survive. A culture for innovation recognizes the occasional need to fail in order to learn.

In my work helping to bring new thinking to organizations of all sizes, I have seen many styles of (supposedly) innovative leadership. Some were, indeed, terrific, but others were lacking. Here are a dozen suggestions I've seen successfully implemented (or implemented myself):

PRSA

THE STRATEGIST/SPRING 2006 PAGE **12**

FIGURE 16.4

Association Publication   *One benefit of membership in the Public Relations Society of America (PRSA) is the magazine The Public Relations Strategist, published quarterly. This article uses an effective "dozen suggestions" format—using numbered paragraphs—that you may find helpful during your public relations career.*

Source: Reprinted with permission of Rich Relations—A Creativity Consultancy.

CREATIVITY · INNOVATION

1. Get over yourself. If you are "the boss," recognize that you are not the only one in your company with good ideas. Neither is your creative department the only source for "out of the box" thinking. Creativity is everyone's business, and everyone in the company should be encouraged to get involved in thinking in new ways.

2. Have your hearing checked. Listen to everyone who offers a new approach or direction. Don't automatically tune out people. If you ignore them, they are not likely to offer their thoughts again. Everyone in your company is entitled to an equal "share of ear." You never know where the good ideas will come from, but they will surely not come from people who know they will not be heard.

3. Set a creative example. If you want people to take risks, do so yourself. You can't tell people to be creative and then stay with the tried and true. Encourage risk taking. Reward risk takers even if they fail. As Samuel Beckett once said, "Try again, fail again, fail better." Painful but true — people learn more from failure than from success.

4. Send out a positive vibe. Treat employees as if they are as smart as you (think you) are. Encourage them to solve their problems in their own ways rather than simply repeat what was done before. Let them know the organization has faith in them and high expectations for their success.

5. Turn the Greek chorus into cheerleaders. Discourage naysayers and pessimists and put "creativity cheerleaders" in every department instead. All ideas need passionate advocates behind them. Let people know that creativity is a meaningful company goal and that it will be rewarded. (Be sure you follow through accordingly.)

6. Excise these expressions. What shouldn't you say? Here are some examples. "That isn't the way we do things." "We tried something like that once, and it didn't work for us." "We don't have that kind of money/man power." "I simply don't like the idea." "If it's that good, why hasn't it been done before?" "What made you come up with an idea like that?" "It's just too creative for us." (That's my favorite.) Add your own "idea killers" to the list, and then do your best to erase them from your personal lexicon.

7. Give employees the time. I can't tell you how many PR professionals have told me they don't have time to think or aren't paid to think, and they honestly believe that is the case. Be certain you make "thinking time" a part of each employee's orientation. Set a line for it on their time sheets. Establish a percentage of time (appropriate to each position) expected to be used for thinking. And if the employee's time is not used accordingly, be sure to point it out during personnel reviews.

8. Give employees a place to think. Create "thinking spaces" where people can go outside of their own offices or cubicles to be left alone to think quietly and comfortably. These should be private places as opposed to creative conference rooms where "group thinks" are held. With regard to creative conference rooms, these should not be your same old meeting rooms. How can you expect people to think up new and different ideas in the same old room?

9. Break from routine. When work lives become routine, ideas tend to become routine as well. People tend to get in a rut when they are too set in their jobs, or have worked too long on a single piece of business. So why not unsettle them on occasion by engaging them in role play? Have people exchange roles/positions/assignments and play someone else's part for a day. You play too. It'll change the way employees think, and once you've been assigned to the mailroom (or whatever) for your own 24-hour stint, you're likely to have some different thoughts as well.

10. Change partners. The less you allow people to circulate, the less likely they are to be stimulated. And the less they are stimulated, the more difficult it is for them to develop ideas that truly challenge convention. So shake up the teams that usually work together. Make it a point to reassign group members on a regular basis. Get people out of their silos so they can see the bigger picture. Cross-fertilization helps grow big ideas.

11. Are you having fun yet? It's important that creativity is not seen as a chore but rather as a challenge. Don't let anxiety breed insecurity and fear. Encourage spontaneity and playfulness. Help your people believe in themselves. Let them dream big. The rewards will follow.

12. Celebrate widely. When a risk taker reaps rewards for the corporation, make a big deal out of it and the person or persons responsible. These are your chances to showcase the value of innovation and demonstrate just how important creative thinking is to the whole organization. Remember, it's brains (not brawn) that drive our business and keep you in charge. So, full speed ahead. Why be hesitant at terrific times like these? ■

Judith Rich is president of Chicago-based Rich Relations — A Creativity Consultancy. She is the former executive vice president and chief creative officer worldwide for Ketchum as well as the former executive vice president and national creative director for Edelman. She currently consults, trains, speaks and leads workshops on creativity and innovation. She can be reached at JRichRelations@aol.com.

FIGURE 16.4 (*continued*)

Source: Reprinted by permission of Dan Reynolds and Cartoon Stock,
www.cartoonstock.com

will result in countless phone calls, emails and letters to the editor. It's nice to be noticed, but it's
better if the notice comes from some creative or inspired writing, rather than from a mistake.

Corporate Publications for the Public

More companies are producing magazines about their product line, offering advice and ser-
vices. Health maintenance organizations (HMOs) publish magazines about their services.
Manufacturers like Sony are likely to have more than one publication. Sony publishes *Sony
Style* and *Sony Electronics.*

Although these are published for customer convenience and information, their purpose
is to establish brand loyalty.[7] Slick and expensive, these publications do have subscriptions,
but the subscriber costs are generally low, intended to cover marketing and distribution costs.
Subscribers also benefit from coupons in the publications and special prices to subscribers.

Another type of corporate magazine sells image. One of the most impressive magazines of this type is *Saudi Aramco World*, published by Aramco Services Company. The oil company uses its magazine to share information about the history, art and culture of the Middle East. There is no charge for this publication, which goes to a limited audience of appreciative readers. Another, a slick four-color magazine, *food&family*, is published by Kraft Foods North America, Inc. and includes feature articles, full-page ads and recipes touting its products while building its image.

Conclusions

- Magazines may be for internal or external publics.
- Magazines remain a powerful public relations tool because of their depth of treatment and "pass-along" qualities that increase exposure.
- Choosing topics for these magazines is critical to capture the "volunteer" readers because public relations publications must compete in the broader marketplace for reader time and attention.
- Substantive stories are important.
- Publications done well can contribute a lot to the success of the organization.
- Look to employees and association members for story ideas. Listen carefully to them.
- Many of the stories readers are most interested in are ones managers least want to talk about. So be prepared for the politics of getting clearance to do certain stories.
- Many magazines now are published only on websites to increase their availability and eliminate printing and distribution costs.
- Trade and industry publications are important and are read carefully by knowledgeable readers.

Exercises

1. You are the vice president of communication at O. Joyitz Funn Manufacturing Systems. OJF is a major producer of plastic toys. The research and development department has recently created and successfully tested a new toy. Tests seem to suggest that the new toy, called "Rotzie," will be a huge seller. OJF is frantically working on a plant expansion to help accommodate the demand it expects when Rotzie is introduced. You are equally busy getting communication plans ready for a formal announcement two months from today. Although some employees are aware of Rotzie, most of them have no clue as to how its potential sales will affect them or OJF. You know that you must put together news releases for local and national media as well as trade journals, and prepare speeches, brochures, sales literature and other things. But right now, you're pondering how to approach a feature story about Rotzie for the OJF employee magazine and the leading toy trade journal. Should the approach be the same for both? Why? Why not? Explain your decision.

2. Your company, Oltorf Chemicals, is approaching its 50th anniversary. The company's products are chemicals and petrochemicals that are used to make thousands of items, from ballpoint pens to telephone housings to auto parts. The company has been an industry leader in environmental protection and social responsibility. As lead writer in the public relations department, you are responsible for planning, writing, producing and distributing a special issue of the company's magazine. What should be in the special issue? Put together a list of story ideas. Remember that the Oltorf family has been important as the company expanded from its one location to a worldwide organization with annual sales of $25 billion and 23,000 employees. Today Oltorf Chemicals delivers a broad range of products to customers in 63 countries.

Use InfoTrac® College Edition to access information on topics in this chapter from hundreds of periodicals and scholarly journals.

Speeches, Presentations and Other Orally Delivered Messages

Speeches are presentations, but the presenter is one person who may or may not use any visuals. Other presentations involve multiple participants, such as panels, or more elaborate affairs with visuals and/or handouts for the audience and sometimes complex productions with music and costumed performers. Other messages that public relations deliver may be in the context of introductions of speakers, presenting awards, acceptance of recognition and recorded messages.

All of these are planned, but then there are the unplanned messages in response to media interviews by phone or on camera. At a news conference, or in an arranged interview, most responses are expected, but not always. Unexpected, though, should not mean unanticipated.

What speeches and all oral presentations have in common for public relations writers is the consideration of two critical elements—the impression the audience will take away from the experience and the information that audience will retain. In some situations, a persuasive element is crucial because of what the audience is expected to do or to think as a result of the experience.

Speeches and presentations are strategic tools. Remember from Chapter 5 that there are three strategies to consider: organizational, business and functional. Each poses some questions that must be answered by the public relations writer.

Regarding organizational strategies, what is the reality within the organization's mission, its goals and objectives, its resources? What strategic function does a speech or presentation serve in fulfilling a goal? How will that speech or presentation be accepted internally? How will the speech or presentation affect the organization's primary publics, those most closely identified with the organization?

In terms of business strategies, what does the organization expect as a result of the speech or presentation? Is direct action a needed consequence? Is delayed response not only anticipated but desired? What has to happen from the organization's investment in the time and trouble to give the speech or make the presentation?

The functional strategy is how the speech or presentation fits into the overall communication tactics. Is publicity a crucial factor? Or is a subtle, low-keyed persuasive approach needed? What effects are anticipated from the various publics who will have direct exposure to the speech or presentation? What about side effects from those who read or hear about the speech or presentation? How will these be measured?

All of these considerations are critical ingredients in preliminary planning. A significant consideration also is how close the audience is to the information being presented. If the speech or presentation is for internal audiences such as employees or related trade or professional groups, some allowances can be made for assumptions about familiarity with the topic. If the audiences are primarily external, nothing can be taken for granted, and some special care needs to be taken to eliminate misunderstandings or misinterpretations. Some speeches or presentations can have negative public relations consequences, often just because of one word or phrase.

Speeches

Delivering a speech is a hazardous undertaking. A speech takes place in real time—once. Although its delivery occurs once, that one presentation may be recorded and represented—out of context and without explanation. Another challenge is that members of the audience may be sending out—in real time by social media—points the speaker is making. It's not unlikely that the content will appear in a blog within minutes of the conclusion of the speech.

Think of the responsibility the writer has. USA President Barack Obama's 27-year-old speech writer, Jon Favreau, has to consider immediate and historical repercussions of what he writes. So do other writers though not in such high-profile jobs. Like the president's speech writer, they too may be working with other speech writers, or nonwriters, to craft an important statement for an administrator to give.

The speech first has to claim the audience. Without audience attention, no communication can occur. A speaker can only send messages, verbally and nonverbally, to an audience. It's the audience that gives those messages meaning.

For this reason, writing speeches and scripts demands more attention and care from the public relations writer than almost any other writing task. You can't simply write your thoughts on a subject and expect them to be delivered successfully by any speaker. Audiences react emotionally to the speaker's authority, trustworthiness, tolerance and friendliness, so the speechwriter must consider these factors when writing. In essence, this means the speech must be personalized. The words must go with the person. A speaker must sound natural and not as though he or she were reading cue cards. A person who feels comfortable with the words being spoken will be a more credible speaker. Direct interaction with an audience in either a speech or a visuals/words presentation brings out the best in most of us. The person preparing the material must remember that, although the audience is the ultimate receiver of the information, the person presenting it is most important. The speaker is both medium and message.

Sometimes public relations writers deliver speeches themselves, and in these cases, it should be easy to write a natural-sounding speech. But there's more to consider than just the speaker. Whether writing for another person or for yourself, you must have an idea of what the audience will be like. What experiences do audience members bring with them? What do they expect from the speaker? What stereotypes do they hold? That is, what are the "pictures in their heads"? If you don't know these things, you won't be able to write an effective speech.

You need to know the language patterns of the audience as well as of the speaker, because certain words used in particular ways can send thoughts down familiar paths. Remember that the connotations of words are as important as the denotations. And keep in mind that meanings change with time and that the same words may mean different things in different contexts or in different parts of the country. This means you can't write like you talk (or like the speaker talks) without considering how the audience talks.

Words, important as they are, aren't the only thing to be considered. Nonverbal cues can help emphasize points or obscure them. Audiences are sensitive to body movements, gestures, facial expressions, physical appearance and displays of personality and emotion. Effective speakers use these nonverbal expressions to hold attention and to help get the message across. Most speakers videotape rehearsals to perfect the blend of words and nonverbal expressions.

Many speechwriters get stalled at the beginning because they don't ask some important questions: Why was the speaker invited to address this particular group? What do the group members expect to hear? What does the speaker want to accomplish by giving a speech to this particular group? What particular topic will meet the speaker's needs and the group's expectations? You have to answer these questions before you start writing.

The next two questions have to be considered together: How long should the speech be, and what is the physical setting? A luncheon group won't tolerate as long an address as a dinner group, for example. People attending luncheons usually have other obligations; people who go to dinner are making an evening of it. Are there other speakers? Who are they and what are their topics? (These last questions are especially important if the speech is part of a seminar.)

Types of Speeches

Public relations people usually deal with four basic types of speeches: informative, persuasive, entertaining and technical. A fifth, less formal type of speech is termed brief remarks.

Informative   The informative speech generally—but not always—makes use of visuals. The subject matter is information that can readily be understood by audiences with little or no background in the subject matter. It thus is an educational opportunity for the organization. Such a speech may consist of telling a civic organization what the speaker's organization does, or it may involve telling an advisory body or an internal public what the organization is planning to do or has done. The speech given by the head of an organization at the annual meeting falls in this category.

Persuasive   The persuasive speech attempts to sell an audience on an idea, a person or a course of action. It could also be used to promote a specific product—anything from T-shirts to season tickets to the opera. More likely, though, the subject is something more abstract and therefore more difficult to sell. The speech might be aimed at convincing employees to take an early retirement opportunity or to contribute to a political action committee. It could be intended to convince a union of the desirability of accepting management's proposal or to favorably impress investor rating agencies with the state of the organization. Presentations like these may also make use of graphs and even handouts or booklets of charts and supporting documentation.

Entertaining   The presentation may be designed primarily to entertain, such as an after-dinner talk or a luncheon speech. In some cases, a keynote address may be classified as chiefly entertaining, although such addresses are generally more purposeful. Even when emphasis is placed on giving the audience an enjoyable experience, information about the organization is presented, and the speaker tries to leave the audience with a favorable impression not only of herself or himself, but also of the organization.

Technical   The technical presentation almost always involves visuals, usually PowerPoint slides and/or videos, and printed handouts. A problem with technical presentations is that the technology often fails. PowerPoint presentations are particularly vulnerable to incompatible components or unfavorable lighting. Videos sometimes don't work as well as planned either, for a variety of reasons. Computers may have compatibility problems and so may disks used in stand-alone projection units. If your speaker will be using a teleprompter, be sure the speaker is well trained and rehearsed in delivery. The teleprompter needs a good technical support team standing by, and a backup system.

Technical presentations are usually for peers at trade or professional meetings, or an official presentation to a regulatory body or a board of directors. The audience is likely to be less forgiving since it wants and needs the information. Be sure to have a backup plan for a verbal-only presentation with handouts.

Brief Remarks   Other speeches fall into the category of brief remarks, which are given on special occasions as introductions, expressions of thanks, welcome, acceptance, recognitions. Although certainly important, these need not be entirely scripted unless the person speaking is uncomfortable without a script. What works best for these occasions is to develop the gist or content of the remarks and have the speaker put them in his or her own words. If it is a highly official function, it may be better to use a script and rehearse the speaker a number of times until she or he is comfortable with the brief remarks. A major problem encountered with these is that the speaker may not be familiar with the pronounciation of names or terms. Be sure that these are spelled in easy-to-read phonetic terms. (See examples in Table 17.2). Another help comes from a website www.pronouncenames.com set up in 2006 and run by volunteers.

Planning

After you know the length and the setting of your speech, make a list of proposed topics and begin your research. If the audience is a general one, the best place to begin is to use a search engine to find what has been said about a topic. Another resouce is the *Readers' Guide to Periodical Literature*. You need to find out what the audience might have been exposed to recently. If the audience is a specialized group, consult the publications that group members receive and find out what is being written. You'll learn their current concerns and get an idea of what the group is like.

Most speeches written for public relations purposes are informative speeches. After you have determined what the audience has already been exposed to, you will need to do research on the topic chosen. Although you may feel you already know the material well enough to write a speech in your sleep, do some secondary research. Some can be done from your computer using various search engines. Most libraries provide access to materials that contain needed information even if you are not a subscriber. All your knowledge of the topic is likely to be from an insider's point of view. You probably have seen some materials that come from competitors and critics, but you should look at what has appeared in the mass media as well. *The New York Times Index* is a good source. Most public libraries in metropolitan areas and in cities with a university have electronic research capabilities if yours are limited. Select your topic and have the literature searched for sources. Remember that, in writing an informative speech, you are charged with offering members of the audience new and valuable information and then helping them understand and retain it. When you are writing a speech for someone else to deliver, you need to meet with the speaker after this initial research to get an idea of what he or she thinks is most important and to determine the slant or approach for the presentation.

Paring and Timing

If you have done your research well, you will have many more ideas than you can or should introduce in a single speech. Begin paring. Cut away until you have no more than three items you want to communicate.

Select the three most important ideas you want people in the audience to carry away with them, and then present the ideas as something fresh and meaningful. (It helps if the ideas are startling in themselves, but don't fake it.) Give the listeners some way to associate these ideas with others they hold. You'll have to repeat the ideas often to make sure they are retained, but don't be redundant. You don't want the audience thinking, "You just said that a few minutes ago." You also have to introduce the ideas in a logical sequence, using relationships that aid retention. It helps if you can break the pace of the presentation, adding some visuals when appropriate. Injecting humor helps people retain information, but problems can arise with this if the speechwriter and the speaker are not the same person. Humor is very personal. It's difficult to write humor for someone else unless both people are real professionals at their jobs. To be safe, use anecdotes—narratives that don't depend heavily on the style of delivery.

At each rehearsal do more trimming. Sometimes you'll find whole chunks of copy to delete. Do that, but add transitions so the speech won't become choppy. You need to physically time the speech with a stopwatch. If you are writing the speech for someone else, attend rehearsals and time the delivery. When visuals are used, you'll have less copy because visuals take more time than the actual showing. There's lost time in the movement from voice to video or slides. You'll lose less time if you have someone else handling the visuals so the speaker can concentrate on delivery and be more attentive to audience reactions. Time the whole presentation at each rehearsal. It should get shorter, up to a point. That's fine. Good presenters always leave the audience wanting more, rather than getting eager for the end.

Persuading

As you convey your three main ideas, keep in mind what you want to accomplish with this message. Do you want to move the audience to take some action? If so, you'd better let the listeners know what you want them to do, how they can do it and what their rewards will be.

Perhaps you want to change their belief about something. Remember, a belief is acceptance of a truth—an acceptance based on experience, evidence and opinions. If you are going to try to persuade people to change a belief, you'll have to offer both logical proof and some emotional appeal.

Alternatively, you may only want to reinforce a belief. Many public relations speeches are of this nature. Give the audience reasons for retaining their belief, and inform them of reference groups who also hold the belief. This will reassure your listeners that they are right in believing what they do.

The Mechanics of Organization

A speech has three parts: an introduction, a body and a conclusion. Contrary to what you've probably done all your life, don't write the introduction first. Just as you wouldn't write an introduction for a speaker until you knew who the speaker was, you shouldn't write an introduction for a speech until you know what will be in it.

Start with a title. The title should keep the main point of the speech in the forefront of your thinking. After you have a title, write down your purpose: to entertain, explain, convince or motivate. Then list the three ideas you want the audience to retain. Next, state precisely what you want the audience to do as a result of hearing the speech. You should then be able to write a conclusion.

Go back now to the three main ideas you want to convey, and devise a theme to tie them together. You ought to be able to tie this theme in with the purpose of the speech. At this point, you should be ready to prepare an outline.

Begin the outline by listing the three main points on separate sheets of paper. Under each point, list the pertinent information you have gathered from your research, along with what you already knew. Keep this list on the left side of the page. On the right side, write a key word for an anecdote or illustration to go with each point. Narratives make points memorable. Now arrange all of the information under each point in a logical sequence, and you are ready to write.

Formal speeches have a format that you need to consider: response to introduction; greetings to audience and effort to build rapport with them; overview of topic; summary of three points to be covered; discussion of each point with verbal and/or visual illustrations; reiteration of three points in light of purpose of speech; desired response from the audience—what to remember and why; conclusion and thanks for the audience's time and attention.

Style

To be effective in stimulating images in the audience's mind, you need to employ vivid words and expressive language. Be clear. Choose your words with precision. Be specific. Keep a thesaurus and a dictionary on hand to find precisely the words you need. For emphasis and retention, use repetition, but use it effectively. Think of a phrase that used for rhetorical emphasis will be recalled by audiences and captured as a sound bite. Use transitions not just to connect thoughts but to underscore a point by reiterating it. Confirm that all your words are appropriate to the purpose of the speech, to the audience and to the speaker. The audience always is global, either actually or potentially, so be sensitive to cultural issues. Remember that words have definitions. People give them meaning.

Involve the audience by using personal pronouns and asking questions that listeners must answer for themselves. Find some way to establish rapport—by citing common experiences or using familiar situations and imagery, for example. Use quotations if they are not long and if they can be integrated with your ideas to give authority. Be direct. If you are ambiguous, an audience may leave wondering what you meant and may come up with the wrong answer.

In delivery, the speech should support its points with various timely, meaningful exhibits—audiovisual aids, statistics (not too many), detailed illustrations and hypothetical or real situations. Comparison and contrast are effective too. Craft the speech to include these.

After you've completed the body of the speech, go back and write an introduction. The introduction is an integral part of the speech. It should lead smoothly, logically and directly into the body. It shouldn't appear to have been pasted on as an afterthought. The introduction must create attention and build rapport. It should give the audience some sign of the direction the rest of the speech will take.

You can use various devices to create an effective introduction. For example, start with an anecdote or illustration to capture the audience's interest. Use a quotation or a bright one-liner that makes a startling assertion or asks a provocative question. You might even use a suspense gimmick, which you can then refer to throughout the speech and finally tie into the conclusion. Some speakers begin with a compliment to help establish rapport, but there is some risk in this. You could come off as patronizing. You never want to apologize for yourself or the speech. You shouldn't have to!

When writing for someone else, keep in mind that person's favorite words, expressions and normal speaking pattern—long sentences or short, snappy ones. One speechwriter records the speech-planning session and plays it during this part of the work. The basic speech is then personalized for the speaker.

After the speech, be prepared for responses from the audience, either formal or informal. Think of questions the audience might ask and have answers ready, in writing if necessary. Provide some examples of the three main points that can be developed extemporaneously and review these with the speaker to rehearse possible responses. If possible, take a real example from the speaker's own background, or use that background to create a story or metaphor that the speaker might have thought of to illustrate the point. Summarize the three points so the speaker can reiterate them.

Part of the job is finding out all you can about the physical location so you can think of appropriate gestures. You need to inform the speaker of the physical arrangements so appropriate delivery can be rehearsed and nonverbal expressions developed to reinforce the message. The physical situation is extremely important. For example, subtle gestures are lost in a large auditorium, whereas the slightest movement is magnified by television cameras.

Be sure the speaker is comfortable with any visual aids or demonstrations. Go over these carefully with the speaker. If the speaker is not experienced in handling such equipment and time for training is limited, get an assistant and write that into the speaker's script. Be sure the technician is familiar with both the speech and the equipment. Mechanical failures can undermine a speaker's authority and poise. Eye contact is important. Audiences don't like to be talked *at*. The speaker needs to find individual people to look at to direct the message to them. Be sure these "point people" are scattered about the room so that attention doesn't seem to be focused in one spot. For a speaker facing a television camera instead of a live audience, the red light is the audience. Such situations occur when a speech delivered by an official is being sent technologically to remote audiences.

Source: Wizard of Id. Reprinted with permission of John L. Hart and Creators Syndicate, Inc.

Setting the Stage and Writing the Finale

In addition to writing the speech, the public relations writer must provide a written introduction of the speaker. How the person with the message is presented is important to audience acceptance. Content has to be controlled. For example, it's common for the person inviting the speaker to ask for a résumé. The problem is that the résumé is often *read*. Such an introduction is lethal. In public relations practice, you should offer to write the introduction for the person who will be presenting the speaker. Since you probably don't know the introducer, keep your introduction short and simple and easy to read. Think about what this particular audience wants and needs to know about the speaker. What will best set the tone and context for the speech? The slant will change for each audience even if the speech is basically the same.

Another part of the presentation that you'll need to write for the speaker is what she or he says immediately following the introduction. The speaker needs to acknowledge the introduction and say something nice about the person who invited him or her to speak, or about the person in charge of the gathering or the members of the audience. It's not only good manners, but it's also good public relations. You'll need to do some research to write something meaningful, such as finding out who issued the invitation and why. The reason to prepare this is because some speakers have destroyed the positive atmosphere for their speech before they begin by some extemporaneous, inappropriate remark. Planning and rehearsing some sort of acknowledgement should have the effect of sincerity.

The other major writing job is to prepare a news release about the speech. Because the audience for the speech may be limited, a news release gives the message broader circulation. For a major address, an institution usually includes publication of the speech in the promotion budget. The format is similar to a brochure, with the introduction of the speaker included, along with a description of the occasion on which the speech was presented. Copies are then mailed to lists of important publics for the message who were unlikely to have been present, usually with a cover memo (rarely a letter) or simply a business card. Specifications for reprint are also usually included.

Reprinting the speech is usually permitted, although in some cases, the speech is copyrighted. When the latter is the case, it should be made clear so that those who want to use the speech or large portions of it will know that permission for use is required. When you post the speeech on the organization's website, be sure to include the copyright symbol and the date if the speech is to be copyrighted material.

Presentation Scripts

Speeches, as discussed here, are presentations that a person delivers before a live or electronic audience. Scripts are formats for integrating visuals into a presentation by one or more persons.

Differences and Similarities

Major differences between preparing a script and a simple speech are the technologies involved and consideration of the audience. A script is not tailored as specifically for a single audience or single event as a speech. Many audiences may be seeing it *individually* (as in the case of employee videos on benefits) or *collectively* (as when salespeople all over the world see it in their own company group). Ordinarily, scripts are expected to have a longer "shelf life" than a speech, even one given frequently. Furthermore, the audiovisual presentation may be an educational tool from which the listener/viewer expects to gain a skill or information to progress in the workplace.

Approach script planning by first determining what you want to accomplish. Then think about the various publics who might be exposed to the presentation. After you have identified these publics, make a list of what each needs to know about the subject.

Types of Presentations

Basically there are two types of presentations that involve public relations writers: the primarily informational and the primarily persuasive.

Informational presentations are generally to employees and/or organizational advisory groups, external advisory groups such as government regulatory or supervisory bodies or nongovernmental groups (NGOs) who are a special public because of their interest in issues related to the organization, educational organizations or associations or trade and professional groups. Some informational presentations are instructional, and these are usually more repetitive in content than strictly informational scripts. Safety instructions or how to use new equipment presentations are in this category.

Persuasive presentations may be directed to any of these groups too, but usually persuasive presentations are a call to action or a particular point of view. These presentations are often given by lobbyists to governmental staff or elected officials themselves or to special-interest groups that the organization is trying to enlist in a joint effort to affect policy. Persuasive presentations may be given to employees too, especially those given in connection with a campaign to get them involved in and supportive of the effort before going to other publics. One type of persuasive presentation that public relations people in agencies or firms are always involved in is new business solicitations in which it is the organization itself that is being promoted with the idea of persuading the prospective client to hire them.

Planning

List the principal ideas you want to convey in the presentation. Arrange these logically so development is easy to follow. Use a narrative approach if you can. Make a master chart of the ideas, listing under each, as you would for a speech, the points you want to make. Beside each, describe in detail how you might present the point visually. Be sure each point has these elements: something to set the scene for the idea, something to carry the action of the line of thought forward and something to relate to a common experience that audiences can identify with.

Because scripts are more like a play than a speech, there must be an element of drama that builds. You can't put your punch lines first. You need to build to climaxes, give comic relief, offer suspense and/or surprise. You are more of a dramatist than a speechwriter—but it's not all that different from writing a television commercial or a PSA. (See Chapter 13 on advertising.)

Development

At the point of developing audiovisuals, there is no single path forward. Often because the speech is composed on the computer, the writer will prepare the major points as a visual or series of visuals. If graphs or charts are important, these are added. Of course, you can incorporate other art from the computer or use art that you scan into the computer. The presentation is projected to a large screen directly from the computer. The speaker can then go from one point to another easily and back up if there's a need to revisit a point. (For suggestions about when to incorporate computer graphics, see Table 17.1.)

If the scriptwriter is not handling the graphics personally, the writer has to work closely with the person preparing the graphics and other visuals, because these tell the story. The words are just there to help. There are two ways to go about this double-track operation: Select your visuals and write a script that fits them, or prepare the script and then "illustrate." When the visuals come from outside the organization, it is logical for the script to come first.

If you are getting help with visuals, plan for a series of conferences. The first adds details not in the proposal. The writer can explain the outline of points and suggest how these might be told with visuals. If specific pictures are needed, a photographer then develops a shooting schedule, interpreting the intent of the script in terms of shots that need to be taken to tell the story. Additional visuals may have to be sought or created elsewhere.

After the first visuals are ready, another conference should be held to ensure that the visuals match your conception of the message. And when all are completed, another conference is needed to see what is missing or needs replacement. At this point, the stronger art should be selected. The most compelling illustrations must be arranged in the best way to tell the story. In addition, the script may have to be revised at this stage. The importance of flexibility can't be overstated—although it is sometimes difficult to be objective about finding the best way to tell the story.

After the art is chosen and the sequences are planned, the script is ready for polishing, if it has been written. If it has not been written, you are ready to start.

Matching Words and Sights

Visuals have the power to set a mood, inject drama and explain in powerful ways. The words of the script should help the visuals do this. Too many words interfere with the listener's ability to absorb the visuals. Allow time for the pictures to have an impact.

The question always arises as to whether the script should carry the same information that is being seen, perhaps on charts or graphs. Usually the audience is given the charts and graphs as a handout. These need to be in a suitable format for keeping as a reference. It's best

---

TABLE 17.1   *Computerized Graphics*

When should you use computer graphics?

- When you want to have a screen show at the touch of a key
- When the equipment is available and the technology would enhance your communication with the audience
- When your competitors are using it or a similar presentation mode

Creating graphics

Graphics can be either static (still) or dynamic (animated).

Examples

Still: Charts—Bar/line, organization, text, pie, area, high/low, etc.
Should be used for communicating information such as budget disbursement.

Animated: Product rotated on the screen, internal view of how something works, simulated growth history of sales in animated form, flow of information in a communication network, etc.
Should be used for communicating information such as product capability.

Hints for effective use

- Use graphic techniques and maintain audience focus and attention.
  Transitions include zooms, fades, overlaps, dissolves, and others.
- Use a different color in graphics to emphasize major points.
- Present only pertinent information. Avoid excessive details.
  Use as a guideline: No less than 28-point type
  Maximum of 33 characters per line
  No more than 6 lines of text per screen
  No more than 3 or 4 screens per minute
- Use upper and lower case (rather than all caps) for text. Headers can be upper case, if desired.
- For readability from across a room, use a very dark background and large, very light-colored type.

Contingency plan

- Before your presentation, check whether equipment is functioning properly.
- Have transparencies, an overhead projector, and a screen ready in case equipment failure prevents your computer screen show.

Know your material well enough that you can still give an organized presentation during a power outage (even if it means giving your presentation in the dark).

Source: Permission Gay Wakefield.

---

to handle charts as they are handled in the print media. First the textual material prepares readers for the illustration by discussing it. Below the illustration there usually is a caption explaining the graph or chart and source or credit lines where necessary. Readers then expect to see the relationship between the illustration and the point being made explained further in the textual matter.

Writers with television-writing skills adjust easily to presentation scripts. Their experience with the medium transfers easily to writing scripts. Sometimes, though, they have difficulty with the time period. Television writers are accustomed to working with fragments of time. In a presentation incorporating visuals, the time is usually about 30 minutes, but it can be twice that. In a long presentation, both unity and pace make the job quite different from that of writing an ordinary television script. For elaborate presentations consider the use of sound. It can add emphasis and recall. Think of music and sound effects to accompany the words.

Pace can be varied in both the script and visuals. And to keep audience interest, it is essential to employ some of the techniques of the dramatist—suspense, dramatic foreshadowing and comic relief among others. In a way, the script constitutes half of a dialogue and the visuals form the other half; together, both tell the story.

Just as in the case of speeches, promotion is involved in calling attention to the ideas presented in the script. Like speeches some presentations may be prepared as publications. A news release may be written if the presentation is for important or large groups or is a "traveling" presentation. If the production is a long presentation going to a number of audiences, a promotional brochure should be developed.

Computer Advantages/Disadvantages

Advantages seem fairly clear—retention and flexibility. Facts and visuals for the speech or script and various versions can all be stored as PDFs on a laptop or on disks for reconsideration. Editing is simplified and printed copies of various versions can easily be produced. Computer graphics programs can produce excellent transferable illustrations to integrate into the presentation. Illustrations can be changed easily on the computer. Some points can be highlighted, colors added, backgrounds changed and designs reconfigured. Digital images and audio can be imported and stored. When an observation calls for use of older visuals, these can be scanned in and used for something such as an historical observation.[1] Sound can be digitalized and imported too.

Computerized presentations can be developed using a program like Adobe software or Microsoft PowerPoint© presentation software. Some computerized presentations are simply stored on a memory stick. A high-intensity overhead projector is needed for the presentation unless the computer is connected directly to a large-screen monitor.

When the presentation version is completed, it's best to copy that and a runtime version to a disk. The runtime version permits the presentation to be run on another computer without the software application, but it doesn't allow for revisions.[2]

Because one major advantage of computer presentations is flexibility, you always want to maintain that and keep open the opportunity for revisions, up to the last minute if necessary. Another advantage of computer-generated presentations is the opportunity to use the projected visuals as prompts for an experienced, knowledgeable speaker for whom the projection is the script. Preparing scripts for experts often means preparing just the points the speaker wants to make along with associated charts, graphs or other visuals. The speaker will use these to keep the presentation on track but will speak extemporaneously. This makes for a very persuasive presentation as long as the speaker's delivery is effective. You'll probably go through a number of designs for this sort of presentation until the speaker is comfortable with all of the computer screens that will be used. This must flow easily and nothing can be overlooked. Here the ability of the speaker to return to previous screens in a question-and-answer session following the presentation makes it necessary to have a script there for reference so the screen can be found promptly.

Disadvantages of computer presentations are not as obvious as the advantages. One disadvantage is having equipment problems. First make sure the equipment needed for the presentation is on-site and working. If the presentation is to a large group, you may be projecting to large screens or even to a remote site. In these cases, you need top-notch technical support. The equipment may check out fine in rehearsals and then break down while the presentation is going on. You want to be sure you have backup equipment, and someone there who knows the mechanics of the setup. That is a delivery problem, though. A not-so-obvious problem for the PR writer is inexperience in using PowerPoint© or another presentation software effectively.

Presentation software offers endless possibilities, and some scriptwriters find it tempting to use all or most of them. The effects can be dazzling and dizzying. Shapes and forms that seem to melt into each other or surprisingly emerge, wonderful color for background and type often are more of a detriment than an asset to the presentation. Before attempting a computer presentation script, reread Chapter 10 on message design concepts and Chapter 8 on writing for websites. Much of the information there pertains to presentation scripts.

Older Types of Presentation Aids

Overhead Projectors   PowerPoint© slides can be printed as transparencies for use on overhead projectors. Information on the individual transparencies needs to be spare for easy reading, and the slide should not be cluttered with art work. If color is used, be sure it will show up well on the transparencies. Also the type should be large enough to be read easily in the back of the room. Normally what you would want to put on the transparencies are graphs, charts and statistics that are difficult to follow verbally.

Flip Charts   If you are giving a presentation that depends on audience participation, use a flip chart. Pages can be torn off and taped around the room. You'll need a good supply of multi-colored markers and masking tape.

Sound   Your presentation may call for sound from a recording. You should get someone to help with the sound systems, including the microphones. Nothing is worse than not being able to hear or for the sound to be overpowering. When prerecorded sound is used, you'll need to be sure the recording is cued so that it will blend into the presentation and not detract from it.

Always rehearse, rehearse, rehearse. And time the presentation with the aids. While aids may add significantly to the presentation, they also will add to the time you'll use.

Other Speech/Presentation Occasions

Introductions and **acknowledgements** are two of the brief speeches that already have been discussed. Others are **award** and **recognition** speeches as well as **acceptance** speeches. Generally, the recipient is aware of the award or recognition and thus can provide biographical information so that it can be added to the speech that introduces the award and names the recipient. Introducing the award involves providing a brief history of the award or its inception. If this is the award's first recipient, explain the award's significance and then give the reason for the choice of recipient. The same pattern follows for types of recognition that don't necessarily have a physical award. Recognition is important, so be sure you know how to pronounce names correctly. Write pronunciation into the script, using the broadcaster's simplified phonics, as in Table 17.2.

Background on recipients of any recognition always is needed because information that can be found about the person through electronic searches may need updating or confirming. A parallel to recognitions is **acceptances**. When someone is receiving an award, an off-the-cuff response is not always as thoughtful as a planned, gracious acceptance that recognizes the organizations giving it.

The organization will have some publicity about the presentation that usually includes the recipient's acknowledgement or acceptance. For that reason, some planning needs to occur so that the acceptance genuine and brief. If you think of the ceremonies for the Oscars and Grammy awards, you will not have much trouble remembering some inappropriate acceptances. Although the recipients will not know that they will be chosen, being nominated suggests that a response be considered.

TABLE 17.2	*Pronunciation Guide for Announcers*	
VOWELS		Use AW for broad O as in fought.
A	Use AY for long A as in mate.	Use OO for O as in fool.
	Use A for short A as in cat.	Use U for O as in foot.
	Use AI for nasal A as in air.	Use OW for O as in how.
	Use AH for short A as in father.	U Use EW for long U as in mule.
	Use AW for broad A as in talk.	Use OO for long U as in rule.
E	Use EE for long E as in meet.	Use U for middle U as in put.
	Use EH for short E as in get.	Use UH for short U as in shut.
	Use UH for hollow E as in the or the French article le.	**CONSONANTS**
	Use AY for the French long E with accent as in Pathé.	Use K for hard C as in cat.
	Use IH for E as in pretty.	Use S for soft C as in cease.
	Use EW for EW as in few.	Use SH for soft CH as in machine.
I	Use EYE for long I as in time.	Use CH or TCH for hard CH as in catch.
	Use EE for French long I as in machine.	Use Z for hard S as in disease.
	Use IH for short I as in pity.	Use S for soft S as in sun.
O	Use OH for long O as in note.	Use G for hard G as in gang.
	Use AH for short O as in hot.	Use J for soft G as in general.

In *A Broadcast News Manual of Style*, these symbols are used. Although getting all sounds on paper is difficult (the TH sounds in *Smith* and *then* differ, for example), this phonetic guide will aid you in understanding the usage guide and help you create useful pronouncers. It is based on the guide used by United Press International (UPI).

Permission of Ron MacDonald, *A Broadcast Manual of Style*, 2nd ed., copyright 1994 Longman, paperback publication by Pearson Education 2002.

Some speaking opportunities are under less-controlled circumstances than what has been discussed so far. Two common situations are media interviews and news conferences.

Media Interviews

All media are included here. Some media interviews from traditional news organizations may come by telephone, landline or mobile, without any warning. That can be true too of interviews solicited by members of the trade press, although less likely. Although there is no specific warning, the calls should not be unanticipated. As issues are being monitored by the organization's public relations people, people likely to be called for comments should be notified and some talking points and positions should be discussed. That gives the persons likely to be called a chance to have at hand or at least in mind the background of the issue. Some news media go through the organization's public relations office to the contact, but often that is not the case. Contact information is easy to come by through websites and search engines. Responses to such unexpected media calls should be brief, but not abrupt, and should be consistent with the organization's mission statement and consider the effect of the comments on all stakeholders. Media training for likely respondents is useful, but speechwriters may get a call too to supply some background or statistics that can be sent quickly in an email. This is where backgrounders and position papers can be especially useful. Staff members fielding questions need to have these on hand, and even in a script format as issues evolve. Television interviews also can be unexpected when TV news crews are covering spot news. For more on this, see Chapter 18 on crisis communication.

However, television interviews are more likely to be structured because they occur in a TV studio. Normally in setting up the interview, you will have covered with the interviewer what you or the organization's representative will be discussing. If it is a friendly interviewing situation, the interviewer will meet with you prior to the show, although sometimes just before airtime or the taping. The interviewer wants a good show, and you want to make certain points, never more than three, and maybe less depending on the length of the interview. Get the most important point you want to make out in the first 15 to 20 seconds.

You need to organize your thoughts mentally because you will be speaking extemporaneously. Think of good sound bites, but use them appropriately. Listen carefully to the questions as they are asked, and respond specifically to the question.

Keep a friendly, open demeanor, even if the questioning gets tough. You need to keep calm and relaxed, but be strong in your voice. You want to engage the audience so they'll remember your points. Be sure you know all of the information you are likely to be asked. Your preparation should seem effortless, though, and come out in a natural conversation.

If you are participating from another location, you will be wearing an earpiece. Be sure that it fits properly before the show or the taping starts. You don't want the distraction of fumbling to adjust the piece to your ear to get the right volume. Usually you'll be wearing a lapel microphone, but the sound staff probably will get this adjusted properly for you and test the pick up of your voice before the interview begins.

News Conferences

Because you will have called the news conference, you have more control than you do in a television interview. It is your choice of site, your setting, your equipment and your staff. However, you want to be sure you have anticipated all of the questions. If you are responsible for having an executive interviewed, go through the types of questions likely to be asked and her/his general response. You should be working with a media-trained executive so she or he has some on-camera experience.

Occasionally news conferences call for demonstrations or injections of visuals. Be sure these work as expected and add significantly to the point of the news conference. Have microphones set up for news media to use them so their questions can be picked up by everyone, and also on your organization's video recording of the news conference that your staff is making. If the news conference is being carried in real time on your website, be sure the set is designed for easy viewing on a computer. The setting will have to be tighter than just for television.

In most news conferences, the executive or you will be speaking from a prepared script, although it should be brief. Afterward, you'll be responding to questions. Don't try to dodge them or be evasive in your response. Also, don't get defensive; it shows.

Since you are controlling the presentation, remember the broadcast rule: tell them what you are going to tell them, tell them, and then tell them what you told them. It's okay to be repetitive, just not redundant.

Some good advice comes from media trainer T.J. Walker who says that to evaluate your performance to improve, watch it within 24 hours of the airing or taping.[3]

Evaluations

Public relations writers, as well as presenters and certainly management, want to know if the speech or presentation was effective. What often is used on-site is a simple evaluation form. It may be handed to attendees at the presentation and either collected at the door or left behind on tables. Sometimes if the presentation is at a conference, the evaluation is sent later to those who attended and includes all of the speeches and presentations for respondents to evaluate.

Remember, these forms are generally distributed and collected by the organization where the speech or presentation was given, and when that organization is different from your own, you may or may not know the results. To assess the evaluation, you need a copy of the questionnaire used, the method for soliciting responses and how many completed responses were used in the assessment. Why? Because your job may be on the line. A presentation can get "bad reviews" that you get blamed for when your part of the job was fine. Or it may be that the opinion "survey" is not a good indicator.

When a presentation is an informative one, the best assessment is an evaluation some time after the presentation to test recall of information as well as what was best appreciated or liked about the presentation. This helps you design better presentations.

If the presentation is a persuasive one, the measures are more complex. You can't always judge long-term effects by short-term reports. However, you certainly can tell something about the presentation by the verbal and written responses the organization gets. You can document these and draw some conclusions from them, so long as you remember that those you don't hear from may be significantly different from those who make the effort to express themselves. Be alert to any pointed criticism about bias or insensitivity that a presentation may have aroused. Even one critic's message can be important here.

Conclusions

- Writing speeches and scripts for presentations is a demanding task because of the combination of words and images and the performance element.
- Direct interaction with an audience in either a speech or a visuals/words presentation brings out the best in most of us.
- Preparing material especially for specific audiences is the key to pleasing them.
- The person preparing the material must remember that, although the audience is the ultimate receiver of the information, the person presenting it is most important. The speaker is both medium and message.
- Speech subjects need to be thoroughly researched, but the main points must be pared to three.
- The effect you want the speech to have on the audience should be the governing factor in how it is constructed.
- You need to be sure you are using words and symbols that are meaningful to the audience and appropriate for the speaker.
- Most public relations people are in the business of preparing materials for others to use, so they must be skilled in this task.
- Preparing material for presentation by others is a hazardous task, but a highly creative one.
- Scriptwriters must be able to visualize the combination of pictures and words that will occur when messages are presented.
- Speeches and scripts must have a sense of pace—a rhythm appropriate for both the material and the speaker.
- The script is a dialogue with visuals. Scripts are more like plays than speeches and are closely akin to television commercials and PSAs.
- Presentation of any kind of audiovisual or speech is a public relations function that demands rehearsal.
- Part of the public relations function is to prepare the introduction for a presentation, acknowledgement of the introduction, releases about the presentation, and brochures (which in the case of a speech may be a reprint of the speech or important graphics from the presentation with captions, to be sent with a cover memo).
- All audio/video presentations and the use of older presentation media such as overhead projectors, flip charts and audio and video will add to the length of the presentation. Time and rehearse.
- Brief speeches such as award and recognition presentations and acceptance speeches need to be prepared so that these are thoughtful and appropriate.
- Many media interviews are instant and, although can't be planned for specifically, can be anticipated.
- Television interviews, live or taped, are another type of opportunity to speak. Organize your points mentally. Carry on a conversation with the interviewer and keep a pleasant demeanor even if the questions get tough.
- A news conference offers more control, but needs to be carefully planned to keep it that say. Be concise and think of sound bites in advance. Don't evade questions in the Q&A that follows.

- Evaluations of speeches and presentations are important because your job may be on the line. When other organizations do the evaluating, you may or may not get the results, so you need to build in mechanisms for your organization to evaluate the value of speeches and presentations.
- Informative speeches and presentations are easier to assess than persuasive ones because the long-term effects of persuasion are more difficult to measure.
- Be alert to any pointed criticism of bias or insensitivity in speeches or presentations, even if it's from only one critic. Sometimes only one word can cause public relations problems.

Exercises

1. You are the vice president of communication at O. Joyitz Funn Manufacturing Systems. OJF is a major producer of children's toys made of plastics. The management team recently got a confidential staff medical report confirming that OJF employees have a much higher incidence of respiratory illnesses than is normal in the surrounding community and region. The report cites as the probable cause a key ingredient used in the manufacture of several OJF products, although more study is necessary to confirm this chemical as the offending agent. Management immediately ordered more study for definitive answers. But it also decided to keep the information confidential until the results of these studies are known. Your task now is to come up with a persuasive rationale that will give support to running a story about the staff medical report in the company magazine now. What arguments will you use? Consult Chapter 3 on persuasion for some clues.
2. How would you treat this subject in writing a speech for the CEO to post on the website and how would you recraft it to present in person to:
    a. employees?
    b. a local civic group?
    c. an activist group for clean air in your city?
3. Develop a presentation script to recruit students to your school.

Use InfoTrac® College Edition to access information on topics in this chapter from hundreds of periodicals and scholarly journals.

PART 6

6

Writing in
Turbulent Times

*W*hen Thomas Paine wrote "These are the times that try men's souls" on December 23, 1776, he might well have been writing about today's trying events. Natural and human-made disasters of all kinds create crises in which public relations people and their writing play important roles. The following chapter is intended to make your crises less trying.

Crisis Communication

Crisis communication isn't what it used to be. In the past, PR people were the first to provide public responses to catastrophes and, therefore, were in charge of what was said about the crisis. No more. As reported by MediaShift, "Nowadays, the type of media that will report on a crisis is often as unforeseen as the crisis itself. When Chesley Sullenberger, the captain of US Airways Flight 1549, executed a near-miraculous water landing in the Hudson River in January 2009, initial news reports came from the unlikeliest of sources—and beat the official corporate response by a long shot. One of the most iconic images of US Airways Flight 1549's bobbing hull came not from a fast-acting photojournalist, but from Janis Krums, a regular guy on a nearby ferry who snapped a picture with his iPhone and uploaded it to his Twitter stream. Before US Airways was able to issue even a preliminary statement confirming the incident, MSNBC had already broadcast the photo and interviewed Krums."[1]

What's it like to experience such a crisis? Only those who have been through such major disasters could possibly know. But we do know that in every disaster people in all types of organizations are immediately and deeply involved. Police, fire and other emergency organizations are instantly impacted, along with government agencies at all levels. Charitable organizations respond immediately, and news media from around the globe cover the crisis.

The highly respected American Red Cross, founded in 1881 by the Civil War nurse Clara Barton and providing disaster relief to the victims of more than 67,000 disasters annually, faced its own major crisis following 9/11. Ray Suarez reported on PBS television's *The NewsHour with Jim Lehrer,* "As the contributions poured in, Red Cross President Bernadine Healy took the unusual step of not putting the money in the agency's general funds, rather in a separate place, the Liberty Fund, which most people assumed would be used solely for September 11 victim relief." But less than one-third of the $543 million pledged was spent on relief efforts. The Red Cross planned to spend more than half of the contributions for other purposes.

This brought heated criticism and a threatened lawsuit by New York's attorney general. The organization's president and chairman resigned, and the American Red Cross was faced with the difficult task of rebuilding its credibility.[2]

Planning for Crisis Situations

No one likes to think about calamities, but public relations people are expected to consider and plan for worst-case possibilities. If you work for a refinery, you need to assume that there will be a fire sometime, somewhere. If you work for a chemical company, there will be a "hazardous substance" case sometime, in some form, somewhere.

But you don't have to be involved in a "dangerous business" to encounter a crisis. The Red Cross crisis points out that crises aren't limited to explosions, fires, storms and earthquakes. For instance, a Dallas CEO was kidnapped and held for ransom; a truck crashed into a busy cafeteria; an angered employee went home, returned with a rifle and killed supervisors and fellow employees. And we're all familiar with tragic events involving shooting of school children. Anything that *can* happen, *will*. You need to be prepared for it.

© Mike Baldwin / Cornered

"You have a major fiasco at 10:30, followed by a shocking scandal at 2:15."

Source: Reprinted by permission of Mike Baldwin and CartoonStock, www.CartonStock.com

The fall of high-flying Enron is another example of "self-inflicted" crises. Mark Palmer, vice president for corporate communications at Enron, said, "We all thought there was no way to go but up. We were a $160 billion company, number seven on the Fortune 500 list and in the top three for innovation, quality of employees and quality of management. Then on October 16, 2001 the wheels came off." That was the day the company announced a $1 billion loss for the third quarter of 2001. A few days later, the SEC began an investigation. Rumors of document shredding circulated. The company was unable to secure the financing it needed, and Enron began the slide toward bankruptcy. "We didn't sleep well," Palmer said. "I lost 30 pounds in six weeks. We marched along that path with our CEO (Kenneth L. Lay) thinking it was just a giant PR problem. 'Enron will never go bankrupt,' he said, 'and anyone who thinks that probably shouldn't be working here.'" Yet on December 2, 2001, Enron *did* go bankrupt, filing for Chapter 11 bankruptcy.[3] In May 2006, former Enron top executives CEO Kenneth L. Lay and Jeffrey K. Skilling were convicted for fraud and conspiracy. *The New York Times* reported, "Mr. Skilling was convicted of 18 counts of fraud and conspiracy and one count of insider trading. He was acquitted on nine counts of insider trading. Mr. Lay was found guilty on six counts of fraud and conspiracy and four counts of bank fraud." Simply put, they "were found guilty of lying—to investors, employees and regulators—in an effort to disguise the crumbling fortunes of their energy empire."[4] Kenneth Lay died of a massive heart attack in Aspen, Colorado, on July 5, 2006 at the age of 64.

Immediately the conspiracy theorists went to work. In Internet sites and blogs, conspiracy theorists and jokesters have floated the idea that the Enron founder's powerful friends helped him fake his death to escape sentencing in one of the biggest corporate frauds in USA history, ignoring a statement from the Colorado coroner who performed an autopsy.[5]

The term *crisis communication* includes within its meanings *issues management*, because it is good public relations to intervene in a developing situation before it becomes a crisis. And issues management, in turn, is primarily a research function, the purpose of which is to identify and track trends and events likely to affect the institution and any of its publics. But beyond issues management, which involves all of the communication tools and planning previously discussed, there is the critical event—the serious unforeseen development. In this chapter, we will use the term *crisis* exclusively to refer to the critical event. Refer to Table 18.1 for a brief outline of what is usually included in planning for and dealing with a crisis.

Research suggests that there are only six types of crises—three in each of two categories. Review these in Table 18.2. The two categories are violent and nonviolent. Within each are crises that are caused by nature, by accidents or by deliberate acts.[6]

Corporate Information

Part of being prepared is a matter of routine. It involves maintaining current corporate fact sheets containing all necessary basic information in the files at all times. See Chapter 9 for more information on fact sheets.

The most important pre-crisis action, though, is getting your positive messages out daily and educating your publics so they are knowledgeable and you can draw on their trust and goodwill when the crisis occurs.

When the Columbia space shuttle disintegrated on February 1, 2003, killing all seven astronauts aboard, NASA immediately put its crisis plan into action. Carl Gustin and Jennifer Sheehy of the Clarke & Company Crisis Communication Center evaluated NASA's communications this way: "One lesson already learned from the Columbia disaster is the value

T A B L E 1 8 . 1	*Outline of Crisis Communication Plan*

Planning

1. Develop a series of scenarios that reflect the kinds of crises your organization may face. Pay particular attention to the worst cases. Evaluate realistically the probability of their happening. Review current policies and strategies that may be impacted.

2. Identify a crisis management team. Assign specific roles to team members. Designate one person to speak to external publics and another to keep internal publics fully informed. Rehearse the crisis management team regularly. Train and retrain the spokespersons, emphasizing the need for them to coordinate and share information so the organization is seen as speaking with one corporate voice.

3. Insofar as is possible, implement policies and strategies designed to minimize the impact of crises. If needed, lobby government and seek public support for changes in laws and/or regulations that may prevent crises or reduce their impact.

4. Review the entire plan at least annually. A quarterly review is better. Make sure that members of the crisis management team have copies of the current plan and can access them immediately.

Triggering Event

1. When a crisis occurs, activate the crisis management team immediately. Designated spokespersons should take charge of all communication functions.

2. Strive for a timely, consistent and candid flow of accurate information to both external and internal publics to allay fears and stifle rumors.

3. The organization should continue to function as normally as possible, leaving it to the crisis management team to contend with the crisis.

4. Make adjustments to policies and strategies as needed to arrest the crisis. Seek public support as needed.

Recovery

1. As needed, make changes in policies and strategies to speed recovery from the effects of the crisis.

2. If necessary, make changes to the structure of the organization. If these changes are needed and the organization has a history of an open management style, such changes are often slight.

3. Seek as soon as possible to re-establish the operation of the organization to the level it had before the crisis or even better.

Evaluation

1. Learn from the crisis experience. Evaluate its causes, the organization's responses to it and the outcomes.

2. Modify policies and strategies in light of this experience.

3. Update the crisis management/communication plan in light of this most recent experience.

TABLE 18.2	*Crisis Typology*	
Source of Crisis	**Violent: Cataclysmic—Immediate Loss of Life or Property**	**Nonviolent: Sudden Upheaval But Damages, If Any, Are Delayed**
Act of nature	Forest fires, floods, earthquakes on land and under the sea, such as the underwater one that created the tsunami December 26, 2004.	Droughts, epidemics, diseases, such as Avian Flu (Bird Flu) and Mad Cow, now seen as a threat to North American deer and elk.
Intentional	Acts of terrorism, including product tampering, when these result in loss of life or destruction of property. An example is the March 11, 2004 train bombing in Madrid, Spain that killed 200 and injured 1,500 or more.	Bomb and product tampering threats, hostile takeovers, insider trading, malicious rumors and other malfeasance. Examples include the Wendy's restaurant in San Jose, California where a woman claimed she "found" a finger tip in her chili.
Unintentional	Explosions, fires, leaks, other accidents, such as the fire, probably caused by a gas leak, in Asunción, Paraguay, that incinerated 464 people in a supermarket.	Process or product problems with delayed consequences, stock market crashes, business failures. For example, Vioxx and Celebrex being blamed for deaths.

Reprinted with permission from Doug Newsom, Judy VanSlyke Turk and Dean Kruckeberg, *This Is PR: The Realities of Public Relations, 10th ed.* (Wadsworth Publishing Company: Belmont, Calif., 2010) p. 318.

of preparation in dealing with a future crisis. NASA's senior management team was obviously ready to put its crisis communication plan into action, and has been getting high marks for its openness, availability, knowledge and sensitivity. . .. NASA management was prepared. It learned lessons from the [1986] Challenger and put in place, and no doubt 'drilled,' its crisis plans. Those plans clearly include communications with clear lines of authority for speaking to media and government officials. That was evident in the frequent updates that NASA started broadcasting within the hour of initial reports of a problem and the speed with which the first press conference was convened. . .. No one would accuse NASA, at least to this point, of remaining silent. NASA should be commended for its two-a-day press conferences and the apparent availability of a smart, talented press staff."[7]

There is never a good time to plan for a crisis, but sooner is better than later. And it is critical not only to a plan but also to make sure that everyone understands it.

In a crisis, the media's first response often is to contact the creators of the institution's public relations image. But before the situation arises, it's important to develop a good plan and be sure everyone likely to be involved knows what to do. Seminars involving role playing can help those who might be responsible in a time of crisis to understand the plan. It's important for you, as the writer of the plan, to know who will play specific roles as well.

Crisis planning by organizations goes beyond communication to specific employee actions.

Most institutions where crises are especially likely—such as chemical plants, hospitals, prisons and banks—have employees who are crisis-trained. The way a situation is handled as it is occurring can make the public relations job easier or more difficult. For example, writing about hostage-taking, which is a fairly common experience in hospitals, clinical psychologist James Turner says that staffs need to be trained in handling the hostage-takers in the first few minutes, before police officers and negotiators arrive.[8]

Designated Spokesperson   The most important strategy in crisis communication is to have only one person communicating with the news media and other external audiences. You may sometimes use both an expert and a management representative, with the crisis determining which is the principal spokesperson. The other person is a support voice and should coordinate messages so these *never* conflict or contradict themselves. When the messages fail to match, a severe credibility problem develops. The best precaution against this is to develop a crisis communication plan.

A Crisis Communication Plan   First, identify people likely to be the principal participants in the communication plan. Then decide what media to use in a crisis: memos, closed-circuit television, computer terminals, intranet telephones—whatever is likely to work in a given situation. You should create a system for checking message statements. Usually, an internal message for employees is developed first, and the external one is composed from that. You don't want employees and others close to the organization to hear about a crisis from outside sources unless this is absolutely unavoidable.

When time is critical and people are not where they are usually found, a telephone operation becomes particularly important. You or the person in charge of communications needs to be highly skilled in getting facts, taking questions and dispensing information accurately. You must act like a reporter first, finding out as much as you can about the situation. Anticipate questions from the news media. Have your own photographers and interviewers out gathering the story. If you don't take these steps, you won't have enough documentation later, and you will not know what the reporters are getting or how accurate their information is.

Your first job will be to get a statement on the severity of the disaster or crisis from someone in authority. You'll need to have the statement both in printed form and on audiotape. Then you'll need to develop a fact sheet telling what is known. Review this information with the organization's attorney to assess the legal ramifications of the information you will be releasing. All information released over the telephone should be drawn only from these prepared and checked sheets. Never speculate.

Crisis Teams   The organization (corporate or nonprofit) involved will create crisis communication teams from staff members—as well as public relations and crisis communications consultants—to create the necessary level of expertise. These teams should be able to deal with the crisis so the organization can go on about its regular activities as normally as possible. Nothing contributes more to the atmosphere of uncertainty than involving all the institution's decision makers in the crisis and thus causing day-to-day business to come to a halt. When this happens, observers can conclude that there is not much depth to management and that the company needs everyone it can get to handle a problem.

"Dark" websites   More and more organizations are setting up "dark" websites for use in the event of a crisis. The URLs of these sites aren't made public unless a crisis situation arises. At that time, information about the situation is posted as it becomes available and the URL is publicized, making possible one central source of information.

Handling the Crisis

When a crisis first occurs, its announcement involves some sort of consultation within the organization. Ordinarily this is a face-to-face meeting, but it could be an electronic one—for instance, a telephone conference call or a video teleconference. Of primary importance at this meeting is that a record be kept—a fairly detailed one—of the points discussed and the responsibilities assigned. In fact, it may be your specific responsibility to write and circulate a memo detailing this.

Almost immediately, and sometimes before such a meeting takes place, you will need to make a response release addressing the situation. The public affairs staff of a Houston-based pipeline company pledges to have a statement in the hands of the local spokesperson within 30 minutes after they are notified of a pipeline rupture or other triggering event, regardless of where it occurs. That involves fast, brief and absolutely accurate interviewing, but they deliver on their promise. You the writer must characterize the crisis in language that will become a symbol of the event. In doing so, you will need to check attributed quotes with the organization's attorney if the release contains any mention of responsibility or damages.

For the broadcast media, you should have an actuality of the statement from the spokesperson. And you will need your own photographer's pictures from the crisis scene—black-and-white and color stills and videos. Some companies maintain ENG (electronic news gathering) equipment so that they can receive pictures of the disaster immediately at corporate headquarters. Here, too, the art chosen should represent the way you want the event symbolized.

You may need to call a news conference so that news media representatives can pose questions. If you do, you should be prepared with a list of the points you want to make, and you should anticipate the reporters' needs and questions.

As news develops, you will be issuing bulletins to keep internal and external publics informed. All of these bulletins should be put on your website or the "dark website" mentioned above, if one is available. Additionally, you will be preparing letters and email messages to various related publics to keep them aware of your control of the situation. For example, a university experiencing a number of fires sent letters to parents, and a company that found a problem with a certain lot of its product sent letters to all affected consumers it could identify through warranty cards. In some cases, you may need to plan special advertising. One utility that had gotten a bad safety review of its nuclear plant and several days of bad publicity thereafter felt it necessary to buy space for its own message.

Often crises involve materials or conditions that the average person (including reporters) may not know much about. With nuclear plant accidents and chemical-related stories, scientists often are called on to help reporters explain these situations. But because of scientists' concerns about being misquoted, Sigma Xi, the Scientists' Institute for Public Information, provides a free service to journalists—a database clearinghouse with a computer file of more than 30,000 scientists, engineers, physicians and policy-makers who have agreed to answer queries from reporters.[9]

Top management's role is critical in crisis communication. Their leadership and "voice" can result in either positive or negative impressions of the organization (see Figure 18.1).

What the Boss Should Really Do in a Crisis

By James E. Lukaszewski, ABC, APR, Fellow PRSA, CCEP

One of the more damaging weaknesses in crisis response is undefined roles and assignments for top management. This critical gap in planning results in the mismanagement of crisis response efforts and occurs too frequently in the plans, responses and scenarios I review with clients. In the course of directing a client's crisis response, analyzing past reactions or developing powerful response strategies, it's clear that prompt, effective crisis response depends on having five essential responsibilities carefully spelled out for top executives:

1. Assert the moral authority expected of ethical leadership.

No matter how devastating a crisis is, in most cultures forgiveness is possible provided the organization, through its early behaviors and leadership, takes appropriate and expected steps to learn from and deal with the issues. The behaviors are:

- **Candor and disclosure**—acknowledgement that something adverse has happened or is happening.
- **Explanation and revelation**—early analysis of the nature of the problem.
- **Commitment to communicate**—even if there are lots of critics.
- **Answer the questions**.
- **Empathy**—intentional acts of helpfulness and compassion.
- **Oversight**—letting outsiders, even victims, know how you're reacting.
- **Commitment to zero**—finding ways to prevent similar events from occurring.
- **Apology**—acceptance of responsibility.

- **Restitution or penance**—paying the price; generally doing more than would be expected.

2. Take responsibility for the care of victims.

The most crucial element in crisis management, aside from ending the victimizing event, is managing the victim dimension. There are only three kinds of victims: people, animals and living systems. Top management is responsible to take appropriate steps to care for their needs. This both preserves reputation and reduces litigation. The worst responses to crises are when victims' needs go unfulfilled or the organization refuses to ease the pain of those afflicted. Of all of the CEO's responsibilities, actively caring for those affected is the most important. Maintain a positive, constructive pressure to get victim issues resolved promptly.

3. Set the appropriate tone for the organizational response.

Tone is determined by management behavior and helps the organization meet the expectations triggered by a crisis. If senior management is defensive, the entire organization will be too. Setting a constructive tone encourages positive attitudes and prompt responses that will protect the organization's relationships during the recovery period, show respect for victims and reduce reputation damage.

4. Set the organization's voice.

Put a face and a voice on the organization as it moves through the crisis for external audiences. Tell how we describe the organization, what we are doing, how the response is going, what responsibilities we are taking and what outside scrutiny we are inviting. Use positive language, be helpful, and suggest early resolution. Avoid demeaning or discrediting anyone. A major leadership communication goal is to avoid producing critics and opponents.

5. Lead at every level.

Leaders need to act like leaders during urgent situations. Literally walk around and talk to people. Focus everyone on the ultimate response process goals. Ninety percent of senior-executive activities should have executives out being leaders and motivators of empathy, not huddling in their offices. Of all of these, preventing similar occurrences will most help victims come to closure and prove that litigation and other forms of public humiliation are not necessary. All crises are management problems first. Planning and rehearsing executive actions can avoid career-deflating moments, making it important to include specific executive instructions in all plans and response scenarios.

Copyright © 2008, James E. Lukaszewski. All rights reserved. Reproduction without written permission is strictly prohibited.

James E. Lukaszewski (loo-ka-SHEV-skee), ABC, APR, Fellow PRSA, CCEP, advises, coaches, and counsels the men and women who run very large corporations and organizations through extraordinary problems and critical high-profile circumstances. See *www.e911.com.*

FIGURE 18.1

What the Boss Really Should Do in a Crisis   *PDF James E. Lukaszewski ABC, APR, Fellow PRSA Communication, CEO of The Lukaszewski Group Inc.*

Source: Copyright © 2009 by The Lukaszewski Group Inc. Used with permission.

10 Steps to Prepare for a Crisis in Social Media Environments
By Kami Watson Huyse, APR

The media has moved well beyond 24/7 news coverage by professional journalists to a communication environment that operates at light speed and is powered by interconnected networks of friends and acquaintances.

The spread of information through word-of-mouth channels of communication and social media networks can be explosive. It is fertile ground for the spread of bad news, rumor and innuendo. Opinions by influential members of online communities can quickly become a firestorm of criticism to which a company and organization must immediately respond in real time.

This presents a challenge to communication programs that follow a traditional structure of deliberation and response. In this environment the cycle must be greatly shortened. The following are ten steps that any organization can take to be better prepared to handle crises that could bubble up in social media channels.

1. **Monitor the chatter**: People are talking about companies and organizations every day. If not, they are surely talking about issues of importance to these entities. In order to keep track of these "conversations," companies, organizations and individuals should set up keyword searches for the company name, any of its variations and competitors, as well as terms or issues of importance.

   Actively watch and respond to both fans and critics. Use free tools like Google Blog Search, Technorati and Twitter Search to get started. Real Simple Syndication enables the user to subscribe to searches and track news more easily though an RSS reader such as Google Reader. There are also many paid services available for companies with more mentions or that have specific needs.

   Companies and organizations can also join and search Facebook for groups or fan pages that might mention them and join them to keep up with what people are saying about them. The same should be done with other popular social networks, such as YouTube. To get a current list of the most popular social networks go to the Wikipedia page for "Social Media" and look under "Social Media Software Applications."

   By actively monitoring the Internet, companies are in a position to catch a crisis boiling up in its nascent stages and address it head on. Companies shouldn't forget forums and user groups that pertain to the organization. There are still many people who participate in these "older" technologies and they should not be discounted in pursuit of newer and more popular social networks. Monitor everything that has a concentration of people that care about your product, service or cause.

2. **Maintain a social "footprint"**: More and more brands and organizations are defined by search engines like Google. When brands use several formats, such as photo sharing, videos, podcasts, popular social

networks, and blogs, they make it easier for people to find them. This content-based strategy is one way to improve the optimization of a Web site for search engines. Both Facebook and LinkedIn, two currently popular networks, provide a mechanism for companies and organizations to create a page and build a community of fans.

Companies, and key individuals within the organization, should maintain several profiles on popular social networks. Choose the two or three that are most relevant to the business or organization. Tie them together by linking to them from a central location, such as a blog. Linking back to the social profiles will strengthen the connection between the branded site and these more generic social networks. Be sure to include links back to the blog or Web site in the social profiles as well.

It might seem like a lot to maintain, but consider that many of these social networks have spent countless dollars to ensure that their pages rank very high in search results, which is critical in a crisis when many high-ranked sites and blogs might write about an organization and push other positive content about the crisis lower in search engine results pages. Optimized social networks are more likely to hold, or more quickly regain, their position in an onslaught of mentions.

3. **Deputize a Quick Response Team:** Similar to the process followed during a traditional crisis, there should be a team tasked with response through social media channels. This team should ideally include management, legal representation and one or more communicators with more than a passing knowledge of social media channels. Preferably the main spokespeople should have accounts with social media networks already in place (see step number 2). It should also include key team members from the main business areas or departments of a company or organization.

Most crises in social networks can reach full blown status within just a few hours. This team should be able to respond to both full blown and mini-crisis situations within that timeframe. In general, the slower the response, the harder it is to recover from the subsequent explosion of criticism and discussion in social media channels. Getting involved early ensures that the point-of-view of the company will at least have a voice at the table of public opinion.

Comment streams on popular blogs and forums can reach into the hundreds within an hour or two. An early response can sometimes turn the tide from negative to positive, or at least neutral. Also, if misinformation is passed, which is often the case during a social media crisis, the correct information can be quickly inserted into the conversation. Finally, the power of an open and forthcoming company representative showing up in the community or comment thread is often enough to tone down the negative slant to the conversation. It's much harder to bash the organization unfairly when its employees are listening and responding.

4. **Incrementally Release Information:** In a crisis that starts in social media channels, there is a need to release a steady and rich diet of information. The old way of gathering information, deliberating on a response and releasing a "statement" needs to be reconsidered. In this new environment, an absence of information leads to speculation and often misinformation becoming the narrative for the crisis.

To avoid this, information should be released in "byte-sized" pieces on a regular cycle,

FIGURE 18.2 *(continued)*

perhaps once an hour or so. A process to quickly digest and release information should be in place—usually best run through the quick response team. When information is still unknown, that too should be disclosed, along with any steps the company will take to rectify the situation.

Admitting liability is a big concern; however, many companies have navigated this concern by deciding in advance of a crisis with legal counsel what can and cannot be said in a crisis situation. A good relationship with the legal department or counsel is critical to delivering information quickly and accurately.

The company should strive to be the first and best source of information about the crisis situation. In becoming the leading source of information, companies can also diffuse speculation and rumor that is typical when companies choose not to engage in social media environments. The downside for such individuals and companies is severe.

Consider that Kryptonite locks was forced into an expensive recall when a video of a lock being picked by a ballpoint pen was widely circulated on the Internet. The company didn't respond through online channels for several days as it determine its course of action. The resulting response and subsequent damage to its reputation took the company years to overcome, even though it is now quite active in the online community.

5. **Formulate a Crisis Escalation Process:** When a crisis, or even just a negative reaction, boils up in social media channels, a company should have a well defined plan to deal with it.

A quick message or rant on a microblogging network should be handled differently than a blog post by a major influencer. And a quick judgment should be made to determine if the person complaining is an angry customer, a disillusioned fan, a determined detractor or just an interested bystander.

There should be a plan to handle each of these, including a basic outline of how, or if, the company will respond. There should also be a rule-of-thumb list of guidelines that all people representing the company agree to follow. Among these should be transparency about communication, adherence to privacy concerns of those involved, full disclosure of affiliation, truthfulness about the situation and willing to give credit to others. There will also be other guidelines specific to the organization or industry of the company.

The Air Force has done a good job of thinking through these issues in its Response Assessment Chart (See Figure 18.3.)

6. **Employ Scalable Technology:** Access to cutting-edge technology is critical for the communicator. The cost of online delivery tools such as blogs, wikis, podcasts, online video and others are very low or zero cost to the communicator. The barriers to entry for all of these tools has been dramatically lowered as technology companies have continued to develop new online tools that are easy to use and are affordable or free.

During a crisis, traditional communication channels will be overwhelmed. The phone and Web site of a company traditionally experience heavy volume in a crisis situation. It is important for companies to invest in technology ahead of time, such as cellular phones with text messaging capabilities and laptop computers with wireless modems.

Off-site hosting of the company Web site, or at least the part of it dedicated for communications, is strongly recommended by most experts to ensure continuity of operations during a crisis. In the first hours of a crisis, most people look to the company Web site as a source of information. If the crisis is a big

FIGURE 18.2 (*continued*)

one, most companies are not up to the influx of traffic and the site can fail, leaving people to look for information elsewhere. A fairly new hosting concept, called cloud computing, allows a company to quickly scale up to a larger bandwidth. This provides adequate coverage, yet allows companies to only pay for the bandwidth they use on a regular basis.

7. **Know Your Audience:** During a crisis, there are several audiences you should keep in mind. The first and most important audience are those **affected** by the crisis, These include customers, employees, shareholders and the physical community in which the crisis occurs. It is a good idea to have a channel of communication set up with each of these stakeholders in advance that can then be utilized during the crisis. The organization should always talk with these stakeholders directly and not through the media. This requires advance planning and relationship building. The company should also be aware of which of these stakeholders are also influential online and use these stronger ties to get information out to the online audience as well.

   The second group is those **influentials** that matter most to your future but aren't directly affected. Politicians, regulators, watchdog groups and popular bloggers, forum leaders and well-known social leaders on networks fall in this group. It is important to have a relationship with as many of these people as possible before the crisis. However, some might not become known to you until the crisis. If these influencers are given access and treated as valuable partners in recovery, the crisis can serve as a bridge to start new relationships that will serve the company well in the future,

   The next two groups are the most problematic and include the vocal bystanders and the determined detractors. In social networks, **vocal bystanders** are those that pass on negative information but don't have a vested interest in a company. These vocal bystanders can be quite impassioned about their opinions, and some of them could be potential customers. Their role in an online crisis situation is to participate in the word-of-mouth firestorm against a company. They can also do the opposite and help calm the crisis. Vocal bystanders can be easily swayed by the facts of the situation. The key is that they are not representative of the stakeholders of the company and should not serve as a proxy for how customers would respond.

   Determined detractors are those that have a disagreement with the company or organization and who will not easily change their mind. Determined detractors can fall into any of the previous categories. They are often embittered ex-employees, competitors, especially angry customers, activists and possibly influentials that have, for one reason or another, formed a deep-seated difference of opinion with the organization or company. All attempts should be made to solve the impasse, but where it is not possible, the company should work with the other groups to try to minimize the impact of the determined detractor. If the relationships with the first three groups are managed correctly, many may come to the aid of the company against determined detractors in social networks, on blogs and in other social media formats.

8. **Speak the Same Language:** One of the biggest mistakes that companies make when responding to a crisis online is that they don't respond in like manner. In other words, they don't speak the same "language" as those who are voicing concern. For instance, they might issue a press release statement in response to a video attack. Or they might answer questions

FIGURE 18.2 (*continued*)

that are bubbling up in a micro-blogging platform like Twitter by making a blog post of their own and not responding directly to the conversation in Twitter.

For better or worse, today's social media environment is made up of multiple channels and communities. Companies must be prepared to respond in a conversational tone on blogs, podcasts, forums, video and in popular social networks. This means that the company should have some experience in these mediums before the crisis. Learning in the midst of the crisis can be fatal to a company's reputation and doing nothing is no longer acceptable.

9. **Prepare Traditional Response:** While the online audience is critical to crisis preparation, it is still important to prepare a traditional media response. Often things that bubble up in social networks are picked up by journalists. In a 2008 Broudeur study nearly 70 percent of reporters surveyed said they check blogs on a regular basis. Journalist can easily pick up a simmering crisis and move it to the mainstream.

During the election campaign of President Barack Obama, many journalists joined the micro-blogging social network to get updates from the campaign. These quickly updated networks will become even more important as their popularity rises. According to Comscore in April 2009, MySpace.com had 71 million visitors, Facebook.com had 67.5 million visitors, an increase of 10 percent from the previous month and Twitter.com had 17 million visitors, a jump of 83 percent. While these networks are sure to change over time, the immense popularity of online communities is sure to grow.

10. **It's About Relationships:** Social media and networking is relational, meaning people use these technologies to connect with those with whom they know or who have similar interests.

As such, social media are not just another marketing channel to be exploited to get more reach for a company's messages. Instead they should be seen as places to know and be known by the customer.

One of the biggest errors made by companies in social media channels is their use of it as a mechanism to disseminate information. During a crisis this becomes compounded by the lack of time. During a crisis, and certainly during non crisis periods, a company should make an effort to talk with people that show interest in the company, organization or brand. By making a plan to dedicate the necessary resources to do this properly, companies can, and do, set themselves apart.

One of the best examples is DELL computers. After popular blogger Jeff Jarvis had a bad experience with his DELL computer, he wrote a scathing post called "Dell Hell" that sent the online community on a rampage against the company. Soon after, CEO Michael Dell made a decision to start directly talking with bloggers and other social media influencers. The company launched a blog and several other social media properties to start a conversation with its customers. They also employed an online support team that looked for customers that complained about their DELL computers and helped them fix their problems. They also launched IdeaStorm where interested people can submit ideas, vote on ideas and see how their ideas are implemented. The site reports adopting literally hundreds of ideas, voted on by thousands of people, every month.

FIGURE 18.2 (*continued*)

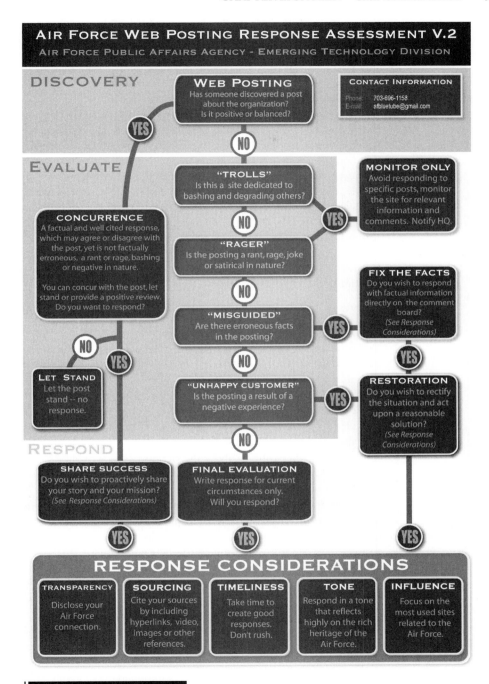

AIR FORCE WEB POSTING RESPONSE ASSESSMENT V.2
AIR FORCE PUBLIC AFFAIRS AGENCY - EMERGING TECHNOLOGY DIVISION

DISCOVERY

WEB POSTING
Has someone discovered a post about the organization?
Is it positive or balanced?

CONTACT INFORMATION
Phone: 703-696-1158
E-mail: afbluetube@gmail.com

EVALUATE

"TROLLS"
Is this a site dedicated to bashing and degrading others?

MONITOR ONLY
Avoid responding to specific posts, monitor the site for relevant information and comments. Notify HQ.

CONCURRENCE
A factual and well cited response, which may agree or disagree with the post, yet is not factually erroneous, a rant or rage, bashing or negative in nature.

You can concur with the post, let stand or provide a positive review.
Do you want to respond?

"RAGER"
Is the posting a rant, rage, joke or satirical in nature?

FIX THE FACTS
Do you wish to respond with factual information directly on the comment board?
(See Response Considerations)

"MISGUIDED"
Are there erroneous facts in the posting?

LET STAND
Let the post stand -- no response.

"UNHAPPY CUSTOMER"
Is the posting a result of a negative experience?

RESTORATION
Do you wish to rectify the situation and act upon a reasonable solution?
(See Response Considerations)

RESPOND

SHARE SUCCESS
Do you wish to proactively share your story and your mission?
(See Response Considerations)

FINAL EVALUATION
Write response for current circumstances only.
Will you respond?

RESPONSE CONSIDERATIONS

TRANSPARENCY	**SOURCING**	**TIMELINESS**	**TONE**	**INFLUENCE**
Disclose your Air Force connection.	Cite your sources by including hyperlinks, video, images or other references.	Take time to create good responses. Don't rush.	Respond in a tone that reflects highly on the rich heritage of the Air Force.	Focus on the most used sites related to the Air Force.

FIGURE 18.3

Air Force Web Posting Response Assessment V.2   *This is a graphic illustration of the process the USA Air Force uses to determine whether to respond to social media posts. If a response is needed, the chart helps determine what type of response to make.*

Getpress.com, a firm that specializes in crisis communications, says the basic tools needed in a crisis situation include the following:

- *"Statement.* This is usually a clear and concise press release that highlights a company or organization's position in a particular situation. Within this statement, a series of messages clearly articulating that position are highlighted."
- *"Media Q&A.* This includes a series of questions most likely to be asked by members of the media, customers and employees regarding the issue/crisis at hand. This document includes direct answers reflecting the company's position and key messages addressing the situation."
- *"Employee Communication.* Recognizing that your employees can be your best spokespeople, clearly articulating the company's position or statement regarding the crisis at hand is instrumental to any well-managed crisis communication plan."
- *"Regulatory Communication.* Depending upon the size and scope of the crisis at hand, communication with various governmental regulators such as the EPA, SEC and FCC may be required."
- *"Customer Service Phone Scripts.* A complete Q&A that addresses and answers anticipated questions."

Getpress.com provides the following basic crisis communications guidelines on its website:

1. Communicate. If you try to hide behind a "no comment" response, you immediately lose control. Even if you can only say that you don't know, say so and why. Reporters look favorably on people who are trying to be helpful.
2. Never lie or speculate. Provide only factual, confirmed information.
3. Assist the people most affected by the crisis. In the case of accidents, remember to deal with victims' families before any other group and, if they desire, intercede on their behalf with the news media.
4. Communicate your concern about the victims.
5. Be available at all times to respond to your various publics. Be aware of media deadlines and try not to rely solely on news conferences.
6. Don't appear defensive. Be prepared for aggressive questioning and realize you might have to provide several answers to the same question.
7. Don't ramble. Especially when broadcast outlets are on the scene, provide brief, precise answers. The short answers also help alleviate nervousness.
8. Take reporters slowly through difficult issues.
9. Monitor media accounts and quickly correct errors by contacting the source of the report.
10. Do not attempt to do legal battle in the media. Express assurances that matters of litigation or potential litigation will be investigated thoroughly.
11. If you have a key point you want to make, prepare it beforehand. Make it short and to the point. Try to repeat it at least once in the news conference or interview.
12. Stay with the crisis throughout its duration.
13. Instigate follow-ups with the news media to update them about what preventive actions have been taken after the crisis ended.[10]

Social media have become increasingly important in crisis communication and must be carefully integrated into your crisis communication plan. (see Figure 18.2.)

Conclusions

- No one likes to think about calamities, but public relations people are expected to consider and plan for worst-case possibilities.
- You need to plan for crises, and when you do, always anticipate the "worst case."
- You don't have to be involved in a "dangerous business" to encounter a crisis.
- Routine corporate communication becomes critical in a crisis and must always be up to date.
- A corporate crisis plan must be developed and placed in the hands of the people who will need it.
- Crisis plans can often be "taught" by role playing.
- There should be no more than one or two designated spokespersons in a crisis.
- These spokespersons should be trained in handling media and individuals who are under stress.
- It is good public relations to intervene in a developing situation before it becomes a crisis.
- Often crises involve materials or conditions that the average person (including reporters) may not know much about.
- Crisis communicators must consciously supply the symbol (visual and verbal) for the crisis, incorporating the symbol in language for a response statement.
- Spokespersons handling internal and external communication must coordinate their messages to avoid discrepancies that would reduce their credibility.
- Crisis teams should take over the crisis situation and permit all others in the organization to go on about their daily work. This will inspire continued confidence in the organization's ability to cope with the problem.
- When a crisis first occurs, its announcement involves some sort of consultation within the organization.
- More and more organizations are setting up "dark" websites for use in the event of a crisis.
- Almost all the communication tools discussed in this book can be used in a crisis.

- Social media have become increasingly important in crisis communication.

Exercise

This is from a real situation in which one of the authors was involved:

You are Director of Public Relations for a petrochemical company headquartered in Dallas, Texas. It's just after midnight, and you get a phone call at home notifying you that your company's largest plant, at the edge of a small West Texas town nearly 500 miles away, has had a major explosion and now is burning. It is believed that three employees have been killed and several injured, but facts are limited. The plant's manager is on vacation and cannot be reached. Your experience and instincts tell you that this is going to be a national news story within hours. *You have a total of 30 minutes* to do the following:

1. Write a brief statement that the assistant plant manager can give to news media who call during the next few hours.

2. List, in sequence, the actions you will take during the next 24 hours.

3. You learn from a second phone call that the plant offices were destroyed, along with all of the public relations files and media lists. List the materials that you will need to reconstruct.

Now assume now that you are able to get a company airplane to take you and your company's president to the town near the plant where the explosion occurred. You are on the plane with the president.

1. Write a statement for the president to read to news media when the plane lands. Remember that the president's first concerns need to be (1) for those directly involved, including employees, firefighters and police, as well as their families and (2) for the safety of employees and neighbors.

2. List the information that you will try to gather. (A good way to do this is to draft the news release that you would like to distribute, leaving blank spaces for the information that you will need.)

Use InfoTrac® College Edition to access information on topics in this chapter from hundreds of periodicals and scholarly journals.

Readability Formulas

Research in readability goes back at least to the 1920s. Early work identified various factors—like sentence length, word length, prepositional phrases—that affected the readability of prose.

In *What Makes a Book Readable*, published in 1935, William Gray and Bernice Leary discussed 64 different aspects of prose that seemed to affect reading difficulty. It would have been nearly impossible to devise a usable formula covering that many variables, so when readability formulas were developed, most emphasized two of the most important factors: sentence length and word length.

Dozens of formulas have been designed to measure readability. In 1959, George Klare identified 31 formulas and 10 variations, and he didn't cover all the different types of formulas. Many more formulas have been designed since then, although only a handful of these are in general use. The three best-known formulas are those devised by Rudolf Flesch, by Robert Gunning and by Edgar Dale and Jeanne Chall.

Flesch's Reading Ease and Human Interest Formulas

The first formula to gain much notice was the one proposed by Flesch in the late 1940s. His formula is based on average sentence length and average number of syllables per word.

To use the Flesch formula, select 100 word samples at random from your text. Divide the number of words by the number of sentences to obtain an average sentence length (*asl*), expressed in words per sentence. Next count the number of syllables in the sample and divide this by the number of words to obtain an average word length (*awl*), expressed in syllables per word. Then insert these values into the Flesch "Reading Ease" formula:

Reading Ease = $206.835 - (84.6 \times awl) - (1.015 \times asl)$

The resulting score should fall between 0 and 100. The higher the score, the easier the material is to read. A score in the 70–80 range is "fairly easy"; a sixth grader could understand it. Scores below 50 are considered difficult reading. Scores below 30 are generally found only in scientific and technical journals.

When using the Flesch formula, count contractions and hyphenated words as one word. When counting sentences, count clauses separated by colons or semicolons as separate sentences.

Recognizing that there is more to easy reading than short words and sentences, Flesch devised a "Human Interest" formula that measures the degree of reader interest. It is not used as often as the Reading Ease formula. Human Interest formula is based on the number of personal words (pw) per 100 words and the number of personal sentences (ps) per 100 sentences. Personal words include personal pronouns and any other words that are either masculine or feminine. Personal sentences are direct quotations, exclamations, questions—sentences that address the reader directly. The formula is as follows:

$$\text{Human Interest} = (pw/100 \text{ words} \times 3.635) + (ps/100 \text{ sentences} \times 0.314)$$

A score below 10 is dull; 20–40 is interesting; above 40 is very interesting.

Gunning's Fog Index

Gunning's formula is much simpler to apply than Flesch's. The "Fog Index," as Gunning calls it, measures reading difficulty rather than reading ease.

Gunning also counts words and divides by the number of sentences to find an average sentence length. But rather than counting syllables, Gunning's method is to count the number of long words—those of three syllables or more. He excludes from this count all proper nouns, verbs in which the third syllable is an -ed or -es and compound words made from two short words, like *worktable*.

To apply the formula, take the average sentence length and add to it the number of long words per 100 words. Multiply the total by 0.4.

The resulting score is roughly equivalent to the grade level of difficulty. A score of 12, for example, indicates that an average high-school senior should be able to read the material. In practice, no general-audience magazine would rate above 12 on the Gunning index. *Time* magazine rates 11, *Reader's Digest* scores about 5 and comic books score 6.

Source: http://www.helpforschools.com/ELLKBase/practitionerstips/Fog_Index_Readability.shtml

Dale-Chall Formula

The Dale-Chall formula is more difficult to apply, because it requires the use of a list of 3,000 words. Words on the list are known by 80 percent of fourth graders. [The list is included as an appendix to Gunning's book, *The Technique of Clear Writing*, rev. ed. (New York: McGraw-Hill, 1968).]

To use the Dale-Chall formula, select 100 word samples and determine the average sentence length (as with the Gunning and Flesch tests). Then count the number of words not on the Dale-Chall list. Here is the formula:

(Average sentence length × 0.0496) +
(Words not on Dale-Chall list × 0.1579) + 3.6365

Dale-Chall scores are usually lower than Gunning scores for a given piece of writing. A Gunning index of 16, for example, indicates readability at the college-graduate level; the same piece would score about 10 on the Dale-Chall test.

Keep in mind that readability scores do not reflect a "recommended" level of reading difficulty. They only indicate the readability level that an average reader (average seventh grader, average high-school senior or whoever) is likely to understand. To make the reading easy, the writing level should be a couple of steps below the educational level of the intended audience. Rarely do popular magazines—even those read by college graduates—score higher than the readability level of a high-school senior.

ELF

The Easy Listening Formula (ELF), developed by Irving Fang, measures readability sentence by sentence, identifying a sentence as a "package of information." Look at each word in the sentence. Subtract 1 from the number of syllables in each word. A one-syllable word counts 0, a two-syllable word counts 1, and so on. If your count passes 12, examine the sentence. It may be all right, or it may be hard to understand. What has pushed up the count? Unnecessary adjectives and adverbs? Clauses that might be better as separate sentences? Abstract words? The more abstract a word, the more difficult it is to understand.

Example:

Communication receivers have preset opinions about certain linguistic features such as pronunciations, sentence structures and words that are outside of their usual vocabulary—that is, "different" words.

Rewrite:

The way words are said and used, and how familiar they are, triggers opinions.

Other Readability Tests

A completely different type of readability test is Wilson Taylor's "Cloze" procedure. This test, first used in the early 1950s, was developed from concepts of Gestalt psychology. It tests readability by seeing how easily a reader can "fill in the blanks" when words are left out of a passage.

For example, readers might be given a passage with every fifth word deleted. From the context, the reader should be able to fill in some of the missing words. The more words the reader can fill in, the more readable the selection is.

This unique readability test has one major drawback: It can't be applied simply by making calculations. The prose must be tested on real readers, and those readers must accurately represent the intended audience. All readability formulas are approximations, because no single formula can cover all the variables that affect readability. With the increased use of computers, though, more complicated formulas may soon come into use. Computers can be programmed to calculate readability automatically when a sample of a story is typed in at a computer keyboard.

An early formula appropriate for computerized use is the Danielson-Bryan formula. It is based on the total number of characters (letters) per word and per sentence. Here is the formula:

$$(1.0364 \times \text{characters per word}) + (0.0194 \times \text{characters per sentence}) - 0.6059$$

Wayne Danielson devised an even more elaborate formula to measure the probable time period of prose. It has long been known that English sentences have, on average, become shorter over the centuries. Taking a random sample of novels published between 1740 and 1977, Danielson found several other variables that have changed with time, such as paragraph length (shorter now than in the past), presence of long words (less frequent now than in the past) and presence of "internal apostrophes" for possessives and contractions (more frequent now than in the past). Using data from his sample of novels, Danielson produced a formula that would predict the publication date for a fiction selection. These predictions work with a fair degree of accuracy on fiction, but the formula in no way predicts the publication year for nonfiction, because only novels were included in the original sample. However, any prose can be given a style year rating by applying the formula. And although the formula is not a readability measure by design, style year scores show a very high correlation to readability scores obtained by standard formulas. (See Table A.1.)

TABLE A.1	Comparison of Readability Scores with Style Year	
Gunning Score (Fog Index)	**Grade Level**	**Style Year**
4	Fourth	1948
5	Fifth	1939
6	Sixth	1929
7–8	Seventh–eighth	1916
9–10	Ninth–tenth	1897
11–12	Eleventh–twelfth	1879
13–15	College	1856
16 and up	College graduate	1838

A computer program has been written to apply this formula, and tests show that a selection with a style year of 1900 or later rates "very readable" on standard readability tests. Style year scores of 1850 or before are not very readable.

The formula, which must be applied to an integral number of paragraphs, is as follows:

$$\text{Style year} = 1949 + (36.41 \times \text{internal apostrophes per sentence})$$
$$- (2.57 \times \text{words per sentence}) - (2.92 \times \text{sentences per paragraph})$$
$$- (16.71 \times \text{long words per sentence})$$

In Danielson's system, long words are defined as words with 10 or more letters.

Software Programs

Most grammar software programs provide more than one readability measure. In addition to word, sentence and paragraph statistics, Grammatik IV offers the Flesch Readability Formula, Gunning's Fog Index measuring years of education and the Flesch-Kincaid Reading Grade Level.

In addition to a qualitative assessment of the writing, *StyleWriter,* a plain-English editorial program, provides word and sentence statistics with an index that gives the percentage of passive verbs plus a count of words in such categories as jargon, legal, abstract, complex and such.

Copyfitting

You need to fit copy accurately for two reasons: (1) to determine how much space a given amount of copy will occupy when set in type and (2) to determine how much copy to write to fill a predetermined space. Occasionally both circumstances are important. If an editor has prepared copy and a layout showing space where the copy is to go, some adjustment will usually be necessary. The copy will have to be cut (or lengthened) to fit the space, the layout will have to be redesigned to allow more (or less) space for copy or both.

In either case, the principles of copyfitting are the same.

Sizing Copy

To fit copy, an editor must know the type specifications. Relevant data include:

1. The typeface, type size and amount of leading
2. A "characters per pica" count for the typeface
3. The column width of the copy after being set in type
4. The total number of characters in the original copy

Computers allow the total number of characters (letters and spaces) in the original copy to be precisely counted.

Computer programs will give you the character count, number of words and number of sentences. If lines are uneven, you may have to determine the average line length by hand. One way to do this is to draw a straight line down the right margin so that half the lines go beyond your line and half don't reach it. Then measure the number of spaces from the left-hand margin to the line you've drawn.

Partial lines should be counted as full lines, because space will appear at the end of paragraphs.

Once you've determined the total number of characters, you must determine the specifications of the type to be used. The *typeface* is simply the name of the style of type you are using—Times New Roman, for example. The *type size* is measured in *points;* it takes about 72 points to make 1 inch. The type size in most general publications ranges from 8 points to 12 points.

Leading refers to the amount of space between lines of type. Sometimes type is set solid—that is, without leading. Often, to improve legibility, the type is leaded 1 or 2 points. This simply means that 1 or 2 points of space are added between each line of type. On the computer, you can use full, expanded or condensed.

Copy space on a layout is usually measured in *picas;* there are 6 picas to the inch. One pica of copy depth is equal to 12 points. Thus one line of 12-point type occupies 1 pica of copy space.

If the type is set solid—no leading—100 lines of 12-point type take up 100 picas, about 16.7 inches. The general formula for determining copy depth is:

$$\frac{\text{lines of type } \times \text{ (point size } + \text{ leading)}}{12} = \text{copy depth in picas}$$

Thus if you use 10-point type with 1-point leading, 100 lines of type will occupy:

$$\frac{100 \times (10 + 1)}{12} = 91.7 = 92 \text{ picas}$$

Notice that, if 10-point type is used and is leaded 2 points, the number of lines of type is equal to the copy depth in picas.

The number of lines of type can be determined only after the width of each line is known. In other words, how many characters will each line contain?

Type books commonly give a "characters per pica" count for different typefaces and type sizes. Ten-point Helvetica, for example, has a count of 2.4 characters per pica. Thus if your copy space is 10 picas wide, the number of characters per line will be 24.

Sample Copyfitting Problems

Suppose you want to set the original copy—calculated at 3,250 characters—in 10-point Helvetica. The width of a column of type will be 14 picas. How many lines of copy will you have?

Step One: Characters per pica times line width in picas gives characters per line:

2.4 × 14 = 33.6

Step Two: Total characters divided by characters per line gives number of lines:

$$\frac{3,250}{3.36} = 96.7 = 97 \text{ lines}$$

Given 97 lines of 10-point type and 1-point leading, what will the depth of the copy be when set in type?

Step One: Point size plus leading times number of lines gives depth in points:

$$(10 + 1) \times 97 = 1,067$$

Step Two: Depth in points divided by 12 gives depth in picas:

$$\frac{1,067}{12} = 89 \text{ picas}$$

If the copy had been 10-point type and 2-point leading instead of 1, the copy depth would have equaled the number of lines: 97.

Suppose the layout is flexible. You have copy with 3,250 characters. The typeface is 10-point Helvetica leaded 2. You want the length of copy when set in type to be 49 lines. How wide will the column of copy have to be?

Step One: Total number of characters divided by number of lines gives characters per line:

$$\frac{3,250}{49} = 66.3$$

Step Two: Characters per line divided by characters per pica gives picas per line:

$$\frac{66.3}{2.4} = 27.6 = 28$$

The column width will have to be 28 picas.

Finally, you are given a layout with columns 21 picas wide, and you have a depth of 120 picas. Copy must be written to fill the space. If you set your margins to provide a 60-space line, how many lines will be needed to fill the space? (Assume type will be 10-point Helvetica leaded 2 points.)

Step One: Characters per pica times line width in picas gives characters per line:

$$2.4 \times 21 = 50.4$$

Step Two: Characters per line times number of lines gives total characters:

$$50.4 \times 120 = 6,048 \text{ characters}$$

(number of lines equals depth in picas because type is set 10 point leaded 2)

Step Three: The number of lines equals the total characters divided by characters per line:

$$\frac{6,048}{60} = 100.8 = 101 \text{ typed lines}$$

Broadcast Copy

Radio

Set margins for a 60-space line. That setting will give three or four seconds per line.

Use 12-point type in Times Roman or a serif type of equal measure that will give you about 10 words per line.

For 30 seconds of copy, there are about seven or eight of these lines.

For one minute, plan for about 15 lines.

If you are going to print out the copy, use triple spacing.

Television

Set margins for about a 30-space line in a column on the right side of the page.

Use 12-point type in Times Roman or a serif type of equal measure that will give you about six words per line.

For 30 seconds of copy, there are about 15 of these lines.

For one minute of copy, plan for about 21 lines read at an average speed.

Print out triple-spaced. (Video information goes in the left-hand column along with other instructions not being read.)

The best gauge for estimating time is to read the copy and time it with a stopwatch. This is more complicated with estimating TV scripts because you have to allow additional time for visuals, even when it is voice-over.

Answer to AP Style Exercises

1. 1) The correct answer is (a). This is a trick question: Dr Pepper is a registered trademark and has no period after the Dr.

   2) (b) is correct. The period is not needed; furthermore, periods should never fall outside quotation marks.

   3) No easy answer. Logic would seem to dictate the punctuation as in example (a), but in practice three punctuation marks in a row are seldom seen. Experts say you should choose the question you most want to emphasize. In this case (b) is probably the best choice.

   4) (b) is correct. This is one of those rare cases where three punctuation marks do follow one another. The exclamation point is part of the title and should not be dropped.

   5) (a) is correct. The quotation is the question, so the question mark falls inside the quotation marks.

   6) Another tricky one. (c) is wrong; (a) seems logical, but (b) is probably the correct choice to avoid awkward appearance. The exclamation is more important than the interrogative.

   7) (a) is correct. When a complete sentence is enclosed in parentheses, so is the period.

   8) (b) is correct. When only part of a sentence is enclosed in parentheses, the period falls outside.

   9) (a) is correct.

   10) (b) is correct. Although the sentence is phrased as an interrogative, there is no question. It is more a command than a request.

   11) (c) is probably the best way to punctuate this. (a) and (b) are clearly wrong; the comma is not needed. Some might use an exclamation point and a question mark together, but most would pick one.

   12) (c) is correct. Commas are not needed in this construction.

   13) (a) is correct.

   14) (c) is correct.

   15) (a) is correct. Semicolons always go outside quotation marks.

   16) (b) is correct.

   17) (b) is correct. The *if* clause is essential to the meaning of the main clause. It is therefore a restrictive *if* clause and should not be set off by a comma.

   18) (a) is correct. The *which* clause is descriptive, not defining. It merely gives more information about a generator. It does not make a distinction between generators in general and the generator under discussion.

   19) Although number is a collective noun, when preceded by *a,* the verb is plural. When *the* is used, the verb form is generally singular. (b) is correct.

   20) *Its* is a possessive, not a contraction. (b) is correct.

2. These revisions are only suggestions. Many other revisions are possible.

    a. Johnson said big money sports forces athletes to cheat in school because they have no time to study.
    b. Like so many wars, this war was largely a result of previous wars.
    c. If today's communication methods had been available, the war would never have started.
    d. Oil and water don't mix.
    e. Work takes up however much time is available.
    f. We have met the enemy, and they are ours.
    g. This machine can do whatever needs to be done.
    h. The company lost **money last year.**
    i. The company does **not have to apply** a year ahead anymore.
    j. CNG reduces vehicle air pollution to below EPA standards. (Or you can spell out CNG and EPA and still have a shorter, clearer sentence.)

Notes

Chapter 1

1. Doug Newsom, Judy VanSlyke Turk and Dean Kruckeberg, *This Is PR: The Realities of Public Relations*, 10th ed. (Boston, MA.: Wadsworth Cengage Learning , 2010), p. 2.
2. Frank Wylie, "The New Professionals." Speech to the First National Student Conference, Public Relations Student Society of America, Dayton, Ohio, October 24, 1976. Published by Chrysler Corporation, p. 5.
3. Edward L. Bernays, *Public Relations* (Norman, Okla.: University of Oklahoma Press, 1952), p. 5.
4. James E. Grunig and Todd Hunt, *Managing Public Relations* (New York: Holt, Rinehart & Winston, 1984), pp. 22–24.
5. Bernays, *Public Relations,* p. 83.
6. William L. Rivers, *The Mass Media* (New York: Harper & Row, 1975), p. 22.
7. David Sturgis et al., "Crisis Communications Management: The Public Opinion Node and Its Relationship to the Environmental Nimbus," *SAM Management Journal* 56(3) (Summer 1991): 22–27.

Chapter 2

1. Bart Ziegler, "Old-Fashioned Ethic of Separating Ads Is Lost in Cyberspace," *The Wall Street Journal*, July 25, 1996, p. B1.
2. John Pavlik and David Dozier, research quoted in "Study Details Bumps to Watch Out for on Info Superhiway," *pr reporter*, August 5, 1996, p. 2.
3. See Lawrence G. Foster, "Tylenol 20 Years later," *The Strategist*, 8(4) (New York: Public Relations Society of America, Fall 2002), pp. 16–20.
4. Terry Maxon, "Weighing the Financial Fallout of Speaking Out," *The Dallas Morning News*, January 14, 1996, p. H1.
5. Go to the USA government websites for information about laws and to the sites of the regulatory institutions for their decisions and new regulations. Also note the following section in this chapter on government regulators.
6. For more information look on the Internet for the Nike case, and see the law chapter of *This Is PR: The Realities of Public Relations*, 10th Edition, Doug Newsom, Judy VanSlyke Turk and Dean Kruckeberg (Boston, MA.: Wadsworth Cengage Learning, 2010).

7. Carrie Dolan, "Wineries and Government Clash over Ads That Toast Health Benefits of Drinking," *The Wall Street Journal*, October 19, 1992, pp. B1, B4.

Chapter 3

1. Edward L. Bernays, *Public Relations* (Norman, Okla.: University of Oklahoma Press, 1952), p. 130.

2. Otto Lerbinger, *Designs for Persuasive Communication* (Englewood Cliffs, N.J.: Prentice Hall, 1972).

3. See, for example, Irving L. Janis, "Personality as a Factor in Susceptibility to Persuasion," in *The Science of Human Communication*, ed. Wilbur Schramm (New York: Basic Books, 1963), pp. 54–64.

4. Milton Rokeach, *The Nature of Human Values* (New York: Free Press, 1973).

5. William J. McGuire, "Persuasion, Resistance, and Attitude Change," in *Handbook of Communication*, eds. Ithiel de Sola Pool et al. (Chicago: Rand McNally, 1973), p. 221.

6. Stanley Lehmann, "Personality and Compliance: A Study of Anxiety and Self-Esteem in Opinion and Behavior Change," *Journal of Personality and Social Psychology* 15 (1970): 76–86. Cited in McGuire, "Persuasion," p. 233.

7. David J. Therkelsen and Christina L. Fiebich, "Message to Desired Action: A Communication Effectiveness Model," *Journal of Communication Management*, 5(4), (2001): 374–390.

8. Everett M. Rogers, *Diffusion of Innovations* (New York: Free Press of Glencoe, 1962). Also see Everett M. Rogers, "Mass Media and Interpersonal Communication," in *Handbook of Communication*, eds. Ithiel de Sola Pool and Wilbur Schramm, et. al. (Chicago: Rand McNally, 1973), pp. 290–310

9. Wilbur Schramm, "The Challenge of Communication Research," in *Introduction to Mass Communication Research*, eds. Ralph O. Nafziger and David M. White (Baton Rouge, La.: Louisiana State University Press, 1963), p. 29.

10. The statement provided is not always true, however. See B. Sternthal, L. Phillips and R. Dholakia, "The Persuasive Effect of Source Credibility: A Situational Analysis," *Public Opinion Quarterly 42* (Fall 1978): 285–314.

11. Lerbinger, *Designs*, p. 25.

12. McGuire, "Persuasion," p. 231.

13. Duangkamol Chartprasert, "How Bureaucratic Writing Style Affects Source Credibility," *Journalism Quarterly* 70 (Spring 1993): 150–159.

14. Aristotle, *Rhetoric*, trans. W. Rhys Roberts (New York: Modern Library, 1954).

15. McGuire, "Persuasion," p. 234.

16. William J. McGuire, "Nature of Attitudes and Attitude Change," in *Handbook of Social Psychology*, eds. Gardener Lindzey and Elliot Aronson (Reading, Mass.: Addison-Wesley, 1969), p. 225.

17. Ibid., pp. 228–229.

18. Everett M. Rogers, "Mass Media and Interpersonal Communication," in *Handbook of Communication*, eds. Ithiel de Sola Pool and Wilbur Schramm, et al. (Chicago: Rand McNally, 1973), pp. 292–298.

19. McGuire, "Nature," pp. 230–231.

20. McGuire, "Persuasion," p. 231.

21. Elliot Aronson, Judith Turner and J. M. Carlsmith, "Communicator Credibility and Communication Discrepancy as Determinants of Opinion Change," *Journal of Abnormal and Social Psychology* 67 (1963): 31–36.

22. James E. Grunig, "Communication Behaviors and Attitudes of Environmental Publics: Two Studies," *Journalism Monographs* 81 (March 1983): 9–14.

Chapter 4

1. Patrick O'Donnell, Ketchum Global Research Network, "PR Research Guru," http://74.125.95.132/search?q=cache:U0YDUsJGq4kJ:www.culpwrit.com/%3Fp%3D169+public+relations+research&hl=en&ct=clnk&cd=14&gl=us (Chicago, IL.: 2008).

2. James E. Grunig, "The Profession's Store of Knowledge," Remarks on Receiving the Arthur Page Society Distinguished Service Award (Chatham, MA.: September 22, 2008).

3. "A Higher Perspective," CEO Survey 2008, *PRWeek*, November 10, 2008.

4. "Wikipedia:About," http://en.wikipedia.org/wiki/Wikipedia:About.

5. "PR Needs Its Own Research Modes, Not Borrowed Ones," *pr reporter,* January 4, 1993, pp. 1–2.

6. Charlene Li and Josh Bernoff, *Groundswell: Winning in a World Transformed by Social Technologies* (Harvard Business Press, Boston, Mass.: 2008), p.89.

7. Ibid., p. 90.

8. Ibid., p. 91.

9. Ibid., p. 84.

Chapter 5

1. Southwest Airlines, "The Mission of Southwest Airlines," January 1988, http://www.southwestairlines.com/about_swa/mission.html (accessed April 28, 2009).

2. Lisa Bradner and Kim Le Quoc with Jaap Favier, Jean Yves Lugo, "Creating Awareness to the Act of Purchase," http://www.forrester.com/Research/Document/Excerpt/0,7211,47054,00.html (accessed April 28, 2009).

Chapter 6

1. William Zinsser, *On Writing Well,* 2nd ed. (New York: Harper & Row, 1980), pp. 56–57.

2. Robert Gunning, *The Technique of Clear Writing,* rev. ed. (New York: McGraw-Hill, 1968), p. 1.

3. David Geary, "The Readability Challenge in Public Relations," *Public Relations Quarterly* 46(4) (Winter 2001), pp. 37–39.

4. Gunning, p. 51. Also see Cynthia Crossen's article, "If You Can Read This, You Most Likely Are a High-School Grad," in *The Wall Street Journal,* December 1, 2000, pp. A1, A11, for a quick history of readability formulas and their uses.

5. Gunning, p. 44.

6. H. W. Fowler, *Modern English Usage* (New York: Oxford University Press, 1965), p. 148.

7. Kenneth E. Andersen, *Persuasion Theory and Practice* (Boston: Allyn & Bacon, 1971), p. 126.

8. Albert Einstein, "On the Electrodynamics of Moving Bodies," *Annalen der Physik* 17 (1905): 891–929, reprinted in *The Principle of Relativity,* trans. W. Perrett and G. B. Jeffrey (New York: Dover, 1952), p. 39.

9. Rudolf Flesch, *The Art of Plain Talk* (New York: Collier Books, 1962), pp. 158, 162.

10. William Zinsser, *On Writing Well,* p. 114.

11. pr reporter, "Panel Issues Guidelines for Reporting Scientific Research," *pr reporter,* March 16, 1998, p. 2.

12. William D. Lutz, "Language Appearance and Reality: Doublespeak in 1984." An excerpt from *The Legacy of Language—A Tribute to Charlton Laird,* ed. Philip C. Boardman (Reno: University of Nevada Press, 1987) appeared with permission in ETC 44(4) (Winter 1987): 382–391.

13. Lauran Neergaard, "Researchers Explore Benefits of Simplifying Jargon," *The Fort Worth Star-Telegram,* November 25, 2002, p. 5D.

14. "Hacking Through the Paper Jungle," *Public Relations Journal* (August 1981): 26.

15. Isaac Asimov, *Opus 100* (Boston: Houghton Mifflin, 1969), pp. 89–90.

16. Steven Krauss, ed., *Your Health Care Planner* (Boston: Madison, 1994), p. 19.

17. Bruce Brown, "Shedding Light on the Aurora," *National Wildlife* (February–March 1985): 51. Copyright © 1985 by the National Wildlife Federation. Reprinted with permission.

18. Paula LaRocque, "This Analogy Clinic Fits Writers' Needs Like Cabretta Gloves," Clinic Column, *Quill,* (September 1996), p. 32.

19. Kathleen Tinkel, "Taking It In," *Adobe Magazine* 7(4) (April 1996): 40–44.

20. Ibid.

21. Ibid., see also Jeffrey M. Laderman, "The Prospectus Tries Plain Speaking," *Business Week* (August 14, 1995), p. 72.

Chapter 7

1. Tom Herman, "Tax Report," *The Wall Street Journal,* June 26, 1996, p. 1.

2. Linda Vaughan, "Weathervane," *The Dallas Morning News,* April 16, 1996, p. J1.

3. Luther Brock, "In Direct Mail, Ignore Friends—Pay Attention to What Pays," *Southwest Advertising and Marketing* (December 1975): 20.

4. Luther Brock, "Two Professionals Disagree on the Need for Purity in Language," *Southwest Advertising and Marketing* (March 1977): 11.

5. Robert Gunning, *The Technique of Clear Writing*, rev. ed. (New York: McGraw-Hill, 1968), p. 265.

6. Stephen Wilbers, "Tarrant Business," *The Fort Worth Star-Telegram*, July 13, 1998, p. 13.

7. Ibid.

8. Ibid.

9. Ibid.

10. Gunning, p. 121.

11. Rudolf Flesch, *The Art of Readable Writing*, 25th anniv. ed. (New York: Harper & Row, 1974), p. 163.

12. Theodore Bernstein, *The Careful Writer* (New York: Atheneum, 1965), p. 288.

13. Flesch, *The Art of Readable Writing*, pp. 9–10.

14. William Strunk and E. B. White, *The Elements of Style*, 3rd ed. (New York: Macmillan, 1979), p. 78.

15. Howard Kahane and Nancy Cavender, *Logic and Contemporary Rhetoric, The Use of Reason in Everyday Life*, 8th ed. (Belmont, Calif.: Wadsworth, 1998). See Chapter 2, "Background Beliefs and World Views."

16. Paula LaRocque, Words & Language column, "Don't Start the New Year Wrong," in *Quill* 97(2), March 2009, p. 27.

17. Christopher J. Moore, *In Other Words: A Language Lover's Guide to the Most Intriguing Words Around the World* (New York: Levenger Press, Division of Walker & Company, 2004).

Chapter 8

1. "Digital Presentation Package," Wieck Media, http://socialmedia.wieck.com/ (accessed March 27, 2009).

2. "Whee! New Numbers on Social Network Usage," http://news.cnet.com/8301-17939_109-10160850-2.html (accessed March 26, 2009).

3. "Open for Questions Wraps Up" from http://www.whitehouse.gov/openforquestions (accessed March 27, 2009).

4. Chris Cobb, "Same Game, New Rules: A Historic Presidential Campaign—and What It Means for Our Digital Future," from "PR Tactics and The Strategist Online," http://www.prsa.org/supportfiles/news/pfNews.cfm?pNewsID=842347706 (accessed March 26, 2009).

5. Ibid.

6. B. L. Ochman, "Debunking Six Social Media Myths," *BusinessWeek*, February 26, 2009, http://www.businessweek.com/technology/content/feb2009/tc20090218_335887.htm (accessed April 6, 2009) and summarized in "The Truth behind Six Social Media Myths" in "PR Tactics and The Strategist Online," February 26, 2009, http://www.prsa.org/supportfiles/news/viewNews.cfm?pNewsID=842347857 (accessed April 6, 2009).

7. Amy Jacques, "In the Driver's Tweet: Making the Most of 140 Characters," *PRSA Tactics*, (New York: February 2009), p. 11.

8. Merry Aronson, Don Spetner and Carol Ames, *The Public Relations Writer's Handbook: The Digital Age*, 2nd ed. (Hoboken, NJ.: Jossey-Bass, 2007), p. 3.

9. Chris Cobb, "Same Game, New Rules: A Historic Presidential Campaign—and What It Means for Our Digital Future," from "PR Tactics and The Strategist Online," http://www.prsa.org/supportfiles/news/pfNews.cfm?pNewsID=842347706 (accessed March 26, 2009).

10. "The Internet as News Central," http://www.emarketer.com/articles/print.aspx?id=1006861, Jan. 13, 2009 (accessed March 26, 2009).

11. Adam Denison, "Face to Face—Virtually: Two PR Professionals Share Their Success on Facebook," *Public Relations Tactics*, October 2005, p. 15.

12. Shel Holtz, "Bring Your Intranet into the 21st Century" in *Communication World*, (San Francisco, CA.: January–February 2008), p. 16.

13. Stephen Humphries, "Companies Warm Up to Social Networks," *The Christian Science Monitor*, September 8, 2008.

14. Andrew Analore, "Sony Blog Improves Public Relations," http://www.ragan.com/ME2/Sites/dirmod.asp?sid=&nm=&type=&tier=4&mod=PublishingTitles&mid=BA4E52387C5D4DBEB81F2F6DF1929188&taxonomyid=BC24700DD431471696FFB81D92542674&SiteID=BDA0C

114585D49D88AE5F9010619FAD9&id=F657 C4BE1EB74C67BA5C26E702E1271C (accessed March 26, 2009).

15. Dianna Dilworth, "Few, Proud and Social," August 4, 2008, http:/www.dmnews.com/Few-proud-and-social/PrintArticle/113253 (accessed January 15, 2009).

16. Newspaper Association of America ad, "The Reality About Newspapers," *The Dallas Morning News* (and other newspapers), May 24, 2009, p. 23A.

17. "2008 Journalist Survey," http://www.pwrnewmedia.com/site08/library/0108_survey.html (accessed March 31, 2009).

18. "How the Press Uses and Values Public Relations and Other Media Resources," a national study by Cision and The George Washington University Graduate School of Political Management, http://www.gwu.edu/~media/research_report.pdf (accessed May 11, 2009).

19. "Just the Fax," *The Wall Street Journal,* May 13, 1993, p. 1.

20. "Final Rule: Selective Disclosure and Insider Trading, Securities and Exchange Commission, 17 CFR Parts 240, 243, and 249, Release Nos. 33-7881, 34-43154, IC-24599, File No. S7-31-99, RIN 3235-AH82, Selective Disclosure and Insider Trading," http://www.sec.gov/rules/final/33-7881.htm (Washington, D.C.: October 23, 2002).

21. Silicon.com Staff, "Lowdown on SOX," http://news.com.com/Sarbanes-Oxley+cheat+sheet/2030-7349_3-5465172.html (San Francisco, Calif., undated).

22. "Media," *PRWeek*, April 29, 2009, p. 8.

23. Eric Alkire, "ABC's of Long-Form Video Edits," *News Photographer*, January 1997, p. 15.

24. David Eisenstadt, "How to Make Video News Releases Work," *Public Relations Quarterly* 47(4) (Winter 2002): 24–25.

25. Tom Moore, "TV News Directors Report High VNR, SMT Usage; Cite Favorite Topics," *PR NEWS* 48(45) (November 16, 1992): 8.

26. Tom Moore, "VNR Producers, Distributors Subscribing to Code of Good Practice," *PR NEWS* 49(13) (March 29, 1993): 7.

27. Suzanne Huffman, "Writing Radio News," Chapter 6, in *Broadcast News Handbook*, C. A. Tuggle, Forrest Carr and Suzanne Huffman (New York: McGraw-Hill, 2001), p. 74.

28. Kelli B. Newman, "A Strategic Subspecialty: Defining the Comprehensive Value of Broadcast Public Relations," *Public Relations Tactics*, June 2006, p. 18.

Chapter 9

1. "National Survey Finds Journalists Use Traditional Newsgathering Sources Just as Extensively as Online Sources," http://us.cision.com/news_room/press_releases/2009/2009-3-2_journalist_survey.asp (accessed April 2, 2009).

2. "2008 Online Newsroom Survey Results," TEKgroup International, http://www.tekgroup.com/pdf/onlinenewsroomsurveyresults_2008.pdf (accessed April 2, 2009).

3. Tony Harrison, "The ABCs of CD-ROMs," *Public Relations Tactics*, September 1996, p. 14.

4. Katharine Q. Seely, "White House Approves Pass for Blogger," *The New York Times*, http://www.nytimes.com/2005/03/07/technology/07press.html?ex=1267938000&en=53aba0fd77cf623d&ei=5090&partner=rssuserland (accessed April 1, 2009).

5. American Society of Plastic Surgeons, "Press Room Guidelines for Plastic Surgery 2009," http://www.plasticsurgery.org/Media/Press_Room_Guidelines_for_Plastic_Surgery_2009.html (accessed October 7, 2009).

6. Todd Brabender, "Turning Your Media Pitch into a Media Hit," http://www.evancarmichael.com/Public-Relations/286/Business-Publicity-Turning-Your-Media-Pitch-Into-A-Media-Hit.html (accessed May 12, 2009).

7. California Association for Health Services at Home, "Media Relations," undated, http://www.cahsah.org/HCMonth/HCmonthmediatips.htm (accessed May 12, 2009).

8. "How the Press Uses and Values Public Relations and Other Media Resources," a national study by Cision and The George Washington University Graduate School of Political Management, http://www.gwu.edu/~media/research_report.pdf (accessed May 11, 2009).

Chapter 10

1. Broxon Sears, personal communication, 2009.

Chapter 11

1. Leslie Brenner, "You've Got Too Much Email," *Los Angeles Times* (Los Angeles, Calif.: July 31, 2008).
2. "2008 Journalist Survey" from *Power Lines*, quarterly e-newsletter of PWR New Media, http://www.pwrnewmedia.com/site08/library/0108_survey.html (accessed February 10, 2009).
3. Sabin Willett, *Present Value* (New York: Random House, 2004).
4. Gale Holland and Seema Mehta, "UC San Diego Admissions Gaffe Dashes Students' Hopes – Again," *Los Angeles Times*, April 1, 2009, http://www.latimes.com/news/local/la-me-ucsd-reject1-2009apr01,0,7943711.story (accessed April 6, 2009).
5. "Sophos Security Threat Report 2009," http://www.sophos.com/sophos/docs/eng/marketing_material/sophos-security-threat-report-jan-2009-na.pdf (accessed April 6, 2009).
6. Ibid.
7. "Text Messaging," *Encyclopedia Britannica*, http://www.britannica.com/EBchecked/topic/1099476/text-messaging (accessed May 13, 2009).
8. Jennifer Steinhauer and Laura M. Holson, "As Text Messages Fly, Danger Lurks," *The New York Times*, September 19, 2008, http://www.nytimes.com/2008/09/20/us/20messaging.html (accessed February 4, 2009).
9. Erin Gifford, news release, "It's 3 A.M. – Are You Checking Your Email Again?" http://corp.aol.com/press-releases/2008/07/it-s-3-am-are-you-checking-your-email-again, July 30, 2008 (accessed February 4, 2009).
10. Ibid.

Chapter 12

1. From the PricewaterhouseCoopers website, "Sarbanes-Oxley and strategies for compliance," http://www.pwc.com/Extweb/NewCoAtWork.nsf/docid/D0D7F79003C6D64485256CF30074D66C (accessed May 11, 2009).
2. The Federalist Society for Law and Public Policy Studies, http://www.fed-soc.org/publications/id.302/default.asp (accessed May 11, 2009).
3. "NIRI Releases Annual Report Survey: For the First Time, a Majority of Companies Use 10-K Wraps, Citing Costs and Ease of Production," http://www.niri.org/irresource_pubs/alerts/eaarchive.cfm (accessed May 11, 2009).
4. U.S. Securities and Exchange Commission, "Annual Report," http://www.sec.gov/answers/annrep.htm (accessed May 11, 2009).
5. Office of Investor Education and Assistance, U.S. Securities and Exchange Commission, "A Plain English Handbook—How to Create Clear SEC Disclosure Documents," http://www.sec.gov/pdf/handbook.pdf (accessed April 29, 2009).
6. "NYSE Revises Listing Standards; Eliminates the Annual Report Physical Delivery Requirements," http://www.mayerbrown.com/securities/article.asp?id=2949&nid=10707 (accessed May 11, 2009).
7. "Rule 14c-4—Presentation of Information in Information Statement," General Rules and Regulations Promulgated Under the Securities Exchange Act of 1934, http://www.law.uc.edu/CCL/34ActRls/rule14c-4.html (accessed May 11, 2009).
8. Robert Gunning, *The Technique of Clear Writing* (New York: McGraw-Hill, 1968), p. 227.
9. Ibid.
10. Rudolf Flesch, *The Art of Readable Writing*, 25th anniv. ed. (New York: Harper & Row, 1974), p. 135.
11. "Sara Lee Finds a Way to Cut Through the Clutter," *inside PR* (November 1992), 6–7.
12. Gunning, p. 244.

Chapter 14

1. Edelman Change and Employee Engagement, "Are Your Employees 'Working with the Volume Off?'" http://www.edelman.com/expertise/practices/employee_change/documents/Edelman_MemotoManagement_vol1issue4.pdf (accessed May 11, 2009).

2. Mark Brownlow, "Email Newsletter Frequency," http://www.email-marketing-reports.com/email-newsletters/frequency.htm (accessed May 5, 2009).

3. Gary F. Grates, "Working with the Volume Off: Cutting Through the Noise of 'Today's' Communications" (New York: Edelman, 2007).

4. Ibid.

5. Jacci Howard Bear, "Top Desktop Publishing Software for Windows," http://www.desktop-pub.about.com/cs/software/tp/dtpsoftware.htm (accessed April 30, 2009).

Chapter 15

1. Noel Ward, "Translating the Languages of Color," *Desktop Publishers Journal* (March 1995): 26–27.

2. Ibid.

Chapter 16

1. Miles Maguire, "Mapping the Size and Scope of a Nonprofit Media Sector: The Case of Magazine Publishing," *Journalism & Mass Communication Quarterly*, (Columbia, SC: Association for Education in Journalism and Mass Communication, Autumn 2008): 647.

2. Ibid., p. 650.

3. "How Word Choice Impacts Employee Communication," *Mid-America Communication Foundation* 2(1) (1996): 47–55.

4. Don Fabun, "Company Publications," in *Lesly's Public Relations Handbook,* ed. Philip Lesly (Englewood Cliffs, NJ.: Prentice Hall, 1971), p. 135.

5. Don Fabun, "Company Publications," in *Lesly's Public Relations Handbook*, ed. Philip Lesly (Englewood Cliffs, NJ.: Prentice Hall, 1971), p. 135.

6. Maguire, p. 649.

7. Eleena DeLisser, "Luring Loyal Customers to Pay for Product News," in "Marketing," *The Wall Street Journal*, August 23, 1993, p. B1.

Chapter 17

1. Barbara A. Ross, Sarah V. Beckman and Linda V. Meyer, "Learning to Produce and Integrate Presentations, Videos and Stills." *T.H.E. Journal* (September 1995): 78–81.

2. Ibid.

3. *tips and tactics*, 41(10), May 5, 2003, pp. 1–2.

Chapter 18

1. Mark Hannah, "In Hudson River Landing, PR Pros Were Not First Responders," http://www.pbs.org/mediashift/2009/02/in-hudson-river-landing-pr-pros-were-not-first-responders036.html (accessed May 9, 2009).

2. Ray Suarez, "The Controversial Liberty Fund," December 19, 2001, http://www.pbs.org/newshour/bb/business/july-dec01/redcross_12-19.html (accessed October 7, 2009).

3. Enron Corporation news release, "http://www.highbeam.com/doc/1G1-80593791.html (accessed October 7, 2009).

4. Alexei Barrionuevo, "Two Enron Chiefs Are Convicted in Fraud and Conspiracy Trial" *The New York Times*, http://www.nytimes.com/2006/05/26/business/businessspecial3/26enron.html?ex=1151121600&en=a7363adba2e997e2&ei=5070 (accessed May 29, 2009).

5. Associated Press, "Conspiracy theories surround Ken Lay's death," July 14, 2006, http://www.msnbc.msn.com/id/13864798/ (accessed May 29, 2009).

6. Doug Newsom, Judy VanSlyke Turk and Dean Kruckeberg, *This Is PR: The Realities of Public Relations*, 10th ed. (Belmont, Calif.: Wadsworth, 2010), p. 319.

7. Carl Gustin and Jennifer Sheehy, Clarke & Company Crisis Communication Center, "Handling a Crisis: Lessons from NASA," *Boston Business Journal*, February 14, 2003, http://www.bizjournals.com/boston/stories/2003/02/17/editorial3.html (accessed May 29, 2009).

8. Jack C. Horn, "The Hostage Ward," *Psychology Today* 21(7) (July 1985): 9.

9. Media Resource Service of Sigma Xi, The Scientific Research Society, http://www.mediaresource.org/ (accessed May 29, 2009).

10. Getpress.com, "Crisis Communications Support," undated, http://www.getpress.com/crisis_communications.htm (accessed May 29, 2009).

Selected Bibliography

Chapter 1

Glen Broom, *Cutlip & Center's Effective Public Relations*, 10th ed. (Englewood Cliffs, NJ: Prentice Hall, 2008).

Arnold S. De Beer, ed., preface by John C. Merrill, *Global Journalism: Topical Issues and Media Systems*, 5th ed. (Boston: Pearson of Allyn and Bacon, 2009).

Hugh M. Culbertson and Ni Chen, eds., *International Public Relations: A Comparative Analysis* (Mahwah, NJ: Lawrence Erlbaum Associates, Inc., 1996).

Hugh M. Culbertson, Dennis W. Jeffers, Donna Besser Stone and Martin Terrell, *Social, Political and Economic Contexts in Public Relations, Theory and Cases* (Hillsdale, NJ: Lawrence Erlbaum Associates, Inc., 1993).

Karla K. Gower, *Public Relations and the Press: The Troubled Embrace* (Evanston, IL: Northwestern University Press, 2007).

Doug Newsom, *Bridging the Gaps in Global Communication* (London, UK: Blackwell Publishing, 2007).

Doug Newsom, Judy VanSlyke Turk and Dean Kruckeberg, *This Is PR: The Realities of Public Relations*, 10th ed. (Boston: Wadsworth Division of Cengage, 2010).

Michael B. Salwen and Don W. Stacks, eds., *An Integrated Approach to Communication Theory and Research*, 2nd ed. (New York: Taylor and Francis Division of Routledge, 2009).

Alison Theaker, *The Public Relations Handbook* (London, UK: Routledge, 2008).

Dennis L. Wilcox and Glen T. Cameron, *Public Relations: Strategies and Tactics*, 9th ed. (New York: Allyn & Bacon, 2008).

Dennis L. Wilcox, *Public Relations: Writing and Media Techniques*, 6th ed. (New York: Allyn & Bacon, 2009).

Chapter 2

Books

Barnaby Conrad and Monte Schulz, eds., *Snoopy's Guide to the Writing Life* (Cincinnati, OH: Writer's Digest Books, 2002).

Tom L. Beauchamp and Norman E. Bowie, eds., *Ethical Theory and Business*, 8th ed. (Englewood Cliffs, NJ: Prentice-Hall, 2008).

Barton T. Carter, Franklin A. Marc and Jay B. Wright, *The First Amendment and the Fourth Estate*, 10th ed. (Westbury, NY: Foundation Press, 2008).

Clifford G. Christians, Kim B. Rotzoll, Mark Fackler, Kathy B. McKee and Robert H. Woods, *Media Ethics: Cases and Moral Reasoning*, 8th ed. (Boston: Allyn & Bacon, 2008).

Ted Crawford, *The Writer's Legal Aid*, 3rd ed. (New York: Hawthorne, 2002).

Charles J. Glasser Jr, ed., *International Libel and Privacy Handbook: A Global Reference for Journalists, Publishers, Webmasters and Lawyers*. (New York: Bloomberg Press, 2006).

Media law annotated bibliographies are published annually by the Law Division of the Association for Education in Journalism and Mass Communication (LeConte College, University of South Carolina, Columbia, SC 29208).

Kent R. Middleton, Bill F. Chamberlin and William E. Lee, *The Law of Public Communication*, 7th ed. (Boston: Allyn & Bacon, 2008).

Don R. Pember, *Mass Media Law*, 16th ed. (with the free student CD-ROM). (New York: McGraw-Hill, 2008).

Dwight L. Teeter, Jr., Harold L. Nelson and Don R. De Luc, *Law of Mass Communications* (Westbury, NY: The Foundation Press, 2008).

Lee Wilkins and Philip D. Patterson, *Media Ethics: Issues and Cases* (New York: McGraw-Hill, 2001).

Journals

Lee Wilkins, ed., *Journal of Mass Media Ethics* (Philadelphia, PA: Taylor & Francis division of Routledge, quarterly).

Wat W. Hopkins, ed., *Communication Law and Policy* (Philadelphia, PA: Taylor & Francis division of Routledge, quarterly).

Others

Government Publications are useful, especially those from regulatory groups such as the U.S. Postal Service, Federal Trade Commission, Food and Drug Administration, Internal Revenue Service, National Investor Relations Institute, Securities and Exchange Commission, and Environmental Protection Agency. Also online, but not free, are Media Law Reporter and World Media Law Report.

Chapter 3

Robert B. Cialdini, *Influence: Science and Practice*, rev. ed. (New York: Collins Business, Division of HarperCollins, 2006).

Noah J. Goldstein, Steve J. Martin and Robert Cialdini, *50 Scientifically Proven Ways to Be Persuasive* (New York: Free Press Division of Simon and Schuster, 2008).

James Haggerty, *In the Court of Public Opinion: Winning Your Case With PR* (New York: John Wiley & Sons, 2003).

Charles U. Larson, *Persuasion: Reception and Responsibility*, 12th ed. (Boston: Wadsworth Division of Cengage, 2009).

Charlene Lei and Josh Bernoff, *Groundswell: Winning in a World Transformed by Social Technologies* (Boston: Harvard Business Press, 2008).

Richard M. Perloff, *The Dynamics of Persuasion* (Hillsdale, NJ: Lawrence Erlbaum Associates, Inc., 2003).

Vincent Price, *Public Opinion* (Newbury Park, CA: Sage Publications, 1992).

Everett M. Rogers, *Diffusion of Innovation*, 5th ed. (New York: Free Press, 2003).

Annette Simmons, *The Story Factor: Inspiration, Influence and Persuasion Through The Art of Storytelling*, 2nd rev. ed. (Cambridge, MA: Perseus Publishing, 2008).

Journals

The International Journal of Public Opinion Research, Oxford Journals Online, Oxford University Press for the World Association of Public Opinion Research and assisted by Stanford University Library HighWire Press.

Media Myths & Realities, annual media research surveys, University of Southern California Annenberg Strategic Public Relations Center and Ketchum and the Media School at Bournemouth University in the UK (Started in 2006).

Public Perspective, A Roper Center Review of Public Opinion and Polling, The University of Connecticut, Roper Center for Public Opinion Research,

Storrs, CT 06269-1164, USA. Back issues only since the publication ceased in 2003.

Chapter 4

Earl Babbie, *The Practice of Social Research*, 12th ed. (Boston: Wadsworth Division of Cengage, 2009).

Leslie A. Baxter and Earl Babbie, *The Basics of Communication Research* (Belmont, CA: Wadsworth, 2004).

Glen M. Broom and David M. Dozier, *Using Research in Public Relations: Applications to Program Management*, 2nd ed. (Englewood Cliffs, NJ: Prentice Hall, 2004).

Daymon C., *Qualitative Research Methods in Public Relations and Marketing Communications* (Florence, KY: Routledge/Taylor & Francis Books Inc., 2002).

Jerry A. Hendrix, *Public Relations Cases*, 8th ed. (Boston: Wadsworth Division of Cengage, 2009).

John E. Hocking, et al., *Communication Research*, 3rd ed. (Boston: Allyn & Bacon, 2002).

Joann Keyton, *Communication Research: Asking Questions, Finding Answers* (New York: McGraw-Hill, 2005).

Charlene Li and Josh Bernoff, *Groundswell: Winning In a World Transformed by Social Technologies* (Boston: Harvard Business Press, 2008).

Mary McGuire, Linda Stilborne, Melinda McAdams and Laurel Hyatt, *The Internet Handbook for Writers, Researchers, and Journalists*, 2002 ed. (New York: Guilford Press, 2002).

Rebecca B. Rubin, Alan M. Rubin and Linda Piele, *Communication Research: Strategies and Sources*, 7th ed. (Boston: Wadsworth Division of Cengage, 2009).

Michael B. Salwen and Don W. Stacks, eds., *An Integrated Approach to Communication Theory and Research*, 2nd ed. (Boston: Wadsworth Division of Cengage, 2009).

Chapter 5

Roger Hawood, *Manage Your Reputation: How to Plan Public Relations to Build and Protect the Organization's Most Powerful Asset*, 2nd ed. (London: Kogan Page Ltd., 2002).

Doug Newsom, Judy VanSlyke Turk and Dean Krukeberg, *This Is PR: The Realities of Public Relations*, 10th ed. (Belmont, Calif.: Wadsworth/Cengage, 2010).

Lester R. Potter, *The Communication Plan: The Heart of Strategic Communication*, 3rd ed. (San Francisco: International Association of Business Communicators, 2008).

Ronald E. Rice and Charles K. Atkin, eds., *Public Communication Campaigns*, 3rd ed. (Thousand Oaks, Calif.: Sage Publications, 2000).

Fraser P. Seitel, *Practice of Public Relations,* 10th ed. (Upper Saddle River, NJ: Prentice Hall, 2006).

Bruce L. Smith, *Engaging Public Relations: A Creative Planning Approach* (Dubuque, Iowa: Kendall Hunt, 2007).

Paul Russell Smith and Jonathan Taylor, *Introduction to Marketing Communication: An Integrated Approach,* 4th ed. (London: Kogan Page Ltd., 2004).

Ronald D. Smith, *Strategic Planning for Public Relations*, 3rd ed. (New York: Routledge, 2009).

Mark Weiner**,** *Unleashing the Power of PR: A Contrarian's Guide to Marketing and Communication* (Hoboken, NJ: Jossey-Bass/Wiley, 2006).

Dennis L. Wilcox, *Public Relations Writing and Media Techniques*, 6th ed. (Boston: Allyn & Bacon, 2009).

Laurie J. Wilson and Joseph D. Ogden, *Strategic Communications Planning: For Effective Public Relations and Marketing*, 5th ed. (Dubuque, Iowa: Kendall Hunt, 2008).

Joseph M. Zappala and Ann R. Carden, *Public Relations Worktext: A Writing and Planning Resource*, 2nd ed. (Mayway, NJ: Lawrence Erlbaum Associates, Inc., 2004).

Chapter 6

Jacques Barzun and Henry F. Graff, *The Modern Researcher*, 6th ed. (Boston: Wadsworth Division of Cengage, 2003).

Rene J. Cappon, *The Word: An Associated Press Guide to News Writing* (Englewood Cliffs, NJ: Prentice Hall, 1991).

Robert L. Chapman and Barbara Ann Kipfer, *The Dictionary of American Slang* (New York: HarperCollins, 1998).

Mary A. DeVries, *Internationally Yours: Writing and Communicating Successfully in Today's Global Marketplace* (Boston: Houghton Mifflin, 1994).

Rudolf Flesch, *The Art of Readable Writing*, rev. ed. (New York: Macmillan, 1986).

Francine Wattman Frank and Paula A. Treichler, *Language, Gender and Professional Writing* (New York: Modern Language Associates, 1989).

Robert Gunning, *The Technique of Clear Writing*, rev. ed. (New York: McGraw-Hill, 1968).

Hayakawa S. I. and Alan R. Hayakawa, *Language in Thought and Action*, 5th ed. (New York: Harcourt Brace Jovanovich, 1991).

Wynford Hicks, *English for Journalists* (New York: Routledge, 1998).

Robert L. Hilliard, *Writing for Television and Radio and New Media*, 7th ed. (Belmont, CA: Wadsworth, 1999).

Lauren Kessler and Duncan McDonald, *When Words Collide: A Media Writer's Guide to Grammar and Style*, 7th ed. (Belmont, CA: Wadsworth, 2003).

Paula LaRocque, *Championship Writing, 50 Ways to Improve Your Writing* (Oak Park, IL: Marion Street Press, Inc., 2000).

Alexander Lawson, *Anatomy of a Typeface* (Boston: David R. Godine, Publisher, 1990).

Michel Lipman and Russell Joyner, *How To Write Clearly: Guidelines and Exercises for Clear Writing* (Concord, CA: International Society for General Semantics, 1979).

Casey Miller and Kate Swift, *The Handbook of Nonsexist Writing for Writers, Editors and Speakers* (London, UK: Women's Press, Ltd., 1995).

Mary Morain, ed., *Enriching Professional Skills Through General Semantics* (San Francisco: International Society for General Semantics, 1989).

Jack A. Nelson, ed., *The Disabled, the Media and the Information Age* (Westport, CT: Greenwood Press, 1994).

The Online Slang Dictionary: http://onlineslangdictionary.com/

Kim Pedersen and Anders Kidmose, *In Black & White: An R&D Report on Typography and Legibility* (Copenhagen: Graphic College of Denmark, 1993).

Rick Poynor and Edward Booth-Clibborn, *Typography Now: The Next Wave* (London, UK: Booth-Clibborn Editions, 1994).

Larry A. Samovar, Richard E. Porter and Lisa Stefani, *Communication Between Cultures*, 5th ed. (Belmont, CA: Wadsworth, 2003).

William Zinsser, *On Writing Well: 30th Anniversary Edition, The Classic Guide to Writing Nonfiction* (New York: HarperPerennial, 2006).

Chapter 7

Grammar Guides

Paul Brian, *Common Errors in English Usage*, 2nd ed. (Wilsonville, OK: Wm. James & Co., an imprint of Franklin, Beedle & Co. 2008).

Jeanette Harris and Donald H. Cunningham, *Simon & Schuster Guide to Writing*, 2nd ed. (New York: Simon & Schuster, 1999).

Lauren Kessler and Duncan McDonald, *When Words Collide: A Media Writer's Guide to Grammar and Style*, 6th ed. (Belmont, CA: Wadsworth, 2003).

Paula LaRocque, *The Book on Writing: The Ultimate Guide to Writing Well* (Oak Park, IL: Marion Street Press, Inc. 2003).

Adam Robinson and Julian Fleischer, *The Princeton Review: Word Smart and Grammar Smart Abridged* (Princeton, NJ: Living Language, 2001). (Audio CD available.)

Irene Schoenberg, *Focus on Grammar: A Basic Course for Reference and Practice*, 3rd ed. (New York: Longman, 2003).

Harry Shaw, *Punctuate It Right!* 2nd ed. (New York: HarperCollins, 1994).

Lynne Truss, *Eats, Shoots & Leaves, The Zero Tolerance Approach to Punctuation!* (New York: Gotham Books, a division of Penguin Group, USA. 2006, first publication 2003).

Dictionaries

The American Heritage Dictionary of the English Language, 4th ed. (Boston: Houghton Mifflin, 2000).

Dictionary.com (free online dictionary and audio pronunciation).

The New American Roget's College Thesaurus in Dictionary Form, 4th rev. ed. (New York: Signet, Division of New American Library, 2009).

The New Oxford American Dictionary (New York: Oxford University Press, 2001).

Shorter Oxford English Dictionary, 5th ed. (New York: Oxford University Press, 2002). (Updated online www.oed.com.)

Webster's Third New International Dictionary Unabridged (Springfield, MA: Merriam-Webster, 2002). (See www.merriam-webster.com for dictionary and translations.)

Word Choice and Style Guides

Brad Kalbfeld and James R. Hood eds., *The Associated Press Broadcast News Handbook, Incorporating the AP Libel Manual* (New York: Associated Press, 2001, ordered through McGraw-Hill).

Norm Goldstein, ed., *The Associated Press Stylebook and Libel Manual* (New York: Associated Press, 2008).

Rene J. Cappon, *AP Guide to News Writing (Study Aids/On the Job Reference)*, 3rd ed. (New York: Arco Publisher, 2000).

Rene J. Cappon, *Associated Press Guide to Punctuation* (New York: Basic Books, 2003).

Rudolf Flesch, *The Art of Readable Writing*, rev. ed. (New York: Macmillan General Reference, 1994).

Robert L. Hilliard, *Writing for Television and Radio*, 7th ed. (Belmont, CA: Wadsworth, 1999).

Norm Goldstein, ed., *AP Stylebook and Brief on Media Law* (New York: Perseus, 2002).

John Grossman, Preface, *Chicago Manual of Style*, 14th ed. (Chicago: University of Chicago, 1993).

Karen Judd, *Copyediting, A Practical Guide* (London, UK: Robert Hale, Ltd., 2002).

Milan D. Meeske, *Copywriting for the Electronic Media: A Practical Guide*, 5th ed. (Boston: Wadsworth Division of Cengage, 2006).

Allan M. Siegal and William G. Connolly, eds., *New York Times Manual of Style and Usage, Revised and Expanded Edition* (New York: Three Rivers Press, Division of Crown Publishing/Random House 1999).

Elsie M. Stainton, *The Fine Art of Copyediting*, 2nd ed. (New York: Columbia University Press, 2002).

William Strunk, Jr. and E.B. White, *The Elements of Style*, 4th ed. (Boston: Allyn & Bacon, 1999).

United Press International (UPI) Stylebook, 4th ed. (Lincolnwood, IN: NTC, 2004).

Barbara Wallraff, *Word Count: Wherein Verbal Virtue Is Rewarded, Crimes Against the Language Are Punished and Poetic Justice Is Done* (New York: Harcourt, Inc., 2002).

"The Write Way: Spotlight on PR Writing," Public Relations Tactics (New York: Public Relations Society of America, February 2009).

Chapter 8

Merry Aronson, Don Spetner and Carol Ames, *The Public Relations Writer's Handbook: The Digital Age*, 2nd ed. (Hoboken, NJ: Jossey-Bass, 2007).

Kathy Bonk, Emily Tynes, Henry Griggs and Phil Sparks, *Strategic Communications for Nonprofits: A Step-by-Step Guide to Working with the Media* (The Jossey-Bass Nonprofit Guidebook Series (San Francisco, CA: Jossey-Bass, 2008).

Deirdre Breakenridge, *PR 2.0: New Media, New Tools, New Audiences* (Upper Saddle River, NJ: FT Press, 2008).

Charles Coates, *Professional TV News Handbook* (Chicago: Bonus Books, 2000).

Norm Goldstein, ed., *The Associated Press Stylebook and Briefing on Media Law*, revised and updated edition (Cambridge, MA: Perseus Publishing, 2002).

Robert L. Hilliard, *Writing for Television and Radio*, 7th ed. (Belmont, CA: Wadsworth, 2002).

Carole M. Howard and Wilma K. Mathews, *On Deadline: Managing Media Relations*, 3rd ed. (Prospect Heights, IL: Waveland Press, 2000).

Gary Hudson and Sarah Rowlands, *The Broadcast Journalist's Handbook* (White Plains, NY: Pearson/Longman, 2007).

Henry Jenkins, *Convergence Culture: Where Old and New Media Collide* (Revised with a New Afterword) (New York: New York University, 2008).

Brad Kalbfeld, *The Associated Press Broadcast News Handbook*, 1st ed. (New York: McGraw-Hill/Contemporary Books, 2000).

Teresa Keller and Stephen A. Hawkins, *Television News: A Handbook for Writing, Reporting, Shooting and Editing* (Scottsdale, Arizona: Holcomb Hathaway, 2005).

Macdonald R. H., *A Broadcast News Manual of Style*, 2nd ed. (White Plains, NY: Longman Publishing Group, 2002).

Doug Newsom, Judy VanSlyke Turk and Dean Kruckeberg, *This Is PR: The Realities of Public Relations*, 10th ed. (Boston: Wadsworth Division of Cengage, 2010).

Robert Thompson, *Broadcast Journalism Handbook: A Television News Survival Guide* (Lanham, MD: Rowman & Littlefield Publishers, Inc., 2003).

Al Tompkins, *Aim for the Heart, Write for the Ear, Shoot for the Eyes: A Guide for TV Producers and Reporters* (New York: Bonus Books, 2002).

Tuggle C. A., Forrest Carr and Suzanne Huffman, *Broadcast News Handbook*, 3rd ed. (New York: McGraw-Hill, 2007).

Ted White, *Broadcast News Writing, Reporting and Producing*, 4th ed. (Amsterdam, The Netherlands: Focal Press, 2005).

Tim K. Wulfemeyer, *Beginning Broadcast Newswriting, A Self-Instructional Learning Experience*, 3rd ed. (Ames, IA: Iowa State University Press, 2003).

Herbert Zettl, *Television Production Handbook*, 10th ed. (Boston: Cengage Learning, 2008).

Chapter 9

George McKenzie, "How to Get Free Publicity by Engaging Journalists with Your Media Kit and Online Press Room" CD-ROM, http://mastermindlearningsystem.com/popup.html (Cedar Knolls, NJ: Mastermind Learning Systems, 2004).

Heil Sheehan, Hendrick Smith, E. W. Kenworthy and Fox Butterfield, *The Pentagon Papers* (Burr Ridge, IL: McGraw-Hill Humanities/Social Sciences/Languages, 1993). Besides being of historical interest, this book is amply illustrated with backgrounders and position papers.

Sally Stewart, *Media Training 101: A Guide to Meeting the Press* (Hoboken, NJ: Wiley & Sons, 2003).

Kate L. Turabian, Wayne C. Booth, Gregory G. Colomb and Joseph M. Williams, *A Manual for Writers of Research Papers, Theses, and Dissertations*, 7th ed. (Chicago, IL: University of Chicago Press, 2007).

Mark Wright, "Writing Media Backgrounders: Help Reporters Find You... Before They Need You," http://www.markwright.com/backgrounder.htm (Washington, DC: Wright Communications, 2003).

David R. Yale, *Publicity & Media Relations Checklists* (New York: McGraw-Hill, 1995).

Chapter 10

Eric Freeman and Elisabeth Freeman with Kathy Sierra and Bert Bates, *Head First Design Patterns* (Sebastopol, CA: O'Reilly, 2004).

Erich Gamma, Richard Helm, Ralph Johnson and John Vlissides, *Design Patterns* (Boston: Addison Wesley, 1995).

Robin Landa, *Graphic Design Solutions*, 2nd ed. (Clifton Park, NY: OnWord Press, 2000).

Potter W. J., *Media literacy* (Thousand Oaks, CA: Sage Publications, 2008).

Marcelle Lapow Toor, *Graphic Design on the Desktop: A Guide for the Non-Designer*, 2nd ed. (Hoboken, NJ: John Wiley & Sons, 1998).

Douglas K. van Duyne, James A. Landay, Jason I. Hong, *The Design of Sites: Patterns, Principles, and Processes for Crafting a Customer-Centered Web Experience* (Boston: Addison Wesley, 2002).

Robin Williams, *The Mac Is Not a Typewriter*, 2nd ed. (Berkley, CA: Peachpit Press, 2003).

Robin Williams, *The Non-Designer's Design Book: Design and Typographic Principles for the Visual Novice* (Berkley, CA: Peachpit Press, 1994).

Chapter 11

Carol Andrus, *Crisp: Fat-Free Writing: Business Writing for the Information Age* (Mississauga, Ontario, Canada: CRISP Publications, 2000).

Dawn-Michelle Baude, *The Executive Guide to E-mail Correspondence: Including Model Letters for Every Situation* (Franklin Lakes, NJ: The Career Press, 2006).

Arthur H. Bell, *Writing Effective Letters, Memos, and E-mail* (Hauppauge, NY: Barrons Educational Series, 2004).

Susan L. Brock, *Better Business Writing: Techniques for Improving Correspondence* (Mississauga, Ontario, Canada: CRISP Publications, 2003).

Janis Fisher Chan, *E-Mail: A Write It Well Guide— How to Write and Manage E-Mail in the Workplace* (Oakland, CA: Write It Well, 2008).

Richard C. Freed and Joe Romano, *Writing Winning Business Proposals: Your Guide to Landing the Client, Making the Sale and Persuading the Boss* (New York: McGraw-Hill, 2003).

Andrea B. Geffner, *How to Write Better Business Letters* (Hauppauge, NY: Barron's Educational Series, 2007).

Sheryl Lindsell-Roberts, *Strategic Business Letters and E-mail* (Boston: Houghton Mifflin, 2004).

Verne Meyer, Pat Sebranek, John Van Rys and Chris Krenzke, *Writing Effective E-Mail: Practical Strategies for Strengthening Electronic Communication* (Burlington, WI: Upwrite Press, 2005).

Jeremy T. Miner and Lynn E. Miner, *Proposal Planning & Writing*, 4th ed. (Westport, CT: Greenwood Press, 2008).

Roy W. Poe, *The McGraw-Hill Handbook of Business Letters*, 4th ed. (New York: McGraw-Hill, 2005).

Tom Sant, *Persuasive Business Proposals: Writing to Win More Customers, Clients, and Contracts* (New York: AMACOM, 2003).

Chapter 12

Patrick Forsyth, *How to Write Reports and Proposals*, 2nd ed. (London, UK: Kogan Page Ltd., 2006).

Lyn M. Fraser and Aileen Ormiston, *Understanding the Corporate Annual Report: Nuts, Bolts and a Few Loose Screws* (Englewood Cliffs, NJ: Prentice Hall, 2002).

George T. Friedlob and Ralph E. Welton, *Keys to Reading an Annual Report*, 4th ed. (Hauppauge, NY: Barron's, 2008).

Angela J. Maniak, *Writing High-Impact Reports: Proven Practices for Auditors and Accountants* (Northport, ME: Skill-Builders Press, February 2005).

William R. Pasewark, *Understanding Corporate Annual Reports*, 7th ed. (New York: McGraw-Hill/Irwin, 2008).

Bruce Ross-Larson, *Writing for the Information Age* (New York: W. W. Norton, 2002).

Caroline Taylor, *Publishing the Nonprofit Annual Report: Tips, Traps, and Tricks of the Trade* (Hoboken, NJ: Jossey-Bass/Wiley, 2008).

Michael Thomsett, *Annual Reports 101: What the Numbers and the Fine Print Can Reveal About the True Health of a Company* (New York: American Management Association, 2006).

Ann Wyle, *Planning Powerful Publications*, 2nd ed. (San Francisco: International Association of Business Communicators, 2002).

Chapter 13

Tom Altstiel and Jean Grow, *Advertising Strategy: Creative Tactics from the Outside/In* (Los Angeles, CA: Sage Publications, 2006).

Robert L. Hilliard, *Writing for Television, Radio and New Media*, 8th ed. (Belmont, CA: Wadsworth, 2007).

Daniel S. Janal, *Online Marketing Handbook*, 3rd ed. (New York: John Wiley & Sons, 1999).

Jerome Jewler and Bonnie L. Drewniany, *Creative Strategy in Advertising*, 8th ed. (Belmont, CA: Wadsworth, 2004).

Barbara K. Kaye and Norman J. Medof, *Just a Click Away: Advertising on the Internet* (Boston: Allyn & Bacon, 2001).

Milan D. Meeske, *Copywriting for the Electronic Media: A Practical Guide*, 4th ed. (Boston: Wadsworth Division of Cengage, 2003).

Roy Moore and Erik Collis, *Advertising and Public Relations Law* (New York: Routledge, 2009).

Sandra Moriarty, Nancy Mitchell and William Wells, *Advertising Principles and Practice*, 8th ed. (Upper Saddle River, NJ: Pearson/Prentice Hall, 2009).

Michael G. Parkinson and L. Marie Parkinson, *Law for Advertising, Broadcasting, Journalism, and Public Relations* (New York: Routledge, 2006).

Gerard J. Tellis and Tim Ambler, *The SAGE Handbook of Advertising* (Los Angeles, CA: Sage Publications, 2008).

Joseph Turow and Matthew McAllister, *The Advertising and Consumer Culture Reader* (New York: Routledge, 2009).

Chapter 14

Peter Anthonissen, *Crisis Communication: Practical PR Strategies for Reputation Management and Company Survival* (London, UK: Kogan Page, Ltd. 2008).

Pamela Brooks, *The Easy Step by Step Guide to Writing Newsletters and Articles* (London, UK: Rowmark Ltd., 2002).

Chuck Green, *Design It Yourself Newsletters: A Step-by-Step Guide* (Gloucester, MA: Rockport Publishers, 2002).

Carol Harris, *Producing Successful Magazines, Newsletters and E-Zines* (Oxford, UK: How to Books, 2005).

Michael J. Katz, *E-Newsletters That Work, The Small Business Owner's Guide To Creating, Writing and Managing an Effective Electronic Newsletter* (Philadelphia, PA: Xlibris Corporation, 2003).

Chapter 15

Perry Chua, *The Best of Brochure Design 10* (Beverly, MA: Rockport Publishers, 2008).

Lisa L. Cyr, *Brochure Design That Works: Secrets for Successful Brochure Design* (Gloucester, MA: Rockport Publishers, 2002).

Stephen A. Kliment, *Writing for Design Professionals: A Guide to Writing Successful Proposals, Letters, Brochures, Portfolios, Reports, Presentations, and Job Applications*, 2nd ed. (New York: W. W. Norton & Company, 2006).

Jenny Sullivan, *Creative Solutions: Brochures: Making a Strong Impression – 85 Strategies for Message-Driven Design* (Gloucester, MA: Rockport Publishers, 2004).

Gordon Woolf, *Publication Production Using Page-Maker: A Guide to Using Adobe PageMaker 7 for the Production of Newspapers, Newsletters, Magazines and Other Formatted Publications* (Hastings, Victoria, Australia: Worsley Press, 2002).

Chapter 16

American Society of Magazine Editors, *The Best American Magazine Writing 2005* (New York: Columbia University Press, 2005).

Society of Publication Designers, *40th Publication Design Annual* (Gloucester, MA: Rockport Publishers, Inc., 2005).

Tim Samara, *Publication Design Workbook: A Real-World Guide to Designing Magazines, Newspapers, and Newsletters* (Gloucester, MA: Rockport Publishers, Inc., 2005).

Ann Wyle, *Planning Powerful Publications*, 2nd ed. (San Francisco: International Association of Business Communicators, 2002).

Chapter 17

Steven Ascher and Edward Pincus, *The Filmmaker's Handbook: A Comprehensive Guide for the Digital Age* (Upper Saddle River, NY: Penguin, A Pearson Co., 2008).

Susan Avallone, comp. and ed., *Film Writers Guide*, 7th ed. (Los Angeles, CA: Lone Eagle, 1998).

Jeanne Tessier Barone with Jo Young Switer (contributor), *Interviewing Art and Skill* (Boston: Allyn & Bacon, 1995).

Douglas Biber, *Variation Across Speech and Writing* (Cambridge, UK: Cambridge University Press, 1992).

Lillian Brown, *Your Public Best: The Complete Guide to Making Successful Public Appearances in the Meeting Room, on the Platform and on TV*, 2nd ed. (New York: W. W. Norton & Company, 2003).

Thomas D. Burrows, Lynne S. Gross and James C. Foust, *Video Production: Discipline and Techniques*, 8th ed. (New York: McGraw-Hill, 2000).

Michel Chion and Claudia Gorbman, ed. and trans., *Audio-Vision: Sound on Screen* (New York: Columbia University Press, 1994).

Mary Ellen Guffey and Dana Loewy, *Essentials of Business Communication*, 8th ed. (Cincinnati, OH: Thomson South-Western, 2009).

Peter Hager, Howard J. Scheiber and Naommi Robbins, *Designing and Delivering Scientific, Technical and Managerial Presentations+Creating More*

Effective Graphs Set (New York: John Wiley & Sons, 2008).

Thomas K. Karam and James Gaut Ragsdale, *Can We Talk?: A Handbook for Public Speakers* (Lanham, MD: University Press of America, 1994).

Milan D. Meeske, *Copywriting for the Electronic Media: A Practical Guide*, 6th ed. (Boston: Wadsworth Division of Cengage, 2009).

Sandra Moriarty with Tom Duncan (contributor), *Creating and Delivering Winning Advertising and Marketing Presentations*, 2nd ed. (New York: McGraw-Hill, 1995).

John Morley, *Scriptwriting for High-Impact Videos: Imaginative Approaches to Delivering Factual Information*, 2nd ed. (Lincoln, NE: iUniverse, Inc., 2008).

Thomas A. Ohanian, *Digital Nonlinear Editing: Editing Film and Video on the Desktop*, 2nd ed. (Boston: Focal Press, 1998).

Linda Seger, *Making a Good Script Great*, 2nd ed. (Hollywood, CA: Samuel French, 1994).

Elizabeth Urech, *Speaking Globally: Effective Presentations Across International and Cultural Boundaries* (Dover, NH: Kogan Page Ltd., 1998).

Kathleen S. Verderber and Rudolph Verderber, *Inter-Act: Interpersonal Communication Concepts, Skills, and Context*, 10th ed. (Oxford, UK: Oxford University Press, 2003).

Rudolph F. Verderber, *The Challenge of Effective Speaking*, 14th ed. (Belmont, CA: Wadsworth, 2008).

John Watkinson, *The Art of Digital Video*, 4th ed. (Boston: Focal Press, 2008).

Chapter 18

Al Czarnecki, *Crisis Communications: a Primer for Teams* (Bloomington, IN: iUniverse, Inc., 2007).

Robert C. Chandler, *Crisis Communication Planning* (St. Louis, MO: BCP Media Inc., 2005).

W. Timothy Coombs, *Code Red in the Boardroom: Crisis Management as Organizational DNA* (Westport, CT: Praeger, 2006).

W. Timothy Coombs, *Ongoing Crisis Communication: Planning, Managing, and Responding*, 2nd ed. (Thousand Oaks, CA: SAGE Publications, Inc., 2007).

Robin Cohn, *The PR Crisis Bible: How to Take Charge of the Media When All Hell Breaks Loose* (New York: St. Martin's Press, 2000).

Kathleen Fearn-Banks, *Crisis Communication: A Casebook Approach*, 3rd ed. (Hillsdale, NJ: Lawrence Erlbaum Associates, Inc., 2007).

Jack A. Gottschalk, ed., *Crisis Response: Inside Stories on Managing Image Under Siege* (Mankato, MN: Capstone Press, 2002).

Roger Hawood, *Manage Your Reputation: How to Plan Public Relations to Build and Protect the Organization's Most Powerful Asset*, 2nd ed. (London, UK: Kogan Page Ltd., 2002).

James E. Lukaszewski, *Crisis Communication Plan Components and Models: Crisis Communication Management Readiness* (White Plains, NY: Lukaszewski Group, 2005).

James E. Lukaszewski, *The Crisis Website* (White Plains, NY: Lukaszewski Group, 2005).

Dan Millar and Larry L. Smith, *Crisis Management and Communication: How to Gain and Maintain Control*, 2nd ed. (San Francisco: International Association of Business Communicators, 2003).

Doug Newsom, Judy VanSlyke Turk and Dean Kruckeberg, *This Is PR: The Realities of Public Relations*, 9th ed. (Boston: Wadsworth Division of Cengage, 2010).

Steve Wilson and Luke Feck, *Real People, Real Crises: An Inside Look at Corporate Crisis Communications* (Winchester, VA: Oakhill Press, 2002).

Index